M000237093

Dr. Mel's Connecticut Climate Book

Garnet Books

Dr. Mel's **Connecticut** Climate Book

Dr. Mel Goldstein

WESLEYAN UNIVERSITY PRESS Middletown, Connecticut

Published by
Wesleyan University Press,
Middletown, CT 06459
www.wesleyan.edu/wespress
© 2009 by Dr. Mel Goldstein
All rights reserved
Printed in the United States of America
5 4 3 2 1

Library of Congress
Cataloging-in-Publication Data
Goldstein, Mel.
Dr. Mel's Connecticut climate book /
Mel Goldstein.
    p. cm. — (Garnet books)
Includes index.
ISBN 978-0-8195-6839-7 (pbk. : alk. paper)
    1. Connecticut—Climate. I. Title. II. Title:
Connecticut climate book.
QC857.U6G65 2009
551.69746—dc22   2009016155

Wesleyan University Press is a member of
the Green Press Initiative. The paper used
in this book meets their minimum
requirement for recycled paper.

Photos courtesy of— Paula Bronstein/
Hartford Courant: p. 92; Joseph Cannata Jr./
Hartford Courant: p. 110; Connecticut
Historical Society: p. 73; Connecticut
National Guard: p. 75 (top); Mary Alice
Dwyer/*Hartford Courant*: p. 90 (bottom);
The Echo, Western Connecticut State Uni-
versity: p. 228 (bottom); Bob Ficks/*Hartford
Courant*: pp. 100 (top), 101; Judy Griesedieck/
Hartford Courant: pp. 85, 90 (top); Hartford
History Center, Hartford Public Library:
pp. 97–98; Arman G. Hatsian/*Hartford
Courant*: pp. 46, 50 (top), 103, 112; John
Long/*Hartford Courant*: pp. 47, 50 (bottom),
51; John Long and Cross Country Aviation
Corp./*Hartford Courant*: p. 89; Raymond
McCrea Jones/*Hartford Courant*: p. 111;
National Weather Service: p. 75 (bottom);
New Haven Historical Society: pp. 30–34;
News Channel 8: p. 229; *News-Times*: p. 228
(top); Cloe Poisson/*Hartford Courant*: 58

Contents

Acknowledgments

This book is dedicated to my wife, Arlene, who has been at my side through the writing and researching of this book. Tirelessly gathering facts and photographs, her contributions made this book possible. She has been by my side throughout my battles with an incurable form of cancer, multiple myeloma, or bone marrow cancer. Thanks for making my life and this book possible.

Also, very important to this book have been the editors at Wesleyan University Press. Suzanna Tamminen, Editor-in-Chief, gave this book direction and structure, and her encouragement was what was needed to get this book written. It has been nearly a half-century since the last complete climate book on Connecticut was put together. Also, helpful have been Leslie Starr in marketing and choosing the book's cover art, and Amanda Dupuis who has assisted me every step of the way. As production editor, she had the thankless task of putting the final form of the book together.

Many members of the community also assisted in immeasurable ways. Claude Albert, Managing Editor of the *Hartford Courant*, opened his doors for our requests of photographs from storms of the past. Kathleen McKula, News Librarian, helped gather the many photographs. Also Michael Iannuzzi, a special neighbor, gathered additional photographs with the help of the New Haven Historical Society.

Finally, I want to acknowledge Theresa (Varga) Kavouras for putting together the various charts, diagrams and illustrations.

Introduction

Connecticut may be one of the smallest states in the nation, but what it lacks in size, it makes up in weather. This 90- by 50-mile state has just about every variety of weather known to Planet Earth. The climate, which is a total sum and average of its weather, manages to deliver snowstorms, heat waves, arctic blasts, floods, droughts, thunderstorms, hurricanes, and tornadoes. Did we leave anything out? Sure, you can find other regions that may feature more tornadoes, but do they also have hurricanes and snowstorms? And other places may have more snowfall, but do they also have hurricanes? And yet other locations are hurricane- and flood-prone, but do these places experience much snow? Connecticut gets it all, or at least, pretty much all.

Connecticut is on the meteorological superhighway. The weather can't get there without coming by here, first. In the tropical latitudes, more heat is collected than is given off by the Earth. In the polar regions, more heat is lost than is received. If this imbalance were left alone, the poles would become colder and colder while the equatorial areas would become warmer and warmer. But this very imbalance sets up a motion that does its best to keep things somewhat steady by bringing warmth away from the superheated tropics toward the superchilled poles. And all of this transport occurs in its greatest volume across midlatitudes . . . just where Connecticut is located. This great energy transfer through Connecticut's backyard causes storms of all varieties to develop. Then, you tack on some hills, Long Island Sound, and the nearby Gulf Stream, and you really are cooking. There isn't a single storm track across the United States that fails to come within striking distance of Connecticut.

In this book, we take a look at Connecticut's rich climate — the storms we remember and can never forget. The heat waves that seemed unrelenting, and the cold snaps, too. The last book that presented a picture of Connecticut's climate was published about a half-century ago. It is time for an update, especially during an era where concern over climate warming is on the front-burner. Is Connecticut's climate really changing and what is the extra-long-range forecast? As they say on TV: Stay tuned.

What Is Climate?

Climate is the average of weather. Climate is a mosaic of day-to-day weather happenings. Sure, there is the hot day, but there is also the cold day. One swallow doesn't make a summer, and nor does one steamy day make for a steamy climate. A flooding rainstorm doesn't indicate a monsoonal climate. The average temperature, rainfall, or snowfall over a long period represents climate. The actual temperature, rainfall, or snowfall on a particular day is just weather. The National Weather Service uses a thirty-year period for its climate averaging. A huge number of factors contribute to climate. You start with the Sun and its exported radiation and look at how that radiation is received by the Earth. Then, there is the tilt of the Earth on its axis and its motion around the Sun. Then, the atmosphere and oceans come into play by distributing heat and energy. All of this is superimposed on a varied topography. And not all factors are of global proportions; some are localized, such as a sea breeze, or even microscopic such as fine particles that become nuclei for precipitation. This chapter is a brief overview of climate. We will see how all these factors come together to make Connecticut's climate very special.

The Earth is always in motion, and moving at a seemingly dizzying rate—80,000 miles per hour. This is how fast the Earth revolves around the Sun. At the same time, the Earth rotates on its axis once each day. The revolution around the Sun helps deliver different seasons, and the rotation brings us day and night. The rotation also delivers a spin to the atmosphere. This spin is called the Coriolis force, and contributes to the air in weather systems moving clockwise or counter-

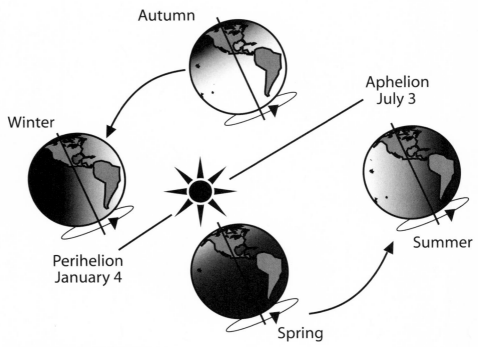

FIGURE 1.1 Earth in motion.

clockwise. Sometimes the weather really does have us going in circles. Figure 1.1 illustrates these motions of the Earth. Even with all these spins and gyrations, we usually don't fall down, or even sense them, because we're grounded by gravity. We can feel the wind, because it blows relative to all the other motions.

Connecticut is located midway between the equator and the poles, at approximately 40 degrees north latitude. Because of the Earth's motion, the length of day will be different during different times of year and at different latitudes. Table 1.1 shows the difference in daylight from latitude to latitude. The solstice occurs on the first day of winter or summer. The day-to-day changes in the Sun's position occur slowly—the Sun seems to stand still, and that is the meaning of "solstice." Notice the great differences in daylight among the different latitudes on the solstices, and the differences among the solstices. In Connecticut, the length of day is about 15 hours around the summer solstice, but just 9 hours on the first day of winter. No wonder it becomes colder in the winter. On the first day of spring or fall, all latitudes receive about 12 hours of daylight—the "equinox," or equal hours of day and night.

The spin, rotation, and as we can see in figure 1.1, the tilt of the Earth's axis all contribute to the seasons. That tilt, by the way, can change, and one

TABLE I.I LENGTH OF DAY IN THE NORTHERN HEMISPHERE

Latitude (in degrees)	Spring equinox	Summer solstice	Fall equinox	Winter solstice
90	12 hrs	6 months	12 hrs	0 hrs
80	12 hrs	4 months	12 hrs	0 hrs
70	12 hrs	2 months	12 hrs	0 hrs
60	12 hrs	18.4 hrs	12 hrs	5.6 hrs
50	12 hrs	16.3 hrs	12 hrs	7.7 hrs
40	12 hrs	14.9 hrs	12 hrs	9.1 hrs
30	12 hrs	13.9 hrs	12 hrs	10.1 hrs
20	12 hrs	13.2 hrs	12 hrs	10.8 hrs
10	12 hrs	12.6 hrs	12 hrs	11.4 hrs
0	12 hrs	12 hrs	12 hrs	12 hrs

theory of climate change focuses around a wobbly axis that can cause fluctuations in direct sunlight, and therefore in temperature.

On the subject of sunlight, let's not forget that the Sun really matters in a huge way. A ray of sunlight heading for the Earth encounters plenty of interference. Actually, only about half of the radiation from that beam finds its way to the Earth's surface. The remainder is scattered, reflected, or absorbed by small particles, droplets, and gases within the atmosphere. The incoming light consists of all colors at different wavelengths, but these very small atmospheric particles will scatter the shorter-wavelength blue light preferentially—so the sky appears blue. But as we know, in the summer, the sky loses some of that deep blue color. It becomes hazy. The air contains more pollution, larger particles that have no preference for scattering light. So, the sky just appears white. Sunrise or sunset can be red because the depth of atmosphere through which the light is passing is greater than at midday, and the blue light is all scattered out, leaving just the red shades. If high, thin clouds are around at sunrise or sunset, the small ice crystals in these clouds add to the scattering, and generate the beautiful red colors.

The amount of scattering, absorption, and reflection become major inputs to climate change computer models. Overall, 30 percent of the radiation that reaches the top of the atmosphere is reflected back to space. When the radiation is absorbed, it turns into longer-wave heat radiation. Most of the incoming radiation is shorter wave, and not heat. When we are outdoors, we might think that the Sun feels hot, but actually, it is the absorption of sunlight by our bodies and by our surroundings that generates heat.

The big item on the climate agenda is carbon dioxide. It is transparent to the shorter-wavelength incoming sunlight, but it is not transparent to the longer wavelengths reflected back. Heat is generated and then trapped within the atmosphere, just like a greenhouse. Other greenhouse gases include methane and old-fashioned water vapor, which absorbs five times as much radiation as all the other gases combined.

Connecticut's climate has changed in recent decades. Is that because of some natural changes to the Sun and the Earth's position with respect to the Sun, or because of more greenhouse gases inadvertently being emitted into the atmosphere? We will look at that a little later, but in the meantime, check out the next figure. Figure 1.2 shows the overall balance of radiation in the atmosphere.

The sunlight that reaches the Earth heats things up with an uneven distribution. The equatorial zones pick up more heat, the poles less. A natural system doesn't like imbalance, so the Earth tries its hardest by redistributing the excesses to places that truly need some help. The relatively less-dense warm air from the Equator rises and spreads poleward, where it

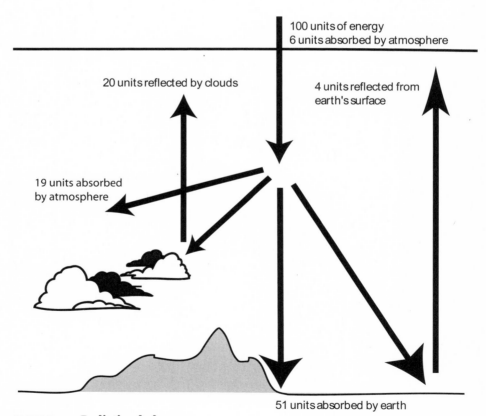

100 units of energy
6 units absorbed by atmosphere

20 units reflected by clouds

4 units reflected from earth's surface

19 units absorbed by atmosphere

51 units absorbed by earth

FIGURE 1.2 Radiation balance.

sinks toward the Earth and spreads southward along the surface. Because of the Coriolis force, and some convergences, the air is deflected off the path so that this "general circulation" takes on some variations. Figure 1.3 shows the ups and downs and the forces that come into play. But thanks to that overall heat transfer, the long-term global temperature variation is fairly steady, unless some outside forces arrive, such as inadvertent human emissions. The poles don't grow progressively colder, and the equator does not become increasingly warmer. And that heat transfer, combined with the spinning Earth and Coriolis force, accounts for the average wind flow at different latitudes.

Notice in figure 1.3 where the rainy climates are located. They generally are found where the air is rising. It can rain only when the air is moving up, not down, and the faster the air rises, the harder the rains fall. When the

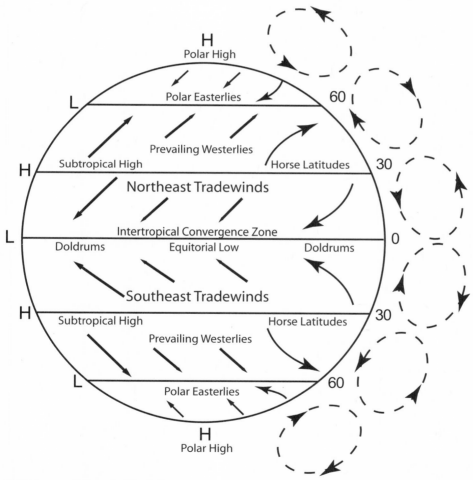

FIGURE 1.3 General circulation.

air rises, invisible water vapor droplets move about less. The droplets stay together. They now transform to visible water as they form around tiny, small nuclei that can be as small as a ten-thousandth of an inch. Small nuclei from the oceans can be a hundred times bigger. Without these nuclei, it would take days and days for rain to happen, if ever. But the absorbing nuclei serve as initial magnets that attract the invisible water vapor and helps them be seen in the form of clouds. Then, the small droplets coalesce and form bigger ones, but at least initially, that too, is a very slow process, except when ice is present. Ice is another precipitation magnet. But for a cloud to contain ice, it must be tall enough and big enough. These thick, large clouds can grow tall only if the air is rising. The ice crystals form at great heights, the droplets latch onto the ice nuclei and become big enough and heavy enough to come down as rain, or cold enough to fall as snow. The most powerful storms have the greatest upward motions.

Those motions, which started the whole process, eventually allow for a balancing of the water budget. Just as the Earth's motions balance its heat budget, atmospheric motions may shape the local water surpluses and deficits, but also keeps them pretty steady. It doesn't get totally out of hand. Figure 1.4 shows the different upward motions that contribute to the different kinds of weather that we experience. Topography can modify the ups and downs of the air and account for local climate differences. The proximity of the sea can do the same for local temperature. Also, anything that

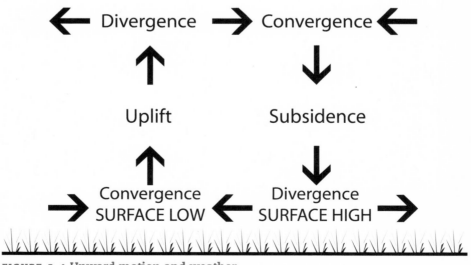

FIGURE 1.4 **Upward motion and weather.**

gets the air in motion has the potential of delivering vertical motions and precipitation. Temperature contrasts can lead to a mixing of the air and help feed energy in storms. After all, the atmosphere just doesn't like those imbalances. Places with the greatest heat transfer will have the biggest storms. Welcome to the midlatitudes and Connecticut.

Now, for Connecticut

Connecticut is on the superhighway of heat-energy transfer. All the excesses of heat energy that are experienced in warmer climates have to pass through the midlatitudes to get to the colder areas and the poles. We live at approximately 41 degrees north latitude, and it doesn't get much more middle latitude than that. The energy of the world can't get there without coming by here, first. No wonder we never seem to run out of energy for storms. Sure, we have our dry spells, and even droughts, but there's no doubt that "Storms 'R' Us."

When you consider the size of the state, you have to wonder how we can experience nearly every form of weather on the face of the Earth, but we do. The state is 90 miles wide (from west to east) and 50 miles tall (from south to north). It is just over 5,000 square miles. Long Island Sound defines the southern border, so the ocean influence is huge. The warm energy source of the Gulf Stream sits just 200 miles offshore, and is poised and ready to set up temperature contrasts that deliver our famous nor'easters, coastal storms of impressive size and duration where the wind can blow out of the northeast for days.

The water can have a benign influence on coastal areas, too. Cooling sea breezes during the hot summer will keep the temperature down. In the winter, the water is warmer than the land, so that an east wind will moderate the temperature and prevent many storms from delivering snow. For snow lovers, they often get robbed, and just rain comes down. Still, we get our share of snow. We get our share of everything.

Places farther from Long Island Sound will pick up

more snow in the winter, and the hills just enhance the snowfall. This is a hilly state. In the northwest portion of Connecticut, the hills rise from 1,000 to 2,000 feet above sea level. The climate in this part of the state is very much like Vermont's climate. The western hills that extend through Fairfield County range in height from a few hundred to 1,000 feet above sea level. Once you reach elevations near 1,000 feet, the weather can vary in a dramatic way, and it can happen within the same town, or even on the same street. King Street in Danbury is just one example where at the top, snow can be coming down fast and furiously, but at the bottom, wet snow and rain are mixed and there is no accumulation. The same experience is reflected in all the towns of western Connecticut. Even by the shoreline, the land becomes hilly in a hurry. I live on the beach, but when I drive to work in New Haven, just 7 miles away, I'll travel along Townsend Avenue. I'll leave with only rain falling, but just as I reach the gentle hill of Townsend Avenue, wet snow is coming down. Try explaining all that in a two-minute television weather forecast! And the eastern hills offer the same challenges. Here elevations vary from 300 to 1,000 feet. How many times have you had a white-knuckled drive down I-84 in the winter when skies open up? Union to Vernon can be slippery and hazardous. In Hartford, you reach the valley, and temperatures will be warmer, but the eastern hills can be clogged with snow and ice. The hills extend right down to New London County, and just like western Connecticut, the same towns can have huge variations in snowfall. The hills are farther north or farther from the warming influence of Long Island Sound, but not far enough away from the coastal storm track to be spared, and the elevation just lifts that east wind further, so snowfall will be tremendous. The highest elevations of the Northwest Hills will pick up an average of 120 inches of snow each year. The shoreline receives an average of just barely 20 inches, and when I say shore, I mean within view of Long Island Sound. Just a few miles back, that average is closer to 40 inches. In New Haven, alone, these variations show up just between Light House Point and the Westville section of town. In northeast Connecticut, I often wonder if a year will come when the snow will fail to melt completely at Union. It had trouble doing that in 1978, the year of one of the greatest blizzards of the twentiety century. Also, during the famous cold year of 1816, snow fell during June in Vernon. More recently, in 1977, on May 9, heavy wet snow to the tune of 10 to 20 inches fell in the Northwest Hills at Norfolk. On that day, snow even fell as far south as the shoreline. In Danbury, I measured 2 inches collected on car rooftops. Table 2.1 lists some of the average snowfalls around the state at particular locations.

The hills do provide a lift to the air, and that enhances all precipitation, so there is a lot—about 47 inches of melted snow and rainfall each year.

TABLE 2.1 SNOWFALL AND PRECIPITATION AT CONNECTICUT STATIONS

Station	Snowfall (in inches)	Total precipitation (in inches)
Bridgeport	24.8	44.15
Burlington	27.8	52.27
Danbury	38.8	51.77
Falls Village	38.2	45.82
Groton	20.4	48.72
Bradley (Hartford)	45.3	46.16
Mansfield Hollow Lake	31.3	51.55
Norfolk	86.9	53.87
Norwich	18.7	52.78
Shepaug Dam	51.4	50.57
Stamford	28.6	52.79
Storrs	30.9	51.64
West Thompson Lake	34.2	51.25

We call that "total precipitation." But again, like snowfall, rainfall can vary widely in the same town from the same storm. Localized summer showers and thunderstorms will cause the differences, but somehow, over the course of twelve months, the total precipitation is pretty uniform from one end of the state to another. The same table includes the totals.

Sure, Connecticut experiences droughts, but only rarely, such as in 1965 to 1966, do they lead to water shortages. The weather comes to the rescue just when you think change will never come. During that period, rainfall was less than a third of normal. But, the rain did come. I remember in 1967, when I started as a graduate student at NYU, the meteorology department had a huge project—the Drought Project. It was heavily funded, but that summer, the rains came, and from that point on, the funds for that research dried up. Many rainmaking experiments were going on at that time, but those efforts evaporated, too. I decided to do research on tornadoes and hurricanes. Those funds never went away. We do get it all.

Although the influence of the ocean is huge, because the average flow of air is from the west, we are in the zone of prevailing westerlies. So, weather systems most often come from the westerly component—sometimes the northwest, sometimes the southwest. Fronts, air masses, storms come from that direction, and whatever seems to form in the west, seems eventually to have some influence here. Sometimes fronts and storms will weaken while approaching, but other times, in combination with the ocean influence and temperature contrast, they will transform and become major coastal wonders. These are called secondary storms, but there is nothing second-rate about them. Most of the big winter storms are secondary ones.

Amazingly, we get our share of thunderstorms and tornadoes, too. July is our biggest month for thunderstorms, but these can happen anytime of year. Tornadoes will be spawned out of violent thunderstorms. Because of the dense population of Connecticut, severe thunderstorms and tornadoes will take quite a toll. In 1979, the great Windsor Locks tornado became the mostly costly single tornado to have hit anywhere in the country for nearly twenty years until the Oklahoma City tornado came along in 1999. In 1989, on July 10, a swarm of tornadoes moved from the Northwest Hills to the shoreline. Hamden and northern New Haven were hit by an F4 tornado with 200 mile per hour winds, strong enough to make brick structures crumble. I was on the air during that storm. Oh, what a night! We may not be Kansas, and Dorothy doesn't live here, but we sure are thrown in a spin from time to time.

We'll get into these storms in more detail later, but the point here is that extreme weather is far from lacking in Connecticut. We are at the hub of the Earth's great energy-transfer machine. We have our famous hills and proximity to the Sound and the Atlantic. No wonder Mark Twain supposedly said, "If you don't like the weather, wait a minute." Actually, it was his friend and editor of the *Hartford Courant*, Dudley Moore, who is thought to have made the observation first. In any case, Twain wrote lots about Connecticut's unique climate. In the spring, he said he could "count at least 132 different types of weather in just twenty-four hours." After trying to forecast the weather here for nearly forty years, I think he has that number just about right.

Winter's Fury

I know of few seasons that can be expected to cause more disruption to our normal day-to-day lives than the winter. Sometimes during a mild El Niño winter, we begin to think that the winter will never come, but even if it is a late bloomer, I always say that two consecutive weeks of winter can be enough winter for most people. Those two weeks will do their best to even the score. But other people, and I am one of them, just can't get enough of winter and its storms. We are just fascinated by the energy, power, excitement, and yes, unpredictability of the season, which in Connecticut can appear just before Thanksgiving and only taper off around Easter. Never mind the astronomical definition of winter: from solstice to equinox, from about December 21 to March 21. In fact, the National Weather Service defines the seasons as three-month periods: winter from December 1 to February 28; spring from March 1 to May 31; summer from June 1 to August 31; and fall—from September 1 to November 30. Seasonal records are kept according to those defined limits, but those of us who have spent more than two hours in Connecticut know that these boundaries are not meant to wall off any other form of weather that might happen by—a winter thunderstorm, a warm, almost summerlike spell, even the threat from a late-season hurricane. And those barriers aren't meant to keep winter weather from arriving in early October, as it did in 1987, or traces from hanging on into May of 1977, or even into June in the famous year of no summer, 1816. Meteorological borders are as porous as they come. We'll be looking into these extreme events, as well as the "normal," which, given our true variety of weather, needs to be taken with a grain of salt, or just a rapidly melting drift of snow.

For a number of years, I worked with the Connecticut Department of Transportation. It was my responsibility to give the department two hours' advanced notice of the arrival of any snow or ice. Those two hours were required to get the trucks out of the garages and onto the roads. It was a very stressful experience, given the variety of climate in Connecticut. Sometimes, I thought I was forecasting for the whole world. If I took my time, the precipitation would break out, and lives would be risked on slippery and icy roads. But if I called for an early beginning, then the trucks and drivers would be out plowing and treating absolutely nothing. For every hour that the trucks are on the roads, the state pays over $75,000! There goes the state surplus with one bad call. But the state doesn't need a massive snowstorm to cause accidents on the roads. Even a glazing patch of frost, or some unseen "black ice," which can form during freeze/thaw periods, can cause havoc. I learned a long time ago that in the winter little things do mean a lot. I would go outside in the middle of the night and personally test the roads by stopping the car and brushing my shoe on various parts of the highways.

Often, when I make a prediction of a bad storm, many in my TV audience will complain that we make too big a deal out of winter storms — too much hype. But at the same time, our ratings reach the highest of the year during winter, and during storms, our numbers of viewers skyrocket. Most people are affected by these storms, and they generate lots of interest and concern. Relatively few children walk to school, and seldom is anyone close enough to their job to be able to walk. So we depend on our cars, and sometimes, busses. Road travel can become treacherous. We are cut off from making our normal, appointed rounds. Schools are closed and often business are forced to close. But the bread and milk thing, I don't really understand. The long-term impact of these storms is most often no more than a day, or maybe two, but prior to these storms, the predictions of a big one will send a blizzard of shoppers to grocery stores. My former students who have worked at the cash registers have told me that they could tell how much snow I was predicting by the length of the checkout line! Some winter storm precautions definitely are warranted, and these are listed in table 3.1, but most of these come under the category of common sense. I don't know if storing two weeks of bread and milk come into play, here.

Winter is a very fickle time of year, but so too, are spring, summer, and fall. Still, because of the extremes and frequency of winter storms, the season generates huge interest, concern, and fascination. Our winter weather can come from many sources. Of course, there are the cold fronts that

TABLE 3.1 WINTER STORM PREPARATIONS

Prepare your home and family
- Prepare in case you are stranded: Stock up on canned food, bottled water, and extra medications. Be sure to have rock salt, sand, and snow shovels or other snow removal equipment on hand and in working order.
- Winterize your home: Insulate walls and windows, install weather stripping, cover windows with plastic if necessary.
- Winterize other structures and property around you: Trim branches and trees, keep footpaths free of obstructions, clean rain gutters.
- Insulate pipes: Use plastic or newspaper, or let cold water drip to avoid freezing.
- Keep fire extinguishers on hand: Check all smoke detectors and carbon monoxide detectors.
- Familiarize yourself with general plumbing abilities (i.e., turning off water flow valves).
- Keep the elderly and disabled and your pets in mind.

Prepare your vehicle
- Antifreeze
- Battery and ignition
- Brakes
- Exhaust
- Fuel: Be sure to have at least a half tank of gas before a storm.
- Heater and defroster
- Lights/hazards
- Oil
- Thermostat
- Windshield wipers
- All-weather radials, chains, or snow tires if required by law
- Winter emergency kit: Shovel, ice scraper, flashlight, batteries, battery-powered radio, bottled water, snack food, matches, winter clothing, first aid kit, pocket knife, extra medications, blanket, tow chain, rope, road salt, booster cables, emergency flares, distress flag, portable cell phone.

Dress for the weather
- Wear several layers of light clothing.
- Wear mittens as opposed to gloves.
- Wear a hat.
- Wear a scarf to cover your mouth.
- Wear insulated boots.

Familiarize yourself with the watch/warning system in your area
- Know the difference between a watch and a warning.
- Invest in a NOAA Weather Radio with battery back-up.

sweep from the northwest. Sometimes they are locked in place and refuse to move, and subzero temperatures descend upon us. Pipes freeze and burst, frostbite on exposed skin can occur in minutes, and cars have trouble starting. It can be quite the challenge for people to get around. If power failures occur, the cold can become just too dangerous. Usually, a storm passing to our north is responsible for drawing the cold air southward toward Connecticut. The winter storms have their origins along the edge of the cold air. Sometimes, they develop across the north-central states and push southward, and then turn northeast around the Jet Stream, which drives storms from place to place. Sometimes the cold air will dip as far south as Texas or Louisiana, where storms will form in an area of rich temperature contrast. These then turn northeastward, too, toward Connecticut. Many other storms will redevelop east of the Carolinas or the mid-Atlantic states near the warm Gulf Stream. These become our big coastal storms. If the storms move northward and their centers pass to our west, we receive warmer air from the ocean and mostly rain, but if they pass to our south or east, we stay in the colder air and receive snow. The greatest snowstorms are linked to those secondary monsters, which can stall and linger for two or three days. These are our famous "nor'easters," or northeasters. Because the wind blows from the northeast in these storms, they have acquired that name. If the storms move more northerly, the wind turns out of the southeast, and the snow changes to rain. These are sometimes called "southeasters." When a potential snowstorm turns to heavy rain, the storm is called an inside runner, moving to our west. Of course, if the storm moves too far to the east, then we come up empty. In Connecticut, a good benchmark is 40 degrees north latitude and 70 degrees west longitude. If the storm moves outside that grid, we'll get off more easily and many snow lovers will be disappointed. Figure 3.1 shows some classic storm tracks and the benchmark.

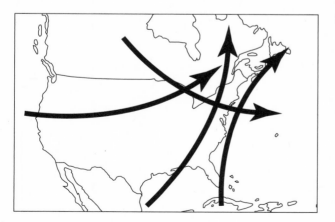

FIGURE 3.1 Storm tracks.

Then, there are shades in between, when snow can transition to ice. Pellets of ice, or sleet, fall upon us, or a glaze of freezing rain will cover trees, wires, roads, and walks. Even the most avid of winter-weather enthusiasts seldom is enamored of a disruptive ice storm, such as the one we had during pre-Christmas week in 1973. A winter never passes without delivering its share of weather.

Winters of Yesteryear

Extreme winter weather has been written about and talked about ever since the Pilgrims landed upon these shores. Actually, during the colonial period, the winters were as harsh as they come. The period was so cold that it has been called the "Little Ice Age." Harbors were frozen routinely as far south as Chesapeake Bay, and snow was measured not by the inch, but by the foot. The Little Ice Age began to show its first life around the fourteenth century, and it did not moderate until the middle of the eighteenth century. Prior to the fourteenth century, the climate was far more moderate, and had it stayed that way, Connecticut most likely would have been settled by the Vikings who were pitching settlements as far west as Greenland and Newfoundland, but the Little Ice Age ended all that. We could all be speaking Swedish if it weren't for the turn of weather events. The warm period prior to the Little Ice Age was just about as warm as our modern-day experience, except industrialization could not have been the cause for that. In any event, early New England settlers had to endure some very harsh conditions. Winter weather was one of their major challenges.

Just as the Vikings abandoned their early settlements because of the Little Ice Age, early English colonists had to do the same. In the early seventeenth century, a colony was being established along the central Maine coast, at the mouth of the Kennebec River. This colony, called Sagadahoc, was under the command of George Popham and Raleigh Gilbert by August 1607. A few months earlier, Jamestown, Virginia was being colonized, but Jamestown, and later, Plymouth, had far better chances of success. The Maine winters were beyond harsh, and the English settlers were not prepared for them. During the first winter, Popham died. At the same time, Gilbert's brother, Sir John Gilbert, died in England, and Raleigh decided to return home to take care of affairs, especially because of the severe winter, which was summed up by William Stratchey: "Many discoveries had likewise been made to the Mayne and unto the neighbour rivers, by the diligence of Captain Gilbert, but the winter proved so extreme and frosty." Gilbert, himself, said, "The fear that all the other winters would prove like the first, the company would by no means stay in the country." So, Jamestown and Plymouth would find their places in colonial history, and the rough winter of 1607–1608 obscured Sagadahoc's future in feet of drifting snow.

Although Plymouth's climate, very similar to coastal Connecticut's, was less severe than the Maine climate, the Pilgrims originally were supposed to be heading for the New York Harbor area. But the weather got in the way. In late November 1620, the Mayflower was in the vicinity of Cape Cod and about to turn toward the south. But the winds were increasing against the ship while strong currents were ripping along the dangerous nearby shoals. The Pilgrims were near Nauset, very close to the elbow of Cape Cod. On November 19, the wind began to increase from the south, and the ship had trouble pushing toward New York. There was concern of an impending storm, and the ship, along with the crew, had endured much during the two-month Atlantic crossing. The Mayflower turned around, headed northward, and moved around the tip of Cape Cod, and then westward, into the more protected waters of Cape Cod Bay. It was time to anchor and form a settlement. As John Winthrop, historian and eventual governor of the Plymouth Plantation wrote, "The season, it was winter, and they that know the winters of that country know them to be sharp and violent, and subject to cruel and fierce storms, dangerous to travel to known places, much more to search for an unknown coast." The Pilgrims reached Plymouth, and the rest became history.

Ironically, all accounts of the first Pilgrim winter indicate a relatively mild experience. One of the Pilgrims, Edward Winslow, came up with a great public relations publication called, "Good Newes from New England." He wrote about the "remarkable mildness" of the winter. Still, you can't beat the Vikings' PR effort in putting "green" into frozen Greenland. For the Pilgrims, maybe, it was just a case of beginners' luck, but even with a little meteorological luck on their side, these early settlers did have plenty of winter descending upon them. By the first week of December, the ground was frozen and snow-covered. In mid-December, freezing spray from the ocean was glazing a shallop being used for exploration. Through the winter, conditions were changeable, with alternating warm and cold spells — typical of southern New England. That in itself took its toll. Nearly half of the passengers and crew of the Mayflower died during that first "mild" winter.

In any case, the winters didn't remain especially mild. While the Massachusetts Bay settlement was underway, severe winter weather became commonplace. In the winter of 1631–1632, frostbite occurred frequently, with bitter cold developing during the first days of December and remaining through late February. Ten years later, a very harsh winter caused harbors to be frozen from late January through early March. Horses were pulling carts across the frozen harbors. Snow was reported to be 3 feet deep. Another historic winter occurred in 1680–1681. Once again, all harbors had frozen over. Another very extreme winter occurred in 1697–1698. Throughout the new colonies, reports were that that winter was the "severest that ever was known in the memory of man." The first snowstorms arrived in late November, and they continued into the second week of April. By late February, snow depth was reported to be more than 40 inches. Eight snowfalls occurred during February alone. Bitterly cold weather accompanied the storms, and the new colonies were solidly encased in ice.

Of course, not every season was extremely harsh. A number of winters were mild and "open," even during the heart of the "Little Ice Age." That pattern continued through the eighteenth century. At least ten winters could be classified as severe, another dozen were harsh, but nearly two dozen were unusually mild. But those severely cold winters have always caught our attention, and the eighteenth century had just gotten underway when two consecutive winters brought Arctic-like conditions to southern New England. In both seasons, 1704–1705 and 1705–1706, winter began by November 21 with heavy snow. Several heavy snowstorms occurred through the 1704 winter, and as late as April 23, 1705, ice remained thick and heavy on the ground. The following winter was just as harsh. Cotton Mather wrote, "there came upon us a very cold season." Deep snow was reported on the ground through early March. A brutally cold air mass settled over the entire Northeast in late December. Around New York, the Hudson River was frozen, and a ship ran aground near Sandy Hook, New Jersey. Over 130 crew members froze to death.

But of all the legendary winters of the 1700s, the standout had to be the winter of 1716–1717, with its great nor'easters of late February and March, historically called "The great snow of 1717." The winter began with a December chill, but a January thaw turned into a three-week springlike experience. It looked like a very early spring. Crops were even being planted, and in New London, the season was described as "very moderate with people comforting themselves on having gotten through the winter." Amazingly, the same thing, but on a smaller scale, happened more recently during January 2007, but during February 2007, and in a huge way in 1717, the weather turned around with the "great snow" arriving in February. For Connecticut, February 1717 brought one of the worst snowstorms in history. John Winthrop of New London wrote, "It continued so long and severe that multitudes of all sorts of creatures perished in the drifts."

From late February through the first week of March, four snowstorms struck the region, with snowfall amounts of 5 to 10 feet! Some of that had to be drifts, but still, the snow depths were monumental. Cotton Mather had this to say: "As mighty a snow, as perhaps has been known in the memory of man, is at this time lying on the ground." The crowning-jewel storm occurred in March. On March 4, Joshua Hempstead of New London wrote in his diary: "A great Storm of Snow. Itt is said to be 4 foot deep in ye woods on a Level. Itt snowed al last night. Knee deep in ye Morning. Itt continued snowing all day tht the drifts were so high thr was no passing to an fro for man or beast." The region was tied up for weeks, and thousands of animals perished, including an estimated 95 percent of the deer population. The storms of 1717 and the snow became the standard by which subsequent storms were compared — just as we might compare our modern-day snowstorms to the blizzard of February 1978.

But 1717 was certainly not the only tough winter of the eighteenth century. Just three years later, the 1719–1720 winter brought enough cold weather to freeze harbors and rivers from Boston to Philadelphia, and in Virginia, the winter was described as "the coldest ever known." The winter brought its share of snow, too, such as a nor'easter on February 10, 1720. Four days after that snowstorm, heavy rain fell, only to be followed by more bitterly cold weather. The ice in the rivers around Philadelphia did not break up until early March.

Then, in 1732–1733, another harsh winter delivered frozen-solid harbors from New England to Virginia. Ice blocks clogged Long Island Sound. The freeze began in late November and didn't melt until the end of March. The waterways were impassable for vessels throughout the colonies. Intense snowstorms added to the harshness of the winter. In Maine, the snow was 4 feet deep until early April.

As rough as these winters were, they managed to be exceeded by the harshest season of all — the winter of 1740–1741. The winter began on November 15 with a 6-inch snowfall across central Connecticut. On November 24 and 25, a foot of snow fell in another storm. But then a major thaw occurred with fourteen days of rain. Severe flooding occurred in the Connecticut River valley — the worst flooding since a spring flood in 1692. In

Maine, mills and bridges were swept away. In Connecticut, the flooding ruined stores of corn, which caused scarcity and contributed to great losses of livestock during the winter, and by late December, winter returned in all its fury.

A strong nor'easter brought gale force winds and knee-deep snow to much of the Northeast. Two more coastal storms pounded the region through the first half of January. Each storm was followed by an outbreak of severe cold, which formed thick ice in the rivers and along the shore. The sleighs came out, and people were able to ride on the shore ice from New London to Newport. An ice bridge formed from Fishers Island in eastern Long Island Sound to Connecticut. One of the signers of the Declaration of Independence, Francis Lewis, rode his sleigh on shore ice from Cape Cod to New York City—200 miles. According to John Bissell, who was serving as town clerk of Bolton, Long Island Sound was completely frozen and people "passed it on ice." His summary of the winter was in town records, and he described more violent snowstorms in late January and February. Even in mid-March, snow was still 3 feet deep. The snow melted very slowly. He wrote, "The weather continued cold and the snow wasted but slowly, so that there was considerable quantity of snow until the middle of April."

Actually, accounts of the winter in New London show that snow was falling as late as April 22. Little Ice Age? This season appeared to be something out of a real, full-blown ice age. New Haven Harbor was still being crossed by wagon in late March, and the ice on the Thames River in New London did not break up until March 26. The winter brought major losses to shipping and livestock, most of which perished. But there were some remarkable survival stories, including that of a sheep in Guilford that had been buried by the snow for more than ten weeks, but according to Bissell, "Came out alive."

The 1740s brought another harsh winter in 1747–1748. The winter was not especially cold, but it was snowy. More than two dozen snowfalls occurred, and snow cover was at least 4 to 5 feet deep during the height of the season. Joshua Hempstead of New London wrote that the first major snowfall occurred on December 14, and the storms were still rolling along as late as March 26. Not every storm brought snow. On February 27, he wrote, "A snowy day, it began before sunrise and held all day and late in ye night." But on the 28th he wrote, "Rainy all day. Ye great quantity of snow knee deep fell yesterday is much of it melted and very sloppy." Of course, it didn't take long for deep snow cover to return. On March 2, he wrote, "A violent storm . . . NE wind and great snow from before sunrise to near sunset . . . the snow drives furiously."

The big winters just kept happening, but there was a break in the extreme winters until 1764–1765. This season was another for the books. It was the snowiest since 1748 and the coldest since 1740. Temperatures reached the lowest levels since the introduction of the thermometer. Around New Year's Day, the temperature dropped to zero and stayed below zero for fifty-seven consecutive hours in New York City. The accuracy of these early thermometers may be called into question, but the cold snap caused ice to form across Chesapeake Bay. The Delaware River at Philadelphia closed on New Year's Eve and did not open until the end of February. Along with the cold came numerous snowstorms. Snow cover reached its maximum in February. In Hartford, the average depth was reported to be 38 inches on February 19. Another big winter occurred in 1772, and again the heavy snow came late. Midwinter had been cold in Connecticut, and perhaps the cold flow forced the storm track to be well to the south. In late January, a massive snowstorm dumped over 30 inches of snow in the mid-Atlantic area. Both Thomas Jefferson and George Washington kept diaries of the storm, which later became known as the Washington and Jefferson Snowstorm. In Connecticut, very little snow occurred, as the storm took that track out to sea. But in March, the storm track shifted north.

The *Connecticut Courant* wrote about the Hartford area weather: "Since the first of March there have been no less that four heavy storms of snow which is very much drifted and has rendered traveling almost impracticable. The snow upon the level in these parts is upwards of three feet. It is said the winter past has been the most severe of any since the year 1740." Even in April, the impact of the harsh weather was experienced, with no mail arriving during the first week of April, and no newspapers being delivered from March 28 to April 7 between Boston and New York.

Through the late eighteenth century, the weather remained harsh, and one of those seasons, 1783–1784, had to be one of the longest and most severe on record. The longest spell of below-zero cold occurred in Connecticut, and in Maine, it was claimed that this was the longest and coldest winter since the colonists arrived. The first signs of a rough winter occurred in November. Often if November is tough, watch out for the rest of the season. Snowstorms occurred as early as November 12–13, and again on the 28–29. Then, a massive snowstorm struck just before New Year's Day, on December 30–31. After the 2-foot storm, an early thaw melted the snow. But more snow arrived in mid-January. That was followed by a major January thaw, which broke the ice and created severe flooding. This up-and-down pattern continued in late January with the arrival of another storm that brought more snow. New Haven reported 15 inches of snow. Then came the cold in February. In Hartford, Noah Webster's diary showed that from February 10 through 17, the temperature in the Hartford area reached 12 degrees below zero. The sunrise temperature during that period ranged from 12 below to 20 below. In New Haven, the records of Ezra Stiles at Yale show that for six consecutive mornings the readings at sunrise ranged from 2 below zero to 10 below. Ice clogged the waterways and navigation was completely shut down. Western Long Island Sound was also jammed with ice, which prevented shipping in and around New York City, even in the Narrows between Staten Island and Long Island. As bad luck may have it, 1786 was a Leap Year, so February had an extra day, and another cold snap arrived. Ezra Stiles' thermometer stayed near zero through all of February 29. Between 1781 and 1870, Yale records show that this winter in New Haven was the fifth coldest—so as bad as it was, the "Little Ice Age" wasn't finished yet. Even then, when spring arrived, spring weather forgot to happen. Noah Webster commented, "Such a winter and spring are seldom known in this climate." His diary shows a series of snowfalls through April 11. On April 22, he was finally able to write, "This is the first pleasant day," but that was only to be followed by another entry on May 1, "At Home. Cold, cloudy, disagreeable weather."

The following season, in 1785, brought a late but harsh experience. It was another one of those years to remember. Major snowstorms came in January and didn't quit until April 19, on the tenth anniversary of the battle of Lexington and Concord. In Connecticut, snow and sleet combined to keep accumulations down to just a couple of inches, but in the Northwest Hills, snow measured 2 feet. That is a classic pattern in Connecticut: the shoreline receiving that wintry mix while the hills are buried in snow, especially in the spring when elevation snow becomes a major item because of the colder temperatures above the ground.

Although the 1785 season came late, the 1786–1787 winter came early. Some snow was peppering the Northeast through November, and in late November a harsh cold wave developed. Some of the low temperatures on Ezra Stiles' thermometer showed New Haven temperatures down to 19 degrees on the 25th, 9 on the 28th, and 4 above on the 29th. On that morning in Hartford, the temperature hit zero. The Connecticut River froze, with dozens of boats locked in place at Middletown. This bitterly cold weather was followed by a series of heavy snowstorms in December. Jeremiah Alling in Hamden reported 20 inches of driving snow on the 4th and 5th. Then, following the nor'easter came more cold weather, with the thermometer down to 4 below zero in New Haven on the 6th. On the same morning in Hartford, the temperature fell to 9 below zero. Another snowfall brought 9 more inches to Hamden on the 8th, and then, on the 9th, another major nor'easter struck. Newspaper accounts described the hardship brought by the storm. The *Connecticut Journal* in New London wrote, "The roads leading to this city have been so filled with the repeated falls of snow since the 5th that here has been little communications with the country during that time, and most of the inhabitants are distressed for want of fuel, and many of them for provisions." In Windham County, roads were filled with up to 4 feet of snow. Ezra Stiles wrote, "Snow above knee deep in the woods—very much drifted—equal to two feet on the level." Noah Webster wrote that he broke his sleigh in the deep December snow. In Newport, press accounts claimed, "There has scarcely been know to the oldest inhabitant living so stormy a week as the last, or so much snow on the ground." The storms also brought very high winds, which pushed extreme tides onto the shore. The rough seas claimed dozens of ships and dozens of lives. More harsh cold followed this storm of December 9.

The *Connecticut Courant* reported morning temperatures in Hartford ranging from 6 above on the 10th to 21 below zero on the 12th. In New Haven, the thermometer ranged between 5 and 6 below on the same morning. Supplies became very scarce. The *New Haven Gazette* published the temperatures but also wrote, "The severity of the weather this past week must be our excuse for publishing but a half of a sheet." Amazingly, after this brutal beginning, the season began to melt very quickly, with major thaws on December 13 to 18, and again around Christmas. Only a few banks of snow remained after Christmas. It was a harsh but short season.

This rough century had one more memorable season to deliver and that occurred in 1798–1799. In New Haven, the winter was rated as the third coldest during the ninety-year period of early weather records. Once again, a harsh November was a harbinger of what was to come. A five-day snowy period included the "Long Storm" of the 19th to the 21st. Upwards of a foot of snow fell along with severe gales, and the storm brought more cold. Noah Webster reported that numerous vessels were sunk at sea. Off Cape Cod, at least twenty-five sailors perished. And this was just November.

Snowstorms continued to strike through the third week of December, and claims were made that there had never been so much snow prior to January 1 on any year in the past. Then, January brought more harsh cold with near or below zero readings. The weather became moderate during February, but then in March the cold waves returned, with a reading of 4 below zero in New Haven on March 5. And of course snow. In Portland, Maine, there was a count of 40 snowstorms during that season. Rough weather continued in April, and even during May. At New Haven, some light snow fell on May 2 and May 8, with the Northwest Hills covered on the morning of the 8th. This brings back memories of what occurred in more recent times. On May 9, 1977, traces of snow fell along the shoreline, with over a foot accumulating in the Northwest Hills.

In the 1970s, harsh winters brought out theories of another impending "Little Ice Age," but a major global warming occurred within ten years, and that melted away those theories. But in early days of the United States, the real "Little Ice Age" continued for nearly another century. The nineteenth century was no slacker. In fact, it brought its share of snowy, cold seasons, along with the snowstorm of all snowstorms in 1888, and one of the oddest, coldest years of 1815–1816, the "Year Without a Summer." Crop failures that year brought worldwide hardship, and led to a great migration from Europe to the United States, and within the United States from the Northeast to the Midwest. It was called "Ohio Fever," but the weather was not much better in Ohio. Prior to 1815, snow did occur in ample quantities, and there was some below-zero cold, but the new century began relatively mildly. Thomas Jefferson wrote that the winters didn't seem to persist as long as in the past, and springs came sooner and more erratically, with alternating thaws and freezes. He attributed the warming to the burning and clearing of the fields for development. Sound familiar? No wonder he was called the first Meterorologist-in-Chief. But if he waited a few years, he might have been a little more reserved in making those comments.

The season of 1804–1805 was icy and snowy. Noah Webster made this account in January of 1805: "Winter commenced about the middle of December and was severe from the 20th with good sleighing. It continued with severe and steady cold through January and most of February. The snow of January 1805 was about three feet deep. This was the severest winter since 1780." Actually, that winter began with strange occurrences as early as October. A strong October storm that could have had tropical characteristics brought severe winds and heavy snow to the western hills of New England, even into Connecticut. The system became known as the "snow hurricane." The storm is reminiscent of another October storm that struck in more modern times during 1987. Rain changed to snow on the night of October 2, 1987, and upwards of a foot of snow fell in Connecticut's western hills as well as through eastern New York and Vermont. Trees that were still in full leaf were damaged severely by the weight of the heavy, wet snow. Similarly, the storm of October 9, 1804, caused extensive tree damage, according to Noah Webster. Connecticut snowfall accumulations ranged from a covering in the New Haven area, to 3 to 12 inches in the Litchfield Hills.

But the biggest snowstorm of the season occurred in late January, and that capped a month that brought as much as 57 inches to Hamden, according to the records of Jeremiah Alling. On January 27–28, alone, 18 inches fell. Yale records show that 14 inches fell in New Haven on the 19th and 20th, and 16 more inches on the 27th to 28th. The *Connecticut Courant* wrote that the snow totals around Hartford likely were even greater than the 30 inches reported by Webster.

In 1807, January brought subzero cold, which lasted all day in late January. Then February brought heavy rain and a flooding thaw. But then, more snow and cold occurred through March. The 1807 season was topped off by a record-setting April Fool Storm. In northwestern Connecticut, Thomas Robbins reported that snow was already "Two feet deep in the woods," before the storm of March 31 and April 1 began. That storm doubled the snow depth and moved across inland hills west of the storm track. On April 2, he wrote, "Was out with most people most of the day breaking paths. The snow between three and four feet deep." The storm carved an inland path from the Midwest to western Connecticut. The Connecticut shoreline was just south of the track, so this area received mixed rain and snow and strong winds that brought considerable damage to Long Wharf. Other damage reports included the blowing down of the steeple of the West Haven Meeting House. The Yale barometer reached a low of 28.75 inches — not unlike the central pressure of a hurricane.

The early nineteenth century brought another rough season in 1811–1812. The largest storm occurred on Christmas Eve, and it turned Long Island Sound into a shambles, with numerous shipwrecks along and off the Connecticut shore. The damage to shipping was likely the greatest impact of the storm. It was one of those classic nor'easters, which stalled long enough to deliver heavy snow and punishing winds. Yet, on December 23, 1811, the weather was relatively mild. The wind was from the southeast, and the temperature was warm enough for just a little drizzle. But cold air worked into the storm on Christmas Eve. Drizzle turned to a heavy, driving snow that fell for twenty-four hours. At Old Lyme, Vine Utley reported that huge snowdrifts made mail delivery impossible for four days. Sentries at Fort Trumbull in New London reported that the temperature fell to 8 degrees during the middle of the afternoon on the 24th, and that the wind almost seemed to increase to that of a "tornado." Professor Jeremiah Day of Yale kept a detailed account of the storm, and confirmed the rapid drop in temperature — from 41 degrees at noon on the 23rd to 14 degrees at sunrise on the 24th. On Christmas morning, the temperature was in the single numbers. While there was a rapid fall in temperature and large snowdrifts, total snowfall was not over the top. In New Haven, snowfall was reported to be 8 inches, and in Hartford, amounts of 12 inches were reported by Thomas Robbins. But the early snow did set the stage for a very cold winter that brought subzero cold in mid-January.

In New Haven, the temperature averaged below normal each month from March to October. The summer of 1812 challenged the cold of the famous "Year Without a Summer" in 1816. Snow even fell in Connecticut on May 4. Up to 12 inches of wet snow fell in the hills of western Connecticut on that day in May, and light accumulation occurred along the shore in New Haven. But remember May 9, 1977? The exact same situation had occurred, with 1 to 2 feet of wet snow accumulating in Connecticut's Northwest Hills. Connecticut's weather is ready to deliver that surprise, regardless of the century.

Some of the strangest weather known to any century occurred during 1815 and 1816. The odd, cold and stormy weather was something that affected much of the world. Famine occurred around the world, helping to accelerate a migration into the United States, where, unfortunately, the weather wasn't much better than elsewhere, and Connecticut was not about to be excluded. The cold and great storminess very likely was enhanced by an increase in volcanism that was occurring. In 1815, Mount Tambora in Indonesia erupted and sent ash and gas into the high atmosphere. The emissions likely blocked enough sunshine to lower worldwide temperature during a period that was already chilled. The enhanced cooling made for some tough going.

Even before the volcano erupted, January and February of 1815 brought subzero cold to Connecticut. In Windsor, Thomas Robbins wrote about January 31: "The Sun shone, but obscurely. I think I never saw a colder day." The noon temperature was just 2 above zero, and by sunset, his thermometer recorded 7 below. Ice completely choked off Long island Sound to marine traffic, and in the Sound, a British warship sank with the loss of 117—only 6 survived. In New Haven, the temperature remained below freezing from the 22nd of January through February 1. Heavy snow fell, too. Fifteen inches fell in January and another 23 inches fell during February. And following this cold, snowy, icy winter came the historic year of 1816, known as the "Year Without a Summer." It was also called the "Poverty Year," because of the extensive crop losses. Some called it the "Mackerel Year," because people used mackerel in place of corn, which became very scarce. Drought didn't help the cause either, and the dryness led to numerous fires such as those in Oxford, North Haven, Bristol, Derby, and New Milford. But the cold was the major item, and some would remember the year as "Eighteen Hundred and Froze to Death.'"

In Connecticut, frost, or freeze, was reported every single month of 1816, with some snow falling in June and a devastating frost at the end of September. The June snow fell heavily in the hills and mountains of northern New England, and lighter amounts were reported in the hills of Connecticut. Two bursts of snow occurred—one on June 6 and the other on June 8–9 that fell farthest to the south. Thomas Robbins of East Windsor reported snow in the hills, and an additional report had snow falling in Plymouth. The cold of that summer created a major failure of the corn crop, and great hardship followed with the threat of starvation.

Europe had a very similar experience. The summer was a horror, and there is little wonder that one of the great horror stories of all times, *Frankenstein*, was penned during that season. Mary Shelley often was confined to the house because of the cold and seemingly endless rainfall. She and her husband, poet Percy Shelly, and their friends Lord Byron and Dr. John Polidori, passed the time away by writing ghost stories. Following one of those writing sessions, Mary Shelley had a dream, and after that, she wrote the famous tale *Frankenstein*.

Amazingly, the autumn of 1816 took a mild and easygoing turn. Even during the most extreme periods, the weather tries to balance the score in Connecticut. I call it the "Law of Weather Averages." An extended Indian Summer occurred through December, and into early January. In December, frost was generally out of the ground. But from mid-January 1817 through early March, winter settled in with a vengeance. Four major cold waves occurred, along with a vicious nor'easter. In New Haven, February averaged nearly 9 degrees below average — making February 1817 the coldest February since records began to be kept in 1780.

The variability of the nineteenth-century climate was on display in the Thomas Robbins account of the 1819–1820 winter at East Windsor. The season seemed relatively mild until late December, when bitter cold developed after Christmas. On the 26th, the temperature was 8 above, and by New Year's Eve, a violent snowstorm arrived. A foot of snow fell, and there was considerable drifting. The weather turned very cold after the storm moved along, with a temperature of 10 below zero on the 7th. Then, came a brief thaw, followed by more snow and severe cold. But by January 27, the temperature reached 50 degrees, and the old-fashioned January thaw continued until February 1, when the arctic cold returned with an afternoon temperature of just 11 above. More snow followed. A series of snowstorms made roads impassable by the eleventh. But on February 13, the temperature reached 60 degrees! The meltdown began. The back of winter was broken. By late March, the temperature reached 83 degrees.

Throughout the nineteenth century, the hits just kept coming. A very cold period occurred from 1831 to 1840. From August 1834 through December 1837, the mean temperature in New Haven was below average for 38 out of 41 months. In 1838, the mean temperature was below average for 7 out of 12 months. In January 1835, the temperature reached 27 below zero in Hartford and 24 below in New Haven. The next year, 1836, was the coldest in two hundred years of recordkeeping in New Haven. Other severe winters occurred in 1867–1868, when the temperature was below average from October through May except during March, and 1880–1881, when the temperature was below average from October through April.

But one of the greatest hits of all—maybe the greatest of all recorded history—was the Blizzard of '88. Ironically, all accounts of the winter of 1887–1888 indicate mild conditions, so mild that crocuses were blossoming early. Shopkeepers who invested in snow shovels didn't exactly know what they would do with their merchandise. Spring was arriving early, and March 11 was warm and balmy. A light rain began to fall with the arrival of a low-pressure system that was tracking eastward from the Midwest. But then, a second center took shape off the mid-Atlantic coast, and its northeast wind began to tap a cold pool of air that was located in eastern Canada. That cold air caused the rain to turn to snow, and it helped to block the rapid motion of the storm. The storm became stationary near Block Island, where it just spun like a top. Most of the rain turned to snow and it snowed from late on the 11th through the 14th. The storm pounded the Northeast from Maine to the nation's capital. For a week, the northeastern states were cut off from the rest of the world. Winds reached hurricane intensity and over four hundred lives were lost, two hundred in New York City alone. Some survivors of the storm, called "Blizzard Men of 1888," held annual meetings in New York City until 1941.

Although the storm began as rain, the temperature plunged to near zero on Monday, the 12th. Slush turned to solid ice. Southeastern Connecticut received more frozen slush than snowfall. Temperatures there were not as cold as in other parts of the state. Snowfall came to about 6 inches. But for the rest of the state, snowfall amounts were historic and monumental. In New Haven, snowfall measured 45 inches. On the 12th alone, New Haven received 28 inches, which became a state record for a single twenty-four-hour period. Both Wallingford and Waterbury received a three-day total of 42 inches, and Middletown picked up the state record for a single storm of 50 inches. These 4-foot accumulations did not account for the drifts, which reached 20 to 40 feet! Statewide, the average snowfall was 30 to 40 inches. The *Stamford Advocate* wrote this account:

By 10 o'clock Sunday night the storm increased, and took the character of a Dakota blizzard. The air was filled with particles of fine snow that even after daybreak Monday morning one could scarcely see a distance of seventy-five feet. There was no intermission in the fury of the wind or the fall of the snow all day Monday nor during the night, nor in fact until daybreak Tuesday morning, though the temperature was low reaching to ten above zero.

More than four feet of snow buries downtown New Haven during the Blizzard of 1888. This view shows the tunnels created by the snowbanks, which were piled on the sides of the road.

The heavy snow could only be transported away by railroad cars. These snow-filled cars line up along Union Station in New Haven.

Many trains were stuck along the snow-covered rail system. Here people are doing their best to clear the railroad tracks following the greatest blizzard of all.

College and Grove streets have changed little since the late nineteenth century, but there has never since been such an inundation of snow as seen in this photo along College Street.

The intersection of Grand and State Street has changed over the years, but this photo across from the current WTNH-TV studio does show some similarities. Still, there has never been such an accumulation of snow outside that TV station as seen in this photo.

Following the blizzard, the great dig-out was underway. All downtown streets were blocked with feet of snow.

The city of New Haven was paralyzed from the Blizzard of 1888.
Notice the snowbanks extend almost as high as the store awnings.

This could be called "The Nightmare on Elm Street." On March 21, 1888, only
a narrow path allowed people to go from place to place. The architecture of
the buildings along Elm Street is very similar to that of today's structures.

The snow hasn't yet stopped falling, but people are doing their best to clear sidewalks and hope that life can go on.

A description of the storm written by Helen Upson in the *Redding Times* indicated that the temperature was close to 70 degrees in Danbury around noon on the 11th but then: "Next morning—how different! Overnight there had been a radical change. The sky was overcast with heavy, sullen clouds. The mercury had catapulted to low levels and the air was filled with large snowflakes. The voices of birds and peepers, so evident a few hours before were silent. There was no more open water." By July 4 of 1888, the ridges around Redding still had enough snow for making gallons of ice cream.

The *New York Times* wrote this account about conditions in New York City on the 12th: "Before the day had well advanced, every horse car and elevated railroad train in the city had stopped running; the streets were almost impassable; the electric wires—telegraph and telephone—were nearly all broken." The storm became known as the "Great White Hurricane," and it led to the building of a subway system and the installation of underground electric cables. The Blizzard of 1888 is the standard by which all other snowstorms are measured.

Connecticut has some of the earliest records of weather and climate in the country, and the long record shows tremendous fluctuation in both summer and winter conditions. When we examine those trends in detail, we will see that a definite change came in the late nineteenth century — after the great blizzard. The "Little Ice Age," which characterized the fourteenth and fifteenth centuries, was melting down. Even then, there were warm periods, such as during 1790 to 1810, when Thomas Jefferson speculated that the clearing of forests accompanied by the burning of the landscape was responsible for the change, but then it became bitterly cold again. In Connecticut, the period from 1811 to 1875 was very cold, with only eleven years averaging above the long-term normal temperatures.

That pattern completely reversed during the first part of the twentieth century. For the next sixty-five years, only eleven averaged colder than the long-term normal. And since then, the weather has become even warmer. Was the climate ready for a natural change after five hundred years of brutal, nearly ice-age cold? Or was the industrial revolution of the late nineteenth century contributing to this trend? Or how about both? We'll look at these questions in more detail later. For now, let's continue our exploration of the winters during the end of one age and the beginning of another.

Winter of the New Age

Although the trend has been in the warmer direction since the late 1800s, Connecticut has experienced its share of "old-fashioned winters," even into the twenty-first century. The twentieth century began with two very cold winters in 1903–1904 and in 1904–1905, when winter set in during November and persisted until March. The change toward colder weather seemed to get underway as early as December 1902, when below-zero temperatures were reported in the first half of December. These winters averaged the third coldest in 150 years of past recordkeeping — a match for any of the chill of the "Little Ice Age." But consistency has never been a characteristic of Connecticut's weather, and after those two winters, the weather warmed sharply, although the total snowfall in 1905–1906 was above average. Severe cold seemed to take a backseat to the action until the brutally cold winter of 1917–1918.

That winter started early, with damaging frosts in early September, and the autumn chill was followed by consistently cold weather from December through the first week of February, when the temperature was 7 to 12 degrees below average, which is a lot during the winter months. This winter was called the "Great World War I Cold Wave." On December 29, the temperature in Hartford was reported at 18 below zero. In northern New England, at Berlin, New Hampshire, the temperatures bottomed out at 44 below! On New Year's Day, New Haven's temperature was 7 below zero — bitterly cold for coastal Connecticut. In both Hartford and New Haven, December and January averaged as the two coldest consecutive months on record, since weather records began to be kept by the National Weather Service in the late 1800s. The two months came to 7 degrees below average in Hartford and 6 degrees below average in New Haven. Even going back to earlier records, the winter surpassed the cold of 1903 and 1904, and the winter became the third coldest since the middle of the 1700s. For most of Connecticut, the record has held since.

Until that time, Connecticut was a major force in the peach-growing industry, but according to John Lyman of Lyman Orchards in Middlefield, the peach crop was wiped out that year, when frost went as deep as 4 feet into the ground. Whole trees were destroyed. The response was to plant more-resilient apple trees, and that is how Connecticut orchard growers got into the apple business. The weather in Europe was rough during that season, too, and that only added to the woes of the war effort.

The brutal winter of 1917–1918 was enough for a full generation to talk about, but another historic year came in 1934, thanks to February of that year, which became one of the snowiest months on record. The month itself was among the coldest on record, and the deep chill spawned a massive coastal storm on the 20th. The storm tracked just east of Connecticut across Rhode Island. Places closest to the center received less snow. Milder air often will wrap around the center of these storms, but even in New London where just 3 inches of snow fell, the landscape turned to frozen slush and traffic was shut down when the wind backed around to the northwest. Winds reached over 40 miles per hour. Likewise, the temperature plummeted at other locations with that wind shift. For much of the storm, which began around daybreak of the 20th, the snow was heavy and wet, but the change in wind direction as the storm slowly pulled northward caused temperatures to fall from near 30 degrees to 11 degrees at midnight in New Haven and down to 3 degrees across northern Connecticut, with the snow still falling. Over 20 inches of snow fell, even along coastal areas such as Norwalk, Bridgeport, and New Haven. By the end of February, 47 inches of snow had fallen in Bridgeport and 46 inches in New Haven. And there was plenty of cold to go around all month long.

For Bridgeport, where "official" National Weather Service readings began in 1905, the two consecutive months of January and February 1934 were the coldest on record, averaging 5 degrees below average at 29.5 degrees. In Hartford, from the same official record, February 1934 became the coldest month of record with an average of 16.5 degrees, about 10 degrees below average. And in New Haven, where the official records extend back to 1871, February 1934 also became the coldest on record, with an average of 17.4, more than 8 degrees below average. During that month, Bridgeport averaged more than 9 degrees below the average.

This cold and snowy spell occurred when social conditions were in their own depression. Many of the "Hooverville" homeless suffered through that depression year. The backdrop of the brutal season became the setting for a popular murder mystery called *Mood Indigo* written by Charlotte Vale Allen in 1998.

The winter might have taken a toll on a teenage John F. Kennedy. The future president had serious health problems from a very young age. While attending Choate in Wallingford during the winter of 1934, he was rushed to New Haven to be treated for a variety of ailments including weight loss, hives, and a cough. At first, the doctors thought he had leukemia. He wrote to a classmate, "It seems that I am much sicker than I thought I was." But by March, as the winter melted away, so, too, did his symptoms. Yet, the summer of that year, digestive problems sent him to the Mayo Clinic. The winter turned out to be more than many could easily handle.

Stores ran out of staples while the luncheonette business thrived. Many people were stranded on snow-clogged roads, but people did come to each other's assistance. In Branford, a stalled bus filled with passengers including many children was about to be rescued by the fire department, but when the emergency workers arrived, they found the bus empty — neighbors came out during the height of the storm and brought the passengers into their homes.

The prolific songmaster Harry Warren wrote many tunes during the 1934–1935 era, including "Shuffle Off to Buffalo." He could have written "Shovel Off to Buffalo." But he did write "Fair And Warmer." Wishful thinking! Other tunes that became popular in 1934 include, "Ill Wind," and the classic "Winter Wonderland." "What a Difference a Day Makes" was also popular, although, in the case of the 1934 storm, three days passed before life started to come back to normal.

After the rough winter of 1934, the weather settled into a less extreme pattern, and the winter of 1936–1937 was exceptionally mild, with the winter temperature more than 5 degrees above average. In northern Connecticut, at Windsor Locks, the official National Weather Service location for Hartford, only 14.7 inches of snow were measured for the entire season. The overall pattern of winters became erratic, with little consistency in snowfall from year to year. During the 1940s, some winters were also very mild. In 1941–1942, only 14.7 inches of snow fell the entire season in Hartford, and just 27 inches fell during the winter of 1943–1944. The average snowfall there is closer to 50 inches. But the 1940s also brought some memorable snows and winters. In 1945–1946, the snowfall total came to 80 inches, and the same occurred the following winter. Two major snowstorms struck Connecticut in December 1945 one on the 19th and 20th, and the other on the 29th. The two storms delivered 36 inches of snow to Hartford, and more than 40 inches of snow fell for the entire month, making it the snowiest December on record for Hartford. Then, two years later, the region was hit by another severe winter. The winter began in earnest the day after Christmas with a blizzard that dropped 1 to 2 feet of snow. The cold that followed set the stage for additional heavy snowstorms through January and February 1948. Even coastal sections of Connecticut received 50 to 70 inches of snow during that season. Amounts ranged up to 120 inches in the Northwest Hills.

The 1940s had its storms to remember, but among my personal favorites was a snowstorm that came along on St. Valentine's Day, 1940. It became heartwarming for my mother and father, who were about to be married. The heavy snowstorm on that February 14 paralyzed travel throughout New England. Busses and trolley traffic completely closed down in a storm that generated knee-deep snow, and even greater drifts. My parents-to-be lived in the Boston area. My father was on a bus traveling from Everett to Lynn where his fianceé lived. The bus broke down in Revere, but he was determined to see his intended. So, he walked more than 7 miles in the drifted snow, and for my family, the rest became history. That storm was the only major snowfall of the entire season.

The warming trend that began in the twentieth century seemed very evident during the 1950s, when only one winter brought above-average snowfall. The entire 1950s was one of the warmest decades of the century. Only the winter of 1955–1956 seemed to be of the old-fashioned type.

The 1955–1956 season began quietly, with only a total of 12 inches of snow falling from November through January. Another easy winter? Well, not exactly. February brought the first major snowfall, and then March brought far more than a full season's worth of winter. Storm after storm clobbered Connecticut. For much of the state, March 1956 was the snowiest March on record. Norfolk, in the Northwest Hills, received a total of 73.6 inches of snow during that month. Major storms struck on the 6th, the 8th, the 14th, and the 16th. In addition, a blizzard hit on the 19th, and more snow fell on the 24th and the 29th. The biggest storm occurred on the 19th, when a storm moved out of the Ohio Valley to a position south of Cape Cod. Generally, 1 to 2 feet of snow fell in that storm. Total snow cover of 4 feet was common by the end of that month. And the snow didn't exactly stop falling during April of that year. On April 7–8, several inches of snow fell in southern Connecticut, but 12 to 20 inches of snow fell in northern sections, where drifts were as high as 14 feet.

Another late-season bloomer occurred during the 1957–1958 winter. Although the season was no match for 1955–1956, late-season storms in 1958 let everyone know that winter could still happen in a big way. On February 17th, a blizzard closed schools for two to three days. Generally, 1 to 2 feet of snow fell in that storm, and then came the lion-sized month of March, which brought two nor'easters — one on the 14th through 16th, and the other on the 20th to 22nd. The late-March storm delivered heavy, wet snow and gale-force winds, which combined to bring down power lines. Electrical service was out for several days. An average of 10 to 20 inches of snow fell in the storm.

So, even if the 1950s turned out to be relatively mild in the winter department, the decade did deliver its share of winter weather. Whatever was lacking during the 1950s seemed to be balanced by the 1960s. Just as the 1950s could be noted for their general warmth, the 1960s were extreme in their overall chill. The 1960s were big. All but two winters delivered above-normal snowfall, and the decade began in a blizzard of storms. Over 80 inches of snow fell in Hartford during the decade opener in 1960–1961. The most memorable storm of that season took place when President Kennedy was inaugurated on January 20, 1961.

The storm moved out of the Midwest and rapidly intensified when reaching the East Coast. The Washington, D.C., area was hit first on the 19th, and in the wake of the snow came bitter cold. More than ten thousand cars were abandoned and airplanes were backed up. In the White House, over thirty members of the Eisenhower staff were snowbound. Still, the parties went on, and sunshine did return to Washington in time for the inauguration on the 20th. Regardless of the cold, one of the most famous inaugural addresses of all time was given outdoors as planned: "Ask not what your country can do for you, but what you can do for your country." Even an elderly Robert Frost made a presentation in the biting cold during the inauguration. But the storm strengthened by the time it reached New England, and on the 20th, Connecticut received a solid 1 to 2 feet of snow. Strong winds caused the snow to drift over 15 feet. Connecticut was shut down.

This storm was far from the only big snowmaker of the season. A blizzard had started the winter season during December. On the 12th, 1 to 2 feet of snow fell, and the powdery snow was whipped into drifts by gale-force winds. Then, after the inaugural storm came a massive storm on February 3–4. Another 12 to 27 inches of snow fell, and the snow was driven by powerful winds. A total of three crippling snowstorms occurred during that very old-fashioned winter.

As soon as we look at the second half of the twentieth century, many of us will have personal recollections of the big ones, and the rip-roaring sixties were just inaugurated by the 1961 snow blitz. Another huge, old-fashioned blizzard occurred in January 1964. I was a freshman at Penn State, and I had an 8:00 a.m. calculus class that was about a mile away from the freshmen dorms. Snow had been falling since late on January 12, and it continued through the 13th. On that Monday morning, I walked through drifts that were over my boots — my knees, too — got to class, only to find out that classes were cancelled because the professors were unable to reach the campus. We were walkers. They were commuters. On a level surface, snowfall came close to 2 feet, and as the storm redeveloped south of Cape Cod, the heavy, blinding storm moved into Connecticut. Because the storm took a track to the south and east of New England, with its center about 150 miles southeast of the shoreline, areas to the south picked up more snow and wind. Manhattan was hit with 6-foot drifts, and New York City travel was shut down. In Connecticut, snowfall amounts were less, but 1-foot amounts were common, with a range of 7 to 15 inches. All planes were grounded at Bradley Field. The worst of the storm hit after 8:00 a.m. on the 13th, with just flurries the night of the 12th. Because of the delayed arrival of the heavy snow, many schools were undecided about closing, and many people hit the roads, only to be stranded later in the day when the brunt of the storm struck. Many drivers hit snow banks that were piled up by road crews. Two New Haven trains stalled and blocked train traffic in southwestern Connecticut. Wind gusts of 35 to 40 miles per hour were common with the storm, and on Block Island, the wind reached a near-hurricane gust of 71 miles per hour. The Connecticut shore was hit hard with high winds and tides reaching 2 to 4 feet above normal. Most companies in Connecticut sent their workers home early in the afternoon. Temperatures were held to the teens. Five deaths were attributed to the storm, four from shoveling the deep snow. The fifth was a veteran state highway worker of twenty-five years who was crushed by a sand truck when he was directing it into a maintenance garage.

The 1960s were filled with meteorological action, and 1966 brought a series of moderate to heavy snowstorms. One was called the "Donner and Blitzen" storm because the snow arrived on Christmas Eve to deliver a White Christmas. Thunderstorms occurred at the time of the heaviest snow. Norfolk in the Northwest Hills received the greatest accumulation of 13 inches. Generally, 6 to 9 inches fell around the state. The heaviest occurred in the higher elevations from the Berkshires to the Catskills, where 20 to 30 inches accumulated. By Christmas morning, the storm had moved into the Gulf of Maine.

Later in the 1966–1967 winter, another very powerful storm hit, very much in line with the 1964 monster. The heavy snow swept into Connecticut on February 8, 1967. The storm also generated thunderstorms as it exploded off the mid-Atlantic coast. The Coast Guard's weather ship at Diamond Shoals, just off Cape Hatteras, North Carolina, was badly damaged by a waterspout that brought major tornado-intensity winds of 140 miles per hour. In Connecticut, the heavy snow was accompanied by bitter cold. High temperatures did not rise out of the teens as the snow piled up on the 8th. At 7:00 p.m. in Norfolk, the temperature was just 2 above zero, and that doesn't include the wind chill, which was in the frostbite area of 50 below. Snowfall amounts ranged up to 19 inches in the Northwest Hills at Norfolk to 12 to 18 inches from Hartford to New Haven. Ten inches were reported at Groton, and up to 16 inches from Norwalk to Stamford. The "quiet corner" of northeast Connecticut picked up 14 inches of accumulation at Putnam. In Enfield, at the state prison, an inmate viewed the storm as an opportunity to escape. He was working on the prison farm, but at 1:00 p.m. conditions were bad enough for the prisoners to be called in early. Between then and a 4:00 p.m. prisoner check, he had escaped by scaling a prison fence, where a portion of his glove was left as evidence as it caught on the barbed wire. He had served one year in a two-to-nine-year sentence for breaking and entering. He got away. Maybe he was determined to travel south to a warmer clime. But he did run into traffic. Hundreds of cars were stranded on Connecticut highways, with the visibility often down to just 50 feet. The cold, heavy, powdery snow was whipped around by wind gusts of 35 to 40 miles per hour. Emergency vehicles were also stuck in the snow and were delayed reaching people in serious need. Schools and businesses were closed. Like so many powerful nor'easters, this one, too, delivered lightning and thunder. During this thunder-snow, most of the accumulation occurred. Not even mail carriers were able to make it to their appointed rounds, and they were called in during the early afternoon when that thunder-snow was blinding the region. Yet, through it all, a brush fire burned in New Britain.

More snowstorms arrived during March 1967, and when winter was finally finished with Connecticut, 89.1 inches of snow had fallen for the season at Windsor Locks, with over 60 inches on the shoreline in Bridgeport. Over 100 inches fell in the Northwest hills. Generally, snowfall was twice as great as the long-term average. The 1966–1967 season brought two winters instead of one.

The 1968–1969 winter was another big snow season. No wonder that articles and books were being written about the arrival of another ice age — never mind global warming. February was a tough month. The storm struck Connecticut on February 9. Snowfall amounts ranged from 1 to 2 feet and completely paralyzed the area. Along the shoreline, 15 inches fell in New Haven, and 18 inches accumulated farther west toward the New York City area, where 2 feet were measured, not counting the drifts. Winds gusted to 70 miles per hour at Bridgeport, and numerous tree limbs were knocked down from Branford to Stonington, causing widespread power outages. Both I-91 and I-95 were closed at times because of the snow, and in New York City, days would pass before residents in Queens were plowed out. The storm became known as the "Lindsay Storm." New York Mayor John Lindsay was criticized heavily for not doing the job, and the storm effectively ended his political career. Snow-removal complaints were still occurring in March! And then, just two weeks later, another major snowstorm hit the region. And this was a strange one.

It became known as the "100-hour storm" because snow managed to fall steadily in eastern New England for nearly 100 hours. In Boston, the snow began at 1:35 a.m. on February 24, and did not end until 12:10 a.m. on February 29. Okay, for Boston's Logan Airport, it was a 99-hour storm, but also one that delivered a record 26.3 inches of accumulation. But up to 40 inches fell in the suburbs near the shore around Boston. Huge drifts pushed snow up to the roofs of homes. The storm was blocked south of Cape Cod, and it only slowly moved out of the picture. Dozens of communities declared States of Emergency. Road crews were exhausted trying to keep highways open. Locations from Rhode Island to Maine received the heaviest snowfall. Pinkham Notch in the White Mountains picked up 77 inches of snow, but snowfall amounts dropped off sharply farther west and southwest.

In Connecticut, a foot of snow fell in the Hartford area and up to 14 inches in Putnam, but just 4 to 6 inches fell along the shore. New York City caught a break this time, with only 2 to 4 inches accumulating. In Connecticut, the storm started on Sunday night, February 23, and it tapered off Monday night. So it was only a 24-hour storm, or less, for the state. But, the snow was heavy and wet and because of high winds, numerous power outages occurred state-wide. Most roads were able to stay opened. Still, the storm helped push the monthly snowfall in Hartford up to 32.2 inches, eclipsing the 31.5 inches that fell during March 1934, and just shy of the record 32.7 inches that fell during February 1934.

The cavalcade of storms continued during the 1969–1970 season, with two of the biggest occurring during the holidays, Christmas and Easter. During Christmas night, the first brought snow into Connecticut from the southwest. By December 26, the storm was centered in southern New Jersey, and it moved east-northeastward offshore on the night of the 26th. By then, the snow had tapered off to a freezing drizzle. In Connecticut, high winds helped pile up the tides and cause local flooding, and snowfall amounts ranged from 9 inches along the shore from New London to New Haven, to 13 to 15 inches in the Hartford area, to 17 inches around Danbury.

At times, the snow fell at a rate of 3 inches per hour. Twenty to 40 inches fell in upstate New York. Nearly every airport in the Northeast was closed at some point during the storm. Bradley was closed for 12 hours. Because Christmas occurred on a Thursday in 1969, many workers were given a long weekend, so that people were already home and off the highways during the height of the storm on Friday. Roads were kept open. Still, local service stations stayed busy pulling cars out of ditches, and rail traffic was delayed from Connecticut to New York. The snow was of the heavy, wet variety and it was difficult to move. Now, that was a very White Christmas, or at least a White Christmas Night and day after. Three people in Connecticut died from the storm, but amazingly, on Saturday the 27th, post-Christmas shoppers were out exchanging and returning presents and looking for some bargains. This was going on while parking bans continued in downtown areas. Cars were towed and owners were given fines of $20, which were not received with much holiday spirit since many were already short on cash from holiday spending.

The holiday spirit might have been a little less than it should have been on Easter Sunday of the 1969–1970 season. The refrain for March 29, 1970, was "In your Easter Bonnet with all the snow upon it." Easter did come early that year, and snowfall set a record for any Easter Sunday. The storm was a surprise and it caught many off guard, including motorists who were stranded on highways. The Merritt Parkway was blocked for 8 miles in the Fairfield area, and Route 15 up to Hartford was impassable. Snow was knee-deep in drifts with 7 to 8 inches on a level surface reported in Danbury, New Milford, Bridgeport, and Haddam. The snow moved in rapidly and road crews were just not prepared for the heavy snowfall. They were not out in full until mid-afternoon, and by then the snow already had piled up. The famous Easter Parade in New York City was snowed-out for the first time since 1885. But some managed to keep their humor. A Newington family decorated a Christmas tree on their lawn, just to keep the Easter Bunny a little more confused.

Although the winters might have appeared to mellow during the 1970s, we still had our share of harsh weather. Snowfall averaged above normal during both the 1970–1971 and 1971–1972 winters. Then, there was the unforgettable pre-Christmas ice storm in 1973, the bitterly cold January of 1976, and the snowstorms of 1978. We had plenty of winter.

One of the most intense storms of the early 1970s occurred during late February 1972. The storm reached its peak on Saturday, February 18, when as much as 18 inches of snow fell in parts of the state. The heaviest accumulation occurred in western Connecticut. Generally, between 12 to 18 inches fell from Ridgefield and Danbury northward to Torrington and Winsted. Eleven inches fell in the Hartford area, but amounts diminished to the east and south of Hartford. Five inches fell along the shoreline from Bridgeport to New Haven and New London. The storm delivered strong east winds, which reached 48 miles per hour in Bridgeport and 60 miles per hour on Block Island. Those winds brought milder air onshore, and in southern and eastern Connecticut, the snow mixed with rain. Accumulations of snow were lower than inland areas. But those same winds piled the water onto beaches and flooding was commonplace during high tide. The heaviest snowfall occurred to the west of Connecticut, across north-central Pennsylvania, where as much as 30 inches was reported. Following the storm, temperatures plunged into the single numbers. Travel was hampered by the storm, but the show did go on — that is, the dog show.

During the height of the storm, hundreds of dog lovers showed up at the 43rd Dog and Obedience Trial that was being held in Hartford at the State Armory. Prize dogs from all over New England managed to make it to the show, regardless of the weather. The judges showed up, too. The storm had plenty of bark, but not enough bite to cancel the show.

Following snowy winters during the 1970–1971 and 1971–1972 seasons, the next two years came up short: about 40 percent below average. The change could have been helped along by a strong El Niño that developed. The El Niño is the warm phase of an oscillation that occurs in the eastern Pacific, near the Equator. When the waters in the eastern Pacific become much warmer than normal, the weather across North America can be affected in a variety of ways. Mild winters are not uncommon in New England during strong El Niño periods, and the El Niño that developed during the early 1970s was one of the strongest on record. But winter didn't entirely forget to occur. Actually, one of the most devastating ice storms in recorded history took place during this "warm" phase.

The pre-Christmas ice storm of 1973 became legendary. In fact, a novel that became a major Hollywood movie was written with this storm playing a key role. Both book and film appropriately were called *The Ice Storm*. Winter-weather enthusiasts may love snow, but hardly anyone is enamored of an ice storm, which can cause fierce weather conditions along with major hazards and disruptions.

Ice storms occur when a layer of above-freezing air occurs above a cold, below-freezing layer close to the ground. Snow may be falling from above, but when it reaches the warm layer, which can be about 5,000 feet above the surface, the snow melts and turns to rain. Then, as the rain falls into the cold layer near the ground, it refreezes. If that cold layer is sufficiently thick, the raindrops turn to bouncing ice pellets, or sleet. But if that layer is very shallow, the rain will freeze only on contact with objects at the sur-

The ice storm in 1973 took a toll on the powerlines.

face; that is freezing rain. A glaze occurs that turns roads and sidewalks into sheets of ice, and as the ice collects on utility wires and tree limbs, they break and create power outages. The power outages in 1973 were the greatest on record, until Hurricane Gloria came along in 1985. More than 250,000 homes lost power.

At first, snow was falling during Sunday, December 16, but it changed to rain as warmer air moved in above the ground. During Sunday night, the temperature at 5,000 feet was 50 degrees, but a stubborn north wind near the ground kept temperatures below freezing at the surface. The layer of cold air was very shallow in southern and central portions of the state — and that is where freezing rain created the most serious problems. In northern and northwestern areas, the cold layer was more extensive, and sleet rather than freezing rain was dominant, so the accumulation of ice on wires and limbs was less. The sleet would just bounce off these surfaces.

While large sections of the state were blacked out, communities such as Torrington escaped with few problems—little more than inconvenience. No traffic accidents or power outages were reported. But elsewhere, the storm created havoc.

Throughout that Sunday night, the temperature at the ground refused to move upward, even though rain was falling, and by daybreak Monday, the temperature began to fall through the twenties and into the upper teens. The rain continued to fall through Monday. More than an inch of rain fell, and ice sheaths of a half-inch had collected on tree branches. Gusty winds added to the problems. Branches snapped, with more tree damage occurring during this storm than during the historic 1938 hurricane. The National Guard was activated and storm shelters and motels began to fill as powerless and freezing residents evacuated their homes. I was one of the victims of the storm, and it didn't take long for me to check myself and my family into a motel that did have power.

The full restoration of power was a very slow process and many Connecticut residents were without power for a week. The lack of power during the winter is far more disruptive than a loss of power during the warmer summer months. While Hurricane Gloria caused more power outages, the impact of this ice storm was greater. In the Hartford area, the Metropolitan District Commission reported that twenty-five of its sewage pumping stations were out because of the loss of power, and the sewage was diverted from the stations into the Connecticut River. Communities

Car damage from the ice storm of 1973.

such as Middletown were completely shut down. Even the fire alarm systems were knocked out and fires had to be phoned into the fire departments, as long as the telephones were working. Smaller towns, too, such as Coventry, Enfield, and Suffield were completely shut down. Shoreline communities were hit just as hard. As the storm passed on Tuesday, the temperature plunged to near zero. For many who persevered through this storm, it was their "Storm of the Century."

The "warming" effect of the 1973 El Niño began to fade by the mid-1970s, and some extremely cold weather occurred during the 1975–1976 and 1976–1977 winters. Both January 1976 and January 1977 were between 8 and 10 degrees below average. As in the days of the Little Ice Age, harbors and rivers had turned to ice. People were able to walk across portions of Long Island Sound, and stories abound about how it was possible to walk from Lighthouse Point in New Haven, across the harbor to West Haven. The cold was as severe as any winter, and the speculation at the time was that another ice age was on the way. Connecticut even experienced its latest snowstorm in modern history on May 9, 1977.

At first, the snow appeared to be just some wet snow and rain showers when it began falling during the morning. But the precipitation became heavier and it brought down very cold air that was moving eastward overhead. That upper-level circulation was as deep and cold as any out of winter. In Danbury, the snow first accumulated on car roofs and grassy surfaces. Then, the slushy snow began to cover pavements. The snow totals for the Danbury area were 2 to 3 inches, but elsewhere in the western hills, the snow piled up. The highest elevations, such as those around Norfolk, picked up a foot and a half of snow. Even along the shore, measurable snow was reported. Of course, the snow melted rapidly, except in the memories of those who watched it accumulate. And it didn't take too much longer for some very big winters to return to Connecticut. Skies opened during the following winter of 1977–1978. During that winter, snowfall totaled more than twice the average. What a season!

For the most part, the 1977–1978 winter began quietly, and it wasn't until January 13, a Friday the Thirteenth, that the weather turned around. A series of three snowstorms hit Connecticut in a single week– the first on the 13th, the next on the 17–18th, and the third on the 19–20th. Two feet of snow fell across much of the state during this particular week, along with sleet and freezing rain. The weight of the accumulating ice and snow actually brought the roof down: During the pre-dawn hours of Wednesday the 18th, the coliseum roof of the Hartford Civic Center collapsed. The collapse of the 1,400-ton roof occurred even before the third, and heaviest, storm in the series arrived late on the 19th. The collapse of the roof was described as the worst financial disaster in Hartford's history. The roof originally was constructed in a single piece on the ground and then raised to an 85-foot height. The roof rested on four concrete posts, and its design was considered unique. Fortunately, the coliseum was empty at the time of the collapse and nobody was injured.

This week of storms wasn't the last big blast of winter. One of the biggest snowstorms on record was waiting to happen in just another two weeks: the blizzard of February 6–7. Hurricane-force winds and heavy snow made this storm one to remember.

Snow began to fall close to daybreak on Monday the 6th in southwestern Connecticut. As the storm developed, it moved slowly, and the snow was very slow to spread across the state and into eastern New England. Schools and businesses closed early on that Monday in western Connecticut, but elsewhere, it was business as usual. But then, the snow did move eastward, and many people were stranded by the storm. They were caught by surprise, even though the storm was predicted. New computer models very accurately predicted this storm as much as 48 hours in advance, but it wasn't until they experienced the reality of the snow falling that most people believed it would really hit. But it did, and thousands of motorists were caught off guard and were trapped in their vehicles. Roads were clogged, and during that evening, Governor Ella Grasso closed down the entire state. Only emergency travel was allowed on the state's highways. Even the governor was forced to abandon her car and walk during the storm. Grasso was on the way from her residence to the armory where she was scheduled to deliver her declaration. When the police car in which she was riding couldn't move any longer, the governor got out on Farmington Avenue and walked a mile through the deep snow to the armory. The storm paralyzed the eastern seaboard from Virginia to New England. Coastal areas were hit with hurricane-force winds and massive, flooding tides. Snowfall measured 1 to 2 feet around the state, with drifts up to 18 feet. The hardest-hit region was in eastern Connecticut, where as much as 36 inches fell, not counting the huge drifts. Two-foot snowfalls occurred around New Haven. Ambulances were unable to get through the clogged streets. School busses were stranded as well. President Jimmy Carter declared a State of Emergency in Connecticut and provided federal assistance in removing the snow and opening highways. Private contractors were mobilized, too, and the effort by these groups was said to be as great as what occurred during the devastating floods of 1955.

The snow tapered off slowly during Tuesday, but it wouldn't be until the next day when roads were finally being opened. For decades, the Blizzard of 1978 became the measure of comparison for all others that followed

Policemen help shovel the snow in Hartford, 1978.

Heavy snows slow the traffic.

Digging out, 1978.

Guardsmen help clean up after the Blizzard of 1978.

A snowy street in Hartford after the Blizzard of 1978.

in the Northeast. There were storms that covered more territory, but in the major urban corridor from Washington, D.C., to Boston, it is tough finding a match. They were certainly not matched during the next few years. The following three winters were outstanding in their warmth and lack of snow.

One major storm did come close to hitting Connecticut in February 1979. This was called the Presidents' Day Blizzard, and it concentrated its fury on the corridor from Washington to New York, with as much as 25 inches of snow reported in Dover, Delaware. Downtown Washington received just under 19 inches, and even New York City picked up over a foot in Central Park. But the storm took a sharp right-hand turn out to sea, and Connecticut received remarkably little snowfall. Only 1 to 3 inches fell, and that occurred mainly in the southwest corner of the state — not exactly our snowstorm. Overall, snowfall for the 1978–1979 winter was 22 percent below average in Connecticut. The snowfall during the 1979–1980 winter was almost nonexistent, with amounts being 67 percent below average, and even less fell during the 1980–1981 season. And it was warm, with mid-winter temperatures averaging 5 to 10 degrees above average. The years were so warm and unusual that Connecticut was hit by one of the most costly tornadoes in the nation's history — but that is a topic for another chapter. Those new-age ice-age theories sure melted away quickly during those seasons, and that is when thoughts of greenhouse warming really came off the back burner. Overall, the warmth continued during the next two seasons, but that didn't prevent some winter from occurring. Above-average snowfalls returned during December and January of the 1981–1982 season, and Connecticut was clobbered by a late-season blizzard on April 6, 1982.

The storm came along in classic fashion — first moving through the Midwest, and then re-centering off the mid-Atlantic coast. The second center became the one that delivered a foot or more of snow from New York City to Maine. While snow was expected, the intensity of the late-season storm caught most people off guard. Highway departments were preparing for spring by taking their sanders off the trucks while cleaning the roads of accumulated sand, and skiing seemed something for another season. Although one ski shop in Willimantic had posted a "Think Snow" sign, during the storm, another sign went up: "We are closed due to the snow." The shop was one of many stores and businesses that were shut down by the storm. Governor William A O'Neill ordered the National Guard to clear roads that were filled with abandoned vehicles. Ninety percent of Hartford-area streets were said to be impassible. The storm was classified as the first true spring blizzard in Connecticut's modern history, which, at that time, extended back to records kept by the National Weather Service for seventy-eight years. Fields that were being prepared for baseball were ruined, and golf courses took a beating as well. The Yankees opener was postponed, and many disappointed sports fans were left stranded at sports bars, going for the jukebox instead of the TV sets. Most drivers and municipal operators had already replaced their snow tires. The ski area operators couldn't have been happier. There would be Easter skiing in 1982. Snowfall measured 10 inches in Danbury, up to 18 inches in the Northwest Hills at Norfolk, up to 14 inches in Windsor Locks, and 15 inches in the Northeast Hills. Amounts dropped to 6 to 9 inches along the coast from Groton to New Haven. I was in knee-deep snow waiting to go on the air outside a Waterbury TV studio. The snow was driven into large drifts by winds that gusted over 50 miles per hour. There was plenty of blowing and drifting of powdery snow as the temperature fell to 19 degrees during the height of the storm. Within a few days, only traces of that snow remained, but it looked like something out of mid-winter while it fell.

The 1982–1983 season finished with near-average snowfall amounts, but only because of a single February storm that came along on the 12th of that month, and it was a surprise storm that produced a record snowfall in Hartford of 21 inches in 15 hours. Three people lost their lives and many more were injured in accidents. Through the day, the storm was expected to curve out to sea—at least, that was what the computers of the day were projecting. But each hour that passed showed the snow advancing farther north—from Washington to Philadelphia and then northward through New Jersey. By dusk, snow had reached New York City. Yet, skies were still partly cloudy in Connecticut as I drove to the Waterbury TV studio in the late afternoon. In those days, we taped some of our weather broadcasts in advance, and I had to make a forecast that would still be relevant at 10:00 that night. Would the snow hit or still go out to sea? The computers had it all wrong, but the observations made it appear that snow was on our doorsteps. I went with the snow, taping at 6:00 p.m.: "Heavy snow is falling across the state." That would be played at 10:00 p.m., yet it was taped before the first flakes of snow arrived. I was probably one of the few happy people to be driving home in the snow that evening. Fortunately, the storm struck on a Friday night, and the state had a weekend to recover. Twelve to 24 inches of snow fell throughout much of the state, except that lesser amounts of 9 inches fell along the shoreline around New London. But New Haven picked up 18 inches, and some of the worst road conditions in the state were reported there. Thirty-inch snowfalls were measured in the hills west of Washington, D.C. Even New York City picked up 22 inches. Overall, in the Northeast corridor, thirty-nine deaths were reported from the storm, including twenty-five people who perished on a coal carrier that sank 30 miles off Chincoteague, Virginia. As it turned out, the snow was powdery and it compressed nicely during the following days. By Monday, above-average temperatures had returned, and the snow rapidly melted away. The relatively easy-going winter pattern continued for the next several seasons. Much below-average snowfall occurred during each winter until 1986–1987. That became a big year with snow falling as early as November, with the crowning jewel coming along during January 22, 1987.

The snow fell heavily at the start, but a change to rain kept final accumulations down to a range of 6 to 14 inches, with the highest amounts falling around Norfolk in the Northwest Hills, and the lowest along the shoreline from Groton to Bridgeport. But just a few miles back from the shore, amounts came to 8 to 12 inches, with Danbury reporting 12 inches. The northeast hills also had snowfall limited to 6 inches. Lightning and thunder accompanied the burst of heavy snow before the changeover to rain. Snow began falling in the late morning, and by mid-afternoon, it was accumulating at a rate of 1 to 2 inches per hour, while winds were gusting over 40 miles per hour. Streets were gridlocked, and cars were abandoned. Tractor-trailers were jackknifing along Interstates 84 and 91. The arrival time of the snow was not the best and many schools along with businesses already had started their day. When the heavy snow arrived, children and workers were sent home early, and that contributed to the gridlock. One state police dispatcher said, "Everyone is abandoning cars. We're towing them left and right." Fortunately, because of the change to rain, most major roads were cleared by 10:00 that evening. This January storm was the heaviest since February of 1983. But 1987 wasn't finished with us. We had the earliest heavy snow on record during early October that year, and nobody was ready for that one.

A steady cold rain was falling on Saturday, October 3, 1987. But during that night, the temperature continued to fall, and at the time, I was consulting for the Connecticut Department of Transportation. Well, I saw that temperatures were falling into the upper 30s while the rain had turned to wet snow in the Catskills during the early hours of Sunday morning. I had trouble believing that we could get hit by such an early-season snowfall. Leaves were still out full on the trees, but all indications pointed to a change to heavy, wet snow, at least for western Connecticut and the hills by daybreak. I called the highway monitor, and he practically hung up on me. He wouldn't believe me. But then at 5:00 a.m., wet snowflakes began to mix with the rain in western Connecticut, and I called the monitor back. This time, his phone was busy. I wasn't the only person calling, and when that happened, it was always too late. The highway department was caught unprepared. By 6:00 a.m., a full-blown snowstorm was striking western Connecticut. The heavy, wet snow collected on leaves and branches and brought limbs down. Hardly a tree was left undamaged by the storm. Up to a foot of snow fell in the Northwest Hills. In Canaan, two people were killed and two were injured when a limb of an oak fell on their vehicle at about 1:00 p.m. Many roads were closed by fallen branches, and those falling branches brought down power lines. Over forty thousand households lost power. Total snow accumulations were very much elevation-driven. In western Connecticut, 12 inches fell in Sharon, 8 inches in Kent, 7 inches in New Milford, and 4 inches in Ridgefield. Even Bridgeport picked up a record half-inch of snow, and New Haven reported an inch. The snowstorm ripped through all of western New England and upstate New York. In Vermont, numerous foliage tourists were caught unaware by the storm, the leaves suddenly turned white from their brilliant reds and oranges. But little or no snow fell around Hartford or points east. Still, for Connecticut, this was the earliest snowstorm on record, and with its tree damage and widespread power outages, its impact was more that of a hurricane than a snowstorm.

The October storm seemed to open the door to a snowy winter, which brought 10 to 15 percent more snow than average. But after those two seasons, 1986–1987 and 1987–1988, snowstorms diminished in frequency and we went into a relative snow drought, with below-average snowfalls for the next four seasons. It wasn't until the 1990s when harsh winter weather resumed, although erratically. The first truly big storm of the decade struck in December 1992.

The storm was notable along the coast not for its snowfall, but for its flooding high tides. Three times the tide rolled in and three times, coastal property and roads were inundated. Water poured down coastal roads, covering cars to their windows in East Haven. The storm's coastal flooding was enhanced by heavy rain and a full moon, and the surges were very much hurricane-like. Rainfall came to more than 2 inches. Coast Guard helicopters swept into Fairfield to evacuate ten people, and the Connecticut National Guard troops evacuated two hundred people cut off by the rising waters in Fairfield, Westport, and Norwalk. This could have been February 1978 all over again had it not been for the rain that fell in southern and eastern Connecticut. Wind gusts were clocked to 60 to 70 miles per hour in New London and Stonington. But in northern sections, the storm was mostly snow, and a lot of it. At our New Haven station WTNH-TV, we were calling this storm the tale of two states. While the south was being flooded, the north was being buried in knee-deep snow drifts. High winds knocked out power to over forty thousand utility customers. The heaviest snow fell in the communities of Burlington, Terryville, and Wolcott. Once again, the heavy snow was elevation-driven with just 4 to 6 inches falling around Hartford, yet 14 inches reported in the higher elevations of West Hartford. Most of the snow fell on Friday, but colder air in back of the storm changed the rain to snow on Saturday morning. Although accumulations were limited in southern Connecticut, roads turned icy and treacherous, and at times the snow showers came down at rates of 1 to 2 inches per hour. The greatest total snowfall reported was in northeastern Connecticut at Union, where 27 inches fell. Twenty-four inches fell in Litchfield, 12 inches in Danbury, 6 inches in Hartford, 5 inches in Norwich, 7 inches in Mansfield, and 17 inches in Putnam, but just 3 inches fell in Milford, 4 inches in New Haven, and 3.5 inches in Old Saybrook. In Canaan, drifts were reported to be 8 feet deep. Three people died in storm-related accidents. This was a storm to remember, regardless of location in the state. And it might have been precursor of a storm that was to hit later that season—a storm that became known across the Northeast as the "Storm of the Century."

For Connecticut, it was not quite the "Storm of the Century," but it did deliver a record-low barometric pressure of 28.3 inches and those records were set as far south as Florida and Alabama. The storm moved in on January 13. The extent of the storm was indeed historic. Snow closed every major airport from Alabama to New England. Numerous tornadoes ripped through Florida. In Connecticut, the heavy snow closed most roads temporarily, and about thirty thousand utility customers lost power. Fortunately, flooding did not pack the punch of the December storm. The shoreline reported no widespread flooding damage, but the snow did pile up. Two feet of snow fell in the northwest corner of state, with drifts of 4 to 5 feet. Twenty inches fell in the Hartford area, and even the New Haven area picked up a foot of snow. One-foot snowfalls were common in eastern Connecticut, except around New London, where amounts were closer to 7 and 8 inches. Most residents took the storm in stride. Patrick Hague, Winsted's public work director, said that regardless of the 20 to 25 inches that fell, there were no major problems. Again, a weekend storm helped make it much easier for road crews—and helped their overtime. In Winsted, overtime charges would come to more than $20,000. Shovelers did have difficulty with the storm, clearing one ton of material from a 12-by-12-foot area. The heavy snow was most remarkable because it extended from Maine to the hills of Alabama. It was definitely one of the most paralyzing storms of the twentieth century, and it affected over 100 million people, producing one of the most significant snowfalls of the century. Storm of the century? Maybe, but not for Connecticut, where recovery was rapid. But the heavy snow of January helped send seasonal snowfalls over 30 percent above average, and it wasn't until the season of 1995–1996 that even higher amounts were reported, with snowfall totals of over 100 inches, making the season of 1995–1996 the snowiest on record.

After a relatively quiet year in 1994–95, the winter unleashed snowstorm after snowstorm upon Connecticut. The snowstorms were not all blockbusters by themselves, but we had our great ones, and as the season wore on, the totals added up. Over 40 inches fell in January alone. A succession of storm tracks brought the snow to Connecticut, and by the time all was totaled, Hartford received an all-time high of 115 inches of accumulation. The storms seemed to strike during the middle of the week, creating havoc with meeting schedules. By the time the twelfth storm struck in March, the headline in the *Hartford Courant* ran: "Let it Stop, Let it Stop, Let it Stop." One of the most powerful storms struck on January 6–8, 1996, and it was called the "Blizzard of '96."

The storm was ranked as one of the most significant of the twentieth century, mainly because it affected the large population center in the Northeast, from the mid-Atlantic states northward. Overall, the Northeast corridor experienced $2 billion dollars of damage and twenty-two people lost their lives. In Connecticut, snowfall up to 18 to 26 inches occurred, even in south-central regions, close to the coast where flooding tides forced evacuations from local communities. The storm struck its greatest blow to Connecticut on Monday the 8th, and businesses generally were closed. It was a "snow day" for much of the state. Bradley International Airport was shut for most of the day, as well. Planes stopped running at 8:00 a.m. and didn't resume until 7:00 p.m. Homeless shelters were filled. Even three of four Connecticut ski areas were closed because of too much snow! According to market research, television viewership doubled during the storm. The storm combined with the previous snow of the winter and exhausted local snow-removal budgets. Schools were closed the following day, on Tuesday, as well. Huge snow banks made visibility very poor around street

Snowy day in Bushnell Park, Hartford, 1996.

corners. The few eateries that remained opened received some storm-sized business. The winter of 1995–1996 was as old-fashioned as any. The shoreline picked up a record 76 inches of snowfall for the season — the average is closer to 25 inches. Record snowfall occurred throughout the region.

The weather began to settle down during the following winter of 1996–1997, but Connecticut did have its storms, including one of the more powerful late-season storms, which became known as the April Fool's Day storm because it hit on March 31 to April 1. Accumulations of the heavy, wet snow were modest along the Connecticut shoreline, with 4 inches reported in New London and 6 inches in New Haven and Bridgeport. But over interior Connecticut, the snowfall piled up, with a foot in Hartford, and over 14 inches at Bradley International Airport. Twenty-one inches fell in Norfolk as well as in Putnam. Portions of Massachusetts were clobbered, with 33 inches at Worcester and 36 inches at Milton, just west of Boston. The Worcester snowfall was a record. In Connecticut, a total of four hundred thousand utility customers were without power, but within two days, temperatures had returned to the 50s and 60s — a New England spring.

Following the April Fool's storm in 1997, Connecticut experienced a lull that lasted well into 2000 and beyond. Very mild El Niño winters seemed to have an impact, and the biggest storm to hit since March 31, 1997, occurred at the very end of 2000: on December 30–31, but even this storm was a modest one. Snowfall in Connecticut ranged from 3 inches around New London to 9 inches in Hartford and New Haven, 10 inches in Torrington, 9 inches in Putnam, and 14 inches in Danbury. Mixed precipitation kept snowfall totals down in eastern and southeastern Connecticut. The storm created some disruption, but there were few power failures and no coastal flooding. The biggest storm in three years didn't seem that big at all in Connecticut, although heavier snowfalls of a foot to a foot and a half did occur throughout eastern New York southward to New Jersey. Newark reported 14 inches of accumulation.

Another two or three years would pass before a super-sized snowstorm would arrive. This one came in February 2003, and it was as big as they get. This occurred during Presidents' Day weekend, February 15 to 18 — another Presidents' Day storm — the last one occurred in 1979. One- to two-foot snowfalls were common in Connecticut. Downtown Hartford received 20 inches along with Danbury and Union. New London had 14 inches, while New Haven and Greenwich had 19 inches. Most of the snow fell on that Monday, which was already a day off for many, and most schools were closed for February vacation. Conditions were blizzard-like, but Connecticut managed through the storm with no fatalities, although twenty-eight storm-related deaths were reported along the Northeast corridor. The main impact in Connecticut was the loss of business from holiday sales. Many stores and malls were looking for a big turnout of customers for Presidents' Day, but the shops and malls were closed. Amtrak was forced to cancel many trips. The winter lingered into spring during 2003. Two additional snowfalls occurred, one on March 6, and the other on April 8. The March storm generally delivered 6 to 9 inches of snow, with specific amounts of 8 inches in Stamford, 7 inches in New Haven and Groton, 9 inches in Hartford, and 8 inches in Putnam. The April storm was lighter, with just 2 to 4 inches generally accumulating around the state.

Late that year, in early December, a very odd storm hit the region. It had all the markings of a major snowfall, but it behaved erratically. The storm hit during the first weekend of December. The snowfall failed to put it together in parts of eastern and south-central Connecticut, where amounts of just 5 to 8 inches were measured—5 inches in Old Saybrook, for example. But a foot of snow fell in Bridgeport and 19 inches fell around Hartford. In the suburbs of Boston, such as Peabody, 35 inches of snow were reported. The snow was long in duration, and its length helped pile up some of those amounts, but radar imagery showed a definite gap in activity over Connecticut, and the total amounts were reduced from what could have been.

The December storm opened the door to a busy season of light to moderate snowfalls. Through March of 2004, snowfalls were never too far from the area, but individually, the storms generally delivered less than 6 inches of snow. The storm that had the most impact occurred in late January, on Wednesday the 27th. The storm was predicted well in advance, and there were high expectations of snowfall accumulations, but after punishing the Midwest with fifty deaths, the storm became less organized. Still, 6 to 12 inches of snow fell throughout the state and many schools were forced to close, along with some businesses. Amounts ranged from 6 inches in New Haven, Waterbury, and Hartford, up to 10 inches in Manchester and 12 inches in Storrs. A light, fluffy snow began during the pre-dawn hours of the 27th, and then, as the day progressed, the storm intensified. Many schools started with a delayed opening, but then were forced to close. Overall, the state managed the storm well. For the season, snowfall totals of 43 inches across interior Connecticut were close to average.

The 2004–2005 season seemed to be off to an ominous start, with the first snowfall occurring as early as November 13th. Amounts of 1 to 2 inches were reported all the way down to the shore, where Bridgeport's 1.5 inches set a record for so early in the season. But after that season opener, the storms that followed were relatively tame until late January 2005. On January 22–23, blizzard conditions occurred across the state for the first time since the April Fool's storm of 1997.

Snowfall totals were close to a foot or more from one end of the state to another. Groton had 15 inches of accumulation, New Haven received 16 inches, and Greenwich picked up 9 inches. In New York City, at one point, the snow was falling at a rate of 4 inches per hour. The Empire State Building was completely obscured. Hartford received 13 inches, but Stafford Spring measured 16 inches while Montville had 19 inches. Amounts increased farther to the east, with up to 36 inches of snow falling in eastern Massachusetts and Cape Cod, where drifts were reported to be 9 feet.

The storm intensified off the New England coast, and fortunately, the snow occurred during a weekend. Also, coastal flooding was minimal in Connecticut and the snow was dry and powdery, so it was easily moveable. By Monday, even with the heavy snow, businesses and schools were getting back to normal. Snowfall totals were historic in parts of New England.

And that wasn't the end of the snow for the season. Several storms came along through late March. Six-inch snowfalls were common in many of these storms. None were blockbuster events, but the snowfall totals for the season were adding up. Season totals were 10 to 20 inches above average.

Winter was also off and running early during the 2005–2006 season. The first snowfall occurred on November 24th with light accumulations. Then, during the first week of December, light to moderate amounts fell on the 5th and 6th. But on December 9, an old-fashioned nor'easter ripped through the region. Winds were clocked as high as 105 miles per hour on Block Island. The snow occurred during an 8-hour period during which thunderstorms developed along with whiteout conditions. A waterspout was even reported near Chatham, Massachusetts. In Connecticut, snowfall totals ranged from 3 inches at Groton to 10 inches in Danbury, Southbury, and Hartford. Bridgeport reported 6 inches, but nearby West Haven received 7 inches. Avon measured 12 inches and Middletown picked up 10 inches. The storm hit like a squall—sharp and fast-moving. Because the snow fell on a Friday, a three-day weekend was in the offing for many. State Police reported 120 accidents and one fatality.

One mega-storm might seem enough for one season, but another major snowstorm struck during the 2005–2006 winter in February. The storm came along on February 11–12, a weekend. Accumulations of snow were massive, with record or near-record totals. Hartford received 22 inches, West Hartford reported 27 inches, and Farmington 26 inches. Amounts decreased toward the shoreline, but New Haven still received 16 inches. Shops were closed and roads were impassable, but road crews worked through the weekend, keeping the state open. Very few power outages occurred, and no storm-related fatalities were reported. The snow was of the light, fluffy variety, and even after the massive snowfall, the state was back to business as usual on Monday. But the combination of this storm with the December nor'easter helped push the season's snowfall to as much as 15 to 20 inches above average for the second consecutive season.

But during the following season, 2006–2007, March 16–17 registered the only heavy snowstorm of the entire season. Even this storm was not exactly a classic—the snow was wet. Rain and sleet were mixed with the snow, and then, sharply falling temperatures turned the snow and sleet cover into a glacier-like surface. The icy surfaces contributed to more than four hundred accidents and forty injuries. Snow totals came to 10 inches at Windsor Locks, 9 inches in Manchester and Middletown, 12 inches in Danbury, and 7 inches in Norwich. Only light to moderate snowfalls occurred on other occasions during the winter. Total snowfall for the season came to just half of average. The season was the first in three years to finish with less snow than average.

The Most Powerful Storm on Earth

Hurricanes are the most powerful and energetic storms on earth, and Connecticut is no stranger to these tropical wonders. Although documentation of hurricanes is sketchy at best prior to the late nineteenth century, there is little doubt that these storms have been much too common and were great hazards to early settlers. Ever since the Pilgrims landed on these shores, one or two hurricanes of the magnitude of 1938 have struck the region each century. The 1938 hurricane devastated coastal property, blew down forests, flooded both shoreline and inland areas, and took the lives of six hundred people. According to statistics, we are due for another 1938 disaster, but we will go into this just a little later. And, of course, lesser but still powerful tropical cyclones have moved into our waters and then onshore. In addition, hybrid storms occur in the fall that are both tropical and non-tropical in nature. They are northeasters, sometimes called equinoctial storms because they occur near the time of the autumnal equinox. The famous "Perfect Storm" of 1991 is an example of one of these hybrids.

Actually, Columbus himself discovered hurricanes, along with the New World, in 1494 during his second voyage. He was fortunate that hurricanes tracked somewhere else during his 1492 voyage, and he didn't encounter these massive storms. After all, his trip occurred during hurricane season, the late summer and early fall, and he sailed through the Trade Wind Belt where hurricanes develop and grow in the warm tropical waters. But during his second voyage in 1494, his fleet of seventeen ships was forced to find refuge on the southeastern portion of Hispaniola when rising waters and winds developed ahead of a storm. Fortunately, Columbus and his fleet found protection near Saona Island from some of the highest winds, and the early explorers experienced little damage. He did have an encounter with a full-blown hurricane during his fourth voyage, but again, the storm-savvy explorer was able to find shelter for himself and his ships, while a nearby fleet of thirty gold-laden ships was almost completely destroyed. The storm struck on July 10, 1502. Only four of those thirty ships survived the hurricane. More than five hundred lives were lost.

These storms thrive on the warm waters of the tropics. The water temperature usually needs to be close to 80 degrees for sufficient energy to be delivered to a developing storm. As the water temperatures decrease, energy is lost from the atmosphere and absorbed by the colder water. The storm weakens. Seldom will the waters off New England reach such warmth. We'll see water temperatures reach into the 70s during the late summer, but 80-degree water is just not part of our environment. So, hurricanes that are caught in the Jet Stream and track northward toward Connecticut usually weaken and dissipate. Also, these storms cover a relatively small area. Our everyday mid-latitude storm can be close to 1,000 miles wide, but hurricanes are usually 200 miles wide or less, and destructive winds seldom reach more than 100 miles from the center. Often, those winds are no more than 25 to 50 miles out from the storm's eye. So, it is common for these storms to be just close calls. They miss Connecticut far more often than they hit, but of course, the few that manage to move out of the tropics, survive the colder water, and lock onto our shores do make quite a name for themselves.

While documentation prior to the eighteenth century is thin, the early settlers in New England did have their encounters with these tropical terrors. In 1635, when Connecticut had only a single settlement of a handful of people in Wethersfield, a hurricane wreaked havoc across New England during the classic hurricane month of August. This storm became known as the "Great Colonial Hurricane." This is the first documented hurricane to have struck New England. The storm made landfall in Narragansett Bay. Accounts of the storm show considerable damage in eastern New England, with thousands of trees uprooted and hundreds of homes destroyed. Tides of 20 feet occurred, and the Narragansett Indians were forced to climb to the tops of trees to avoid the rising water. The storm also caused several shipwrecks and the drowning of children and adults who were onboard. The exact number of lives lost is unknown, but on one ship alone, eighteen of twenty passengers were swept away. The corn crop was also destroyed by the storm, which lasted about six hours. William Bradford, governor of Plymouth Plantation, documented the storm and said that no person living, English or Indian, had ever experienced a storm equal to this one, and no part of the country escaped its wrath.

While the storm of 1635 might have been the first documented hurricane in New England, it certainly would not be the last. The "Second Colonial Hurricane" struck in 1675. In New London, numerous ships were wrecked or driven aground. The following year brought another massive fall storm that could have been one of those hybrid systems. The famous adventure of Captain Ephraim Howe was spawned by this storm, which struck around September 12, 1676. The violent storm sunk numerous vessels in the New England waters. At the time, Howe, a sea captain from New Haven, was making his normal return cargo run from Boston to New Haven. He had onboard two of his sons, who were also seamen, and three passengers, one of whom was a boy. The storm struck when they had reached near Cape Cod. The boat was driven near rocks and nearly stranded. The rudder broke, and the vessel, torn and tattered, was tossed about in the tall seas. As the story is told, the ship wandered aimlessly for three months until it reached an island near Cape Sable, Nova Scotia — far from its Connecticut destination. Numerous other storms pounded Howe's ketch. The rudder was fixed, only to be broken again, and the boat was completely ruined on the rocks along the island. One by one, the passengers and crew died from exposure. Howe was the only person found alive later that spring. He had to make it through the rough winter until a vessel from Salem picked him up. Other vessels caught his signals earlier and sailed away, fearing an attack by Indians. But the Salem fishing boat came close enough to see that he was seriously hurt, and on July 8, 1677, he arrived in Salem. Soon after, he was reunited with his family and friends in New Haven, where he was hardly recognizable because of the effects of exposure. His miraculous homecoming occurred ten months after he first set sail.

In 1683, during August 23, another serious hurricane struck New England and Connecticut. In Stonington, all trees were said to have been blasted by the storm, and severe flooding resulted when the Connecticut River rose to 26 feet above normal — similar to levels that occurred during the 1938 hurricane.

During the eighteenth century, accounts of these monster storms continued. The first major storm to hit New England in the eighteenth century occurred on August 13, 1713. It was called the "New London Hurricane" because it made a landfall there and caused tremendous damage to the growing city. Scores of buildings were flattened and numerous trees were blow down. Fruit trees were so badly blasted that the damage was compared to that of a devastating frost. The storm continued on a destructive northward course that brought it through Massachusetts and New Hampshire.

On September 27, 1727, heavy rain and "horrible wind" struck southeastern Connecticut. This storm, too, damaged many trees in New London and Stonington and caused structure damage as well as shipping loses. The storm then tracked through Narragansett Bay and eastern Massachusetts.

One of the more famous hurricanes of the century occurred in November 1743. Barometers had just come along by then, and the first barometric reading ever taken in a New England hurricane occurred with this storm on November 2 as the hurricane passed Cambridge, Massachusetts. The barometer recorded 29.35 inches. High winds, heavy rain, and flooding accompanied the storm as it pushed northeastward from the mid-Atlantic States to New England. The storm did its share of damage. It was called "Franklin's Hurricane" or the "Eclipse Hurricane." Benjamin Franklin was in Philadelphia on November 2, hoping to observe a lunar eclipse. The wind was howling from the northeast and the sky was overcast. He never was able to observe the eclipse through the cloud layers. But in later correspondence with his brother who was in Boston, he found that areas to his north that also were hit by the storm managed to catch some of the eclipse before the skies closed in upon them. So, he concluded that the storm must have tracked northward out of the tropics even if the winds were coming from the opposite direction, from the northeast. The storm hit Philadelphia before Boston. All of this later suggested to scientists that storms have a counter-clockwise rotation while they track northward in a different current of air. But these conclusions would not be made definitive until well into the nineteenth century. As usual, Franklin's thinking was well ahead of his time.

Another violent storm struck New England and the waters of Long Island Sound on October 19, 1749. This became known as the "October Hurricane of 1749." Its center moved offshore and caused much damage to ships. It drove seven vessels ashore on Martha's Vineyard.

Connecticut had another blast from a major storm on October 23–24, 1761. The storm was called "Winthrop's Hurricane," after Professor John Winthrop, who wrote extensively about it in his meteorological diary. He described the hurricane that swept through southeastern New England as the most violent storm in thirty years. Trees were ripped from their roots and shipping losses were great. The storm collapsed a wooden bridge over Narragansett Bay and toppled the wooden spire of a church in Newport. The storm continued its path of destruction northward to Portsmouth, New Hampshire, and into eastern Maine.

On October 20, 1770, another hurricane, following a similar track to Winthrop's Hurricane, created extensive damage. It became known as the "Late Season Hurricane of 1770" and the "Stiles' Hurricane," because Rev.

Ezra Stiles wrote extensively about it in his diary. Rainfall of 3 inches was measured. In New London, alone, two merchant ships were run ashore and then beaten to pieces. Numerous other vessels were damaged or destroyed. Fort William, along New London Harbor, was heavily damaged, losing its sentry boxes, timber stocks, and several chimneys. Small boats were smashed against the fort's ramparts. The barometric pressure was measured at a very low 28.96 inches, and the storm continued to maintain its strength during its destructive track northward through eastern New England. In Boston, the tide was said to have been the greatest in nearly fifty years.

Another hurricane moved offshore on August 12–13, 1778. Although it did not strike Connecticut directly, it did have an impact on the Revolutionary War effort. It became known as the "French Storm" because it damaged French and British warships and prevented the start of a sea battle. Masts were ripped off many ships. In addition to causing damage to ships, the storm destroyed the corn crop near the coast. Hardship and hunger followed.

On August 19, 1788, a powerful hurricane ripped through western New England. It took an inland track through eastern New York and northwestern Connecticut. Strong south winds swept through Long Island Sound, causing massive waves, flooding, and damage along the Connecticut shore. In New Haven Harbor, strong winds brought numerous vessels onto Long Wharf. In Connecticut, houses and barns were blown down, and many more were damaged. Apple trees were destroyed along with grain. Fields of corn were completely flattened as the storm progressed northward through western New England and eventually into Vermont. Several people were killed as trees toppled or buildings collapsed. Amazingly, the storm had a relatively small core, with much of its damage at any location lasting for less than 30 minutes over its 75-mile-wide track. The storm became known as the "Western New England Hurricane," and was the last recorded historic hurricane of the eighteenth century, although numerous other blasts occurred during that century, probably not of tropical origin but causing plenty of wind damage. One especially odd one hit a year earlier in 1787.

This storm seemed to resemble a tornado, but a very large one. It first swept out of a darkening sky over New Britain on Wednesday, August 15, 1787. It then tracked to Wethersfield, where it swept away trees and crushed buildings. The residence of Wait Robbins was destroyed. He was traveling to Dartmouth to make arrangements for his oldest son to enter college, but the son, who was home with his mother and family, was killed by the storm.

His mother, who was holding an eighteen-month-old child in her arms, was also killed. The baby was severely injured but survived along with another brother who was three years old. Two silk dresses were blown out of Mrs. Robbins' drawer and landed at her brother's house, across the Connecticut River in Glastonbury, 3 miles away. The storm caused structural damage in Glastonbury, too, and it tracked into East Windsor. Huge trees were twisted and destroyed along with crops. The storm also spawned damage and destruction through the remainder of New England.

The nineteenth century brought its share of tropical fury to New England, and as population and technology advanced, so too did the accounts of these storms. Many of the storms were close calls in Connecticut, with much of their damage offshore or in eastern New England, but some did make historic hits on the state.

The "Storm of the Century" for Connecticut occurred in 1815. Overall, the summer of 1815 was packed with storms and rain. This was the unpleasant summer that preceded the famous "Year Without a Summer" in 1816 when frost occurred every month and snow fell in Connecticut during June. This was the heart of the "Little Ice Age," but that didn't prevent tropical cyclones from reaching our shores, such as the storm that struck on September 23, 1815.

The storm persisted for two days, and in that sense it seemed more of a northeaster than the typical fast-moving hurricane. The storm was probably a hybrid, having both tropical and nontropical characteristics by the time it reached Connecticut. It became one of those classic equinoctial storms, occurring close to the time of the equinox. Its rain and wind were first experienced on Friday morning, the 22nd, and the storm peaked twenty-four hours later. The wind was so fierce that fires would not light inside homes, buildings of various sizes were destroyed, and salt water was carried more than 40 miles inland. Foliage and vegetation were wiped out by the salt. Sea birds were driven miles inland. The tide along Connecticut's shore was the highest known at the time—so high that any moveable property on Long Wharf in New Haven was picked up and destroyed. At Yale, the temperature rose from 48 degrees in the early morning to 65 degrees as the storm's center approached in the afternoon. In Stonington, twenty anchored vessels in the harbor ran aground or sank. The tide rose 17 feet higher than normal. First, everything along the wharves was destroyed, and then, the wharves themselves were washed away. The storm completely changed the landscape. Gardens and fields became sandy beaches. In New London, trees were adrift on Main Street, and nearly every vessel in the Thames River was destroyed. Several buildings in Norwich were washed away, and in eastern Connecticut, Plainfield churches were blown down or destroyed. The storm swept through all of New England,

and the total extent of the damage and loss of life could never be determined. The destruction could hardly be comprehended.

A poem, "September Gale," by Oliver Wendell Holmes, who was six years old at the time of the storm, described the impact of this storm:

Lord! How the ponds and rivers boiled,
And how the shingles rattled!
And oaks were scattered on the ground
As if the Titans battled;
And all above was in a howl, And all below a clatter—
The Earth was like a frying pan,
Or some such hissing matter.

Noah Webster called it a "Perfect Hurricane." This September gale became as celebrated as the 1938 hurricane of the twentieth century, but other storms became famous, including another hurricane that arrived on September 3, 1821. This one caused extensive damage to buildings and trees. Long Island was especially hard hit. Ships were sunk in Long Island Sound, and the storm became part of meteorological history when a Connecticut resident surveyed the damage and derived, for the first time, an explanation of storm circulation.

William Redfield lived above his dry goods store in Cromwell. He was an avid weather watcher, and became one of the most accomplished meteorologists of the nineteenth century. He systematically retraced the tracks of hurricanes by examining logbooks of ships that ran into these storms. Following the 1821 storm, he noticed that the trees in Cromwell had fallen toward the northwest, indicating that the wind blew from the southeast. Later, while surveying the damage, he also noticed that 100 miles to the northwest, trees had fallen in a southeasterly direction, indicating a wind from the northwest. So, the same storm brought opposing winds in different locations. That observation led to his famous conclusion that a storm has a circulation that spins in a counterclockwise fashion. The hurricane of 1821 became known as "Redfield's Storm," and he spent the following decade constructing the first realistic model of a hurricane. In 1831, he published his work, which became very controversial, but it completely revolutionized the understanding of storms. His paper also pointed to the presence of a calm eye at the center of circulation. Meteorology was never quite the same after Redfield's Storm.

During the next several decades, relatively "mild" tropical systems came along, but one of these made a name for itself when it toppled a famous tree. The "Charter Oak Hurricane" struck on August 21, 1856. Although the storm tracked east of Connecticut, it delivered winds of 77 mph and several inches of rain. The wind was enough to bring down numerous trees, including the historic Charter Oak tree in Hartford. This was the ancient oak tree in which the Connecticut Charter had been hidden during a period of political instability in the 1680s. The tree stood for more than three hundred years, until this hurricane came along and broke the tree 6 feet from the ground.

Another hurricane moved to the east of Connecticut on September 8, 1869. Damage was extensive in eastern New England. The center of the storm moved through Narragansett Bay, and Providence was completely flooded. The hurricane then went through eastern Massachusetts carving an extensive path of destruction. The storm was only 50 miles wide, and much of Connecticut escaped serious damage, but the storm did exact a toll in eastern Connecticut, with a number of vessels washing ashore in Stonington.

Only one month later, on October 4, another hurricane shifted to the east of Connecticut and slammed into northern Maine and Nova Scotia. Flooding did occur in Connecticut, but the storm made a name for itself because a British naval officer, Lieutenant S. M. Saxby, predicted the exact date of the storm a year in advance. He warned that the eastern seaboard and Canada would experience an intense hurricane on October 4, 1869. His prediction was close enough, and the storm quickly became known as "Saxby's Gale," but he never really explained his method.

Connecticut had another brush, but not a direct hit, with a hurricane in early October 1878. This storm tracked to the west, rather than east. The storm moved northward from Chesapeake Bay through eastern Pennsylvania and New York, and then crossed into central New England, from Albany to Concord, New Hampshire. Numerous trees were blown down across interior sections, and very high tides caused flooding on the shore. A number of ships were damaged or destroyed along the Connecticut shore and in Long Island Sound.

After a quiet period, storms became active again in 1893, when three hurricanes came within striking distance of Connecticut in a single month. On August 21, a storm moved well to the east of Connecticut but was close enough to generate heavy rains and gale-force winds. Then, just three days later, another hurricane approached, this one much closer. The center moved ashore near Stamford and then tracked toward Pittsfield. In New Haven alone, three hundred elms were toppled, and throughout Connecticut, crops were destroyed including much of the tobacco. Then, on the 29th, another hurricane approached, but tracked slightly to the west, from Harrisburg, Pennsylvania, to Bennington, Vermont. Connecticut escaped the worst damage, but the oyster beds were destroyed. There was a fourth hurricane during October, but that, too, took a track west of Connecticut through central Pennsylvania and New York. Still, strong winds did bring down numerous trees, especially in western Connecticut. The storm was similar to Hurricane Hazel, which also was an October storm in 1954, and like Hazel, was part of a series of hurricanes.

The nineteenth century came to an end without any additional hurricanes directly hitting Connecticut, although a massive late-November northeaster in 1898 caused considerable damage in eastern portions of the state. Actually, the lull in hurricane activity continued well into the twentieth century, and that peacefulness caught everyone off guard when the real big one came along in 1938. Sure, we had some storm activity, but it was limited until the Great One smashed into Connecticut. On September 16, 1903, a hurricane made landfall near Atlantic City, New Jersey, and then quickly dissipated. New Haven recorded winds of 47 miles per hour, which wasn't of hurricane proportions but was the highest registered in thirty years. Then, on October 21, 1904, gale-force winds brought down a number of trees as a storm moved offshore. And that was just about it—until 1938 when truly the hurricane of the century arrived.

Most people had no idea that a major catastrophe was on the way. Those storms usually curve eastward, out to sea, and why should this storm behave differently? Charlie Pierce had a different view.

Pierce was a young forecaster at the Weather Bureau in 1938, and he was uncomfortable with the overly optimistic forecasts that were being issued on the morning of September 21. Just the previous night, the White Star Liner, *Carinthia*, had reported an extremely low pressure of 27.85 inches in the Atlantic, east of Jacksonville, Florida. And, for over a week, Pierce's office had received reports of a major hurricane tracking from the Cape Verde islands off Africa through the Atlantic. He also noticed a low-pressure system moving eastward from the Midwest and a strong high-pressure area setting up in the Canadian Maritimes. Both weather systems would have the effect of channeling the hurricane rapidly northward along the coast. But his superiors overruled his concern, and no hurricane warnings were issued that morning.

On the same day, another lone voice was being heard on Boston radio. Don Kent stopped at the Weather Bureau's office to check the weather maps before going to his unpaid radio job. Kent was just twenty years old, and he was convinced that the hurricane was heading for New England. He went on the radio and gave his own warning. Over the years, Kent became the dean of weather broadcasters, but in 1938, his opinion and that of Charlie Pierce were drowned in the overall expectation that massive hurricanes just don't happen in New England.

At daybreak, the storm was centered east of Cape Hatteras. By early afternoon, the vicious storm was slamming into Long Island and Connecticut. One Long Islander had just unpacked a new barometer and saw a very low reading. He thought the instrument was broken, and he wanted to return it. So, he repacked it and brought it to the post office. When he returned home, his house was gone.

Katharine Hepburn's family summer home in Old Saybrook was gone, too, and she just missed being washed away into the furious Long Island Sound by about one hour. Ironically, Hepburn was playing a round of golf that morning, which was sunny, and she managed to hit a hole-in-one. But her early afternoon swim was interrupted by threatening skies and she returned to her house. She later wrote, "We began to realize that we were in for something special." She was with her mother, her brother Richard, a family friend, and a cook. Windows were breaking and the house was shaking in the increasingly furious wind. The five tied themselves together, climbed through a broken window and struggled to somewhat higher ground. Looking back, they saw the house disappear into Long Island Sound. She said, "It just sailed away as easy as apple pie, and soon nothing was left . . . like the beginning and end of the world." Hepburn's home was among the forty-five hundred buildings that were destroyed and the fifteen thousand that were seriously damaged from Long Island through New England as the storm rapidly raced northward at 50 to 60 miles per hour. In Misquamicut, only five of five hundred summer homes were left standing after the storm surge. Countless trees were toppled. Carla Carlson of Guilford was stalled on a road by the fallen trees and she decided to do some reading. A tree fell on her car, killing her. What was she reading? *Gone with the Wind*.

The 1938 hurricane was truly the "perfect storm." It moved onshore in Milford at about 3:00 p.m. that Wednesday. Most of Connecticut was on the dangerous right-hand sector where the storm's circulation combines with the storm's northward motion to enhance the force of the wind. The storm was moving at nearly 60 miles per hour, so that flow from the south combined with the strong south wind in the eastern sector to deliver winds well in excess of 100 miles per hour. At Blue Hill Observatory, outside Boston, the wind gusts reached 186 miles per hour. That fierce south wind drove the waters of Long Island Sound onto Connecticut's shore and created gigantic storm surges of 12 to 25 feet that washed away everything in their path — railroad tracks, trees, utility poles, and buildings. In addition, the storm came along at high tide and close to the autumnal equinox, when the tide is already running higher than normal. And that's not all.

Katharine Hepburn helps the cleanup effort after the Hurricane of 1938.

Devastation at White Sands beach, 1938.

Many homes in Westbrook were lost in the Hurricane of 1938.

The Connecticut River reached far beyond its banks at Hartford in the aftermath of the Hurricane of 1938.

Prior to the storm's arrival, tropical-like downpours had been occurring for several days, so the ground was totally saturated even before the storm hit. Between September 13 and 20, 7 to 10 inches of rain had fallen and localized flooding had been occurring. Many rivers were already at flood stage. Then, the storm brought another 7 inches of rain and flooding became massive. Not only was the shore inundated by the storm surge, but inland areas were flooded by the raging rivers and streams. The Connecticut River reached a stage of 35.4 feet, almost 20 feet above flood stage. The Park River went over its banks and much of Hartford was under water. In northeastern Connecticut, the Quinebaug River flooded Putnam. Just as structures were swept away by the surge along the shore, buildings were destroyed by the swollen rivers across interior Connecticut. Not a single part of Connecticut was left untouched by the combination of wind, storm surge, and flood. This was the worst natural disaster ever to have hit Connecticut during recorded history.

New London received just about everything the storm had to offer, and something else—a fire that nearly destroyed the entire downtown area. The 500-foot sailing ship, *Marsala*, washed into a warehouse complex along the docks. The fire began there and set off explosions while engulfing downtown buildings. The fire was out of control for seven hours and completely destroyed 25 percent of downtown New London. All of downtown would

The bandshell in Bushnell Park after the hurricane, September 22, 1938.

have been destroyed if it hadn't been for a shift in the wind as the storm center moved north.

The storm obliterated much of Connecticut's infrastructure. The shoreline railroad was destroyed, and inland tracks that could have provided an alternate route were flooded by the overflowing rivers and streams. Over a third of the state's telephone system was knocked out of service. Five thousand utility poles were down and another two thousand were damaged. Cables were left in a dangerous tangle. One hundred and forty miles of cable, and 600,000 pounds of wire needed replacing. Hundreds of thousands of trees were toppled. Bridges and roads were impassable. In Connecticut, ninety people died. Nearly three hundred people lost their lives in Rhode Island. Overall, six hundred people were killed along the storm's path from Long Island through New England. Nearly two thousand people were injured. No doubt, the Hurricane of 1938 was Connecticut's "Katrina."

After this historic storm, the region needed a breather from these tropical wonders, and a definite break did occur in the action, but during September 14–15, 1944, another intense hurricane made its way through eastern New England. The storm made landfall near Point Judith, Rhode Island, and tracked to South Weymouth, Massachusetts. The storm's dangerous eastern sector swept through eastern Massachusetts, including Cape Cod, but Connecticut was on the western edge and was spared the harshest winds. Also, the storm came through at low tide. Still, late in the evening of the 14th, Hartford recorded a wind gust of 109 miles per hour and rainfall came to 3 to 6 inches. Damage was confined mainly to fruit trees and to power and telephone lines. But it was a close call. Twenty-six people were killed in New England and many people lost their lives at sea. The 1,850-ton Navy destroyer *Warrington*, and the Cuttyhunk lightship were hit directly by the storm and more than three hundred sailors drowned.

It would be another ten years before a hurricane hit Connecticut, but it did, and in a very big way. Actually, the mid-1950s ushered in a swarm of hurricanes, and by that time, hurricanes became personalized—they had names. The policy of naming hurricanes after women began in 1953. The concept might have originated in a 1941 novel written by George Stewart, *Storm*. The novel's storm was called "Maria." Prior to 1953, hurricanes were identified simply by their position—latitude and longitude—and that method was cumbersome. Later, storms were named "Alpha," "Baker," "Charlie," but the method lacked variety and the technique became confusing. So, beginning in 1953, female names were used. In 1978 in the Pacific and 1979 in the Atlantic, male names were added and alternated with the female names. Now, the National Weather Service and the World Meteorological Agency draw up annual lists for each of five years. The list of names reflects the native languages of the countries through which the storms pass. The list is repeated every sixth year, unless a storm in the list makes a particular name for itself, and then it is forever put into retirement. Hurricane Carol, which struck Connecticut in 1954, is one of those storm names that will live in infamy.

I was eight years old at the time and anxiously waiting for my father to come home from work. As I looked out the window, I could see branches falling from trees along the street, and pieces of our roof flying off with the wind. My father came home in time to set up pails for catching the water that was pouring through the fracturing roof. Our roof was only one of thousands that were destroyed by the storm that made landfall in Connecticut near Old Saybrook on August 31. Over ten thousand buildings were seriously damaged or destroyed by the hurricane as it carved out a path from Long Island through New England. In Connecticut, wind gusts reached 125 miles per hour. Downtown Providence was hit especially hard with flooding that occurred in a near-record tide. The relatively shallow waters of Narragansett Bay allow for flooding when the wind drives the water toward shore. Throughout its path, the storm took the lives of sixty people. Two people in New York City were killed, but many more lost their lives on Long Island and in New England. In Montauk, four thousand five hundred people were stranded. In Boston, a television transmission tower and the steeple of the Old North Church toppled in the storm. In the harbor near our home, boats were in splintered shambles, and overall, throughout Carol's path, more than three thousand boats were destroyed. New Haven, Middlesex, and New London counties were declared disaster areas. In Connecticut alone, property losses totaled $50 million, and crop losses came to $3 million—all of this in 1954 dollars—but generally, areas west of the Connecticut River were spared serious damage.

Eleven days later, another hurricane threatened the area. But this storm took a more easterly track, and Connecticut was on the less-powerful side and just received a glancing blow. On September 11, Hurricane Edna crossed Martha's Vineyard and Cape Cod. While southeastern New England was hit hard by the storm, west of the storm track, many wondered what might have happened to the storm. Still, along its path and to the east, there was no question that this was a major disaster. Wind gusts reached over 125 miles per hour, rainfall measured 6 inches, and twenty-two people were killed, many of whom were fisherman. Overall damage came to $50 million in 1954 dollars. The storm moved northward from just east of the Carolinas and made a direct hit on Martha's Vineyard, just after dawn. Seven-foot storm tides accompanied the storm along with its 125-mph sustained winds and gusts as high as 145 miles per hour on its eastern semi-circle.

Edna was a major category 3 storm. After Martha's Vineyard, the storm struck Cape Cod with its harshest fury, causing severe damage to homes, piers, and boats. Then, the storm went on to Maine and the Canadian Maritimes. Three-quarters of Nova Scotia's apple crop was destroyed. Connecticut might have been spared from serious damage, but Edna's name has been retired, too.

And 1954 was not yet finished with us. Another powerful storm ripped northward from the tropics. This was a late-season storm—Hurricane Hazel. The storm baffled forecasters from its very beginning in the southern Caribbean. It first showed up in Granada and swung northward erratically. Even just before landfall in the United States, the area thought to be in its path was Florida and Georgia. Instead, it pounded North and South Carolina with its 106-mile per hour sustained winds first coming ashore at Myrtle Beach on October 15. Nearly 80 percent of the exclusive property on Myrtle Beach was damaged or destroyed. And then, Hazel moved on an inland track through Virginia, Pennsylvania, and New York. Yet, the storm maintained strong winds that uprooted tall pine trees, brought down power lines, and damaged crops. In western Connecticut and Massachusetts, power outages were widespread, even with the passage of the storm well to the west. Most of Connecticut was spared serious damage, but strong wind gusts in western Connecticut did take a toll on the power grid. And the storm maintained plenty of strength, bringing 70-mile per hour wind gusts to Burlington, Vermont, and carrying its fury into Canada, where some of its greatest damage occurred. The Great Lakes helped intensify the storm even more. Toronto was stunned by its now 100-mile per hour wind gusts. Numerous rail lines and roads were washed away by rising waters. In Toronto alone, Hazel was responsible for the loss of sixty-nine people. It was the storm that refused to give up.

After 1954, you might think that the region deserved another ten-year break from devastating hurricanes, but this was not to be the case. In August 1955, the one-two punch of Hurricanes Connie and Diane brought the worst natural disaster to Connecticut in history—even worse than the Hurricane of 1938. Connie was first on the scene and it took an inland track through interior Pennsylvania and New York. Winds were not a big problem, but 3 to 8 inches of rain completely saturated the ground and caused localized flooding. Its main impact was to set the stage for Diane, which followed less than a week later. The storm moved northward along the coast and then out to sea, just south of Long Island. Rainfall amounts were variable but up to 16 inches fell, bringing the two-storm total to over 20 inches in some places. In Torrington, the August rainfall total came to more than 27 inches, most of that from the two storms. The greatest Connecticut disaster followed, with not a single one of the state's 138 towns being unaffected. Putnam, Winsted, Torrington, Waterbury, Ansonia, and Derby were particularly hard hit. Winsted was completely flooded as the Mad River truly lived up to its name. The Naugatuck Valley was hardest hit when the Naugatuck River went over its banks, washing away roads, bridges, buildings, and a number of people. Severe flooding also occurred along the Still River in the Danbury area and the Mill River farther east. In Putnam, the flooding Quinebaug River collapsed and helped set fire to a magnesium processing plant that belonged to the Metal Sellers Corporation. Hundreds of barrels of burning magnesium then swept through town, setting off pyrotechnic displays when they exploded.

Seventy people were killed by the raging waters in Connecticut. Many were children. In Waterbury, the mayor said he saw twelve bodies floating down the swollen Naugatuck. Rescue helicopters came into service from all branches of the military. Many personnel had been at Sikorsky Airport in Stratford waiting to pick up and transport new helicopters to their home bases. Instead, dozens of helicopters and these veteran pilots from the Korean War were called into rescue mode. Families were plucked off rooftops, similar to scenes from Katrina. The helicopters were used mainly through the Naugatuck Valley, and also in Canton and Farmington. Over three hundred people were rescued by the Sikorsky helicopters. It was a disaster that few could forget. In the Hartford area, the Park River went over its banks, and two children were swept away by the Farmington River. The City of Hartford was declared a State of Emergency. Dams washed away and roaring waters came through the Thompsonville section of Enfield. Marshall law was declared in the state. One day later, President Eisenhower declared Connecticut a federal disaster area. Dozens of railroad bridges were wrecked and some rail lines never came back into service. Old river mills never reopened either. It was a disaster that few could forget.

Nearing my tenth birthday, I could remember being in the flooding basement of my parents' home trying to help my grandfather bail out the water that was climbing higher and higher. We lived close enough to the ocean so that we wondered if the water was from the ocean tide or just rainwater bubbling up through cracks in the cellar floor. My grandfather was from the old school, and he gave the water the old "taste test." He stuck his finger into the water, tasted it, and said, "It's not from the ocean." We were losing the battle and were forced to retreat upstairs. But we were among the lucky ones who survived the storm. The fire department came and rescued us along with the house and pumped out the basement, where the water came up over 6 feet. But the floods left mass destruction of power and telephone lines. Washouts occurred where there were no streams before. The infrastructure of the state was in shambles. Small boats became the main means of transportation. Many towns were left without any potable water. In addition to the seventy deaths, forty-seven hundred people were injured in Connecticut alone.

The wind was never the issue with these storms, but the rain became historic. Diane was "downgraded" to a tropical storm as it made its elliptical track from near Myrtle Beach through Virginia and curved out to sea off New Jersey on August 18–19, but that is when Connecticut was inundated. Southwestern Connecticut was spared the brunt of the August hurricane flooding, but this was not the case in October when a nontropical storm came along. We'll have more on that later in our flood section, but without doubt the 1950s was a decade with some of the most devastating storms in Connecticut's history.

The next hurricane to have an impact on Connecticut was Donna, in 1960. The storm was massive, but fortunately it weakened during its northward track along the East Coast. When it hit the Florida Keys, the storm had 180-mile per hour wind gusts, and it delivered 12 inches of rain to Miami on September 10. The storm crossed the Florida peninsula twice, once from the east, and then after recurving, from the west. Although it arrived in the Northeast in weakened fashion, it did bring an 11-foot storm tide to New York Harbor, where there was extensive pier damage. The final landfall of the storm occurred near New London on the morning of September 12. Over Block Island, winds reached 95 miles per hour, but no sustained winds of hurricane intensity were reported in Connecticut, although a few gusts reached 75 miles per hour in eastern sections. Rainfall came to 3 to 8 inches, with the highest in south-central areas. Flooding was limited to some crops, and wind damage to some trees and power lines. Donna tracked through eight countries and thirteen states along a 5,000-mile course. The storm claimed 168 lives, 50 in the United States, and 137,000 people were left homeless. In the scheme of hurricanes, Donna was huge, but it was a relatively minor storm in Connecticut.

Hurricane activity in Connecticut settled down in the 1960s. During 1961, three late-season storms threatened, but only Esther on September 21 brought heavy rain to Connecticut. Some flash flooding occurred in Connecticut and Rhode Island with its maximum 7 to 8 inch rainfall. But no lives were lost and damage was minimal. The storm was unusual in that it made a loop 400 miles off Cape Cod and came back to the Cape in weakened fashion and eventually to Maine. The storm was also noteworthy because it was the first hurricane to be seeded by silver iodide crystals in the attempt to disperse the energy from its eyewall. This was the first experiment of Project Stormfury, but the results were mixed. At first, the storm weakened when chemical canisters were dropped into the eye, but then on a second attempt, there was little change when the chemicals were dispersed just outside the eyewall.

After the early 1960s, there was a definite period of hurricane-free weather in Connecticut. Many offshore storms were out there, and there were a few tropical storms, but none had a major impact. The most serious threat did not come along until Hurricane Belle on August 10, 1976, and even that was called a poor excuse for a hurricane. The storm first crossed Long Island near Jones Beach and the moved onto the Connecticut shore near Bridgeport, where it brought 74-mile per hour winds with gusts to 77. The storm rapidly weakened, with winds diminishing to 45-mile per hour gusts in Hartford. But heavy preceding rains that already had saturated the ground accompanied the 2- to 5-inch storm rainfall, and the combination helped to bring about local flooding, with the gusty winds destroying fruit trees and bringing down some power lines. In Connecticut, one fatality occurred when a car skidded into a tree in Barkhamsted. But the storm came close to low tide, and tides were only running 3 feet above normal. The storm weakened from its potential because it moved relatively slowly at 25 miles per hour through colder waters. The 1938 hurricane carved a similar path but it didn't have a chance to weaken much. It tracked northward from off the Carolina coast at speeds of 60 to 70 miles per hour.

In 1972, a powerful storm, Hurricane Agnes, weakened to a tropical storm but caused historic flooding in New York and Pennsylvania through its inland track. Some residual flooding occurred in western Connecticut, but the state received only fringe effects from the devastating storm. Bridgeport's peak wind was 37 miles per hour.

After Hurricane Belle, the 1970s remain quiet for Connecticut, and it wasn't until Hurricane Gloria came ashore on September 27, 1985, that we had one of those old-fashioned hurricanes, but even that had less impact than many storms of old. This storm had the potential to be a huge disaster. It had been tracking for nearly two weeks out of the tropics, and at one point, was a category 4 storm. The circulation remained to the east of the Carolinas as it set its sights on Connecticut on the night of September 26. The storm already was labeled another "Storm of the Century," but it certainly failed to live up to its billing. On the evening before the storm hit, I was on the telephone with Carolina Power and Light Company, with whom I had been consulting. As the eye of Gloria passed east of Cape Hatteras, I asked about weather conditions. The response from a dispatcher was this: "It isn't any worse than a summer thunderstorm here." As it was, a maximum rainfall of 9 inches was reported in eastern North Carolina—tough enough, but at that point, I knew that this storm would be much less than advertised.

The storm crossed near Milford, but during low tide on the early afternoon of the 27th. I called it the lunch-hour storm—if you had a long lunch, you could have missed the entire storm. Gloria's intensity diminished to a category 2 storm while crossing Long Island, and the storm had broken up significantly by the time it reached the Connecticut shoreline. Still, storm tides of 5 feet destroyed fishing piers, and strong wind gusts helped create the single greatest power outage in the history of Connecticut up until that time, with 669,000 homes losing power—some for well over a week. Two people were killed from falling trees, including one six-year old. Of the eight fatalities from Gloria, two occurred in Connecticut, which seemed to receive its share of problems from the weakening storm. Governor O'Neil, while I was working with him as a special assistant, described it to me as a bad blow, but manageable, and he received kudos for his measured response. Major evacuations were underway in other states that received little or no impact from the storm, and Connecticut was one of the few states that did not declare emergency declarations along the storm's path, although federal disaster declarations were designated after the storm for Connecticut. The state's major impact was from falling trees and long-term power outages. The greatest wind gust reported was from Waterbury: 83 miles per hour. That was enough to turn the lights off.

From 1985 through the beginning of the twenty-first century, Connecticut continued to be threatened but spared major blows from these furious products of the tropics. Hurricane Bob did make a direct hit upon New England in 1991, but it focused its energy upon eastern portions of the region, Cape Cod and the Islands. Less-populated coastal communities were hardest hit. The storm made landfall near Block Island on August 18, 1991. Sustained winds of 105 miles per hour were reported there with gusts to 125 miles per hour. This storm caused vicious damage reminiscent of Hurricane Carol of 1954 across Cape Cod and Rhode Island. Six-foot storm surges and the 125-mile per hour wind gusts caused extensive damage to piers along the shores of Narragansett Bay. Several homes and buildings fell into the ocean, and as much as 10 inches of flooding rain fell northward along the storm's path into Maine. In Connecticut, 7 inches of rain fell in the Groton area, and several fatalities were reported. Two tornadoes were reported in eastern Long Island. In New England, the storm was smaller but more powerful than Gloria, and if it had stayed closer to land, the damage would have been historic. But Connecticut came out of this storm with relatively minor damage—some outages along with downed branches and power lines. Connecticut was lucky, this time.

Another storm unleashed some fury in 1999 when Tropical Storm Floyd pushed its way northward from the Carolinas. The storm made a category

4 run for Cape Fear, North Carolina, on the night of September 16. It created a major disaster as it poured rain down at amounts of 15 to 20 inches. Dozens of people drowned and six thousand homes were lost as the storm moved northward along the coast and directly across Connecticut late at night on the 16th. But by the time the storm reached Connecticut, it had weakened to a tropical storm and low astronomical tides prevented any serious coastal damage. Early on the 17th, the storm lost tropical characteristics.

Still, parts of Connecticut received flooding rains. Generally, 6 to 10 inches of rain flooded small streams and rivers. Rainfall of 9.14 inches was reported in Southington, and 10.80 inches occurred in Bristol. Flooding occurred along the Quinnipiac River in Southington along with other rivers and small streams. The hardest hit area was western Connecticut, where Danbury received 8 to 12 inches of rain, with isolated amounts over a foot. Extensive flooding occurred around the Danbury Fair Mall, and this part of Connecticut eventually was declared a federal disaster area. The flooding and lack of power closed the mall. The torrential rain also created havoc in southeastern New York—Putnam and Westchester counties—where people were rescued off the roofs of their homes and even through the roofs of trapped busses. One person was reported to have drowned in Connecticut while kayaking along the swollen Quinnipiac River the day after Floyd passed.

Through the first decade of the new century, hurricanes continued to take a back seat to the heavy action that was occurring elsewhere in the tropics, including the greatest disaster of all, Hurricane Katrina. Sure, we have had some brushes with these storms. On September 2, 2006, Tropical Storm Ernesto brought 50- to 60-mile per hour winds onshore during high tide. Waves crashed to the second story of homes along the shore. Seaweed came up to the second story of our own beachfront home.

Connecticut is vulnerable.

7

Tornadoes —
Dorothy Would Be at Home

Tornadoes are far less common in Connecticut than in some other portions of the country, but a very high population density raises the chances that we will be affected by these storms to a level that can match the damage anyplace else in the nation. Ever since 1682, tornadoes have been recorded in Connecticut. The threat rating of someone, property included, being injured in Connecticut and western Massachusetts by a tornado is as high as most places in tornado country. Of course, as population continues to expand in the Plains and Midwest, the odds of a Midwesterner experiencing a tornado do increase — our more stable population means that the threat rating locally decreases with respect to other parts of the country, but up through the 1970s, Connecticut and Western Massachusetts had the highest threat rating in the entire country.

As an example, the 1979 tornado that hit Windsor Locks had the distinction of being the most destructive single tornado up to that time — until the Oklahoma City tornado came along on May 3, 1999. Our 1979 Windsor Locks storm generated an estimated $632 million of damage, adjusted to 1997 dollars. For twenty years, that level of damage was just about tied with the $635 million damage associated with a Grand Island Nebraska storm that struck in 1980, but seven different funnels were associated with that outbreak. No other single tornado matched the Windsor Locks single storm until the Oklahoma City storm hit with over $1 billion of damage in 1999. To this day, the Windsor Locks tornado remains among the top-ten costliest tornadoes to have hit in the country. The tornadoes that seem to favor a Northeast tornado alley

Connecticut has its share of tornadoes. This photo shows some of the damage from the F4 tornado that hit Windsor Locks in 1979.

take a toll in terms of life as well as property. The tornado that struck Worcester, Massachusetts, and its suburbs in 1953 remains in the top-twenty list of killer tornadoes, with ninety lives being lost.

On the average, Connecticut will experience two or three tornadoes each year. A total of eighty-two tornadoes have struck between 1980 and 2007. These are typically "weak," with winds estimated up to 100 miles per hour, but those gusts are enough to bring branches down, cause roof damage, and even topple mobile homes. In addition to these tornadoes, severe thunderstorms, minus the tornado, are just as destructive and more fre-quent. These occur on the average of five days each year. Then, every two years on the average, a major tornado has occurred — the bottom of the na-tional count, but as we see when they do occur, watch out.

A Fujita scale, developed by T. Theodore Fujita, has been used to estimate wind speed from observed damage. A major tornado has been classified as one with an F2 or higher rating. F3 ratings bring estimated wind gusts up to 206 miles per hour, winds up to 268 miles per hour are rated F4, and the most powerful tornados, with winds of 261 to 318 miles per hour, are F5. The Wind-sor Locks storm was estimated as a strong F4. Ten years later, on July 10, 1989, another F4 storm hit Hamden. Whole structures crumbled. More re-cently, the National Weather Service has developed a modified version of the F-scale to better correlate wind with damage. It is called the FE scale, the enhanced Fujita Scale, which generally moves a storm up the old scale by one rank for the same estimated speeds in major tornadoes. So the old F3 storm would be an FE4, or close to it, on the enhanced scale, and an F4 would be elevated to an FE5. Although there is room for an FE5 on the enhanced scale, one has yet to be confirmed by the National Weather Service.

So without question, Connecticut experiences our share of tornadoes, and our landscape is scarred by these vicious storms. Dorothy would be surprised.

One of the most violent early documented tornadoes in Connecticut occurred in 1786, and once again, western Massachusetts and Connecticut were hit together. The storm erupted at the typical hour of 5:00 p.m. on August 23, 1786, first in Sturbridge, and then tracked to Southbridge before crossing into Connecticut. The storm swept through the towns of Woodstock, Pomfret, and Killingly. The sky grew nighttime dark in a destructive path about a quarter mile wide. Fences and heavy stone walls were tossed about. More than one hundred buildings, many of them barns, were blown down and destroyed. Cattle were killed by falling timbers. One story made reference to a wagon that was carried up by the wind and dropped upon an apple tree. Killingly seemed to receive the brunt of the storm. There, a new home was destroyed and one of its family members was killed. When the storm struck, six persons were in the new home of Othniel Brown, and all escaped except Mrs. Brown as the house was blown to pieces. A second fatality occurred inside a crushed home in Woodstock when two large elm trees were uprooted and dropped upon the house. The storm then tracked into Rhode Island.

As is usual, violent thunderstorms accompanied the tornado, and several places in Connecticut experienced severe weather damage, other than directly from the tornado. In Wethersfield, a person was struck and killed by lightning. In Windham, crops were set on fire by the lightning. In New London, the thunderstorms persisted for three hours. Frequent cloud-to-ground lightning strikes hit structures, including the home of Jonathan Brooks. Lightning entered through a chimney and struck and killed his only daughter, who was just fifteen.

Another day of horror occurred in 1794, when a vicious tornado made a huge sweep through western Connecticut from New Milford southeastward to Branford on Long Island Sound. The storm hit during the late afternoon of June 19, and it carved a path of destruction through New Milford, Newtown, Watertown, Waterbury, Northford, and Branford. Houses, barns, and other structures were destroyed by the storm, which was reported to emit strange loud sounds. A number of people were sucked into the whirling funnel and killed after plunging back to the ground. The storm also did considerable damage to forest and fruit trees. Its path was irregular—sometimes touching down and other times lifting off the ground, but wherever it tracked, it took its toll. The path of destruction is reminiscent of the July 10, 1989, tornado outbreak that made a very similar sweep from the Northwest Hills to New Haven.

One of the great catastrophes in Connecticut's history occurred on Friday, August 9, 1878. A tropical weather pattern had spawned heavy thunderstorms for about three weeks, but on the 9th of August, close to 6:00 p.m., the most deadly tornado outbreak in New England up until that time occurred in Wallingford. The storm's severe path of destruction was in a populated and developed area about 2 miles long and a half mile wide, about a quarter mile north of the railroad station.

Thirty-four persons lost their lives, twenty-eight more were severely injured, and 160 buildings were completely ruined. Forty homes and fifty barns were among the totally destroyed structures, and dozens were at least partially destroyed. Many of the people were killed by the falling and collapsing structures. Telephone and telegraph wires were down, and it was left for a twelve-year old boy, John Hoey, to ride on horseback to Meriden to seek help. Thanks to Hoey, by 7:00 that evening, steam cars began to come from Meriden to the victims' rescue. Seven physicians arrived by 7:30 p.m., and bodies were searched out. The town hall became a hospital for the wounded, who suffered concussions, broken arms, broken legs and backs, and fractured skulls. Two days later, on Sunday, twenty-five of the victims were buried in the town cemetery, and as many as ten thousand people were present at the service. People came together to respond to the needs of the heavily Catholic community. In several towns around Wallingford, meetings were held to raise funds for the victims of the catastrophe. All but one of the victims was Catholic. The Catholic Church and a newly built brick high school were among the buildings completely in ruins.

It would be a long while before another catastrophic tornado would strike Connecticut. In 1953, Connecticut was just missed by one of the most powerful New England tornadoes on record—the 1953 Worcester tornado. That storm remained in Massachusetts, but its dark clouds could be seen from Connecticut. At the time, I was a youngster, seven years old, and traveled with my parents to see what that storm had done to the Worcester area. Weather-watching runs in my family. I remember being at a coffee shop and listening to an eyewitness explain that if he hadn't crossed the street as the storm swept by, he wouldn't be telling any story. His pock-marked face was visibly shaken by the event that took the lives of ninty-four people. Brick structures were reduced to rubble, and the National Guard had cordoned off the city. The storm was easily in the F5 category, and it remains among the top-twenty killer list for tornadoes in all of U.S.

history. The storm easily could have been a Connecticut system, but it remained in Massachusetts. Another destructive tornado did hit Connecticut in 1962. This storm struck between 5:30 and 6:00 p.m. on May 24, 1962, and for the time, became the most destructive tornado to have hit the state. The storm carved a 12-mile path from Middlebury through Waterbury and Wolcott, and then into Southington. Seventy buildings were destroyed, and another 175 were heavily damaged. Six hundred more were moderately damaged. One person was killed and fifty were injured. Damage in 1962 dollars came to $1,500,000. Hailstones of an inch and a half in diameter accompanied the storm. This was no Worcester tornado, but it did take its toll.

A number of tornadoes occurred between 1962 and 1979. In 1973 alone, six separate days brought tornadoes to the state, but none reached the historic magnitude of what occurred on October 3, 1979. This was a very strange storm, which turned out to be one of the most costly in this nation's history. I was conducting a class during that early morning and demonstrating the use of a tornado prediction index that I had developed a few years earlier as a graduate student. It was a very stormy morning across all of Connecticut, including in Danbury where I was teaching, and where the Danbury State Fair was located prior to the construction of the large shopping mall. Heavy showers were pouring out of the dark clouds that were rolling in from the south. Gusty winds accompanied the rain. After class, one of my students insisted that we go into the lab and calculate the index. I didn't want to . . . after all, this was early October, and tornadoes are rare enough, let alone during a cooler autumn month. But he didn't want a theoretical discussion of the index, he wanted some practical application. So, reluctantly, I agreed, but after making the calculation, I couldn't believe the results. The index was near the top of the scale. I never saw it become much higher, even for the super-tornadoes of the Midwest.

Immediately, I called the Office of Emergency Operations in Danbury, and spoke to the director, Peter Winter. I told him of the potential. He then had the fire department empty out the big tent at the fairgrounds. This was Governor's Day at the fair, and hundreds of young people were bussed in, free of charge. Governor Ella Grasso came, too. My first call was logged in at the operation's center at about 10:00 a.m., and I made several calls up until early afternoon when the tornado itself struck. No official watches were posted, and most people were completely surprised by the storm. The index couldn't specify where in Connecticut that tornado would hit. It only could indicate an area that was most likely to receive activity—and that was most of the state. No tornado hit Danbury, but the governor was sent home. Ironically, she lived in Windsor Locks, where the tornado touched down. I was serving as a special aide to the governor at the time. She didn't fire me.

A cold, dry pocket of air located above 10,000 feet over the mid-Atlantic States was pushed northward into Connecticut's supersaturated air mass. The resulting turbulence was more than the atmosphere could handle, and severe thunderstorms were unleashed. These led to the massive tornado that ripped through Windsor Locks and the Poquonock section of Windsor. Winds were estimated to have reached over 200 miles per hour, making this an F4 storm. These vicious storms form when the warm, lighter, moist air near the ground rises through the heavier, colder air aloft. The greater the temperature difference, the greater the rising motion. The air rises like a cork through a basin of water. Then, in the upper atmosphere, air is exhausted outward by strong winds, and often these winds provide an initial rotation to the rising turbulent column. All the conditions were there on that October day in 1979.

The storm devastated the Bradley Air Museum where vintage aircraft were flipped over, crushed, and torn apart. A hangar that housed some of the airplanes was blown to pieces with its roof torn off. Aircraft such as a C-133B transport, F108-F8 fighters, and a CH 37 helicopter were ruined. A B29A smashed into a SP2-E Neptune, and the damage just went on and on. As the storm moved into Windsor, it struck an elementary school, which by good fortune was nearly empty because of early administrative dismissal that day. The roof of the school was destroyed. Had there been a regular day at the school, the loss of life would have been huge. As it was, three people

Aircraft devastated at Windsor Locks, 1979.

Plane blown from Bradley Air Museum at Windsor Locks, 1979.

Tornado's Toy. A Navy plane lies upside down in the aftermath of the tornado at Windsor Locks in 1979.

An F4 tornado hit Hamden in 1989.

were killed by the tornado and five hundred were injured. Damage came to nearly $500 million in 1997 currency, making this single tornado one of the mostly costly in history, anywhere in the country. It ranked as the single most costly storm for nearly twenty years, until the Oklahoma storm struck with $1 billion of damage in May 1999.

About ten years later, on July 10, 1989, Connecticut once again was hit with an F4 storm. Like the 1979 storm, this one came as a surprise to most people. I was working on WTNH-TV. During the noon show, I pointed out a cluster of heavy thunderstorms that were hovering around the Berkshires of western Massachusetts. It looked like we could be in for an active afternoon, with some of the storms reaching severe proportions. For most of the afternoon, the storms stayed to the north, but by late afternoon, the most violent activity tore southeastward and carved out the longest path of tornado damage in Connecticut's history. At least three tornadoes were spawned from the northwest corner of the state in Cornwall, where the beautiful forest called the Cathedral of the Pines was destroyed, to Litchfield, where the Bantam section of town was flattened, to the New Haven area, where the most powerful of all storms struck. In Watertown, where a tornado was confirmed, strong thunderstorm winds struck Black Rock State Park, killing a twelve-year-old girl. The squalls even crossed Long Island Sound and hit Long Island at East Moriches. In southern Hamden, right on the New Haven border, the tornado reached F4 status.

Wreckage in Hamden, 1989.

I was on the air at 5:30 p.m., just about when the tornado hit. I remarked to the news anchor that I never saw the sky become so dark on a summer's afternoon. The anchor replied, "Dr. Mel, I never saw you perspire on the air as you are right now." The tornado had lifted off the ground and was moving over our building. We quickly lost power, but switched to emergency backup, and we remained on the air through that evening. I continued to perspire, as we had little or no air conditioning.

Just blocks from our studio, in the Newhall section of Hamden, brick structures were turned into rubble. Homes were in shambles. In this area alone, four hundred buildings were destroyed, including an industrial park. Tree damage could be seen for years after the storm, and residents were shocked by the intensity of the storm. The roof of the middle school was torn away. Hail was measured 2.5 inches in diameter, and at nearby Oxford Airport, 4.4 inches of rain fell in just 30 minutes. Throughout the Northeast, including Connecticut, seventeen tornadoes were confirmed on that mighty day, extending from New York State through New Jersey.

During the next fifteen years, tornadoes continued to appear, but none reached the F4-status of the Hamden tornado. In fact, all but one was either F0 or F1. The exception was an F2 storm that hit Torrington on June 23, 2001. No injuries or deaths occurred with that storm, although property damage reached $250,000.

Floods—
When It Rains, It Pours

Connecticut is without question a flood-prone location. The beautiful hills, streams, lakes, and shoreline contribute to sources of pride, but also to huge problems during times of excessive rain, melting snow, or tidal surges. Connecticut is as prone to flooding damage as nearly anywhere in the country. Over the past twenty years, FEMA has issued over a dozen disaster declarations for flooding in Connecticut. Rain is distributed fairly evenly through the twelve months of the year, but every so often, skies open up. Flooding seems to be a disaster waiting to happen.

Just as I was writing this chapter, on the first weekend of March 2008, a major storm was about to run up the spine of the Appalachians. Before it arrived in full, I couldn't help being anxious, thinking about another weekend flood that hit during the first weekend of June in 1982. The latest threat was coming on the heels of one of the wettest Februarys on record. My leaking skylights can attest to that. And just a few days later, 3 to 4 inches of rain fell. The ground was supersaturated, and just another 2 inches of rain would cause many streams and rivers to go over their banks. The computers were promising at least that amount. The rain came, and the flooding, but the rainfall was no match for the 15 inches of rain that fell during that weekend in 1982, or the nearly 20 inches in 1955. We dodged a close call.

The sources for flooding are almost too numerous to list. Coastal residents are most familiar with hurricane surges, which can elevate the tide to 8 or 10 feet above normal. On top of the surge is wave action, which can send waves crashing as high as second-story windows. These same hurricanes bring torrential downpours that flood inland areas and can wipe out entire communities, as was the case in 1955.

A full-blown tropical system is far from the only source of coastal and inland flooding. There isn't a single storm track in North America that fails to come within striking distance of Connecticut. Coastal storms are often the most dramatic. These develop along the East Coast with the warm water of the Gulf Stream serving as an energy source. The rip-roaring northeasters can generate high winds that pile up the waters on the shore and very heavy precipitation that floods the landscape. In December 1992, a northeaster did all of that. Three times, the tide rolled in, and for all three cycles, water poured down coastal streets, inundating cars up to their rooftops.

During the summer months, fronts deliver thunderstorms that can cause localized downpours, and often, these squalls develop one after another. The major circulation stalls, and for hours, these squalls develop and move through a town as if the heavy pockets of rain were railroad cars chugging along a track. The phenomenon is even called training, and in June 1982, this is exactly what took place. In south-central Connecticut, flooding reached the worst levels in fifty-five years. A dozen people were killed in the river and by flash flooding. Antecedent rain of 4 inches didn't help the cause, either.

Then, there are the famous spring floods along the major rivers. The combination of snowmelt, ice jams, and heavy rain can send rivers to record levels, as was the case in the devastating floods of 1936. And that snowmelt can occur hundreds of miles to the north in the river basin. The Connecticut River reached its highest level on record that year, and flooding in Hartford was monumental. Fourteen thousand people were left homeless. Flooding is part of our weather heritage, thanks to geology and climatology. Here is a chronology of some of the bigger ones in our history:

One of the earliest documented heavy floods occurred in 1770. This was an early winter flood when the combination of a heavy rainstorm with strong southeast winds combined with the meltdown of snow and ice. The storm struck on a Sunday, January 7. The weather in December was cold and dry and thick ice had formed along all the rivers, but most of it gave way on January 7. After a day of violent wind and rain, the Sun returned, but the water piled up, reaching 10 feet above normal.

In Hartford, the Connecticut River flooded a half mile on either side, causing considerable damage. The river was impassible for several days. The Farmington River also flooded, and in Simsbury, the buildings of an iron works floated away in the swollen river. Similar flooding occurred through much of New England.

Another tragic flood occurred in 1801, on March 19–20. The Connecticut

River rose to 27.5 feet, enough to cause severe flooding. Flood stage is at 16 feet. The storm began on a Wednesday, and the rain did not finally move out until Saturday. Along the Farmington River, fourteen bridges, seven grist-mills, two barns, two shops, a home, and several outbuildings were swept downstream. Great quantities of lumber and fencing materials were part of the debris. Two young people were killed by the raging waters.

Two young boys were also on a highway in Thompson, Cushion Brown and Otis Lamed. They tried to cross the swollen Quinebaug River, which had swept across the road. Lamed went first, but he fell into a hole that had been dug out by the flooding waters. The current swept him into the middle of the stream and that was the last seen of him. Brown was more fortunate, and managed to make the crossing safely.

In another flooding tragedy, two children, a brother and sister, the children of Josiah Adkins of West Simsbury, went into a mill to take down an old weaver's loom that was owned by the family. But as they were working, the foundation of the building began to give way, and the mill began to float downstream. The girl was first to try to escape along a plank that extended to the riverbank, but when she went onto the plank, it became unstable because of the moving building and she was swept into the raging current. She then grabbed onto some shrubs that were hanging by the banks and eventually was able to pull herself to safety. Her brother's fate was less fortunate. He could not escape the building, and as people watched along the banks, he was seen screaming for help from the doorway. But the onlookers could do little to rescue the boy. Even his family watched as their son was being swept away. Eventually the building collapsed, and the boy was killed. His body was found broken and bruised among the debris and returned to his parents. He was buried the next day.

A few years later, another flood swept through New England. The damage occurred mostly in eastern New England during February 1807. Buildings, mills, and numerous bridges were swept away from Maine to eastern Connecticut. Heavy rain and melting snow contributed to the swollen rivers and streams. In Connecticut, the ice on the Willimantic and Mount Hope rivers began to break up on the night of February 7. The cracking of the ice sounded like thunder. In Norwich, several bridges were swept away, and additional ones were damaged. The river overflowed and went into the first stories of structures. When the water reached the second stories, boats were used to rescue those who were trapped. The flooding continued from East Main Street to Franklin Street. Prior to the storm, an embankment had been constructed with every bit of material that would prevent leakage. The embankment contained wood, rails, stones, hay, straw, and canvas. It was constructed from the Wauregan Hotel to the opposite side of the valley. Where the embankment was located, the river was held back. There, only some water trickled over.

Another flood, caused by the breakup of snow and ice combined with heavy rain, occurred in Connecticut in 1823, where, once again, eastern portions were hit hard. Heavy snow had piled up during February. But on March 5, the thaw began with heavy rain that fell for twenty-four hours. That was just too much. Six bridges spanning the Yantic River washed away. Three were in Norwich and two in Bozrah. In Norwich, the Wharf Bridge was broken up and buildings on the bridge were moved, including a church that stood on the bridge. The chapel floated down the river until it met up with the Thames River and headed toward New London. According to accounts, it maintained its frame until it reached Long Island Sound. A schooner in New London Harbor nearly collided with the church, and that even inspired a poem, "The Captain," by Brainard. The schooner was on its way from Charleston, South Carolina, to Bridgeport. The captain turned out of the harbor and rushed toward Bridgeport. He was never so frightened in all his days at sea.

Western Connecticut was not exactly left out of the flooding that occurred with frequency during the 1800s. For example, very heavy rain fell during the middle of November 1853, and the heaviest fell on Sunday the thirteenth. The Connecticut River and its tributaries were swollen, and considerable damage was done along the Housatonic and Naugatuck rivers. Numerous railroad bridges were damaged or destroyed. That night, at Seymour and Ansonia, bridges across the Naugatuck River collapsed. Many people on the bridge, watching the raging river in Ansonia, were thrown into the water when the bridge gave way. Several people drowned, while others were fortunate enough to cling to shrubs and bushes until they were rescued. Cries for help were heard through that dark night. Boats were sent out to try to rescue some of the drowning people. In one case, fifteen people were picked up by a boat that braved the raging river filled with the debris of floating trees, timber, and bridges. But many others could no longer hold out and drowned.

The Connecticut River flooded on numerous occasions during the 1800s, and at times severe flooding occurred. Some of the flooding was helped along by tropical storms, as in 1869, when up to a foot of rain poured down in the Connecticut Valley. Still, through the century, the crest of the river remained below 30 feet, generally rising 25 to 26 feet. But during the twentieth-century, some massive flooding occurred.

The greatest flood of all time on the Connecticut River occurred in March 1936, when the river reached a record crest of 37.6 feet. Records of these crests have been kept for over three hundred years. Melting snow across all

Elderly lady gets rescued, flood of March, 1936.

of New England combined with frequent rains over a thirteen-day period
was responsible for the historic flood. Four distinct storms came along from
March 9 through March 22. The water equivalent of the melting snow and
rainfall was averaging 16 inches, but was as high as 30 inches in the White
Mountains of New Hampshire. Ten inches of water over an acre weighs
1,130 tons. That was too much. Ice jams formed, dams failed, and bridges
collapsed. The Connecticut River, the Farmington River, and their tributaries overflowed beyond the flood plain into populated portions of Hartford.
Fourteen thousand people were left homeless and two-thirds of the phone
service was knocked out. A massive power failure occurred when the power
plant flooded, leaving much of the city in darkness. The *Hartford Courant*
was forced to publish from New Britain, although its reporters remained at
the flooded downtown location. Three partially filled gas tanks were ripped
from their moorings on the Connecticut River, and the Coast Guard ordered
three cutters up the river to clear them, or as a last resort, to blow them up.
Four feet of water filled Hartford's central business section, and the swollen
Park River threatened the city from the west. And Hartford was not the only
community affected. In New Hartford, a bursting dam contributed to loss

A flooded street scene in Hartford, during the flood of March 1936.

of property and homes. An earlier flood in 1927 had not been as serious, although it caused water to spill over into East Hartford, flooding roads, buildings, and shrubbery. Rescuers came in rowboats with water knee-deep through the community. Many commercial buildings were at least partially destroyed. In Hartford, the Park River reached nearly the top of the arch on the Trumbull Street Bridge. Roads along the river were flooded. But the 1936 flood was the granddaddy of river flooding.

Only two years later, another massive flooding experience occurred, although this one was associated with the great Hurricane of 1938. The 1938 hurricane crest on the Connecticut River was 2 feet below the record 1936 level. Flooding can occur from many sources in Connecticut, and in 1938, when the historic hurricane arrived, very heavy rain already had saturated the ground across the state. The storm made landfall on September 21, but from September 13 to 20, antecedent rainfall measured 7 to 10 inches. Another 3 to 7 inches fell with the arrival of the hurricane, so not only was the coastline devastated by storm surges and wave action, but inland areas also were inundated with near-record floods. That additional rain filled small streams and rivers and flooded adjacent areas. Roads and bridges were washed out. In the Hartford area, crops were wiped out, and of course, those rains combined with massive winds that blew down forests and property.

A year seldom passed without some flooding, but the next major flood waited until 1949, when a winter storm flooded areas near the Housatonic and Naugatuck rivers. The storm was actually a New Year's deluge, coming along on December 28 and stalling in the Hudson Valley. By January 1, as much as 13 inches of rain had fallen in the Berkshires, and that water drained into the Housatonic Basin. Towns in western Connecticut experienced severe flooding, which was classified as a hundred-year storm. The Connecticut River reached a crest of 25.2 feet — nearly 10 feet below the crests in 1936 and 1938, but high enough to cause some flooding.

Historically, 1955 was the most devastating year for flooding in Connecticut. Two great floods occurred — one during August, and the other occurred in October. The August flooding was hurricane-related, and the flooding delivered the greatest disaster in Connecticut history. Nearly 20 inches of rain fell in parts of the state when back-to-back hurricanes Connie and Diane came along during August 12 through 19. Neither storm brought much wind, but the combination brought more rain than could be contained by the state's streams and rivers. The entire state was hit hard, and no community escaped the wrath of these storms. Some towns were especially hard hit, such as those in the Naugutuck Valley: Winsted, Torrington, Waterbury,

Thousands of people were forced to evacuate during one of the 1955 floods.

Flood day. 1955.

1955 flood, Putnam fire (buildings burn, from above).

Unionville Bridge after one of the floods of 1955.

Ansonia, Derby, and Seymour. The Naugatuck River ran violently through these communities. Putnam in northeastern Connecticut experienced severe damage, too, when the Quinebaug Dam burst in Massachusetts and flood waters flowed through northeastern Connecticut. Putnam was split into two by the flood, and a major fire occurred at the Blooms Mills. Structures of all kinds were swept away by the raging waters. At least four major dams burst and two dozen bridges collapsed. In Connecticut, seventy people died and forty-seven hundred were injured. Numerous people were trapped on their roofs, pleading for help. Helicopters were able to rescue many, but many adults and children were swept away by the raging waters in full view of their parents. Areas around the Farmington River were also hit very hard, with numerous lives lost. One family was being rescued by a boat, but the boat was swamped and capsized by the water. Three children

Hartford policeman assists a woman and her baby during one of the floods of 1955.

High-wire rescue, 1955.

who were in the boat were then tied to trees while their parents searched for help. When help did arrive by boat and helicopter, two of the children were rescued, but the third child was never found. Rail service was wiped out. In Waterbury alone, forty to fifty boxcars were washed away by the raging waters. The New Haven Railroad gave an accounting of its damage: twenty-four washouts, six landslides, one derailment, ten bridges washed out along with four trestles.

Flooding occurred throughout New England, but Connecticut was hit the hardest. Overall, in the memory of those who survived the August 1955 flood, no other flood could even come close to matching its devastation, and downtown areas were never quite the same.

But the weather raged once again during October 1955, when a storm of tropical origin produced 12 to 14 inches of rain between October 14 and 16. Although much of Connecticut was hit hard during the August floods, the southwest part of the state was spared some of the violent damage. This was not the case in October, and for Fairfield County, the impact of the Oc-

A National Guardsman looks down a wrecked street in Winsted, 1955.

Assessing the damage in Winsted, 1955.

tober flooding was far greater than the August flood. The Norwalk River raged through communities. Route 7 was under water. On the Branchville line, a train was stalled for fourteen hours. Its eighty-three passengers were rescued by three helicopters. Georgetown was destroyed when the dam of Gilbert and Bennet Manufacturing burst and water raced through town. Thousands of cellars flooded and water reached the first floor, or higher, in seventy houses.

Many flood-control projects were put into place following the 1955 floods, but these didn't prevent another flooding disaster from unfolding nearly thirty years later. The worse flooding since 1955 occurred during the weekend of June 5–6, 1982. This storm was not of tropical origin, and it was unrelated to melting snow or a spring thaw. Instead, a series of squalls ripped through the state, especially in south-central Connecticut. A train of thunderstorms rolled along, one squall after another. The individual squalls moved from southwest to northeast, and they kept forming in the same area. Each thunderstorm brought it is own monsoonal downpour, and after one passed, another came along. It was a brutal weekend. Rainfall measured 8 to 16 inches in a 48-hour period. Most of the rain fell on Saturday, June 5. Up to 10 inches occurred during that day alone. Also, 4 inches of rain had occurred during the previous week, so the ground was nearly saturated before the storm arrived. The flooding was massive. Seventeen dams failed and another thirty-one were damaged. Twelve people were killed. The larger rivers such as the Connecticut and Housatonic were not affected as much as the smaller rivers and streams, such as the Yantic, Farmington, West, and Park rivers. The lower portion of the Naugatuck was hardest hit — this is where the heaviest rain fell. Most of the rain was concentrated in Connecticut and not in the northern watershed areas of the large rivers. Thousands of homes were damaged by the storm and seven hundred companies reported losses, with four reporting losses of over $1 million. Nearly every community in the lower portion of Connecticut reported serious

Water was rationed in the wake of one of the 1955 floods.

damage. The Milford City Hall was flooded and evacuated. Portions of the Merritt Parkway, Route 1, and I-95 were closed. More that thirty-five thousand utility customers lost power. Armories were opened in Ansonia, Norwich, Naugatuck, and New Haven and the National Guard was called up to help evacuees. Total losses came to $230 million.

In one of the ironies of the storm, the Northeast River Forecast Center, which monitors rivers throughout the Northeast, was flooded in the storm. The office was forced to move from its Bloomfield location during the deluge to the home of one of their senior hydrologists, Dr. David Curtis. The computers were not working, the telephones were down. The office had been located in a basement, and fourteen hours of down time passed before the new location was up and running. Even though a flood warning had been issued on Friday, before the heaviest rain, the intensity of the storm came as a surprise to most people, and an automated state-wide river and stream monitoring and warning system was instituted following the disaster.

The 1982 flooding might have been the most serious since the 1955 deluge, but just two years later, in late May and early June 1984, a five-day stalled low-pressure system caused the waters to rise once again. Authorities were warning that this flood could become just as bad as what hit two years earlier. As it turned out, it was bad, but the rain was less concentrated, more spread out, and flooding didn't turn out to be as serious. But it was bad enough. The rain seemed to never end, and areas near the larger rivers, such as the Connecticut and Housatonic, took the brunt of the damage. New Milford, which has the Housatonic running through the middle of town, was one of the hardest-hit communities. More than 8 inches of rain damaged more than one hundred homes and forced five hundred people to evacuate. Major roads, such as Route 7, were cut off. The entire town was isolated. Also, the Connecticut River was running at near-record levels of 30 feet. In Hartford, the river crested at 30.74 feet, the third highest on record, only exceeded by the floods from the 1938 hurricane and the huge 1936 rainstorm and meltdown. But flood-control projects were credited with keeping damage limited. Down the river, in Middletown, the river was running about 13 feet above flood stage, and much of Middletown was also cut off by the rising water. The river's crest of 21.27 feet was also the third highest on record. Most of the city's forty thousand residents escaped to higher ground, but Routes 9, 72, and 66 were all blocked. Only Route 17 offered an opening to the south. Over a hundred National Guardsmen were positioned in the town. Fortunately, there were no reports of deaths or serious injuries.

In 1992, one of the oddest storms I worked with came along during December 11–12. It was a true northeaster, ripping northward along the East Coast. Most of the problems were related to wind and heavy snow over inland areas, but along the shoreline, the problem was tidal flooding. Three times the tide rolled in, and three times the tide flooded to hurricane proportions. One person drowned in Bridgeport from the suddenly rising water. Mansions and small cottages were inundated by the flood. Protective seawalls seemed transparent to the surging water. Automobiles that were parked within a block or two from the shore were flooded to their door handles or even higher. The water simply poured through access roads from the beaches. Water crashed over and through those seawalls and brought feet of water pounding against homes of all magnitudes and status. More than sixty thousand homes lost electricity. In Westport's Metro-North commuter railroad station, more than three hundred cars were flooded at high tide. The tide also washed into Westport's downtown section along Main Street. The National Guard brought out huge 20-ton vehicles to help evacuate coastal residents. Coast Guard helicopters were called in, as well. Sikorsky Airport in Stratford was closed when the tides rolled in and flooded the facility. In every community along the shore, severe tidal flooding brought heavy damage. Additional damage occurred over inland Connecticut, where 2-foot flood waters turned to 2-foot snows. It seemed to be a tale of two states. Northern Connecticut received heavy snow—knee-deep in many spots, with even higher drifts in northwestern Connecticut, while southern Connecticut received mainly rain, wind, and those punishing tides. On the northern Connecticut/Massachusetts border, 20 to 40 inches of snow was measured. Heavy snow extended to the suburbs of Boston, and 1-foot snows fell as far south as the Merritt Parkway. But on the shore, snowfall came to just 1 to 2 inches. Damage tallied more than $2 billion.

In 2005, a variety of extreme weather hit the nation, and Connecticut was not exactly left high and dry. This was the year that brought a record number of tropical storms and hurricanes through the Atlantic and Gulf. We didn't have enough letters in the alphabet to account for the more than two dozen storms that blossomed, and we needed to dig into the Greek alphabet to account for the additions. It was the year that brought the most-costly national disaster on record—Hurricane Katrina—which devastated New Orleans and much of the Gulf coast. That storm occurred in late August and did not directly affect our area, but during October, some wild weather did occur in our backyards and basements. This was the month that brought record rain to Connecticut. The remnants of Tropical Storm Tammy early in the month, a strong northeaster during mid-month, and the remnants of Hurricane Wilma at month's end helped generate 16.32 inches of rain in Hartford, washing away the old monthly record of 11.61 inches. Most cities in the Northeast broke rainfall records dating back to 1895. Wilma actually contributed to heavy snow across the interior of the Northeast.

But the greatest disaster for Connecticut came along from the nor'easter that hit October 14 to 16. The storm came in a torrential rage on Friday night. Rainfall from this storm came to 5 to 9, inches with some locally higher amounts in north-central parts of the state where flooding seemed to be worse. Two people were killed. In Enfield and Somers, comparisons were being made with the big floods of 1955. Major roads were closed for hours such as I-91 around Windsor and Enfield. In eastern Connecticut, the Willimantic River went over its banks, flooding neighborhoods and basements. West Hartford had over three hundred calls for assistance from flooded homes and basements. Amtrak cancelled Shoreline East service from New Haven because of water going over the tracks. Southern Connecticut had its share of problems, too. Thousands of homes in the Bridgeport area lost power, a mudslide in Naugatuck cut off rail service, and the Housatonic swept through the towns south of the Stevenson Dam, including Oxford, Ansonia, Derby, and Shelton. All required evacuations.

Just six months later, another major flood hit the state. This East Coast storm struck on Sunday, April 15. Five to 7 inches of rain and high winds created plenty of havoc. Rainfall in Stamford came to 6.84 inches, Bridgeport measured 5 inches, and 5.25 inches fell in Middletown. Most of this rain occurred on April 16. Winds gusted to 52 miles per hour in Groton.

Eastern Connecticut was hit hard by the wind. Power outages occurred to more than fifty thousand homes and businesses, much of that in eastern Connecticut. In western Connecticut, the main problem was too much water. The Housatonic, Still, Saugatuck, Norwalk, Quinnipiac, Farmington, and Naugatuck rivers spilled over their banks. Two feet of water flooded into homes in Darien as well as in many other communities. Governor of Connecticut, Jodi Rell, was watching the Still River, and said she never saw so much water coming out of the river in thirty-five years of living nearby in Brookfield. Propane tanks and debris were floating down Route 7. Farther east, the Connecticut, Mill, and Rooster rivers were flooding, too. Sandbags went up around Long Meadow Pond Dam in Bethlehem as the water began to overflow and threaten nearby Woodbury and Southbury. Three days after the storm hit, on Wednesday, Route 7 was still under water in New Milford, and several other town roads were closed indefinitely. Ironically, the storm turned into a heavy, wet snowmaker through central and northern New England.

A year hardly passes without some flooding in Connecticut. Even though many flood-control projects have been put into operation over the years, water has a way of getting around these, especially when it falls in excessive quantities. There really is no specific flood season. River flooding occurs during colder months with melting snow and northeasters, but hurricanes add their impact during the late summer and fall. Then, the severe thunderstorm season can bring its squalls and flash flooding during the summer. Huge variability occurs from year to year in the intensity of the flooding. Some years pass relatively quietly, but other years are unforgettable.

Getting Steamed!

Big heat, humidity, and even drought are often part of our summer landscape, and lately, many feel an even greater trend in that direction. This is a heated issue. Fortunately, the big heat of Connecticut does not go to the extremes of some other sections of the country. For example, Hartford has an average of eighteen days of 90-degree weather each year, and Bridgeport experiences six such days. For the sake of comparison, Saint Louis, Missouri, will have forty days of 90-degree heat and Fort Smith, Arkansas, experiences an average of seventy-two of these sweltering experiences annually.

Connecticut often will receive relief from big heat from a number of sources. Long Island Sound's sea breezes can be the most comforting, but these often are confined to the shoreline, sometimes only a few blocks from the water. Yet, many times, a steady southwest flow from a steamy tropical weather circulation will have a long enough fetch to cover most of the state. A high-pressure system sets up offshore. That is the "Bermuda High," and it can cook the entire eastern half of the country as it builds in from the western Atlantic. But the relative coolness of the Sound in the summer will moderate the overheated air mass, at least locally, and we experience at least a little breather. Because of the influence of the Sound, our hottest days usually occur when the flow is from the west, or even northwest, and not from the south or southwest.

Then, we have the famous New England "backdoor cold fronts," which come down from the north and northeast, from the cold waters off Northern New England. The conventional cold front comes from the west—the front door—but this one sneaks through

People flock to the beaches, trying to beat the heat. Rocky Neck State Park.

the back door, the east. Often when you expect it the least, a dense area of cold air builds over the cold North Atlantic waters, high pressure develops, and pushes under the superheated tropical air masses. The warm air masses are much deeper and can extend for miles into the atmosphere, but just enough cold air collects near the ground with these backdoor events to offer a welcomed change. A shallow surge of cool comes along.

And, of course, our latitude is far enough to the north to benefit from the passage of the garden-variety cold fronts that slip southward from central Canada, even during the summer. The storm track and frontal parade do shift northward in the summer, but every few days a front will make a run for us and do its best to keep the atmospheric thermostat down several notches. Unfortunately, these changes do not come along quietly. Heavy thunderstorms and severe weather are often part of the exchange. July is our hottest month, and the month with the most thunderstorms.

Despite these mitigating factors, we do have our days of unforgettable heat. For example, there was August 1988, when Hartford experienced fifteen of sixteen days with 90-degree temperatures. We could have had six-

A lifeguard surveys the crowded beach.

teen consecutive days of 90-degree weather, but on August 8, 1988, the temperature failed to hit 90—it just hit, you guessed it, 88. And sometimes, big heat doesn't wait until the summer. In mid-April of 1976, the thermometer reached the upper 90s in Connecticut, and the Patriot's Day run of the Boston Marathon began with the thermometer in Hopkinton, Massachusetts, checking in at 100 degrees! Stories and records of excessive heat in Connecticut and New England go back a long time.

During the colonial period, temperature records were not very accurate, but an effort was made to import various thermometers from Europe. Benjamin Franklin, George Washington and Thomas Jefferson were all avid collectors of weather data. One month of note was June 1749. The hottest day of that month was on Sunday the 29th, when the temperature came close to 100 degrees. Ezra Stiles, who was one of the early weather experts and Connecticut observers, often would speak of that day, his first day preaching a sermon. One thermometer that was used was an inverted instrument that recorded the warmest temperatures near the lower bulb and the coldest temperatures at the top. Because that day was so hot, it was difficult to discern the reading because the fluid had collected at the bottom. Also, many thermometers were just not set up for such heat and they burst. Franklin did record 100 degrees in Philadelphia.

Also, while the Revolutionary War raged, the big heat occasionally would do the same. In late June and July 1778, during the Battle of Monmouth, an extreme heat wave struck the Northeast. By time, Ezra Stiles had become president of Yale, and his diary is superheated during that period. He set up his thermometer on July 29, when the heat was already going strong for nearly a week. He recorded successive daily high temperatures of 94, 97, 95, and 94 degrees through July 2, when some relief came. But then, from July 7 through July 12, his thermometer recorded 86.5, 95, 95, 94, 93, and 87 —and all of this on the "cooler" Connecticut shoreline!

The nineteenth century had its warmth, too, even with the "Little Ice Age" still going strong. In June 1816, snow fell as far south as northern Connecticut, but in 1825, the region definitely cooked, once again. During both June and July, the temperature topped 90 degrees frequently, and in the Boston area, the temperature reached 100 degrees on three occasions. Late in the century, in 1870, the National Weather Service became organized and records became more accurate and reliable.

It did not take long for the twentieth century to turn on the heat. The weather data for summers show some very warm seasons from 1911 to 1920 and again during the mid- and late 1930s and part of the 1940s and 1950s. But the warmest summers of the twentieth century without question have occurred since 1980. The five-year running average has been consistently near or over 70 degrees. In July 1991, at Brainard Field, the temperature hit a record high of 100 degrees or greater on four consecutive days. Record highs also were set for four consecutive days in June 1984, when

Seeking relief in a 138-degree city.

each day of the heat wave, the temperature hit 96 degrees. The hottest day on the official record books occurred in Danbury on July 15, 1995, when the thermometer hit 106 degrees. On the day before, the temperature reached a record 101. During 1991, in July, the Danbury temperature reached records of 100 degrees or above on three consecutive days. The appendix lists the daily climate extremes for a number of Connecticut communities. It is clear that we have had our most sweltering seasons since 1980. The appendixes also list the daily average temperatures, average degree days, frost periods, snowfall, and snow depth for numerous communities in the state. The data is derived from the National Climate Data Center and the Northeast Regional Climate Center.

While hurricanes, tornadoes and snowstorms capture the headlines, in the United States, with the exception of cold, heat takes the greatest toll on life. An average of 173 lives are lost to heat each year. In the heat wave of 1980, more than twelve thousand lost their lives. From 1936 to 1975, over twenty thousand people succumbed to heat. And if climate scientists are correct, plenty more heat is yet to come. A European heat wave in 2003 alone took 37,451 lives. Big heat is serious business.

Climates Made to Be Broken

One of the great controversies of modern times is whether climates are changing, and whether we have a hand in those changes. Are recent changes part of a natural cycle, or are the changes anthropogenic — a result of human activity? The question may be a scientific one, but the entire area of climate change is a hotbed of social, political, and economic issues. Then, of course, even if the overall worldwide climate is changing, what does it all mean for local regions, such as Connecticut? Are we in for more storms, more extremes in temperatures and precipitation, more hurricanes, more sea-level rises, more disease? And can anything realistically be done about it? Do we really want to do something about it?

Let's start off by saying that climates have been changing naturally since the beginning of time, and change is far more natural than an environment that is stable. The Earth is an ancient place. Materials collected from all over the world show that the climate has been changing for hundreds of millions of years. In the earliest days of the Earth, there probably wasn't even an atmosphere. Microorganisms and plants were able to take in carbon dioxide that was being vented by volcanoes. Eventually, the atmosphere took shape with its unique blend of mainly nitrogen and oxygen. More than 99 percent of the atmosphere consists of those two gases. But the atmosphere, and the climate, have been evolving ever since then. There is a lot of evidence of change.

Records of change from the past few hundred years to the past two thousand years can be found in historical documents. For example, George Washington maintained a weather diary until the day before he died. Thomas Jefferson was an avid weather-watcher and has even been called the first "Meteorologist-in-Chief." Fossils, pollens, coal beds, and sand dunes also provide clues of past climates. Evidence of change goes back millions of years, and we turn to some very interesting techniques in unearthing those changes.

For example, the study of tree rings, dendrochronology, is helpful in the study of climate change because thicker layers of wood will form beneath the bark of tree when climates are relatively wet and mild. Also, cores of deep-sea sediments will show shells of old organisms that were once near the surface. The type of organism provides clues to the temperature. In addition, these cores contain certain chemicals in specific ratios that can only exist in particular climate conditions. For example, oxygen comes in different forms. The oxygen we breathe contains a chemical structure of eight neutrons and eight protons. The number of neutrons and protons is called the atomic weight—we are talking about oxygen-16. But there is a heavier form of oxygen that contains two more neutrons, so its atomic weight is 18, or oxygen-18.

It turns out that there is one oxygen-18 molecule for every thousand oxygen-16 molecules in the atmosphere. During cold times, ocean levels will be drawn down by the formation of ice. At the same time, a greater amount of oxygen-18 forms in the atmosphere. So, by examining the ratio of oxygen-18 and oxygen-16 contained in the shells of ancient organisms within core samples, scientists can have an idea of changes that have occurred. If the proportion of oxygen-18 to oxygen-16 is higher in one sample, we know the sample was from a colder period. This radioactive dating becomes a powerful tool in determining the age and character of a sample. Also, carbon dating is used to determine the age of a particular material.

Carbon dating all starts with cosmic rays that bombard the Earth's atmosphere. When the rays arrive in the upper atmosphere, they charge the atoms present and scatter protons and neutrons. Some of the neutrons will combine with nitrogen, which contains seven protons and seven neutrons. The addition of an extra neutron to nitrogen dislodges a proton. The new element contains six protons and eight neutrons, and creates carbon-14, which is unstable. It is an unstable isotope of regular carbon, carbon-12. The carbon-14 eventually goes back to nitrogen, but it takes 5,760 years for half the sample to stabilize, that is, the half-life of carbon-14 is 5,760 years. Because plants take in carbon dioxide and animals eat plants, all living things contain carbon. There is about one carbon-14 for every 100 billion carbon-12 atoms. As long as an organism is alive, carbon-14 will continue to form, but as soon as a plant or animal dies, that's it. No additional carbon-14 will form. The percentage of carbon-14 that remains will depend upon its half-life, and the amount that remains tells something about the sample's age. If only one-quarter remains, the old bones will be 11,520 years old—twice the half-life. This may seem fairly straightforward, but in reality there are complications, such as the amount of cosmic ray bombardment and the amount of carbon dioxide in the atmosphere. The dating process can become complex. Uranium is also used for dating samples. The half-life of U-238 is 4,510 million years!

So, from radioactive dating and examination of deep-sea core samples or tree rings, much can be learned about the Earth and its past. And it has quite a past.

Figure 10.1 represents the geologic time scale. The Earth's history is divided into different eras, periods, and epochs. The eras consist of the Paleozoic ("ancient life"), Mesozoic ("middle life"), and Cenozoic ("recent life"). Prior to the Paleozoic is the Precambrian ("hidden life"). The Precambrian goes from 570 million years ago to 4.5 billion years ago, when the Earth is thought to have formed. Abundant life appeared 570 million years ago, which begins the Paleozoic era. Different forms of life define the different eras, periods, and epochs, and of course, that life was shaped by climate. For example, the Mississippian and Pennsylvanian periods, 280 to 345 million years ago, were warm and moist, and that climate allowed for lush vegetation and dense swamps that became the source for coal beds. Also, the climate provided for giant insects, including massive cockroaches and dragonflies with 3-foot wingspans.

Based upon the evidence of ancient life and materials, figure 10.2 provides a broad picture of climate during the past two million years. The relative temperature has had plenty of ups and downs. Those downs represent ice ages or glacial periods, and the warmer spells represent glacial recessions or interglacial periods. During the cold spells, more snow would fall than would melt. The snow piled up, and then, under pressure, it would spread southward as a glacier. Landscapes would be carved out, only to be revealed during the interglacial periods.

Figure 10.3 shows a more detailed picture of the past 500,000 years. Deep-sea cores and oxygen dating provide this picture, which shows numerous glacial advances and retreats. The temperature shown is sea-surface temperature, which is a pretty good clue of sea-level air temperature. The last very warm interglacial period occurred 120,000 years ago, and then the temperature dropped, putting the world into the most recent ice age, which ended about 10,000 years ago. The warmest period of the past 10,000 years occurred about 5,000 years ago, with a sea-surface temperature of 61 degrees, and that is very close to our current temperature of 59 degrees. That warm period is called the "climatic optimum." If climate projections are

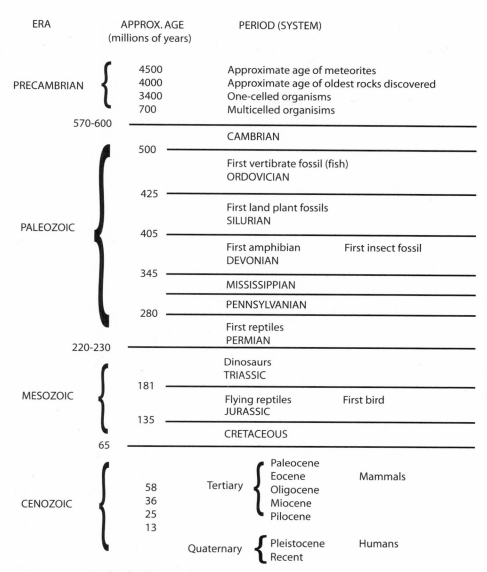

FIGURE 10.1 Geologic time scale.

correct, world temperature soon will exceed the "climate optimum" of the past 10,000 years. Yet, regardless of occasional glacial recessions, the overall picture of the past 100,000 years is cold, and of ice-age proportions.

Changes in climate have had a great impact on life. During the last ice age, 10,000 to 20,000 years ago, the first people arrived in North America. At the time, two giant ice sheets covered North America—one from Alaska to the Pacific Northwest, and the other from the Arctic southward along the eastern slopes of the Rockies and eastward to New York and New England. The glacier moved as far south as present-day Long Island, helping to carve

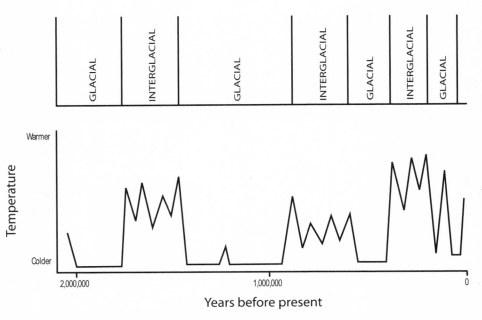

FIGURE 10.2 Temperature of the past two million years.

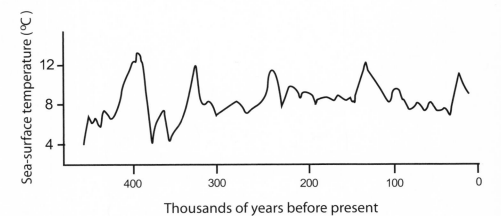

FIGURE 10.3 Variation of sea-surface temperatures.

out both Long Island and Long Island Sound. The ice was as much as 200 to 1,000 feet thick, and sea level was as much as 350 feet lower. This lowered sea level also exposed a plain between Siberia and Alaska. The plain became a land bridge across the Bering Sea, and provided for the passage of people from Asia to America. Huge mastodons, saber-toothed tigers, and wooly rhinoceroses were hunted by these early settlers, but over-hunting and subsequent climate warming made many species extinct. By 7,000 years ago, the ice sheets were gone.

Figure 10.4 shows the overall temperature pattern of the past 3,000 years. Again, fluctuation of temperature seems to be the norm. The warm period around AD 1000 is striking, along with a cold spell that lasted from about 1400 to 1850. This period was cold enough to be given a name—the "Little Ice Age." The warmth around AD 1000 allowed for vineyards to flourish in England. The summers were warm and dry. During that period, the first Europeans, the Vikings, migrated to North America. But the colonies were abandoned or died out when the Little Ice Age arrived. As early as A.D. 1200, the weather showed increasing fluctuations. In Europe, frequent droughts and floods occurred. Some winters were extremely cold, and others were mild. By the 1400s, major famines occurred, and by the 1500s, the cooling trend became very well-defined. Glaciers began to expand, winters were long and hard while summers were short. The vineyards in England disappeared and farming in northern latitudes became difficult.

The historical accounts during the American colonial period describe winters with major harbors freezing from Maine to Chesapeake Bay and

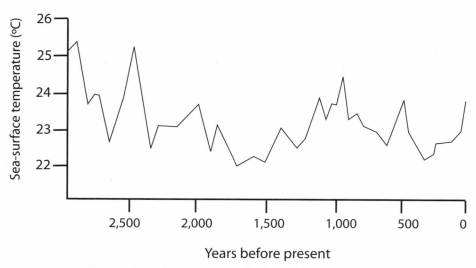

FIGURE 10.4 Fluctuation of temperature during past three thousand years.

snow that was several feet deep. The year 1816 became known as the "Year Without a Summer," when frosts and freezes occurred each month in New England and snow fell as far south as Connecticut during June. Famine and crop failure became widespread, and many people began to migrate westward, but those with "Ohio Fever" found the weather to be just as harsh in Ohio as in New England. In Europe, too, crop losses and famine were common. Most recently, since the late 1800s, the weather has been showing a warming trend. The "Little Ice Age" is well in the past.

Figure 10.5 shows the average worldwide annual temperature trend since the mid-1800s. These trends come from the Intergovernmental Panel on Climate Change, the IPCC, which is a worldwide effort to gather information and make assessments of climate warming. There are plenty of ups and downs, but strong warming has been occurring since the 1970s and 1980s.

Now, the closer we look at these records, the closer we get to describing weather, and not climate, which is the long-term average of weather. The old saying that "one swallow doesn't make a summer," holds true here. Likewise, a cold winter or two doesn't mean an ice age is on the way. The convention is to use a thirty-year average to describe climate. In this analysis, comparisons are made with the 1961 to 1990 period. The current "averages" or "normals" are those of this thirty-year period. Until 1950, worldwide, most of the years since 1900 were averaging below the 1961 to 1990 average. Since 1980, all the years have been averaging above.

How about Connecticut? The trend is similar. If year-to-year tempera-

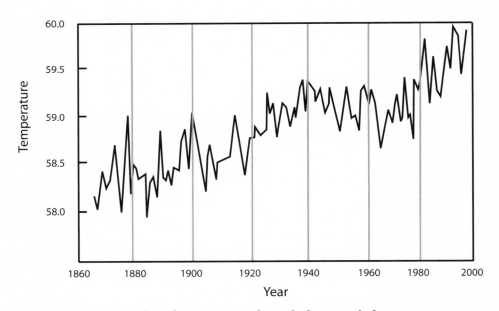

FIGURE 10.5 Fluctuation of temperature through the twentieth century.

tures are compared, it is difficult to see that trend—there is considerable year-to-year fluctuation. We have a lot of weather in Connecticut. But a five-year average of temperature for summers and winters shows that trend. Storrs is one location where weather data is available from the turn of the twentieth century.

These time series are shown in figure 10.6a–f. Even in the five-year series, it is hard to find a trend during the first part of the twentieth century. The winters, especially, have shown tremendous variations. Other locations with long-standing records are also shown—Hartford and Connecticut's famous icebox, Norfolk. The latest spell of cold winters occurred during the 1960s and early 1970s, but since then, the warming is evident. The last five-year average shows a slight cooling. Could this be the beginning of a new trend, or just a pause in the overall warming? Even with the pause, the average summer and winter temperatures remain warmer than anything experienced since 1980.

According to the IPCC, there is little doubt that the general trend will be up, up, and away. Although nearly as many theories on climate change have been developed as there are climatologists, the consensus of the IPCC is that greenhouse gases are to blame for the trend, and those gases aren't going away anytime soon. These gases allow short-wave, ultraviolet radiation into the lower atmosphere, where it is absorbed and transformed into longer-wave heat radiation. The greenhouse gases then trap the heat just as the glass in a greenhouse traps escaping heat and warms its environment. These greenhouse gases are numerous and consist of carbon dioxide, methane, and nitrous oxides. Look at the trend of these gases since 1800! Figure 10.7 shows a dramatic rise through 2005. The numbers represent parts of a particular gas per million parts of air (ppm) or per billion parts of air (ppb). So, we are talking about small quantities here. One gas that is hard to pin down as a factor for warming is water vapor. By itself, it is a greenhouse gas, but its presence can lead to clouds, which would reduce incoming radiation. The IPCC says that its "level of scientific understanding" or LOSU of water vapor is low. In one sense, it could cause runaway greenhouse warming because more heat will cause more evaporation, which will release more water vapor and additional heating. But its release could cause more clouds and precipitation, which will moderate that warming. On the other hand, the LOSU of carbon dioxide is considered to be high.

Natural global changes, too, cause long-term change—solar radiation output, the tilt of the Earth's axis, its wobbling like a top, even continental drift and volcanism. Many of the climate fluctuations of the past can be attributed to these geophysical changes, and these will be part of the future,

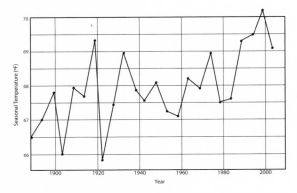

FIGURE 10.6a Summer temperatures in Storrs, twentieth century.

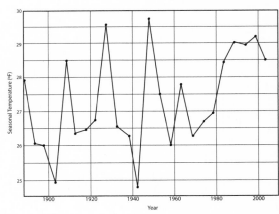

FIGURE 10.6b Winter temperatures in Storrs, twentieth century.

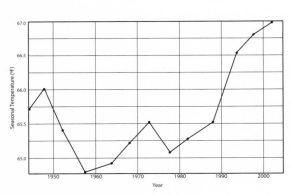

FIGURE 10.6c Summer temperatures in Norfolk, twentieth century.

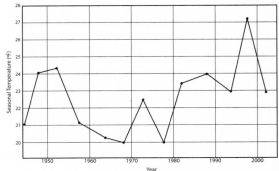

FIGURE 10.6d Winter temperatures in Norfolk, twentieth century.

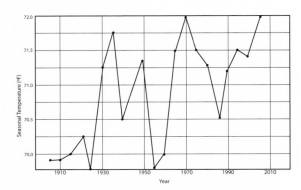

FIGURE 10.6e Summer temperatures in Hartford, twentieth century.

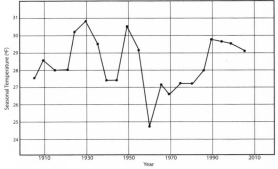

FIGURE 10.6f Winter temperatures in Hartford, twentieth century.

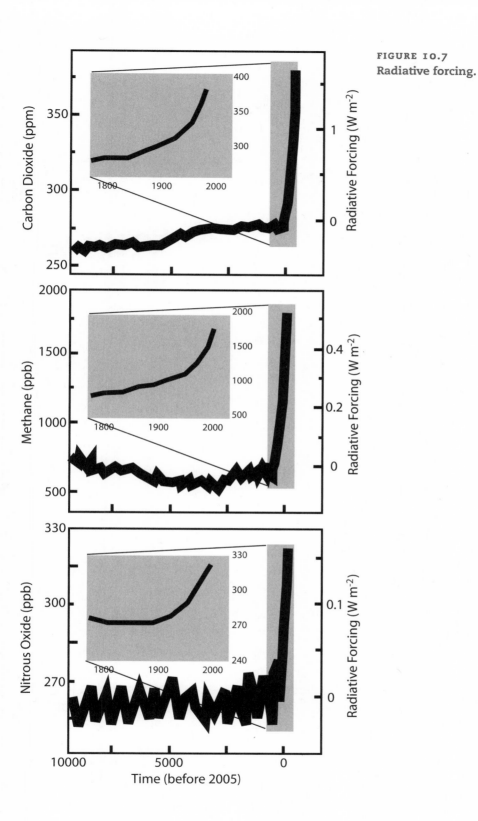

FIGURE 10.7
Radiative forcing.

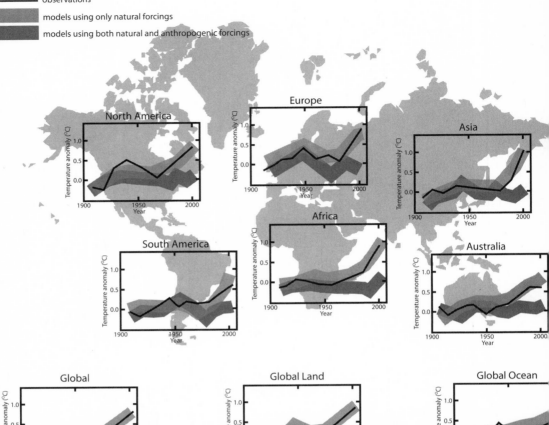

FIGURE 10.8 **Global and continental temperature change.**

as well. But according to the IPCC, the impact of recent greenhouse gas emissions far outweigh these natural forcing mechanisms even if the LOSU is low. Figure 10.8 shows the current trends of global temperature, with both natural and anthropogenic factors compared to natural mechanisms alone.

Climatologists take all the forcing mechanisms, natural and anthropogenic, and these become coefficients in forecast equations. There is enough uncertainty for many to raise questions about the amount of confidence that can be placed in the trends. The LOSU for the various factors are shown in figure 10.9. Also, the basic forecast equations have trouble predicting the weather over the next five days, let alone the next fifty or one hundred years. Of course, the equations are modified, but then, they are made more complex by the addition of the greenhouse forcing mechanisms. The coef-

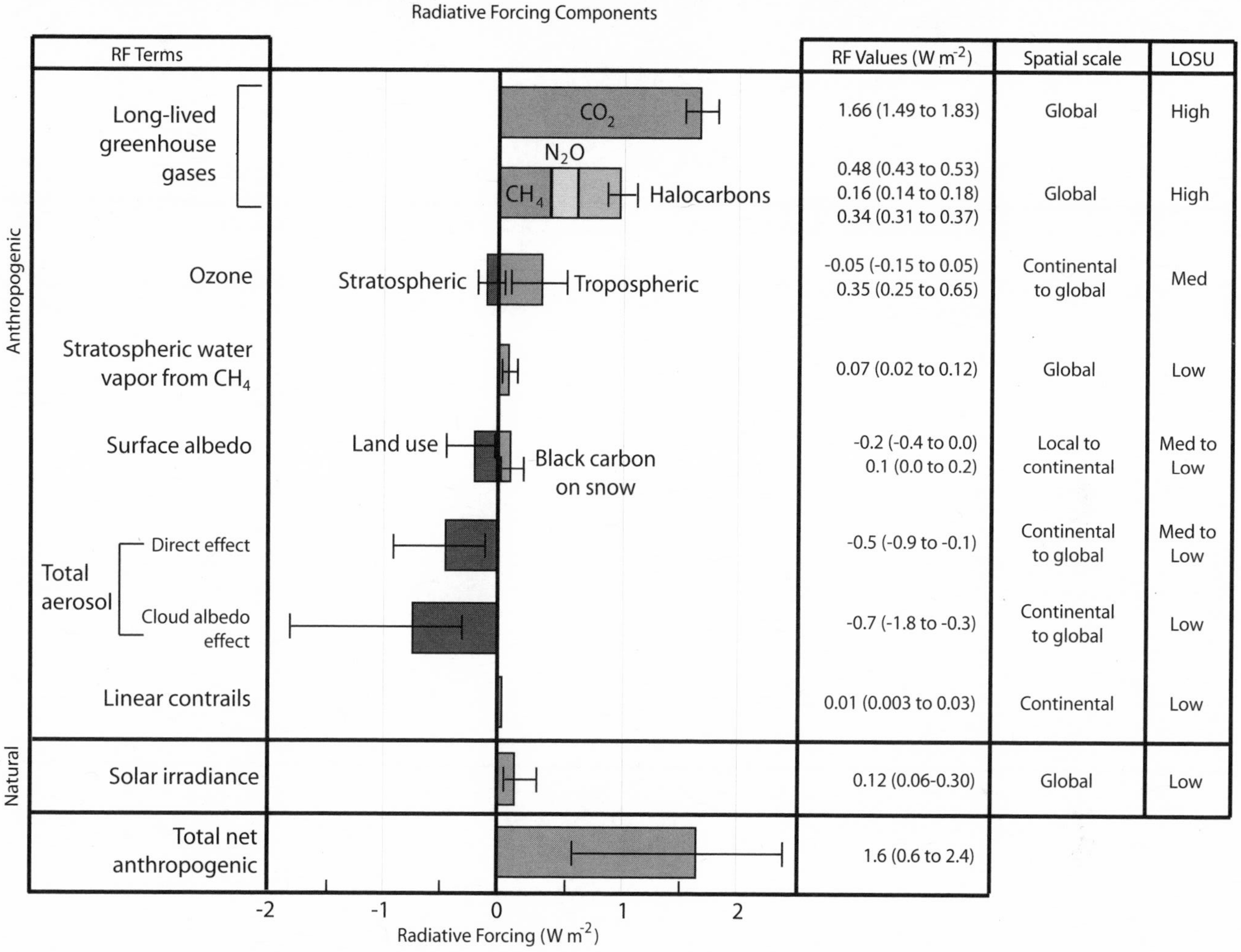

Radiative Forcing Components

RF Terms		RF Values (W m⁻²)	Spatial scale	LOSU
Long-lived greenhouse gases	CO_2	1.66 (1.49 to 1.83)	Global	High
	N_2O CH_4 Halocarbons	0.48 (0.43 to 0.53) 0.16 (0.14 to 0.18) 0.34 (0.31 to 0.37)	Global	High
Ozone	Stratospheric Tropospheric	-0.05 (-0.15 to 0.05) 0.35 (0.25 to 0.65)	Continental to global	Med
Stratospheric water vapor from CH_4		0.07 (0.02 to 0.12)	Global	Low
Surface albedo	Land use Black carbon on snow	-0.2 (-0.4 to 0.0) 0.1 (0.0 to 0.2)	Local to continental	Med to Low
Total aerosol	Direct effect	-0.5 (-0.9 to -0.1)	Continental to global	Med to Low
	Cloud albedo effect	-0.7 (-1.8 to -0.3)	Continental to global	Low
Linear contrails		0.01 (0.003 to 0.03)	Continental	Low
Solar irradiance		0.12 (0.06-0.30)	Global	Low
Total net anthropogenic		1.6 (0.6 to 2.4)		

Anthropogenic / Natural

Radiative Forcing (W m⁻²)

FIGURE 10.9
Radiative forcing components/radiative forcing.

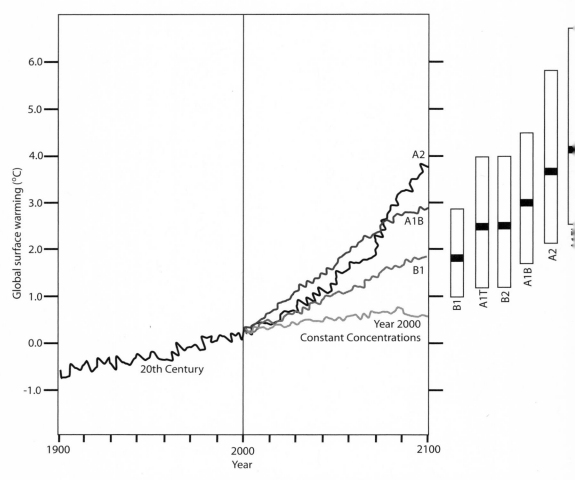

FIGURE 10.10 Multi-model averages and assessed ranges for surface warming.

ficients may fit the present trend, but will they hold for the future? To some, it seems something like predicting future trends from past experience on Wall Street. But the IPCC shows plenty of confidence in a warming trend relative to 1980–1999 averages for a variety of scenarios through the next one hundred years. None show a decrease in temperature, and the only scenario that keeps our temperature fairly flat is the one where concentrations are kept constant at 2000 values. Otherwise, the warming trend ranges from 1.8 degrees Celsius to 3.6 degrees Celsius. And that is on top of the warmest period in over a hundred years! Figure 10.10 breaks down the various scenarios with the IPCC's best estimate and likely temperature range. If these trends pan out, snow cover will be reduced and widespread thawing will occur in the permafrost areas. Sea ice is projected to shrink, and the IPCC says that it is very likely that extremes of heat and precipitation will occur. Already, these impacts are being observed, such as a reduction in the extent of mountain glaciers with the reduction of snow cover in both the Northern and Southern Hemisphere. Also, the IPCC says that recent melting ice sheets in Greenland and Antarctica very likely have contributed to rising sea levels. The changes in snow cover and sea level are shown in figure 10.11. In addition, precipitation patterns have been variable around the world. Increases have occurred in North and South America, Europe, and northern Asia, but drying has occurred in Africa, the Mediterranean, and southern Asia. Mid-latitude winds also have increased during this warm period. Table 10.1 shows the IPCC conclusions on some of the current impacts and the certainty or likelihood of these continuing.

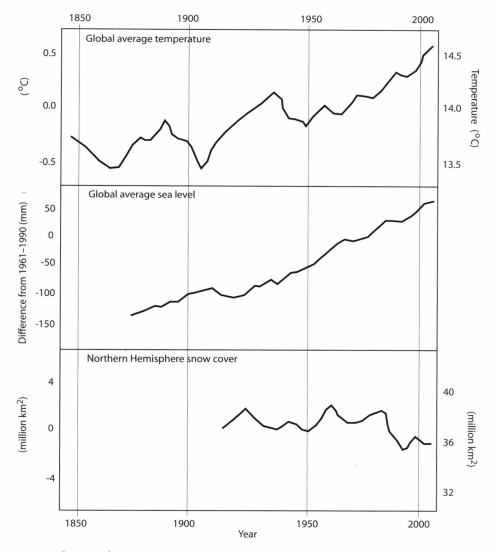

10.11 **Changes in temperature, sea level, and northern hemisphere snow cover.**

TABLE 10.1 LIKELIHOOD OF CLIMATE TRENDS

Phenomenon and direction of trend	Likelihood that trend occurred in the late twentieth century (typically post-1960)	Likelihood of a human contribution to observed trend	Likelihood of future trends based on projections for twenty-first century using SRES scenarios
Warmer and fewer cold days and nights over most land areas	Very likely[a]	Likely[b]	Virtually certain[b]
Warmer and more frequent hot days and nights over most land areas	Very likely[c]	Likely (nights)[b]	Virtually certain[b]
Warm spells/heat waves. Frequency increases over most land areas	Likely	More likely than not[d]	Very likely
Heavy precipitation events. Frequency (or proportion of total rainfall from heavy falls) increases over most areas	Likely	More likely than not[d]	Very likely
Area affected by droughts increases	Likely in many regions since 1970s	More likely than not	Likely
Intense tropical cyclone activity increases	Likely in some regions since 1970	More likely than not[d]	Likely
Increased incidence of extreme high sea level (excludes tsunamis)	Likely	More likely than not[d,f]	Likely[g]

a. Decreased frequency of cold days and nights (coldest 10%).
b. Warming of the most extreme days and night each year.
c. Increased frequency of hot days and nights (hottest 10%).
d. Magnitude of anthropogenic contributions not assessed. Attribution for these phenomena based on expert judgment rather than formal attribution studies.
e. Extreme high sea levels depend on average sea level and on regional weather systems. It is defined here as the highest 1% of hourly values of observed sea level at a station for a given reference period.
f. Changes in observed extreme high sea level closely follow the changes in average sea level.
g. In all scenarios, the projected global average sea level at 2100 is higher than in the reference period.

Specific local variations affecting Connecticut can't be determined from the global trends, but as we see in the pattern of local temperature since 1980, Connecticut has shared in the overall warming. Still, even with the knowledge that warming is now part of our modern era, and the confidence of the IPCC that the trend will continue, there will be controversy. The forcing mechanisms are numerous, and even the basic equations have limitations. Change is what makes our weather famous.

Appendixes

APPENDIX A
Daily/Monthly Station Normals 1971–2000
Minimum/Maximum Temperatures*

FALLS VILLAGE, CT

Minimum Temperature in °F

	1	2	3	4	5	6	7	8	9	10	11	12	13	14	15	16	17	18	19	20	21	22	23	24	25	26	27	28	29	30	31	Month
Jan	15	15	14	14	14	14	14	14	13	13	13	13	13	13	13	13	13	13	13	13	13	13	12	13	13	13	13	13	13	13	13	13.3
Feb	13	13	13	13	14	14	14	14	14	14	14	15	15	15	15	16	16	16	16	17	17	17	17	18	18	18	19	19				15.5
Mar	19	20	20	20	21	21	21	22	22	22	23	23	23	24	24	24	24	25	25	25	26	26	26	27	27	27	27	28	28	28	29	24.1
Apr	29	29	30	30	30	31	31	31	31	32	32	32	33	33	33	34	34	34	35	35	35	36	36	36	37	37	37	38	38	39		33.6
May	39	39	40	40	40	41	41	41	42	42	43	43	43	44	44	44	45	45	45	45	46	46	46	47	47	47	48	48	48	49	49	44.1
Jun	49	49	50	50	50	51	51	51	51	52	52	52	52	53	53	53	53	54	54	54	54	54	55	55	55	55	55	56	56	56		52.8
Jul	56	56	57	57	57	57	57	57	57	58	58	58	58	57	57	57	58	58	58	58	58	58	58	58	58	58	58	58	58	58	58	57.6
Aug	58	58	58	58	58	58	58	58	57	58	57	57	57	57	57	57	57	56	56	56	56	55	55	55	55	55	55	54	54	54	54	56.4
Sep	54	53	53	53	52	52	52	52	51	51	51	50	50	50	49	49	49	48	48	47	47	47	46	46	45	45	44	44	43	43		48.8
Oct	43	42	42	42	41	40	40	39	39	39	38	38	38	38	37	37	37	36	36	35	35	35	34	34	34	34	33	33	33	33	33	36.9
Nov	33	32	32	32	32	32	31	31	31	31	30	30	30	30	29	29	29	28	28	28	28	27	27	27	26	26	26	25	25	24		29.0
Dec	24	24	23	23	23	22	22	22	22	21	21	20	20	20	19	19	19	19	18	18	18	17	17	17	17	16	16	16	16	15	15	19.3

Maximum Temperature in °F

	1	2	3	4	5	6	7	8	9	10	11	12	13	14	15	16	17	18	19	20	21	22	23	24	25	26	27	28	29	30	31	Month
Jan	35	35	35	35	35	35	35	35	35	35	35	35	35	35	35	35	35	35	35	35	35	35	35	35	35	35	35	35	35	35	35	35.0
Feb	36	36	36	36	36	36	36	37	37	37	37	37	38	38	38	38	39	39	39	39	40	40	40	41	41	41	42	42				38.3
Mar	42	43	43	43	44	44	44	45	45	45	46	46	47	47	47	48	48	48	49	49	50	50	50	51	51	51	52	52	53	53	53	47.7
Apr	54	54	55	55	55	56	56	57	57	57	58	58	59	59	59	60	60	61	61	62	62	63	63	63	64	64	65	65	66	66		59.8
May	66	67	67	68	68	69	69	69	70	70	71	71	71	72	72	72	73	73	73	73	74	74	74	75	75	75	75	76	76	76	76	71.9
Jun	76	76	77	77	77	77	77	78	78	78	78	78	79	79	79	79	79	79	80	80	80	80	80	81	81	81	81	81	82	82		79.0
Jul	82	82	82	82	83	83	83	83	83	83	84	84	84	84	84	84	84	84	84	84	84	84	84	84	84	84	84	84	84	84	84	83.6
Aug	84	84	84	83	83	83	83	83	83	83	83	82	82	82	82	82	82	81	81	81	81	81	80	80	80	80	79	79	79	79	78	81.5
Sep	78	78	78	77	77	77	76	76	76	75	75	75	74	74	74	73	73	73	72	72	72	71	71	71	70	70	70	69	69	69		73.5
Oct	68	68	67	67	67	66	66	65	65	65	64	64	64	63	63	62	62	62	61	61	61	60	60	59	59	58	58	58	57	57	56	62.4
Nov	56	56	55	55	54	54	54	53	53	52	52	52	51	51	50	50	49	49	49	48	48	47	47	47	46	46	45	45	45	44		50.1
Dec	44	43	43	43	42	42	41	41	41	40	40	40	40	39	39	39	38	38	38	38	38	37	37	37	37	37	36	36	36	36	36	39.1

*All information in Appendix A provided by the National Climatic Data Center-NOAA.

GROTON, CT

Minimum Temperature in °F

	1	2	3	4	5	6	7	8	9	10	11	12	13	14	15	16	17	18	19	20	21	22	23	24	25	26	27	28	29	30	31	Month
Jan	20	21	21	21	21	21	21	20	20	20	20	20	20	20	20	20	20	20	20	19	19	19	19	19	19	19	19	20	20	20	20	20.0
Feb	20	20	20	20	20	20	20	21	21	21	21	21	21	21	22	22	22	22	22	23	23	23	23	24	24	24	24	25				21.8
Mar	25	25	26	26	26	26	27	27	27	28	28	28	28	29	29	30	30	30	30	31	31	31	32	32	32	32	33	33	33	33	34	29.3
Apr	34	34	34	35	35	35	36	36	36	36	37	37	37	38	38	38	38	39	39	39	40	40	40	41	41	41	42	42	42	43		38.1
May	43	43	43	44	44	45	45	45	46	46	46	46	47	47	47	48	48	48	49	49	49	50	50	50	51	51	51	51	52	52	52	47.7
Jun	53	53	53	53	54	54	54	55	55	55	55	56	56	56	57	57	57	57	58	58	58	58	59	59	59	59	60	60	60	60		56.6
Jul	61	61	61	61	61	62	62	62	62	62	63	63	63	63	63	63	63	63	63	64	64	64	61	61	61	61	61	64	64	64	64	62.9
Aug	64	64	64	64	64	64	63	63	62	62	63	63	63	63	63	62	62	62	62	62	62	61	61	61	61	61	60	60	60	60	59	62.2
Sep	59	59	59	58	58	58	57	57	57	57	56	56	56	55	55	55	54	54	53	53	53	52	52	52	51	51	50	50	49	49		54.5
Oct	49	48	48	47	47	47	46	46	45	45	45	44	44	44	43	43	43	42	42	42	42	41	41	41	41	40	40	40	39	39	39	43.4
Nov	39	39	39	38	38	38	38	37	37	37	37	36	36	36	36	35	35	35	34	34	34	33	33	33	32	32	32	31	31	31		35.2
Dec	30	30	30	30	29	29	29	28	28	28	27	27	27	26	26	26	25	25	25	24	24	24	24	23	23	23	23	22	22	22	22	25.7

Maximum Temperature in °F

	1	2	3	4	5	6	7	8	9	10	11	12	13	14	15	16	17	18	19	20	21	22	23	24	25	26	27	28	29	30	31	Month
Jan	39	39	39	39	39	38	38	38	38	38	38	38	38	38	38	37	37	37	37	37	37	37	37	37	37	37	37	37	37	37	38	37.7
Feb	37	38	38	38	38	38	38	38	38	38	39	39	39	39	39	39	40	40	40	40	40	41	41	41	41	42	42	42				39.4
Mar	43	43	43	44	44	44	44	45	45	45	46	46	46	47	47	47	47	48	48	48	49	49	49	49	50	50	50	51	51	51	51	47.1
Apr	52	52	52	53	53	53	54	54	54	55	55	55	55	56	56	56	57	57	57	58	58	58	59	59	59	60	60	60	61	61		56.3
May	61	62	62	62	63	63	64	64	64	64	65	65	65	65	66	66	66	67	67	67	68	68	68	69	69	69	70	70	70	71	71	66.3
Jun	71	71	72	72	72	72	73	73	73	74	74	74	74	75	75	75	75	76	76	76	76	77	77	77	77	78	78	78	78	78		74.9
Jul	79	79	79	79	80	80	80	80	80	80	80	80	80	80	80	81	81	81	81	81	81	81	81	82	82	82	82	82	81	81	81	80.7
Aug	81	81	81	81	81	81	81	81	81	80	80	80	80	80	80	80	80	80	79	79	79	79	78	78	78	78	78	78	77	77	77	79.6
Sep	77	77	76	76	76	76	75	75	75	74	74	74	74	73	73	73	72	72	72	71	71	71	71	70	70	70	69	69	69	68		72.7
Oct	68	67	67	67	66	66	65	65	65	64	64	64	63	63	63	62	62	62	61	61	61	60	60	60	60	59	59	59	58	58	58	62.5
Nov	57	57	57	56	56	56	56	55	55	55	54	54	54	53	53	53	52	52	52	51	51	51	50	50	50	49	49	48	48	48		52.7
Dec	47	47	47	46	46	45	45	45	44	44	44	44	43	43	43	42	42	42	42	41	41	41	41	41	40	40	40	40	40	39	39	42.7

HARTFORD BRADLEY INTERNATIONAL AIRPORT, CT

Minimum Temperature in °F

	1	2	3	4	5	6	7	8	9	10	11	12	13	14	15	16	17	18	19	20	21	22	23	24	25	26	27	28	29	30	31	Month
Jan	18	18	18	18	18	18	17	17	17	17	17	17	17	17	17	17	17	17	17	17	17	17	17	17	17	17	17	17	17	17	17	17.2
Feb	17	18	18	18	18	18	18	18	19	19	19	19	19	20	20	20	20	20	21	21	21	21	22	22	22	23	23	23				19.9
Mar	24	24	24	25	25	25	25	26	26	26	27	27	27	28	28	28	29	29	29	30	30	30	30	31	31	31	32	32	32	33	33	28.3
Apr	33	34	34	34	35	35	35	35	36	36	36	37	37	37	37	38	38	39	39	39	40	40	40	41	41	41	42	42	42	43		37.9
May	43	43	44	44	44	45	45	46	46	46	47	47	47	48	48	48	49	49	49	49	50	50	50	51	51	51	52	52	52	53	53	48.1
Jun	53	53	54	54	54	55	55	55	55	56	56	56	57	57	57	57	58	58	58	58	59	59	59	59	60	60	60	60	60	60		57.0
Jul	61	61	61	61	61	61	62	62	62	62	62	62	62	62	63	63	63	63	63	63	63	63	63	62	62	62	62	62	62	62	63	62.4
Aug	63	63	63	63	62	62	62	62	62	62	62	62	61	61	61	61	60	60	60	60	60	60	60	59	59	59	59	58	58	58	57	60.7
Sep	57	57	57	56	56	56	55	55	55	55	54	54	53	53	52	52	51	51	51	51	50	50	49	49	48	48	48	47	47	46		52.1
Oct	46	45	45	45	44	44	43	43	43	42	42	42	41	41	41	40	40	40	39	39	39	39	38	38	38	38	37	37	37	37	36	40.6
Nov	36	36	36	36	36	35	35	35	35	34	34	34	34	33	33	33	32	32	32	32	31	31	31	30	30	30	29	29	28	28		32.6
Dec	27	27	27	26	26	26	25	25	25	24	24	24	23	23	23	22	22	22	21	21	21	21	20	20	20	20	20	19	19	19	19	22.6

Maximum Temperature in °F

	1	2	3	4	5	6	7	8	9	10	11	12	13	14	15	16	17	18	19	20	21	22	23	24	25	26	27	28	29	30	31	Month
Jan	35	35	35	34	34	34	34	34	34	34	34	34	34	34	34	34	34	34	34	34	34	34	34	34	34	34	34	34	34	34	34	34.1
Feb	35	35	35	35	35	36	36	36	36	36	37	37	37	37	38	38	38	38	39	39	39	40	40	40	40	41	41	42				37.7
Mar	42	42	43	43	43	44	44	45	45	45	46	46	47	47	47	48	48	48	49	49	50	50	50	51	51	52	52	52	53	53	54	47.7
Apr	54	54	55	55	56	56	56	57	57	58	58	58	59	59	60	60	61	61	61	62	62	63	63	63	64	64	65	65	65	66		59.9
May	66	67	67	67	68	68	69	69	69	70	70	71	71	71	72	72	72	73	73	74	74	74	74	75	75	75	76	76	76	76	76	71.7
Jun	77	77	77	77	78	78	78	78	79	79	79	79	79	80	80	80	80	81	81	81	81	81	82	82	82	82	83	83	83	83		80.0
Jul	83	84	84	84	84	84	85	85	85	84	85	85	85	85	85	85	85	85	85	85	85	86	86	85	85	85	83	83	83	85	85	84.9
Aug	85	85	85	85	84	84	84	84	84	84	84	83	83	83	83	83	83	82	82	82	82	81	81	81	81	81	80	80	80	79	79	82.5
Sep	79	79	78	78	78	77	77	77	76	76	76	76	75	75	75	74	74	74	73	73	73	72	72	71	71	71	70	70	70	69		74.3
Oct	69	68	68	68	67	67	67	66	66	65	65	65	64	64	64	63	63	62	61	62	61	61	60	60	60	59	59	58	58	58	57	63.1
Nov	57	56	56	56	55	55	54	54	54	53	53	52	52	52	51	51	50	50	50	49	49	49	48	47	47	46	46	46	45	45		50.9
Dec	44	44	43	43	43	42	42	41	41	41	40	40	40	39	39	39	38	38	38	37	37	37	37	37	36	36	36	36	35	35	35	39.0

HARTFORD BRAINARD FIELD, CT

Minimum Temperature in °F

	1	2	3	4	5	6	7	8	9	10	11	12	13	14	15	16	17	18	19	20	21	22	23	24	25	26	27	28	29	30	31	Month
Jan	18	18	17	17	17	17	17	17	16	16	16	16	16	16	16	16	16	16	16	16	16	16	16	16	16	16	16	16	16	16	16	16.3
Feb	17	17	17	17	17	17	18	18	18	18	18	18	19	19	19	19	20	20	20	20	21	21	21	21	22	22	22	22				19.2
Mar	23	23	23	24	24	24	24	25	25	25	26	26	26	27	27	27	28	28	28	28	29	29	29	30	30	30	31	31	32	32	32	27.3
Apr	33	33	33	34	34	34	35	35	35	36	36	36	37	37	37	38	38	38	39	39	39	40	40	41	41	41	42	42	42	43		37.6
May	43	43	44	44	44	45	45	45	46	46	46	47	47	47	47	48	48	48	49	49	49	50	50	50	51	51	51	52	52	52	53	47.8
Jun	53	53	54	54	54	55	55	55	56	56	56	57	57	57	57	58	58	58	59	59	59	59	60	60	60	60	61	61	61	61		57.4
Jul	61	62	62	62	62	62	63	63	63	63	63	63	64	64	64	64	64	64	64	64	64	64	64	64	64	64	64	64	64	64	64	63.4
Aug	64	64	64	63	63	63	63	63	63	63	63	63	64	62	62	62	61	61	61	61	60	60	60	60	59	59	59	58	58	58	57	61.2
Sep	57	57	56	56	56	55	55	54	54	54	53	53	52	52	52	51	51	51	50	50	49	49	49	48	48	47	47	46	46	45		51.4
Oct	45	45	44	44	43	43	43	42	42	41	41	41	40	40	40	39	39	39	38	38	38	37	37	37	37	37	36	36	36	36	36	39.8
Nov	36	36	35	35	35	35	35	34	34	34	34	34	33	33	32	32	32	32	32	31	31	31	30	30	30	29	29	28	28	28		32.3
Dec	27	27	27	26	26	25	25	25	24	24	24	23	23	23	22	22	22	21	21	21	20	20	20	20	19	19	19	19	18	18	18	22.2

Maximum Temperature in °F

	1	2	3	4	5	6	7	8	9	10	11	12	13	14	15	16	17	18	19	20	21	22	23	24	25	26	27	28	29	30	31	Month
Jan	36	36	36	36	36	36	36	36	36	36	35	35	35	35	35	35	35	35	35	35	35	35	35	35	35	35	36	36	36	36	36	35.5
Feb	36	36	36	36	36	37	37	37	37	37	37	38	38	38	38	39	39	39	39	39	40	40	40	41	41	41	41	42				38.4
Mar	42	42	43	43	43	44	44	44	45	45	45	46	46	46	47	47	47	48	48	48	49	49	50	50	50	51	51	51	52	52	52	47.1
Apr	53	53	54	54	54	55	55	56	56	56	57	57	57	58	58	59	59	59	60	60	61	61	61	62	62	63	63	64	64	64		58.5
May	65	65	65	66	66	67	67	67	68	68	69	69	69	70	70	70	71	71	71	72	72	72	72	73	73	73	73	74	74	75	75	70.1
Jun	75	75	76	76	76	76	77	77	77	77	78	78	78	78	78	79	79	79	80	80	80	80	80	81	81	81	81	81	82	82		78.6
Jul	82	82	83	83	83	83	83	83	84	84	84	84	84	84	84	84	84	84	84	84	84	85	85	85	85	84	84	84	84	84	84	83.8
Aug	84	84	84	84	84	84	83	83	83	83	83	83	83	82	82	82	82	82	82	81	81	81	81	81	80	81	80	80	79	79	79	81.9
Sep	79	78	78	78	78	77	77	77	76	76	76	75	75	75	74	74	74	73	73	73	72	72	72	71	71	71	70	70	69	69		74.1
Oct	69	68	68	67	67	67	66	66	65	65	65	64	64	63	63	63	62	62	62	61	61	61	60	60	59	59	59	58	58	58	57	62.8
Nov	57	57	56	56	55	55	55	54	54	54	53	53	53	52	52	51	51	51	50	50	49	49	49	48	48	47	47	47	46	46		51.5
Dec	45	45	44	44	44	43	43	43	42	42	41	41	41	41	40	40	40	39	39	39	39	38	38	38	38	37	37	37	37	37	37	40.3

MANSFIELD HOLLOW LAKE, CT

Minimum Temperature in °F

	1	2	3	4	5	6	7	8	9	10	11	12	13	14	15	16	17	18	19	20	21	22	23	24	25	26	27	28	29	30	31	Month
Jan	15	15	15	14	14	14	14	14	14	13	13	13	13	13	13	13	13	13	13	13	13	13	13	13	13	13	13	13	13	13	13	13.4
Feb	13	13	13	13	14	14	14	14	14	14	15	15	15	15	15	16	16	16	16	17	17	17	18	18	18	19	19	19				15.6
Mar	20	20	21	21	21	22	22	22	23	23	23	24	24	25	25	25	25	26	26	26	27	27	27	28	28	28	29	29	29	29	30	25.0
Apr	30	30	30	31	31	31	32	32	32	32	33	33	33	34	34	34	34	35	35	35	36	36	36	37	37	37	38	38	38	39		34.1
May	39	39	40	40	40	41	41	41	42	42	42	43	43	43	43	44	44	44	45	45	45	46	46	46	47	47	47	48	48	48	49	43.8
Jun	49	49	49	50	50	50	51	51	51	51	52	52	52	53	53	53	54	54	54	54	55	55	55	55	55	55	56	56	56	56		52.8
Jul	57	57	57	57	57	57	58	58	58	58	58	58	58	59	59	59	59	59	59	59	59	59	59	59	59	59	59	59	59	59	59	58.9
Aug	59	59	59	59	59	58	58	58	58	58	58	58	58	57	57	57	57	57	56	56	56	56	56	55	55	55	54	54	54	54	53	56.7
Sep	53	53	52	52	52	51	51	51	50	50	49	49	49	48	48	47	47	47	46	46	45	45	45	44	44	43	43	42	42	41		47.5
Oct	41	40	40	39	39	39	38	38	37	37	37	36	36	36	35	35	35	34	34	34	34	33	33	33	33	33	32	32	32	32	32	35.5
Nov	32	32	32	32	32	31	31	31	31	31	31	30	30	30	30	30	29	29	29	28	28	28	27	27	27	27	26	26	25	25		29.2
Dec	25	24	24	24	23	23	23	22	22	21	21	21	20	20	20	20	19	19	19	18	18	18	17	17	17	17	16	16	16	16	15	19.7

Maximum Temperature in °F

	1	2	3	4	5	6	7	8	9	10	11	12	13	14	15	16	17	18	19	20	21	22	23	24	25	26	27	28	29	30	31	Month
Jan	36	36	36	35	35	35	35	35	35	35	35	35	35	35	35	35	35	35	34	34	34	35	35	35	35	35	35	35	35	35	35	35.0
Feb	35	35	35	35	35	36	36	36	36	36	36	37	37	37	37	37	38	38	38	38	39	39	39	40	40	40	41	41				37.4
Mar	41	42	42	42	43	43	44	44	44	45	45	45	46	46	46	47	47	47	48	48	48	49	49	49	50	50	50	51	51	51	52	46.6
Apr	52	52	53	53	54	54	54	55	55	55	56	56	56	57	57	58	58	58	59	59	60	60	60	61	61	62	62	62	63	63		57.5
May	64	64	65	65	65	66	66	67	67	67	68	68	68	69	69	70	70	70	70	71	71	71	72	72	72	72	73	73	73	73	74	69.2
Jun	74	74	74	75	75	75	75	75	76	76	76	76	76	77	77	77	77	78	78	78	78	78	79	79	79	79	79	80	80	80		77.0
Jul	80	80	81	81	81	81	81	81	82	82	82	82	82	82	82	82	82	82	82	82	82	82	82	82	82	82	82	82	82	82	82	81.7
Aug	82	82	82	82	82	82	82	82	82	81	81	81	81	81	81	80	80	80	80	80	80	79	79	79	79	78	78	78	78	78	77	80.2
Sep	77	77	76	76	76	76	75	75	75	75	74	74	74	73	73	73	72	72	72	72	71	71	70	70	70	69	69	69	68	68		72.7
Oct	68	67	67	67	66	66	66	65	65	65	64	64	63	63	63	62	62	62	61	61	61	60	60	60	59	59	58	58	58	57	57	62.4
Nov	57	56	56	56	55	55	54	54	54	53	53	52	52	52	51	51	50	50	50	49	49	48	48	48	47	47	46	46	46	45		51.0
Dec	45	44	44	43	43	43	42	42	42	41	41	41	40	40	40	39	39	39	38	38	38	38	38	37	37	37	37	37	36	36	36	39.7

MIDDLETOWN 4 W (MERIDEN), CT

Minimum Temperature in °F

	1	2	3	4	5	6	7	8	9	10	11	12	13	14	15	16	17	18	19	20	21	22	23	24	25	26	27	28	29	30	31	Month
Jan	22	21	21	21	21	21	20	20	20	20	20	20	20	20	20	20	20	20	20	20	20	20	20	20	20	20	20	20	20	20	20	20.3
Feb	20	20	20	20	20	21	21	21	21	21	22	22	22	22	22	22	22	23	23	23	23	23	24	24	24	25	25	25				22.1
Mar	25	26	26	26	27	27	27	27	28	28	28	29	29	29	29	30	30	30	31	31	31	31	32	32	32	33	33	33	33	34	34	29.7
Apr	34	35	35	35	35	36	36	36	37	37	37	38	38	38	39	39	39	39	40	40	40	41	41	41	42	42	42	43	43	43		38.7
May	44	44	44	45	45	45	46	46	46	47	47	47	48	48	48	49	49	49	49	50	50	50	51	51	51	52	52	52	53	53	53	48.5
Jun	53	54	54	54	55	55	55	55	56	56	56	57	57	57	57	58	58	58	58	59	59	59	59	59	60	60	60	60	61	61		57.3
Jul	61	61	61	61	62	62	62	62	62	62	62	62	63	63	63	63	63	63	63	63	63	63	63	63	63	63	63	63	63	63	63	62.5
Aug	63	63	63	63	63	63	63	62	62	62	62	62	62	62	62	61	61	61	61	61	61	60	60	60	60	60	59	59	59	59	58	61.2
Sep	58	58	58	57	57	57	56	56	56	56	55	55	55	54	54	54	53	53	53	52	52	51	51	51	50	50	50	49	49	48		53.6
Oct	48	48	47	47	46	46	46	45	45	45	44	44	44	43	43	43	42	42	42	41	41	41	40	40	40	40	40	39	39	39	39	42.9
Nov	39	39	38	38	38	38	37	37	37	37	37	36	36	36	35	35	35	35	34	34	34	33	33	33	32	32	32	31	31	31		35.1
Dec	30	30	30	29	29	29	28	28	28	27	27	27	26	26	26	26	25	25	25	25	24	24	24	24	23	23	23	23	22	22	22	25.8

Maximum Temperature in °F

	1	2	3	4	5	6	7	8	9	10	11	12	13	14	15	16	17	18	19	20	21	22	23	24	25	26	27	28	29	30	31	Month
Jan	37	37	37	37	37	37	37	36	36	36	36	36	36	36	36	36	36	36	36	36	36	36	36	36	36	36	36	36	36	36	36	36.2
Feb	37	37	37	37	37	37	37	37	38	38	38	38	38	39	39	39	39	39	40	40	40	40	41	41	41	41	42	42				38.9
Mar	42	43	43	43	44	44	44	45	45	45	46	46	46	47	47	47	48	48	48	49	49	50	50	50	51	51	51	52	52	53	53	47.5
Apr	53	54	54	54	55	55	56	56	56	57	57	58	58	58	59	59	59	60	60	61	61	62	62	62	63	63	64	64	64	65		58.9
May	65	66	66	66	67	67	68	68	68	69	69	69	70	70	70	71	71	71	72	72	72	73	73	73	74	74	74	75	75	75	76	70.6
Jun	76	76	76	77	77	77	77	78	78	78	78	79	79	79	79	80	80	80	80	81	81	81	81	81	82	82	82	82	82	83		79.4
Jul	83	83	83	83	83	84	84	84	84	84	84	84	84	84	85	85	85	85	85	85	85	85	85	85	84	84	84	84	84	84	84	84.2
Aug	84	84	84	83	83	84	84	83	84	84	82	82	82	82	82	81	81	81	81	80	80	80	80	80	79	79	79	79	78	78	78	81.2
Sep	77	77	77	77	76	76	76	75	75	75	74	74	74	73	73	73	72	72	72	71	71	71	70	70	69	69	69	68	68	67		72.7
Oct	67	67	66	66	65	65	65	64	64	64	63	63	63	62	62	62	61	61	61	60	60	60	59	59	59	58	58	58	57	57	56	61.5
Nov	56	56	55	55	55	54	54	54	53	53	53	52	52	52	51	51	51	50	50	49	49	49	48	48	48	47	47	46	46	46		51.0
Dec	45	45	44	44	44	43	43	43	42	42	42	41	41	41	41	40	40	40	40	39	39	39	39	38	38	38	38	38	38	37	37	40.6

NORFOLK 2 SW, CT

Minimum Temperature in °F

	1	2	3	4	5	6	7	8	9	10	11	12	13	14	15	16	17	18	19	20	21	22	23	24	25	26	27	28	29	30	31	Month
Jan	14	14	14	13	13	13	13	13	12	12	12	12	12	12	12	12	12	11	11	11	11	11	11	11	11	11	11	11	11	11	11	11.9
Feb	11	11	11	12	12	12	12	13	12	12	12	13	13	13	13	13	14	14	14	14	15	15	15	15	16	16	16	17				13.4
Mar	17	18	18	18	18	18	19	19	19	20	20	20	21	21	22	22	22	23	23	23	24	24	24	25	25	25	26	26	26	27	27	21.9
Apr	27	28	28	29	29	29	30	30	30	31	31	31	32	32	33	33	33	34	34	34	35	35	36	36	36	37	37	38	38	38		32.8
May	39	39	40	40	40	41	41	41	42	42	43	43	43	44	44	44	45	45	45	46	46	46	47	47	47	48	48	48	48	49	49	44.2
Jun	49	50	50	50	50	51	51	51	52	52	52	52	53	53	53	53	53	54	54	54	54	55	55	55	55	55	56	56	56	56		53.0
Jul	56	57	57	57	57	57	57	57	58	58	58	58	58	58	58	58	58	58	58	58	58	59	59	59	59	59	59	58	58	58	58	57.9
Aug	58	58	58	58	58	58	58	58	58	58	57	57	57	57	57	57	56	56	56	56	56	56	55	55	55	55	55	54	54	54	54	56.4
Sep	53	53	53	52	52	52	52	51	51	50	50	50	50	49	49	49	48	48	48	47	47	46	46	46	45	45	44	44	44	43		48.6
Oct	43	42	42	41	41	41	40	40	40	39	39	38	38	38	38	37	37	37	36	36	36	35	35	35	35	34	34	34	34	34	33	37.5
Nov	33	33	33	33	32	32	32	32	31	31	31	31	30	30	30	29	29	29	29	28	28	27	27	27	26	26	26	25	25	24		29.3
Dec	24	24	23	23	22	22	22	21	21	20	20	20	19	19	19	18	18	18	17	17	17	16	16	16	16	15	15	15	15	14	14	18.6

Maximum Temperature in °F

	1	2	3	4	5	6	7	8	9	10	11	12	13	14	15	16	17	18	19	20	21	22	23	24	25	26	27	28	29	30	31	Month
Jan	30	30	30	29	29	29	29	29	29	29	29	29	29	29	29	29	29	29	29	29	29	28	29	29	29	29	29	29	29	29	29	29.1
Feb	29	29	29	29	29	30	30	30	30	30	30	30	31	31	31	31	32	32	32	32	33	33	33	33	34	34	34	35				31.3
Mar	35	36	36	36	37	37	37	38	38	39	39	39	40	40	40	41	41	42	42	42	43	43	44	44	44	45	45	46	46	46	47	40.9
Apr	47	47	48	48	49	49	50	50	50	51	51	52	52	52	53	53	54	54	55	55	55	56	56	57	57	58	58	58	59	59		53.1
May	60	60	61	61	62	62	62	63	63	64	64	64	65	65	65	66	66	66	67	67	67	68	68	68	69	69	69	69	70	70	70	65.5
Jun	70	71	71	71	71	72	72	72	72	72	73	73	73	73	73	74	74	74	74	75	75	75	75	75	75	76	76	76	76	76		73.5
Jul	77	77	77	77	77	77	77	78	78	78	78	78	78	78	78	78	78	78	79	79	79	79	79	79	79	79	79	79	78	78	78	78.1
Aug	78	78	78	78	78	78	78	78	78	78	77	77	77	77	77	77	76	76	76	76	75	75	75	75	75	76	74	74	74	74	73	76.3
Sep	73	73	72	72	72	71	71	71	71	70	70	70	69	69	69	68	68	68	67	67	66	66	66	65	65	65	64	64	64	63		68.3
Oct	63	62	62	62	61	61	60	60	59	59	59	58	58	58	57	57	56	56	56	55	55	54	54	54	53	53	53	52	52	52	51	56.9
Nov	51	50	50	50	49	49	48	48	48	47	47	47	46	46	45	45	45	44	44	43	43	43	42	42	41	41	40	40	40	39		45.1
Dec	39	38	38	38	37	37	36	36	36	35	35	35	34	34	34	34	33	33	33	33	32	32	32	32	31	31	31	31	31	30	30	33.9

NORWALK GAS PLANT, CT

Minimum Temperature in °F

	1	2	3	4	5	6	7	8	9	10	11	12	13	14	15	16	17	18	19	20	21	22	23	24	25	26	27	28	29	30	31	Month
Jan	20	20	20	20	20	20	19	19	19	19	19	20	20	20	19	19	19	18	18	18	18	18	18	18	18	18	18	18	18	19	19	18.8
Feb	19	19	19	19	19	19	19	19	19	19	20	20	20	20	20	21	21	21	21	21	22	22	22	23	23	23	23	24				20.6
Mar	24	24	25	25	25	26	26	26	27	27	27	28	28	28	29	29	29	30	30	30	30	31	31	31	32	32	32	32	33	33	33	28.8
Apr	34	34	34	34	35	35	35	36	36	36	36	37	37	37	38	38	38	38	39	39	39	40	40	40	40	41	41	41	41	42		37.7
May	42	42	43	43	43	43	44	44	44	45	45	45	45	46	46	46	47	47	47	48	48	48	49	49	49	50	50	51	51	51	52	46.5
Jun	52	52	53	53	53	54	54	54	55	55	55	56	56	56	57	57	57	58	58	58	58	58	59	59	59	60	60	60	60	60		56.5
Jul	61	61	61	61	61	62	62	62	62	62	62	63	63	63	63	63	61	61	61	61	60	63	63	63	63	63	63	63	63	63	63	62.5
Aug	63	63	63	63	63	63	62	662	62	62	62	63	62	62	61	61	61	61	63	61	60	60	60	60	59	59	59	59	59	58	58	61.0
Sep	58	57	57	57	57	56	56	56	55	55	55	54	54	54	53	53	52	52	52	51	51	50	50	49	49	48	48	48	47	47		52.7
Oct	46	46	45	45	45	44	44	43	42	42	42	41	41	41	40	40	40	39	39	38	38	38	38	38	37	37	37	37	37	37	36	40.4
Nov	36	36	36	36	36	36	35	35	35	35	35	34	34	34	34	34	33	33	33	32	32	32	31	31	31	30	30	30	29	29		33.2
Dec	29	28	28	28	27	27	27	26	26	26	25	25	25	24	24	24	24	23	23	23	22	22	22	22	22	21	21	21	21	21	20	24.1

Maximum Temperature in °F

	1	2	3	4	5	6	7	8	9	10	11	12	13	14	15	16	17	18	19	20	21	22	23	24	25	26	27	28	29	30	31	Month
Jan	38	38	38	37	37	37	37	37	37	37	37	37	37	37	37	36	36	36	36	36	36	36	36	36	37	37	37	37	37	37	37	36.8
Feb	37	37	37	37	37	38	38	38	38	38	38	38	39	39	39	39	40	40	40	40	41	41	41	42	42	42	42	43				39.3
Mar	43	43	44	44	44	45	45	45	46	46	46	47	47	47	48	48	49	49	49	50	50	50	51	51	52	52	52	53	53	54	54	48.3
Apr	54	55	55	56	56	56	57	57	57	58	58	59	59	59	60	60	60	61	61	61	62	62	63	63	63	64	64	64	65	65		59.8
May	65	65	66	66	66	67	67	67	68	68	68	69	69	69	70	70	70	71	71	71	72	72	72	73	73	73	74	74	74	75	75	70.0
Jun	75	76	76	76	76	77	77	77	78	78	78	78	79	79	79	80	80	80	80	80	81	81	81	81	82	82	82	82	82	83		79.2
Jul	83	83	83	83	83	84	84	84	84	84	84	84	84	84	84	85	85	85	85	85	85	85	85	85	85	85	85	85	84	84	84	84.2
Aug	84	84	84	84	84	84	84	84	84	84	84	84	84	83	83	83	82	82	82	82	82	82	81	81	81	81	81	80	80	80	80	82.4
Sep	79	79	79	79	78	78	78	77	77	77	76	76	76	76	75	75	75	74	74	74	73	73	72	72	72	71	71	71	70	70		74.9
Oct	69	69	69	68	68	67	67	67	66	66	65	65	65	64	64	64	63	63	62	62	62	61	61	61	60	60	60	59	59	58	58	63.6
Nov	58	57	57	57	56	56	56	55	55	54	54	54	53	53	53	52	52	52	51	51	50	50	50	49	49	48	48	48	47	47		52.4
Dec	46	46	46	45	45	45	44	44	43	43	43	42	42	42	42	41	41	41	40	40	40	40	40	39	39	39	39	39	38	38	38	41.6

NORWICH PUBLIC UTILITY PLANT, CT

Minimum Temperature in °F

	1	2	3	4	5	6	7	8	9	10	11	12	13	14	15	16	17	18	19	20	21	22	23	24	25	26	27	28	29	30	31	Month
Jan	19	17	17	19	19	18	18	18	18	17	17	17	17	17	17	17	17	17	17	17	17	17	16	16	16	16	17	17	17	17	17	17.3
Feb	17	17	17	17	17	17	18	18	18	18	18	18	18	19	19	19	19	19	20	20	20	20	21	21	21	22	22	22				19.0
Mar	23	23	23	24	24	24	24	25	25	25	26	26	26	27	27	27	28	28	28	29	29	29	30	30	30	31	31	31	32	32	32	27.4
Apr	33	33	33	33	34	34	34	35	35	35	36	36	36	37	37	37	38	38	38	39	39	40	40	40	41	41	41	41	42	42		37.3
May	43	43	43	44	44	44	45	45	45	46	46	46	47	47	47	48	48	48	49	49	49	50	50	50	51	51	51	51	52	52	52	47.6
Jun	52	53	53	53	53	54	54	54	55	55	55	55	56	56	56	56	56	57	57	57	57	58	58	58	59	59	59	60	60	60		56.3
Jul	61	61	61	61	61	62	62	62	62	62	62	63	63	63	63	61	63	63	63	60	63	63	63	60	63	63	63	63	63	63	63	62.5
Aug	63	63	63	63	63	62	62	62	62	62	62	63	63	61	61	61	61	61	60	60	60	60	60	60	59	59	59	59	58	58	58	60.8
Sep	58	57	57	57	56	56	56	56	55	55	55	54	54	54	53	53	52	52	52	51	51	50	50	49	49	49	48	48	47	47		52.7
Oct	46	46	45	45	44	44	43	43	42	42	42	41	41	40	40	40	39	39	39	38	38	38	37	37	37	36	36	36	35	35	35	40.0
Nov	35	35	35	34	34	34	34	33	33	33	33	33	32	32	32	32	31	31	31	31	30	30	30	29	29	29	29	28	28	28		31.6
Dec	27	27	27	27	26	26	26	25	25	25	25	24	24	24	24	23	23	23	22	22	22	22	21	21	21	21	20	20	20	20	19	23.3

Maximum Temperature in °F

	1	2	3	4	5	6	7	8	9	10	11	12	13	14	15	16	17	18	19	20	21	22	23	24	25	26	27	28	29	30	31	Month
Jan	39	38	38	38	38	38	38	38	38	38	38	38	38	38	38	38	38	37	37	37	37	37	37	37	37	38	38	38	38	38	38	37.8
Feb	38	38	38	38	38	38	38	39	39	39	39	39	39	40	40	40	40	40	41	41	41	42	42	42	42	43	43	43				40.0
Mar	44	44	44	45	45	45	46	46	46	47	47	47	48	48	48	49	49	50	50	50	50	51	51	51	52	52	52	52	53	53	53	48.6
Apr	54	54	54	55	55	55	56	56	56	57	57	57	58	58	59	59	59	60	60	60	61	61	62	62	63	63	63	64	64	65		58.9
May	65	65	66	66	67	67	68	68	68	69	69	69	70	70	70	71	71	71	72	72	72	73	73	73	73	74	74	74	75	75	75	70.5
Jun	75	75	76	76	76	76	77	77	77	77	77	78	78	78	78	79	79	79	79	80	80	80	80	80	81	81	81	81	82	82		78.5
Jul	82	82	82	83	83	83	83	83	84	84	84	84	84	84	84	84	84	84	84	84	85	85	85	85	85	84	84	84	84	84	84	83.8
Aug	84	84	84	84	84	84	83	83	83	83	83	83	84	84	84	84	84	84	84	84	85	85	85	81	81	84	80	80	80	79	79	82.0
Sep	79	79	78	78	78	78	77	77	77	77	76	76	75	75	75	75	74	74	73	73	73	73	72	72	72	71	71	70	70	70		74.6
Oct	69	69	69	68	68	68	67	67	66	66	66	65	65	64	64	64	63	63	63	62	62	62	61	61	61	60	60	60	59	59	59	63.9
Nov	58	58	58	57	57	56	56	56	55	55	55	54	54	54	53	53	52	52	52	51	51	50	50	50	49	49	49	48	48	47		52.9
Dec	47	46	46	46	45	45	45	44	44	44	43	43	43	42	42	42	42	41	41	41	41	40	40	40	40	40	39	39	39	39	39	42.2

SHEPAUG DAM, CT

Minimum Temperature in °F

	1	2	3	4	5	6	7	8	9	10	11	12	13	14	15	16	17	18	19	20	21	22	23	24	25	26	27	28	29	30	31	Month
Jan	14	14	13	13	13	13	13	13	12	12	12	12	12	12	12	12	12	11	11	11	11	11	11	11	11	11	11	11	11	11	12	11.9
Feb	11	12	12	12	12	12	12	12	12	12	13	13	13	13	13	14	14	14	14	15	15	15	15	16	16	16	16	17				13.6
Mar	17	18	18	18	19	19	19	19	20	20	20	21	21	21	22	22	22	23	23	23	24	24	24	25	25	25	25	26	26	26	27	22.0
Apr	27	27	28	28	28	29	29	29	29	30	30	31	31	31	32	32	32	33	33	33	34	34	35	35	35	36	36	36	37	37		31.9
May	38	38	39	39	39	40	40	40	41	41	42	42	42	43	43	43	44	44	44	45	45	45	46	46	46	47	47	47	47	48	48	43.2
Jun	48	48	49	49	49	50	50	50	50	51	51	51	51	52	52	52	52	53	53	53	53	54	54	54	54	54	55	55	55	55		51.9
Jul	56	56	56	56	56	56	57	57	57	57	57	57	57	58	58	58	58	58	58	58	58	58	58	58	58	58	58	58	58	58	58	57.4
Aug	58	58	58	58	57	57	57	57	57	57	57	57	57	56	56	56	56	56	56	55	55	55	55	55	55	54	54	54	54	53	53	55.9
Sep	53	53	52	52	52	52	51	51	50	50	50	50	50	49	49	48	48	48	47	47	47	46	46	46	45	45	44	44	43	43		48.4
Oct	43	42	42	41	41	41	40	40	39	39	39	38	38	38	37	37	37	36	36	36	35	35	35	35	34	34	34	34	34	33	33	37.3
Nov	33	33	33	32	32	32	32	31	31	31	31	30	30	30	29	29	29	29	28	28	27	27	27	26	26	26	25	25	24	24		29.0
Dec	24	23	23	22	22	22	21	21	21	20	20	19	19	19	18	18	18	18	17	17	17	16	16	16	16	15	15	15	14	14	14	18.4

Maximum Temperature in °F

	1	2	3	4	5	6	7	8	9	10	11	12	13	14	15	16	17	18	19	20	21	22	23	24	25	26	27	28	29	30	31	Month
Jan	35	35	34	34	34	34	34	34	34	34	34	34	34	34	34	34	34	33	33	33	33	33	34	34	34	34	34	34	34	34	34	33.9
Feb	34	34	34	34	35	35	35	35	35	35	35	36	36	36	36	36	37	37	37	37	38	38	38	39	39	39	39	40				36.4
Mar	40	40	41	41	41	42	42	43	43	43	44	44	44	45	45	45	46	46	46	47	47	48	48	48	49	49	49	50	50	51	51	36.4
Apr	51	52	52	52	53	53	54	54	54	55	55	55	56	56	57	57	57	58	58	59	59	59	60	60	61	61	62	62	62	63		56.9
May	63	64	64	64	65	65	66	66	66	67	67	67	68	68	68	69	69	69	70	70	70	71	71	71	71	72	72	72	72	72	73	68.4
Jun	73	73	73	73	74	74	74	74	74	74	75	75	75	75	75	76	76	76	76	76	77	77	77	77	77	77	78	78	78	78		75.5
Jul	78	79	79	79	79	79	79	80	80	80	80	80	80	80	80	80	80	80	80	80	77	80	80	81	81	81	80	80	80	80	80	79.8
Aug	80	80	80	80	80	80	80	80	80	79	79	79	79	79	79	79	78	78	78	78	78	77	77	77	77	76	76	76	76	75	75	78.2
Sep	75	75	74	74	74	73	73	73	72	72	72	72	71	71	71	70	70	70	69	69	69	69	68	68	68	67	67	67	66	66		70.5
Oct	66	65	65	65	64	64	64	63	63	63	63	62	62	61	61	61	60	60	60	59	59	59	58	58	58	57	57	57	56	56	56	60.7
Nov	55	55	54	54	54	53	53	53	52	52	52	51	51	51	50	50	49	49	48	48	48	47	47	47	46	46	45	45	44	44		49.7
Dec	43	43	43	42	42	41	41	41	40	40	39	39	39	38	38	38	38	38	37	37	37	37	36	36	36	36	36	35	35	35	35	38.5

STAMFORD 5 N, CT

Minimum Temperature in °F

	1	2	3	4	5	6	7	8	9	10	11	12	13	14	15	16	17	18	19	20	21	22	23	24	25	26	27	28	29	30	31	Month
Jan	21	21	20	20	20	20	20	20	19	19	19	19	19	19	19	19	19	19	19	19	19	18	18	18	18	19	19	19	19	19	19	19.2
Feb	19	19	19	19	19	20	20	20	20	20	20	20	21	21	21	21	21	21	22	22	22	22	23	23	23	24	24	24				21.0
Mar	24	25	25	25	26	26	26	26	27	27	27	28	28	28	28	29	29	29	30	30	30	30	31	31	31	32	32	32	32	33	33	28.7
Apr	33	34	34	34	34	35	35	35	36	36	36	36	37	37	37	38	38	38	39	39	39	40	40	40	41	41	41	41	42	42		37.6
May	43	43	43	44	44	44	45	45	45	45	46	46	46	47	47	47	48	48	48	49	49	49	50	50	50	51	51	51	51	52	52	47.4
Jun	52	53	53	53	54	54	54	54	55	55	55	56	56	56	56	57	57	57	57	57	58	58	58	58	58	59	59	59	59	60		56.2
Jul	60	60	60	61	61	61	61	61	61	61	62	62	62	61	62	62	62	62	62	62	62	62	62	62	62	62	63	62	62	62	62	61.6
Aug	62	62	62	62	62	62	62	62	62	62	62	61	61	61	61	61	61	61	60	60	60	60	60	60	59	59	59	59	59	58	58	60.6
Sep	58	58	57	57	57	56	56	56	56	55	55	55	54	54	54	53	53	53	52	52	51	51	51	50	50	49	49	48	48	48		53.2
Oct	47	47	46	46	46	45	45	45	44	44	43	43	43	42	42	42	41	41	41	40	40	40	39	39	39	39	38	38	38	38	37	41.6
Nov	37	37	37	36	36	36	36	35	35	35	35	35	34	34	34	34	33	33	33	32	32	32	32	31	31	31	30	30	30	29		33.5
Dec	29	29	28	28	28	28	27	27	27	26	26	26	25	25	25	25	24	24	24	24	23	23	23	23	22	22	22	22	22	21	21	24.8

Maximum Temperature in °F

	1	2	3	4	5	6	7	8	9	10	11	12	13	14	15	16	17	18	19	20	21	22	23	24	25	26	27	28	29	30	31	Month
Jan	39	39	39	39	38	38	38	38	38	38	38	38	38	38	38	38	38	38	38	38	38	38	38	38	38	38	38	38	38	39	39	38.2
Feb	39	39	39	39	39	39	40	40	40	40	40	41	41	41	41	41	42	42	42	42	43	43	43	43	44	44	44	44				41.3
Mar	45	45	46	46	46	47	47	47	48	48	49	49	49	50	50	50	51	51	51	52	52	53	53	53	54	54	54	55	55	56	56	50.4
Apr	56	57	57	58	58	58	59	59	60	60	60	61	61	62	62	62	63	63	64	64	64	65	65	65	66	66	66	67	67	68		62.1
May	68	68	69	69	69	70	70	70	71	71	71	72	72	72	73	73	73	74	74	74	74	75	75	75	76	76	76	76	77	77	77	72.8
Jun	77	78	78	78	78	79	79	79	79	80	80	80	80	80	81	81	81	81	81	82	82	82	83	83	83	83	83	83	84	84		80.7
Jul	84	84	84	84	84	85	85	85	85	85	85	85	85	86	86	86	86	86	86	86	86	86	86	86	86	86	86	86	86	86	85	85.4
Aug	86	85	85	85	85	85	85	85	85	85	84	84	84	84	84	84	83	83	83	83	83	82	82	82	82	82	81	81	81	80	80	83.3
Sep	80	80	79	79	79	79	78	78	78	77	77	77	76	76	76	75	75	75	75	74	74	73	73	73	72	72	72	71	71	71		75.5
Oct	70	70	70	69	69	68	68	68	67	67	67	66	66	65	65	65	64	64	64	63	63	62	62	62	61	61	61	60	60	60	59	64.7
Nov	59	58	58	58	57	57	57	56	56	55	55	55	54	54	54	53	53	52	52	52	51	51	50	50	50	49	49	48	48	48		53.3
Dec	47	47	46	46	46	45	45	45	44	44	44	43	43	43	42	42	42	42	41	41	41	41	40	40	40	40	40	40	39	39	39	42.5

STORRS, CT

Minimum Temperature in °F

	1	2	3	4	5	6	7	8	9	10	11	12	13	14	15	16	17	18	19	20	21	22	23	24	25	26	27	28	29	30	31	Month
Jan	19	19	18	18	18	18	18	18	17	17	17	17	17	17	17	17	17	17	17	17	16	16	16	16	17	17	17	17	17	17	17	17.2
Feb	17	17	17	17	17	18	18	18	18	18	18	18	19	19	19	19	20	20	20	20	21	21	21	21	22	22	22	23				19.3
Mar	23	23	24	24	24	25	25	25	26	26	26	27	27	27	28	28	28	28	29	29	29	30	30	30	31	31	31	32	32	32	32	27.8
Apr	33	33	33	34	34	34	34	35	35	35	36	36	36	37	37	37	38	38	38	38	39	39	39	40	40	40	41	41	41	42		37.1
May	42	42	43	43	43	44	44	44	45	45	45	46	46	46	47	47	47	48	48	48	48	49	49	49	50	50	50	50	51	51	51	46.8
Jun	52	52	52	52	53	53	53	54	54	54	54	55	55	55	55	56	56	56	56	57	57	57	58	58	58	58	58	58	59	59		55.4
Jul	59	59	60	60	60	60	60	60	61	61	61	61	61	61	61	61	61	61	61	61	61	62	62	62	62	62	62	61	61	61	61	60.9
Aug	61	61	61	61	61	61	61	60	60	60	60	60	60	60	60	60	59	59	59	59	59	58	58	58	58	58	57	57	57	57	56	59.3
Sep	56	56	55	55	55	55	54	54	54	54	53	53	53	52	52	52	51	51	51	50	50	50	49	49	48	48	48	47	47	47		51.7
Oct	46	46	45	45	45	44	44	43	43	43	42	42	42	41	41	41	41	40	40	40	39	39	39	38	38	38	38	38	37	37	37	41.1
Nov	37	37	37	36	36	36	36	36	35	35	35	35	34	34	34	33	33	33	32	32	32	32	31	31	31	30	30	29	29	29		33.3
Dec	28	28	27	27	27	26	26	26	25	25	25	24	24	24	23	23	23	22	22	22	21	21	21	20	20	20	20	20	19	19	19	23.2

Maximum Temperature in °F

	1	2	3	4	5	6	7	8	9	10	11	12	13	14	15	16	17	18	19	20	21	22	23	24	25	26	27	28	29	30	31	Month
Jan	35	35	35	34	34	34	34	34	34	34	34	34	34	34	34	33	33	33	33	33	33	33	33	33	33	33	33	34	34	34	34	33.7
Feb	34	34	34	34	34	34	34	34	35	35	35	35	35	35	36	36	36	36	37	37	37	38	38	38	38	39	39	39				36.0
Mar	40	40	40	41	41	41	42	42	42	43	43	43	44	44	44	45	45	45	46	46	47	47	47	48	48	48	49	49	49	50	50	44.8
Apr	50	51	51	51	52	52	53	53	53	54	54	54	55	55	56	56	56	57	57	57	58	58	59	59	59	60	60	61	61	62		55.8
May	62	62	63	63	64	64	64	65	65	66	66	66	67	67	67	68	68	68	68	69	69	69	70	70	70	70	71	71	71	71	72	67.3
Jun	72	72	72	73	73	73	73	73	74	74	74	74	74	75	75	75	75	76	76	76	76	76	77	77	77	77	77	78	78	78		75.0
Jul	78	78	79	79	79	79	79	79	79	79	80	80	80	80	80	80	80	80	80	80	80	80	80	80	80	80	80	80	80	80	80	79.6
Aug	80	80	80	80	80	79	79	79	79	79	79	79	79	78	78	78	78	78	78	77	77	77	77	77	77	76	76	76	76	75	75	77.9
Sep	75	75	74	74	74	74	74	73	73	73	72	72	72	71	71	71	70	70	70	69	69	69	68	68	68	68	67	67	66	66		70.7
Oct	66	66	65	65	64	64	64	63	63	63	62	62	62	61	61	61	60	60	59	59	59	58	58	58	57	57	57	56	56	56	55	60.5
Nov	55	54	54	54	53	53	53	52	52	52	51	51	50	50	50	49	49	48	48	48	47	47	47	46	46	45	45	45	44	44		49.4
Dec	43	43	43	42	42	41	41	41	40	40	39	39	39	39	38	38	38	38	37	37	37	37	36	36	36	36	36	35	35	35	35	38.5

WEST THOMPSON LAKE, CT

Minimum Temperature in °F

	1	2	3	4	5	6	7	8	9	10	11	12	13	14	15	16	17	18	19	20	21	22	23	24	25	26	27	28	29	30	31	Month
Jan	15	14	14	14	14	14	13	13	13	13	13	13	12	12	12	12	12	12	12	12	12	12	12	12	12	12	12	12	12	12	12	12.6
Feb	12	12	12	12	13	13	13	13	13	13	14	14	14	14	14	15	15	15	15	16	16	16	17	17	17	18	18	18				14.6
Mar	19	19	20	20	20	21	21	21	22	22	22	23	23	24	24	24	24	25	25	25	26	26	26	27	27	27	28	28	28	28	29	24.0
Apr	29	29	29	29	30	30	31	31	31	31	32	32	32	33	33	33	34	34	34	35	35	35	35	36	36	36	37	37	38	38		33.2
May	38	39	39	39	40	40	40	41	41	41	42	42	42	43	43	44	44	44	44	45	45	45	46	46	46	47	47	47	48	48	48	43.4
Jun	49	49	49	49	50	50	51	51	51	51	52	52	52	52	53	53	53	53	54	54	54	54	55	55	55	55	56	56	56	56		52.7
Jul	56	57	57	57	57	57	58	58	58	58	58	58	58	58	58	59	59	59	59	59	59	59	59	59	59	59	59	59	59	59	59	58.3
Aug	59	59	59	59	59	59	59	58	58	58	58	58	58	58	58	57	57	57	57	57	56	56	56	56	56	55	55	55	55	54	54	57.1
Sep	54	53	53	53	52	52	52	51	51	51	50	50	50	49	49	48	48	48	47	47	46	46	45	45	44	44	43	43	43	42		48.3
Oct	41	41	40	40	40	39	39	38	38	37	37	37	36	36	36	35	35	35	35	34	34	34	34	34	33	33	33	33	33	33	33	36.0
Nov	32	32	32	32	32	32	32	32	31	31	31	31	31	30	30	30	30	29	29	29	28	28	28	28	27	27	26	26	26	25		29.6
Dec	25	24	24	24	23	23	22	22	22	21	21	21	20	20	19	19	19	18	18	18	18	17	17	17	16	16	16	16	15	15	15	19.4

Maximum Temperature in °F

	1	2	3	4	5	6	7	8	9	10	11	12	13	14	15	16	17	18	19	20	21	22	23	24	25	26	27	28	29	30	31	Month
Jan	36	36	36	36	36	36	36	36	36	36	35	35	35	35	35	35	35	35	35	35	35	35	35	35	35	35	35	35	35	36	36	35.4
Feb	36	36	36	36	36	36	36	36	36	37	37	37	37	37	37	38	38	38	38	39	39	39	39	40	40	40	41	41				37.7
Mar	41	42	42	42	43	43	43	44	44	44	45	45	45	46	46	46	47	47	48	48	48	49	49	49	50	50	50	51	51	51	52	46.5
Apr	52	53	53	53	54	54	54	55	55	55	56	56	57	57	57	58	58	59	59	59	60	60	61	61	61	62	62	63	63	64		57.7
May	64	64	65	65	66	66	66	67	67	68	68	68	69	69	69	70	70	70	71	71	71	71	72	72	72	73	73	73	73	74	74	69.4
Jun	74	74	75	75	75	75	76	76	76	76	77	77	77	77	77	78	78	78	78	79	79	79	79	79	80	80	80	80	80	80		77.3
Jul	81	81	81	81	81	82	82	82	82	82	82	82	82	82	83	83	83	83	83	83	83	83	83	83	83	83	83	83	83	83	83	82.4
Aug	83	83	82	82	82	82	82	82	82	82	81	81	81	81	81	81	80	80	80	80	80	79	79	79	79	79	78	78	78	78	77	80.4
Sep	77	77	76	76	76	76	75	75	75	74	74	74	73	73	73	73	72	72	72	71	71	71	70	70	70	69	69	68	68	68		72.6
Oct	67	67	67	66	66	66	65	65	64	64	64	63	63	63	62	62	62	61	61	61	60	60	60	59	59	58	58	58	57	57	57	62.0
Nov	57	56	56	55	55	55	54	54	54	53	53	53	52	52	51	51	51	50	50	49	49	49	48	48	47	47	47	46	46	45		51.1
Dec	45	44	44	44	43	43	42	42	42	41	41	41	40	40	40	39	39	39	39	38	38	38	38	37	37	37	37	37	37	36	36	39.8

WIGWAM RESERVOIR, CT

Minimum Temperature in °F

	1	2	3	4	5	6	7	8	9	10	11	12	13	14	15	16	17	18	19	20	21	22	23	24	25	26	27	28	29	30	31	Month
Jan	15	15	14	14	14	14	14	13	13	13	13	13	13	12	12	12	12	12	12	12	12	12	12	12	12	12	12	11	11	11	12	12.6
Feb	11	12	12	12	12	12	12	12	12	12	12	13	13	13	13	14	14	14	14	15	15	15	16	16	16	17	17	18				13.7
Mar	18	18	19	19	20	20	20	21	21	22	22	22	23	23	23	24	24	24	25	25	25	26	26	26	27	27	27	27	28	28	28	23.5
Apr	28	29	29	29	29	30	30	30	31	31	31	31	32	32	32	33	33	33	34	34	34	35	35	35	36	36	37	37	37	38		32.7
May	38	38	39	39	39	40	40	41	41	41	42	42	42	43	43	43	44	44	45	45	45	46	46	46	47	47	47	48	48	48	48	43.4
Jun	49	49	49	50	50	50	51	51	51	51	52	52	52	53	53	53	53	53	54	54	54	54	55	55	55	55	55	56	56	56		52.7
Jul	56	56	57	57	57	57	57	57	57	57	58	58	58	58	58	58	58	58	58	58	58	58	58	58	58	58	58	58	58	58	58	57.6
Aug	58	58	58	58	58	57	57	57	57	57	58	57	57	56	56	56	56	56	56	55	5	55	55	55	54	54	54	54	54	53	53	55.9
Sep	53	53	52	52	52	51	51	51	51	50	50	50	49	49	49	48	48	47	47	47	46	46	45	45	45	44	44	43	43	42		48.1
Oct	42	42	41	41	40	40	39	39	39	38	38	37	37	37	36	36	36	35	35	35	35	34	34	34	33	33	33	33	32	32	32	36.4
Nov	32	31	31	31	31	31	30	30	30	30	29	29	29	29	28	28	28	28	27	27	27	26	26	26	26	25	25	25	24	24		28.1
Dec	24	23	23	23	23	22	22	21	21	21	21	20	20	20	19	19	19	19	18	18	18	17	17	17	17	16	16	16	16	15	15	19.2

Maximum Temperature in °F

	1	2	3	4	5	6	7	8	9	10	11	12	13	14	15	16	17	18	19	20	21	22	23	24	25	26	27	28	29	30	31	Month
Jan	35	35	35	34	34	34	34	34	34	34	34	34	34	34	34	34	34	34	34	34	34	34	34	34	34	34	34	34	34	34	34	34.1
Feb	34	34	35	35	35	35	35	35	35	36	36	36	36	36	37	37	37	37	38	38	38	38	39	39	39	40	40	40				36.8
Mar	41	41	42	42	42	43	43	43	44	44	44	45	45	45	46	46	47	47	47	48	48	48	49	49	49	50	50	50	51	51	52	46.2
Apr	52	52	53	53	53	54	54	54	55	55	56	56	56	57	57	58	58	59	59	59	60	60	61	61	62	62	62	63	63	64		57.6
May	64	65	65	66	66	67	67	67	68	68	69	69	69	70	70	70	71	71	71	72	72	72	73	73	73	73	74	74	74	74	74	70.0
Jun	75	75	75	75	75	76	76	76	76	77	77	77	77	77	78	78	78	78	79	79	79	79	79	80	80	80	80	81	81	81		77.8
Jul	81	82	82	82	82	82	82	83	83	83	83	83	83	84	84	84	84	84	84	84	84	84	84	84	84	84	84	84	84	83	83	83.3
Aug	83	83	83	83	83	83	83	83	83	83	83	83	83	84	84	84	81	81	81	80	80	79	79	79	79	79	78	78	78	78	78	80.8
Sep	78	77	77	77	77	76	76	76	75	75	75	75	74	74	74	73	73	73	72	72	71	71	71	70	70	70	69	69	68	68		73.2
Oct	68	67	67	66	66	65	65	65	64	64	64	63	63	62	62	61	61	60	60	60	60	59	59	59	58	58	58	57	57	57	56	61.7
Nov	56	56	55	55	54	54	54	53	53	53	52	52	51	51	51	50	50	49	49	49	48	48	47	47	46	46	45	45	45	44		50.3
Dec	44	43	43	42	42	42	41	41	40	40	40	39	39	39	38	38	38	37	37	37	37	36	36	36	36	35	35	35	35	35	35	38.5

APPENDIX B
Daily/Monthly Station Normals 1971–2000
Average Temperature/Heating Degree Days*

FALLS VILLAGE, CT

Average Temperature in °F

	1	2	3	4	5	6	7	8	9	10	11	12	13	14	15	16	17	18	19	20	21	22	23	24	25	26	27	28	29	30	31	Month
Jan	25	25	25	25	25	25	24	24	24	24	24	24	24	24	24	24	24	24	24	24	24	24	24	24	24	24	24	24	24	24	24	24.2
Feb	24	25	25	25	25	25	25	25	26	26	26	26	26	26	27	27	27	27	28	28	28	29	29	29	29	30	30	30				26.9
Mar	31	31	31	32	32	32	33	33	33	34	34	35	35	35	36	36	36	37	37	37	38	38	38	39	39	39	40	40	40	41	41	35.9
Apr	41	42	42	42	43	43	43	44	44	45	45	45	46	46	46	47	47	48	48	48	49	49	50	50	50	51	51	52	52	52		46.7
May	53	53	54	54	54	55	55	55	56	56	57	57	57	58	58	58	59	59	59	59	60	60	60	61	61	61	61	62	62	62	62	58.0
Jun	63	63	63	63	64	64	64	64	65	65	65	65	65	66	66	66	66	66	67	67	67	67	68	68	68	68	68	68	69	69		65.9
Jul	69	71	70	70	70	70	70	70	70	70	70	70	70	70	69	69	69	69	69	71	71	71	71	71	71	71	71	71	71	71	71	70.6
Aug	71	71	71	71	71	70	70	70	70	70	70	70	70	70	69	69	69	69	69	69	68	68	68	68	68	67	67	67	67	66	66	69.0
Sep	66	66	65	65	65	64	64	64	64	63	63	63	62	62	62	61	61	60	60	60	59	59	59	58	58	57	57	57	56	56		61.2
Oct	55	55	55	54	54	53	53	53	52	52	51	51	51	50	50	50	49	49	48	48	48	47	47	47	46	46	46	46	45	45	45	49.7
Nov	44	44	44	43	43	43	43	42	42	42	41	41	41	40	40	40	39	39	38	38	38	37	37	37	36	36	36	35	35	34		39.6
Dec	34	34	33	33	32	32	32	31	31	31	30	30	30	29	29	29	29	28	28	28	28	27	27	27	27	26	26	26	26	26	26	29.2

Heating Degree Days in °F

	1	2	3	4	5	6	7	8	9	10	11	12	13	14	15	16	17	18	19	20	21	22	23	24	25	26	27	28	29	30	31	Month
Jan	40	40	40	40	41	41	41	41	41	41	41	41	41	41	41	41	41	41	41	41	41	41	41	41	41	41	41	41	41	41	41	1267
Feb	41	41	41	40	40	40	40	40	39	39	39	39	39	38	38	38	38	38	37	37	37	36	36	36	36	35	35	35				1067
Mar	34	34	34	33	33	3	32	32	32	31	31	30	30	30	29	29	29	28	28	28	27	27	27	26	26	26	25	25	25	24	24	902
Apr	24	23	23	23	22	22	21	21	21	20	20	20	19	19	19	18	18	17	17	17	16	16	15	15	15	14	14	14	13	13		549
May	12	12	12	11	11	11	10	10	9	9	9	8	8	8	8	8	7	7	6	6	6	6	5	5	5	5	4	4	4	4	4	233
Jun	3	3	3	3	3	3	3	2	2	2	2	2	2	2	1	1	1	1	1	1	1	1	1	1	1	1	1	1	1	0		50
Jul	M	M	M	M	M	M	M	0	0	0	0	0	0	0	0	0	0	0	0	0	0	0	0	0	0	0	0	0	0	0	0	6
Aug	0	0	0	0	0	M	0	0	0	0	0	0	0	0	0	1	1	1	1	1	1	1	1	1	1	1	1	1	1	1	2	17
Sep	2	2	2	2	2	2	2	3	3	3	3	3	4	4	4	4	5	5	5	5	6	6	6	7	7	8	8	8	9	9		139
Oct	10	10	10	11	11	12	12	13	13	13	14	14	14	15	15	16	16	16	17	17	18	18	18	18	19	19	19	20	20	20	20	477
Nov	21	21	21	22	22	22	23	23	23	23	24	24	24	25	25	25	26	26	27	27	27	28	28	28	29	29	29	30	30	31		763
Dec	31	31	32	32	32	33	33	34	34	34	35	35	35	35	36	36	36	37	37	37	37	38	38	38	38	39	39	39	39	39	40	1109

*All information in Appendix B provided by the National Climatic Data Center-NOAA.
M indicates missing data wherever it appears.

GROTON, CT

Average Temperature in °F

	1	2	3	4	5	6	7	8	9	10	11	12	13	14	15	16	17	18	19	20	21	22	23	24	25	26	27	28	29	30	31	Month
Jan	30	30	30	30	30	30	29	29	29	29	29	29	29	29	29	29	29	29	28	28	28	28	28	28	28	28	28	29	29	29	29	28.9
Feb	29	29	29	29	29	29	29	29	29	30	30	30	30	30	30	31	31	31	31	31	32	32	32	32	33	33	33	34				30.6
Mar	34	34	34	35	35	35	36	36	36	36	37	37	37	38	38	38	38	39	39	39	40	40	40	41	41	41	41	42	42	42	43	38.2
Apr	43	43	43	44	44	44	45	45	45	45	46	46	46	47	47	47	48	48	48	49	49	49	50	50	50	50	51	51	51	52		47.2
May	52	53	53	53	54	54	54	54	55	55	55	56	56	56	57	57	57	58	58	58	59	59	59	60	60	60	60	61	61	61	62	57.0
Jun	62	62	62	63	63	63	64	64	64	64	65	65	65	65	66	66	66	67	67	67	67	68	68	68	68	69	69	69	69	69		65.8
Jul	70	70	70	70	70	71	71	71	71	71	71	72	72	72	72	72	72	72	72	72	72	73	73	73	73	73	73	73	73	73	73	71.8
Aug	73	73	73	72	72	72	72	72	72	72	72	72	72	71	71	71	71	71	71	71	70	70	70	70	70	69	69	69	69	68	68	70.9
Sep	68	68	67	67	67	67	66	66	66	65	65	65	65	64	64	64	63	63	63	62	62	62	61	61	60	60	60	59	59	59		63.6
Oct	58	58	57	57	57	56	56	56	55	55	54	54	54	53	53	53	52	52	52	52	51	51	50	50	50	50	50	49	49	49	49	53.0
Nov	48	48	48	47	47	47	47	46	46	46	46	45	45	45	44	44	44	43	43	43	42	42	42	41	41	41	40	40	40	39		44.0
Dec	39	38	38	38	37	37	37	36	36	36	35	35	35	35	34	34	34	33	33	33	33	32	32	32	32	31	31	31	31	31	31	34.2

Heating Degree Days in °F

	1	2	3	4	5	6	7	8	9	10	11	12	13	14	15	16	17	18	19	20	21	22	23	24	25	26	27	28	29	30	31	Month
Jan	35	35	35	35	35	35	36	36	36	36	36	36	36	36	36	36	36	37	37	37	37	37	37	37	37	37	37	37	36	36	36	1121
Feb	36	36	36	36	36	35	36	36	36	35	36	36	36	35	35	34	34	34	34	34	33	33	33	33	32	32	32	32				964
Mar	31	31	31	30	30	30	29	29	29	29	28	28	28	27	27	27	27	26	26	26	25	25	25	25	24	24	24	23	23	23	22	832
Apr	22	22	22	21	21	21	20	20	20	20	19	19	19	18	18	18	17	17	17	16	16	16	15	15	15	15	14	14	14	13		534
May	13	12	12	12	11	11	11	11	10	10	10	9	9	9	8	8	8	7	7	7	7	6	6	6	6	5	5	5	5	4	4	254
Jun	4	4	3	3	3	3	3	2	2	2	2	2	1	1	1	1	1	1	1	1	1	1	0	0	0	0	0	0	0	0		42
Jul	M	M	0	0	0	0	0	0	0	0	0	0	0	0	0	0	0	0	0	0	0	0	0	0	0	0	0	0	0	0	0	2
Aug	0	0	0	0	0	0	0	0	0	0	0	0	0	0	0	0	0	0	0	0	0	0	0	0	0	0	M	M	M	M	M	4
Sep	0	0	1	1	1	1	1	1	1	1	1	2	2	1	2	2	3	3	3	3	4	4	4	5	5	5	6	6	6	7		83
Oct	7	7	8	8	8	9	9	10	10	10	11	11	11	12	12	12	13	13	13	14	14	14	14	15	15	15	16	16	16	16	17	376
Nov	17	17	17	18	18	18	18	19	19	19	20	20	20	20	21	21	21	22	22	22	23	23	23	24	24	24	25	25	26	26		632
Dec	26	27	27	27	28	28	28	29	29	29	30	30	30	30	31	31	31	32	32	32	32	33	33	33	33	33	34	34	34	34	35	955

147

HARTFORD BRADLEY INTERNATIONAL AIRPORT, CT

Average Temperature in °F

	1	2	3	4	5	6	7	8	9	10	11	12	13	14	15	16	17	18	19	20	21	22	23	24	25	26	27	28	29	30	31	Month
Jan	27	26	26	27	26	26	26	26	26	26	26	26	26	25	25	25	25	25	25	25	25	25	25	25	26	26	26	26	26	26	26	25.7
Feb	26	26	26	27	27	27	27	27	27	28	28	28	28	28	29	29	29	29	30	30	30	31	31	31	31	32	32	32				28.8
Mar	33	33	33	34	34	35	35	35	36	36	36	37	37	37	38	38	38	39	39	39	40	40	40	41	41	41	42	42	43	43	43	38.0
Apr	44	44	44	45	45	45	46	46	46	47	47	48	48	48	48	49	49	50	50	51	51	51	52	52	52	53	53	54	54	54		48.9
May	55	55	55	56	56	57	57	57	58	58	58	59	59	59	60	60	60	61	61	61	62	62	62	63	63	63	63	64	64	64	65	59.9
Jun	65	65	65	66	66	66	66	67	67	67	68	68	68	68	68	69	69	69	69	70	70	70	70	71	71	71	71	71	72	72		68.5
Jul	72	72	73	73	73	73	73	73	74	74	74	74	74	74	74	74	74	74	74	74	74	74	75	71	74	74	74	74	74	74	74	73.7
Aug	74	74	74	74	74	73	73	73	73	73	73	73	72	72	72	72	72	71	71	71	71	71	70	70	70	70	69	69	69	69	68	71.6
Sep	68	68	67	67	67	66	66	66	66	65	65	65	64	64	64	63	63	62	62	62	61	61	61	60	60	59	59	59	58	58	58	63.2
Oct	57	57	57	56	56	55	55	55	54	54	54	53	53	52	52	52	51	51	51	50	50	50	49	49	49	49	48	48	48	47	47	51.9
Nov	47	46	46	46	45	45	45	45	44	44	44	43	43	42	42	42	41	41	41	40	40	40	39	39	38	38	38	37	37	36		41.8
Dec	36	35	35	35	34	34	34	33	33	32	32	32	31	31	31	30	30	30	30	29	29	29	29	28	28	28	28	27	27	27	27	30.8

Heating Degree Days in °F

	1	2	3	4	5	6	7	8	9	10	11	12	13	14	15	16	17	18	19	20	21	22	23	24	25	26	27	28	29	30	31	Month
Jan	38	38	39	38	39	39	39	39	39	39	39	39	40	40	40	40	40	40	40	40	40	40	40	40	40	40	39	39	39	39	39	1218
Feb	39	39	39	39	39	38	38	38	38	38	38	37	37	37	37	37	36	36	36	35	35	35	35	34	34	34	33	33				1024
Mar	33	32	32	32	31	31	30	30	30	29	29	29	28	28	28	27	27	26	26	26	25	25	25	24	24	24	23	23	23	22	22	844
Apr	21	21	21	20	20	20	19	19	19	18	18	17	17	17	16	16	16	15	15	15	14	14	14	13	13	13	12	12	11	11		486
May	11	10	10	10	9	9	9	8	8	8	7	7	7	7	6	6	6	5	5	5	5	5	4	4	4	4	4	3	3	3	3	195
Jun	3	3	3	2	2	2	2	2	2	2	2	1	1	1	1	1	1	1	0	0	1	1	1	1	0	0	0	0	0	0		38
Jul	M	M	M	0	0	0	0	0	0	0	0	0	0	0	0	0	0	0	0	0	0	0	0	0	0	0	0	0	0	0	0	3
Aug	0	0	0	0	0	0	0	0	0	0	0	0	0	0	0	0	0	0	0	1	1	1	1	1	1	1	0	0	0	0	1	12
Sep	1	1	2	2	2	2	2	2	2	3	3	3	3	3	4	4	4	4	4	5	5	5	6	6	6	6	7	7	8	8	8	120
Oct	8	9	9	9	10	10	10	11	11	11	12	12	13	13	13	13	14	14	14	15	15	15	16	16	16	17	17	17	18	18	18	413
Nov	18	19	19	19	20	20	20	21	21	21	21	22	22	23	23	23	24	24	24	25	25	25	26	26	27	27	27	28	28	29		697
Dec	29	29	30	30	31	31	31	31	32	32	32	33	33	33	34	34	34	35	35	35	36	36	36	36	37	37	37	37	37	38	38	1054

HARTFORD BRAINARD FIELD, CT

Average Temperature in °F

	1	2	3	4	5	6	7	8	9	10	11	12	13	14	15	16	17	18	19	20	21	22	23	24	25	26	27	28	29	30	31	Month
Jan	27	27	27	27	26	26	26	26	26	26	26	26	26	26	26	25	25	25	25	25	25	25	26	26	26	26	26	26	26	26	26	25.9
Feb	26	26	26	27	27	27	27	27	28	28	28	28	28	28	29	29	29	29	30	30	30	30	31	31	31	31	32	32				28.8
Mar	32	33	33	32	34	34	34	35	35	35	35	36	36	36	37	37	37	38	38	38	39	39	40	40	40	41	41	41	42	42	42	37.2
Apr	43	43	43	43	44	45	45	45	46	46	46	47	47	48	48	48	49	49	49	50	50	51	51	51	52	52	52	53	53	53		48.1
May	54	54	55	55	55	56	56	56	57	57	57	58	58	58	59	59	59	60	60	60	61	61	61	62	62	62	63	63	63	64	64	59.0
Jun	64	64	65	65	65	66	66	66	66	67	67	67	67	68	68	68	69	69	69	69	69	70	70	70	70	71	71	71	71	72		68.0
Jul	72	72	72	72	73	73	73	73	73	74	74	74	74	74	74	74	74	74	74	74	74	74	74	74	74	74	74	74	74	74	74	73.6
Aug	74	74	74	74	74	73	73	73	73	73	73	73	72	72	72	72	72	72	71	71	71	71	70	70	70	70	69	69	69	68	68	71.6
Sep	68	68	67	67	67	66	66	66	65	65	65	64	64	63	63	63	62	62	62	61	61	60	60	60	59	59	58	58	58	57		62.8
Oct	57	56	56	56	55	55	54	54	54	53	53	52	52	52	51	51	51	50	50	50	49	49	49	49	48	48	48	47	47	47	47	51.3
Nov	46	46	46	46	45	45	45	44	44	44	44	43	43	43	42	42	42	41	41	41	40	40	39	39	39	38	38	37	37	37		41.9
Dec	36	36	36	35	35	34	34	34	33	33	33	32	32	32	31	31	31	30	30	30	30	29	29	29	29	28	28	28	28	27	27	31.3

Heating Degree Days in °F

	1	2	3	4	5	6	7	8	9	10	11	12	13	14	15	16	17	18	19	20	21	22	23	24	25	26	27	28	29	30	31	Month
Jan	38	38	38	38	39	39	39	39	39	39	39	39	39	39	39	40	40	40	40	40	40	40	40	39	39	39	39	39	39	39	39	1213
Feb	39	39	38	38	38	38	38	38	37	37	37	37	37	37	36	36	36	36	35	35	35	35	34	34	34	34	33	33				1014
Mar	33	32	32	32	31	31	31	30	30	30	30	29	29	29	28	28	28	27	27	27	26	26	25	25	25	24	24	24	23	23	23	862
Apr	22	22	22	21	21	20	20	20	19	19	19	18	18	18	17	17	16	16	16	15	15	14	14	14	13	13	13	12	12	12		509
May	11	11	11	11	10	10	9	9	9	8	8	8	7	7	7	7	6	6	6	5	5	5	5	5	4	4	4	4	3	3	3	210
Jun	3	3	3	2	2	2	2	2	2	1	1	1	1	1	1	1	1	1	1	0	0	0	0	0	0	0	0	0	0	0		32
Jul	M	0	0	0	0	0	0	0	0	0	0	0	0	0	0	0	0	0	0	0	0	0	0	0	0	0	0	0	0	0	0	1
Aug	0	0	0	0	0	0	0	0	0	0	0	0	0	0	0	0	1	1	1	0	0	0	0	0	0	0	0	0	0	0	0	3
Sep	1	1	1	1	1	1	1	1	2	2	2	2	3	3	3	3	3	4	4	4	5	5	5	5	6	6	7	7	7	8		103
Oct	8	9	9	10	10	10	11	11	11	12	12	13	13	13	14	14	14	15	15	15	16	16	16	17	17	17	17	18	18	18	19	428
Nov	19	19	19	20	20	20	20	21	21	21	22	22	22	23	23	23	24	24	25	25	25	25	26	26	26	27	27	28	28	28		698
Dec	28	29	30	30	30	31	31	31	32	32	33	33	33	33	34	34	34	35	35	35	36	36	36	36	36	37	37	37	37	38	38	1048

MANSFIELD HOLLOW LAKE, CT

Average Temperature in °F

	1	2	3	4	5	6	7	8	9	10	11	12	13	14	15	16	17	18	19	20	21	22	23	24	25	26	27	28	29	30	31	Month
Jan	25	25	25	25	25	25	24	24	24	24	24	24	24	24	24	24	24	24	24	24	24	24	24	24	24	24	24	24	24	24	24	24.2
Feb	24	24	24	24	25	25	25	25	25	25	25	26	26	26	26	27	27	27	27	28	28	28	28	29	29	29	30	30				26.5
Mar	31	31	31	31	32	32	33	33	33	34	34	34	35	35	36	36	36	37	37	37	38	38	38	39	39	39	39	40	40	40	41	35.8
Apr	41	41	42	42	42	43	43	43	43	44	44	44	45	45	46	46	46	47	47	47	48	48	48	49	49	49	50	50	51	51		45.8
May	51	52	52	52	53	53	54	54	54	55	55	55	56	56	56	57	57	57	58	58	58	59	59	59	59	60	60	60	61	61	61	56.5
Jun	61	62	62	62	62	63	63	63	63	64	64	64	64	65	65	65	65	66	66	66	66	66	67	67	67	67	68	68	68	68		64.9
Jul	68	71	70	69	70	70	69	69	70	70	70	70	70	70	70	70	70	70	71	71	71	71	71	71	71	71	71	71	71	71	71	70.1
Aug	69	68	69	69	69	69	69	69	70	70	70	69	69	69	69	69	69	68	68	68	68	68	67	67	67	67	66	66	66	66	65	68.5
Sep	65	65	64	64	64	63	63	63	63	62	62	61	61	61	60	60	60	59	59	59	58	58	57	57	57	56	56	56	55	55		60.1
Oct	54	54	53	53	53	52	52	52	51	51	50	50	50	49	49	49	48	48	48	48	47	47	47	46	46	46	46	45	45	45	45	49.0
Nov	44	44	44	44	43	43	43	43	42	42	42	41	41	41	41	40	40	40	39	39	38	38	38	37	37	37	36	36	35	35		40.1
Dec	35	34	34	33	33	33	32	32	32	31	31	31	30	30	30	29	29	29	29	28	28	28	28	27	27	27	27	26	26	26	26	29.7

Heating Degree Days in °F

	1	2	3	4	5	6	7	8	9	10	11	12	13	14	15	16	17	18	19	20	21	22	23	24	25	26	27	28	29	30	31	Month
Jan	40	40	40	40	40	40	41	41	41	41	41	41	41	41	41	41	41	41	41	41	41	41	41	41	41	41	41	41	41	41	41	1265
Feb	41	41	41	41	40	40	40	40	40	40	40	39	39	39	39	38	38	38	38	37	37	37	37	36	36	36	35	35				1078
Mar	34	34	34	33	33	33	32	32	32	31	31	30	30	30	29	29	29	28	28	28	27	27	27	26	26	26	26	25	25	25	24	904
Apr	24	24	23	23	23	22	22	22	21	21	21	21	20	20	20	19	19	18	18	18	17	17	17	16	16	16	15	15	14	14		576
May	14	13	13	13	12	12	11	11	11	10	10	10	9	9	9	9	8	8	8	7	7	7	7	6	6	6	6	5	5	5	5	271
Jun	4	4	4	4	4	4	3	3	3	3	3	3	2	2	2	2	2	2	2	2	1	1	1	1	1	1	1	1	1	1		68
Jul	1	1	1	1	1	1	1	0	0	0	0	0	0	0	0	0	0	0	0	0	0	0	0	0	0	0	1	0	0	0	0	7
Aug	0	0	0	0	0	0	0	0	0	0	0	0	0	0	0	0	0	1	0	1	1	1	1	1	0	0	1	1	1	0	2	18
Sep	2	2	2	3	3	3	3	3	3	4	4	4	4	5	5	5	6	6	6	6	7	7	8	8	8	9	9	9	10	10		162
Oct	11	11	11	12	12	13	13	13	14	14	15	15	15	16	16	16	17	17	17	18	18	18	18	19	19	19	20	20	20	20	20	497
Nov	21	21	21	21	22	22	22	22	23	23	23	24	24	24	24	25	25	25	26	26	27	27	27	28	28	28	29	29	30	30		747
Dec	30	31	31	32	32	32	33	33	33	34	34	34	35	35	35	36	36	36	36	37	37	37	37	38	38	38	38	39	39	39	39	1095

MIDDLETOWN 4 W (MERIDEN), CT

Average Temperature in °F

	1	2	3	4	5	6	7	8	9	10	11	12	13	14	15	16	17	18	19	20	21	22	23	24	25	26	27	28	29	30	31	Month
Jan	30	29	29	29	29	29	29	28	28	28	28	28	28	28	28	28	28	28	28	28	28	28	28	28	28	28	28	28	28	28	28	28.3
Feb	28	28	29	34	35	29	29	29	28	29	30	30	30	30	30	31	31	31	31	31	32	32	32	32	33	33	33	34				30.5
Mar	34	34	35	35	35	35	36	36	36	37	37	37	38	38	38	39	39	39	40	40	40	41	41	41	41	42	42	42	43	43	43	38.6
Apr	44	44	44	45	45	45	46	46	46	47	47	48	48	48	49	49	49	50	50	50	51	51	51	52	52	53	53	53	54	54		48.8
May	54	55	55	56	56	56	57	57	57	58	58	58	59	59	59	60	60	60	61	61	61	62	62	62	63	63	63	64	64	64	64	59.6
Jun	65	65	65	66	66	66	66	67	67	67	67	68	68	68	68	69	69	69	69	70	70	70	70	70	71	71	71	71	71	72		68.4
Jul	72	72	72	72	72	73	73	73	73	73	73	73	73	74	74	74	74	74	74	74	74	74	74	74	74	74	74	74	74	74	73	73.4
Aug	73	73	73	73	73	73	73	73	73	72	72	72	72	72	72	71	71	71	71	71	71	70	70	70	70	69	69	69	69	68	68	71.2
Sep	68	68	67	67	67	66	66	66	65	65	65	65	64	64	64	63	63	62	62	62	61	61	61	60	60	60	59	59	58	58		63.2
Oct	58	57	57	56	56	56	55	55	54	54	54	53	53	53	52	52	52	51	51	51	50	50	50	49	49	49	49	48	48	48	48	52.2
Nov	47	47	47	47	46	46	46	46	45	45	45	44	44	44	43	43	43	43	42	42	41	41	41	40	40	40	39	39	39	38		43.1
Dec	38	37	37	37	36	36	36	35	35	35	34	34	34	33	33	33	33	32	32	32	32	31	31	31	31	31	30	30	30	30	30	33.2

Heating Degree Days in °F

	1	2	3	4	5	6	7	8	9	10	11	12	13	14	15	16	17	18	19	20	21	22	23	24	25	26	27	28	29	30	31	Month
Jan	36	36	36	36	36	36	36	36	37	37	37	37	37	37	37	37	37	37	37	37	37	37	37	37	37	37	37	37	37	37	37	1139
Feb	37	37	36	31	30	36	36	36	37	36	35	35	35	35	35	34	34	34	34	34	33	33	33	33	32	32	32	31				966
Mar	31	31	30	30	30	30	29	29	29	28	28	28	27	27	27	26	26	26	25	25	25	24	24	24	24	23	23	23	22	22	22	818
Apr	21	21	21	20	20	20	19	19	19	18	18	17	17	17	16	16	16	15	15	15	14	14	14	13	13	12	12	12	11	11		486
May	11	10	10	10	9	9	9	8	8	8	7	7	7	7	6	6	6	5	5	5	5	4	4	4	4	3	3	3	3	3	3	195
Jun	3	2	2	2	2	2	2	2	2	1	1	1	1	1	1	1	1	1	1	1	1	0	0	0	0	0	0	0	0	0		30
Jul	M	M	2	0	0	0	0	0	0	0	0	0	0	0	0	0	0	0	0	0	0	0	0	0	0	0	0	0	0	0	0	2
Aug	M	M	0	0	0	0	0	0	0	0	0	0	0	0	0	0	0	0	0	0	0	0	0	0	0	1	1	1	1	1	0	5
Sep	0	0	0	0	0	0	1	1	1	2	2	2	3	3	3	4	4	4	5	5	5	6	6	6	7	7	7	7	8	8		105
Oct	7	8	8	9	9	9	10	10	11	11	11	12	12	12	13	13	13	14	14	14	15	15	15	16	16	16	16	17	17	17	17	400
Nov	18	18	18	18	19	19	19	19	20	20	20	21	21	21	22	22	22	22	23	23	24	24	24	25	25	25	26	26	26	27		658
Dec	27	28	28	28	29	29	29	30	30	30	31	31	31	32	32	32	32	33	33	33	33	34	34	34	34	34	35	35	35	35	35	987

NORFOLK 2 SW, CT

Average Temperature in °F

	1	2	3	4	5	6	7	8	9	10	11	12	13	14	15	16	17	18	19	20	21	22	23	24	25	26	27	28	29	30	31	Month
Jan	22	22	22	21	21	21	21	21	21	21	21	20	20	20	20	20	20	20	20	20	20	20	20	20	20	20	20	20	20	20	20	20.5
Feb	20	20	20	21	21	21	21	21	21	21	21	22	22	22	22	22	23	23	23	23	24	24	24	24	25	25	25	26				22.4
Mar	26	26	27	27	27	28	28	28	29	29	30	30	30	31	31	31	32	32	32	33	33	34	34	34	35	35	35	36	36	37	37	31.4
Apr	37	38	38	38	39	39	40	40	40	41	41	42	42	42	43	43	44	44	44	45	45	46	46	46	47	47	48	48	48	49		43.0
May	49	50	50	51	51	51	52	52	53	53	53	54	54	54	55	55	56	56	56	56	57	57	57	58	58	58	59	59	59	59	60	54.9
Jun	60	60	60	61	61	61	61	62	62	62	62	63	63	63	63	64	64	64	64	64	65	65	65	65	65	66	66	66	66	66		63.3
Jul	66	67	67	67	67	67	67	68	68	68	68	67	67	68	68	68	68	68	68	68	69	69	69	69	69	69	69	69	68	68	68	68.0
Aug	68	68	68	68	68	68	68	68	68	68	67	67	67	67	67	67	66	66	66	66	66	66	65	65	65	65	64	64	64	64	63	66.4
Sep	63	63	63	62	62	62	61	61	61	61	60	60	60	59	59	59	58	58	57	57	57	56	56	56	55	55	54	54	54	53		58.5
Oct	53	52	52	52	51	51	50	50	50	49	49	48	48	48	47	47	47	46	46	46	45	45	45	44	44	44	43	43	43	43	42	47.2
Nov	42	42	41	41	41	40	40	40	40	39	39	39	38	38	38	37	37	36	36	36	35	35	35	34	34	33	33	33	32	32		37.2
Dec	31	31	31	30	30	29	29	29	28	28	27	27	27	26	26	26	25	25	25	25	25	24	24	24	24	23	23	23	23	22	22	26.3

Heating Degree Days in °F

	1	2	3	4	5	6	7	8	9	10	11	12	13	14	15	16	17	18	19	20	21	22	23	24	25	26	27	28	29	30	31	Month
Jan	43	43	43	44	44	44	44	44	44	44	44	45	45	45	45	45	45	45	45	45	45	45	45	45	45	45	45	45	45	45	45	1381
Feb	45	45	45	45	44	44	44	44	44	4	4	43	43	43	43	43	42	42	42	42	41	41	41	40	40	40	40	39				1193
Mar	39	39	38	38	38	37	37	37	36	36	35	35	35	34	34	34	33	33	33	32	32	31	31	31	30	30	30	29	29	29	28	1042
Apr	28	27	27	27	26	26	25	25	25	24	24	24	23	23	22	22	21	21	21	20	20	19	19	19	18	18	17	17	17	16		661
May	16	15	15	14	14	14	13	13	13	12	12	11	11	11	10	10	10	9	9	9	8	8	8	8	7	7	7	7	6	6	6	319
Jun	6	5	5	5	5	5	4	4	4	4	4	3	3	3	3	3	3	3	2	2	2	2	2	2	2	2	2	1	1	1		93
Jul	1	1	1	1	1	1	1	1	1	1	1	1	1	1	1	1	1	1	0	0	0	0	0	0	0	0	2	1	1	0	0	17
Aug	0	0	0	0	0	0	0	0	0	1	1	1	1	1	1	1	1	1	1	1	1	2	2	2	2	2	2	2	3	3	3	35
Sep	3	3	3	4	4	4	4	5	5	5	5	5	6	6	6	7	7	7	7	8	8	9	9	9	10	10	10	11	11	12		202
Oct	12	13	13	13	14	14	15	15	15	16	16	17	17	17	18	18	18	19	19	19	20	20	20	21	21	21	22	22	22	22	23	552
Nov	23	23	24	24	24	25	25	25	25	26	26	26	27	27	28	28	28	29	29	29	30	30	30	31	31	32	32	32	33	33		835
Dec	34	34	34	35	35	36	36	36	37	37	37	38	38	38	39	39	39	40	40	40	41	41	41	42	42	42	42	42	42	43	43	1202

NORWALK GAS PLANT, CT

Average Temperature in °F

	1	2	3	4	5	6	7	8	9	10	11	12	13	14	15	16	17	18	19	20	21	22	23	24	25	26	27	28	29	30	31	Month
Jan	29	29	29	29	29	28	28	28	28	28	28	28	28	28	28	28	27	27	27	27	27	27	27	27	27	27	27	28	28	28	28	27.8
Feb	28	28	28	28	28	28	28	29	29	29	29	29	29	30	30	30	30	31	31	31	31	32	32	32	32	33	33	33				30.0
Mar	34	34	34	35	35	35	36	36	36	36	37	37	37	38	38	39	39	40	40	40	40	41	41	41	42	42	42	43	43	43	44	38.6
Apr	44	44	45	45	45	46	46	46	47	47	47	48	48	48	49	49	49	50	50	50	51	51	51	52	52	52	53	53	53	53		48.8
May	54	54	54	54	55	55	55	56	56	56	57	57	57	58	58	58	59	59	59	60	60	60	60	61	61	61	62	62	63	63		58.3
Jun	64	64	64	65	65	65	66	66	66	66	67	67	67	68	68	68	68	69	69	69	70	70	70	70	70	71	71	71	71	72		67.9
Jul	72	72	72	72	72	73	73	73	73	73	73	73	73	73	74	74	74	74	74	74	74	71	74	74	74	74	74	74	74	74	74	73.4
Aug	74	74	74	73	73	73	73	73	73	73	73	73	72	72	72	72	72	72	72	71	71	71	71	70	70	70	70	70	69	69	69	71.7
Sep	69	68	68	68	67	67	67	67	66	66	66	65	65	65	64	64	63	63	63	62	62	62	61	61	60	60	59	59	59	58		63.8
Oct	58	57	57	56	56	56	55	55	54	54	54	53	53	52	52	52	51	51	51	50	50	50	49	49	49	49	48	48	48	48	47	52.0
Nov	47	47	47	46	46	46	45	45	45	45	44	44	44	43	43	43	43	42	42	42	41	41	40	40	40	39	39	39	38	38		42.8
Dec	38	37	37	37	36	36	35	35	35	34	34	34	34	33	33	33	32	32	32	32	31	31	31	31	30	30	30	30	30	29	29	32.9

Heating Degree Days in °F

	1	2	3	4	5	6	7	8	9	10	11	12	13	14	15	16	17	18	19	20	21	22	23	24	25	26	27	28	29	30	31	Month
Jan	36	36	36	36	37	37	37	37	37	37	37	37	37	37	37	37	38	38	38	38	38	38	38	38	38	37	37	37	37	37	37	1153
Feb	37	37	37	37	37	37	37	37	37	36	36	36	36	35	35	35	35	34	34	34	34	34	33	33	33	32	32	32				982
Mar	32	31	31	31	30	30	30	29	29	29	28	28	27	27	27	26	26	25	25	25	25	24	24	24	23	23	23	22	22	22	21	820
Apr	21	21	20	20	20	19	19	19	18	18	18	17	17	17	16	16	16	16	15	15	14	14	14	13	13	13	13	12	12	12		487
May	11	11	11	11	10	10	10	10	9	9	9	8	8	8	8	7	7	7	6	6	6	6	5	5	5	5	4	4	4	4	3	228
Jun	3	3	3	2	2	2	2	2	1	1	1	1	1	1	1	1	0	0	0	0	0	M	0	0	0	0	0	0	0	0		27
Jul	0	0	0	0	0	0	0	0	0	0	0	0	0	0	0	0	0	0	0	0	M	0	0	0	0	0	0	0	0	0	0	1
Aug	0	0	0	0	0	0	0	0	1	0	0	0	0	0	0	0	0	0	0	0	0	M	0	0	0	0	0	0	0	M	M	3
Sep	0	0	0	1	1	1	1	1	1	1	1	2	2	2	2	2	3	3	3	4	4	4	4	5	5	6	6	6	7	7		85
Oct	8	8	8	9	9	10	10	10	11	11	11	12	12	13	13	13	14	14	14	15	15	15	16	16	16	16	17	17	17	17	18	405
Nov	18	18	18	19	19	19	19	20	20	20	21	21	21	22	22	22	22	23	23	23	24	24	25	25	25	26	26	26	27	27		665
Dec	28	28	28	29	29	29	30	30	30	31	31	31	31	32	32	32	33	33	33	34	34	34	34	34	35	35	35	35	36	36	36	998

NORWICH PUBLIC UTILITY PLANT, CT

Average Temperature in °F

	1	2	3	4	5	6	7	8	9	10	11	12	13	14	15	16	17	18	19	20	21	22	23	24	25	26	27	28	29	30	31	Month
Jan	29	29	29	29	29	28	28	28	28	28	28	28	28	28	27	27	27	27	27	27	27	27	27	27	27	27	27	27	27	27	27	27.6
Feb	27	27	28	28	28	28	28	28	28	28	29	29	29	29	29	29	30	30	30	30	31	31	31	32	32	32	32	33				29.5
Mar	33	33	34	34	34	35	35	35	36	36	36	37	37	37	38	38	38	39	39	39	40	40	40	41	41	41	42	42	42	43	43	38.0
Apr	43	43	44	44	44	45	45	45	46	46	46	47	47	47	48	48	49	49	49	50	50	50	51	51	52	52	52	53	53	54		48.1
May	54	54	55	55	55	56	56	56	57	57	58	58	58	59	59	59	60	60	60	61	61	61	62	62	62	62	63	63	63	63	64	59.1
Jun	64	64	64	65	65	65	66	66	66	66	67	67	67	67	68	68	68	68	68	68	69	69	69	69	70	70	70	70	71	71		67.4
Jul	71	71	72	72	72	72	72	73	73	73	73	73	73	73	73	73	74	74	74	74	74	74	74	74	74	74	74	74	74	74	73	73.2
Aug	74	73	73	73	73	73	72	73	73	73	72	72	72	72	72	72	71	71	71	71	71	70	70	70	70	70	69	69	69	69	69	71.4
Sep	68	68	68	68	67	67	67	66	66	66	65	65	65	64	64	64	63	63	63	62	62	62	61	61	60	60	60	59	59	58		63.7
Oct	58	57	57	57	56	56	55	55	54	54	54	53	53	53	52	52	51	51	51	50	50	50	49	49	49	48	48	48	48	47	47	52.0
Nov	47	46	46	46	46	45	45	45	44	44	44	43	43	43	42	42	42	42	41	41	41	40	40	40	39	39	39	38	38	38		42.3
Dec	37	37	36	36	36	36	35	35	35	34	34	34	33	33	33	33	32	32	32	32	31	31	31	31	30	30	30	30	30	29	29	32.8

Heating Degree Days in °F

	1	2	3	4	5	6	7	8	9	10	11	12	13	14	15	16	17	18	19	20	21	22	23	24	25	26	27	28	29	30	31	Month
Jan	36	36	36	37	37	37	37	37	37	37	37	37	38	38	38	38	38	38	38	38	38	38	38	38	38	38	38	38	38	38	38	1162
Feb	38	38	38	37	37	37	37	37	37	37	37	36	36	36	36	35	35	35	35	35	34	34	34	33	33	33	33	32				994
Mar	32	32	31	31	31	30	30	30	29	29	29	28	28	28	27	27	27	26	26	26	25	25	25	24	24	24	23	23	23	22	22	837
Apr	22	22	21	21	21	20	20	20	19	19	19	18	18	18	18	17	16	16	16	15	15	15	14	14	13	13	13	12	12	12		508
May	11	11	10	10	10	9	9	9	8	8	8	7	7	7	7	6	6	6	5	5	5	5	4	4	4	4	4	3	3	3	3	201
Jun	3	2	2	2	2	2	2	2	2	1	1	1	1	1	1	1	1	1	1	1	0	0	0	0	0	0	0	0	0	0		30
Jul	M	M	2	2	2	1	0	0	0	1	1	0	0	1	0	1	1	1	1	1	0	0	0	0	0	0	0	0	0	0	0	2
Aug	0	0	0	0	0	0	0	0	0	0	0	0	0	0	0	0	0	0	0	1	0	0	0	0	0	0	0	0	0	0	0	3
Sep	1	1	1	1	1	1	1	1	1	1	2	2	2	2	2	3	3	3	3	4	4	4	5	5	5	6	6	6	7	7		91
Oct	8	8	8	9	9	10	10	10	11	11	11	12	12	13	13	13	14	14	14	15	15	15	16	16	16	16	17	17	17	18	18	406
Nov	18	19	19	19	19	20	20	20	21	21	21	22	22	22	23	23	23	24	24	24	24	25	25	25	26	26	26	27	27	28		683
Dec	28	28	29	29	29	30	30	30	30	31	31	31	32	32	32	32	33	33	33	33	34	34	34	34	35	35	35	35	36	36	36	999

SHEPAUG DAM, CT

Average Temperature in °F

	1	2	3	4	5	6	7	8	9	10	11	12	13	14	15	16	17	18	19	20	21	22	23	24	25	26	27	28	29	30	31	Month
Jan	24	24	24	24	24	24	23	23	23	23	23	23	23	23	23	23	23	22	22	22	22	22	22	22	22	22	22	23	23	23	23	22.9
Feb	23	23	23	23	23	23	24	24	24	24	24	24	24	25	25	25	25	25	26	26	26	27	27	27	27	28	28	28				25.0
Mar	29	29	29	30	30	30	31	31	31	32	32	32	33	33	33	34	34	34	35	35	35	36	36	36	37	37	37	38	38	39	39	33.7
Apr	39	39	40	40	40	41	41	42	42	42	43	3	43	44	44	45	45	45	46	46	46	47	47	48	48	48	49	49	50	50		44.4
May	50	51	51	52	52	53	53	53	54	54	54	55	55	55	56	56	56	57	57	57	58	58	58	58	59	59	59	60	60	60	60	55.8
Jun	60	61	61	61	61	62	62	62	62	63	63	63	63	64	64	64	64	64	64	65	65	65	65	66	66	66	67	67	67	67		63.7
Jul	67	67	67	68	68	68	69	68	68	68	68	68	69	69	69	69	69	69	67	67	66	65	65	66	69	69	69	69	69	69	69	68.6
Aug	69	69	69	69	69	69	69	68	68	68	68	68	68	68	67	67	67	67	67	67	66	66	66	66	66	65	65	65	65	64	64	67.1
Sep	64	64	63	63	63	63	62	62	62	61	61	61	60	60	60	59	59	59	59	58	58	57	57	57	56	56	56	55	55	55		59.5
Oct	54	54	53	53	53	52	52	52	51	51	51	50	50	49	49	49	49	48	48	48	47	47	47	46	46	46	45	45	45	45	44	49.0
Nov	44	44	44	44	43	43	42	42	42	42	41	41	40	40	40	39	39	39	38	38	38	37	37	37	36	36	35	34	34	34		39.4
Dec	34	33	33	32	32	32	31	31	30	30	30	29	29	29	28	28	28	27	27	27	27	26	26	26	26	25	25	25	25	25	25	28.5

Heating Degree Days in °F

	1	2	3	4	5	6	7	8	9	10	11	12	13	14	15	16	17	18	19	20	21	22	23	24	25	26	27	28	29	30	31	Month
Jan	41	41	41	41	41	41	42	42	42	42	42	42	42	42	42	42	42	43	43	43	43	43	43	43	43	43	42	42	42	42	42	1305
Feb	42	42	42	42	42	42	42	41	41	41	41	41	41	40	40	40	40	40	39	39	38	38	38	38	38	37	37	37				1120
Mar	36	36	36	35	35	35	34	34	34	33	33	33	32	32	32	31	31	31	30	30	30	29	29	29	28	28	28	28	27	27	26	971
Apr	26	26	25	25	25	24	24	23	23	23	22	22	22	21	21	20	20	20	19	19	19	18	18	17	17	17	16	16	15	15		617
May	14	14	14	13	13	13	12	12	11	11	11	10	10	10	9	9	9	8	8	8	7	7	7	7	7	6	6	6	6	5	5	289
Jun	5	5	5	4	4	4	4	4	4	3	3	3	3	3	3	3	2	2	2	2	2	2	2	1	1	2	2	1	1	1		84
Jul	1	1	1	1	1	1	1	1	1	1	1	1	1	1	1	1	1	1	1	1	1	1	1	1	0	0	0	0	0	0	0	24
Aug	0	0	0	0	0	0	0	1	1	1	1	1	1	1	1	1	1	1	1	1	1	1	1	1	0	0	0	0	0	0	2	33
Sep	2	3	3	3	3	3	4	4	4	4	5	5	5	5	5	6	6	6	6	7	7	7	8	8	8	9	9	10	10	10		174
Oct	11	11	11	12	12	13	13	13	14	14	14	15	15	16	16	16	17	17	17	17	18	18	18	19	19	19	20	20	20	20	21	496
Nov	21	21	21	22	22	23	23	23	23	24	24	24	25	25	25	26	26	26	27	27	27	28	28	29	29	29	30	31	31	31		769
Dec	31	32	32	33	33	33	34	34	35	35	35	36	36	36	37	37	37	37	38	38	38	39	39	39	39	40	40	40	40	40	40	1132

155

STAMFORD 5 N, CT

Average Temperature in °F

	1	2	3	4	5	6	7	8	9	10	11	12	13	14	15	16	17	18	19	20	21	22	23	24	25	26	27	28	29	30	31	Month
Jan	30	30	30	30	29	29	29	29	29	29	29	29	29	28	28	28	28	28	28	28	28	28	28	28	28	28	29	29	29	29	29	28.7
Feb	29	29	29	29	29	30	30	30	30	30	30	30	31	31	31	31	32	32	32	32	32	33	33	33	34	34	34	34				31.2
Mar	35	35	35	36	36	36	37	37	37	38	38	38	39	39	39	40	40	40	41	41	41	41	42	42	42	43	43	44	44	44	45	39.6
Apr	45	45	46	46	46	47	47	47	48	48	48	49	49	49	50	50	50	51	51	51	52	52	52	53	53	56	56	56	55	55		49.9
May	55	56	56	56	57	57	57	58	58	58	59	59	59	60	60	60	60	61	61	61	62	62	62	63	63	63	63	64	64	64	65	60.1
Jun	65	65	65	66	66	66	67	67	67	67	68	68	68	68	68	69	69	69	69	70	70	70	70	70	71	71	71	71	72	72		68.5
Jul	72	72	72	72	73	73	73	73	73	73	73	73	74	74	74	74	74	74	74	74	74	74	74	74	71	71	71	71	72	72	74	73.5
Aug	74	74	74	74	74	73	73	73	73	73	73	73	74	74	74	72	72	72	72	72	71	71	71	71	71	70	70	70	70	69	69	72.0
Sep	69	69	68	68	68	68	67	67	67	66	66	66	65	65	65	64	64	64	63	63	63	62	62	62	61	61	60	60	60	59		64.4
Oct	59	58	58	58	57	57	56	56	56	55	55	54	54	54	53	53	53	52	52	52	51	51	51	50	50	50	49	49	49	49	48	53.2
Nov	48	48	47	47	47	46	46	46	46	45	45	45	44	44	44	43	43	43	42	42	42	41	41	41	40	40	40	39	39	38		43.4
Dec	38	38	37	37	37	36	36	36	36	35	35	35	34	34	34	33	33	33	33	32	32	32	32	32	31	31	31	31	31	30	30	33.7

Heating Degree Days in °F

	1	2	3	4	5	6	7	8	9	10	11	12	13	14	15	16	17	18	19	20	21	22	23	24	25	26	27	28	29	30	31	Month
Jan	35	35	35	36	36	36	36	36	36	36	36	36	36	36	37	37	37	37	37	37	37	37	37	37	37	37	36	36	36	36	36	1125
Feb	36	36	36	36	36	36	36	35	35	35	35	36	36	34	34	34	34	33	33	33	33	32	32	32	31	31	31	31				948
Mar	30	30	30	29	29	29	28	28	28	27	27	27	26	26	26	25	25	25	25	24	24	24	23	23	23	22	22	21	21	21	20	788
Apr	20	20	19	19	19	18	18	18	17	17	17	16	16	16	15	15	15	14	14	14	13	13	13	12	12	12	11	11	11	10		455
May	10	10	9	9	9	8	8	8	7	7	7	6	6	6	6	5	5	5	5	5	4	4	4	4	3	3	3	3	3	3	2	176
Jun	2	2	2	2	2	2	2	1	1	1	1	1	1	1	1	1	1	1	0	0	0	0	0	0	0	0	0	0	0	0		24
Jul	0	0	0	0	0	0	0	0	0	1	0	0	0	1	1	0	0	0	0	0	0	0	0	0	0	0	0	0	0	0	0	1
Aug	0	0	0	0	0	0	0	0	0	1	0	0	0	1	1	0	0	0	0	0	0	0	0	0	0	0	0	0	M	M	M	3
Sep	0	0	0	0	1	1	1	1	1	1	1	1	1	2	2	2	2	3	3	3	3	4	4	4	4	5	5	5	6	6		72
Oct	7	7	7	8	8	9	9	9	10	10	10	11	11	11	12	12	12	13	13	13	14	14	14	15	15	15	16	16	16	16	17	370
Nov	17	17	18	18	18	19	19	19	19	20	20	20	21	21	21	22	22	22	23	23	23	24	24	24	25	25	26	26	27	27		648
Dec	27	27	28	28	28	29	29	29	29	30	30	30	31	31	31	32	32	32	32	33	33	33	33	33	34	34	34	34	35	35	35	972

STORRS, CT

Average Temperature in °F

	1	2	3	4	5	6	7	8	9	10	11	12	13	14	15	16	17	18	19	20	21	22	23	24	25	26	27	28	29	30	31	Month
Jan	27	27	27	26	26	26	26	26	26	26	26	26	26	25	25	25	25	25	25	25	25	25	25	25	25	25	25	25	25	25	25	25.5
Feb	25	26	26	26	26	26	26	26	26	27	27	27	27	27	28	28	28	28	28	29	29	29	29	30	30	30	31	31				27.7
Mar	31	32	33	32	33	33	33	34	34	34	35	35	35	36	36	36	37	37	37	38	38	38	39	39	39	40	40	40	40	41	41	36.3
Apr	42	42	42	42	43	43	43	44	44	45	45	45	46	46	46	47	47	47	48	48	48	49	49	49	50	50	51	51	51	52		46.5
May	52	52	53	53	54	54	54	55	55	55	56	56	56	57	57	57	58	58	58	58	59	59	59	60	60	60	60	61	61	61	62	57.1
Jun	62	62	62	63	63	63	63	64	64	64	64	64	65	65	65	65	66	66	66	66	66	67	67	67	67	68	68	68	68	68		65.2
Jul	68	69	69	69	69	69	70	70	70	70	70	70	70	70	70	71	71	71	71	71	71	71	71	71	71	71	71	71	71	71	71	70.3
Aug	71	71	70	70	70	70	70	70	70	70	69	69	69	69	69	69	69	69	68	68	68	68	68	67	67	67	67	66	66	66	66	68.6
Sep	65	65	65	65	65	64	64	64	63	63	63	62	62	62	62	61	61	61	60	60	60	59	59	59	58	58	57	57	57	56		61.2
Oct	56	56	56	55	54	54	54	53	53	53	52	52	52	51	51	51	50	50	50	49	49	49	48	48	48	48	47	47	47	47	46	50.8
Nov	46	46	45	45	45	45	44	44	44	43	43	43	42	42	42	41	41	41	40	40	40	39	39	39	38	38	37	37	37	36		41.4
Dec	36	35	35	35	34	34	34	33	33	32	32	32	32	31	31	31	30	30	30	29	29	29	29	29	28	28	28	28	27	27	27	30.9

Heating Degree Days in °F

	1	2	3	4	5	6	7	8	9	10	11	12	13	14	15	16	17	18	19	20	21	22	23	24	25	26	27	28	29	30	31	Month
Jan	38	38	38	39	39	39	39	39	39	39	40	40	40	40	40	40	40	40	40	40	40	40	40	40	40	40	40	40	40	40	40	1227
Feb	40	40	39	39	39	39	39	39	39	38	38	38	38	38	38	37	37	37	37	36	36	36	36	35	35	35	34	34				1047
Mar	34	33	33	33	32	32	32	31	31	31	30	30	30	29	29	29	28	28	28	27	27	27	26	26	26	25	25	25	25	24	24	890
Apr	23	23	23	23	22	22	22	21	21	21	20	20	20	19	19	18	18	18	17	17	17	16	16	16	15	15	14	14	14	13		557
May	13	13	12	12	12	11	11	10	10	10	9	9	9	9	8	8	8	8	7	7	7	6	6	6	6	5	5	5	5	4	4	254
Jun	4	4	4	3	3	3	3	3	3	3	2	2	2	2	2	2	2	1	1	1	1	1	1	1	1	1	1	0	0	0		60
Jul	1	1	1	1	1	0	0	0	0	0	0	0	0	0	0	0	0	0	0	0	0	0	0	0	0	0	0	0	0	0	0	5
Aug	0	0	0	0	1	0	0	0	0	0	0	0	0	0	0	0	0	0	1	1	1	0	0	0	1	0	1	0	0	0	2	15
Sep	2	2	2	2	2	2	2	3	3	3	3	3	4	4	4	4	4	5	5	5	6	6	6	7	7	7	8	8	8	9		136
Oct	9	10	10	10	11	11	11	12	12	12	13	13	13	14	14	14	15	15	15	16	16	16	17	17	17	17	18	18	18	19	19	442
Nov	19	19	20	20	20	21	21	21	21	22	22	22	23	23	23	24	24	24	25	25	25	26	26	26	27	27	28	28	28	29		709
Dec	29	30	30	30	31	31	31	32	32	33	33	33	34	34	34	34	35	35	35	36	36	36	36	37	37	37	37	37	38	38	38	1059

WEST THOMPSON LAKE, CT

Average Temperature in °F

	1	2	3	4	5	6	7	8	9	10	11	12	13	14	15	16	17	18	19	20	21	22	23	24	25	26	27	28	29	30	31	Month
Jan	25	25	25	25	25	25	24	24	24	24	24	24	24	24	24	24	24	24	24	23	23	23	23	23	23	24	24	24	24	24	24	24.0
Feb	24	24	24	24	24	24	25	25	25	25	25	25	26	26	26	26	26	27	27	27	28	28	28	28	29	29	29	30				26.2
Mar	30	30	31	31	32	32	32	33	33	33	34	34	34	35	35	35	36	36	36	37	37	37	38	38	38	39	39	39	40	40	40	35.3
Apr	41	41	41	41	42	42	42	43	43	43	44	44	45	45	45	46	46	46	47	47	47	48	48	48	49	49	50	50	50	51		45.5
May	51	52	52	52	53	53	53	54	54	54	55	55	56	56	56	57	57	57	57	58	58	58	59	59	59	60	60	60	61	61	61	56.4
Jun	61	62	62	62	62	63	63	63	63	64	64	64	65	65	65	65	65	66	66	66	66	67	67	67	67	68	68	68	68	68		65.0
Jul	69	69	69	69	69	69	70	70	70	70	70	70	70	70	71	71	71	71	71	71	71	71	71	71	71	71	71	71	71	71	71	70.4
Aug	71	71	71	71	71	70	70	70	70	70	70	70	70	69	69	69	69	69	69	68	68	68	68	67	67	68	67	66	66	66	66	68.8
Sep	65	65	65	65	64	64	64	63	63	63	62	62	62	61	61	60	60	60	59	59	59	58	58	57	57	57	56	56	55	55		60.5
Oct	54	54	54	53	53	52	52	52	51	51	50	50	50	49	49	49	48	48	48	47	47	47	47	46	46	46	46	45	45	45	45	49.0
Nov	44	44	44	44	44	43	43	43	43	42	42	42	41	41	41	41	40	40	40	39	39	38	38	38	37	37	37	36	36	35		40.0
Dec	35	34	34	33	33	33	32	32	32	31	31	31	30	30	30	29	29	29	28	28	28	28	27	27	27	27	26	26	26	26	26	29.6

Heating Degree Days in °F

	1	2	3	4	5	6	7	8	9	10	11	12	13	14	15	16	17	18	19	20	21	22	23	24	25	26	27	28	29	30	31	Month
Jan	40	40	40	40	40	40	41	41	40	41	40	41	41	41	41	41	41	41	41	42	42	42	42	42	42	42	41	41	41	41	41	1272
Feb	41	41	41	41	41	41	41	40	40	40	40	40	40	39	39	39	39	38	38	38	38	37	37	37	36	36	36	35				1089
Mar	35	35	34	34	34	33	33	33	32	32	31	31	31	30	30	30	29	29	29	28	28	28	27	27	27	26	26	26	25	25	25	923
Apr	24	24	24	24	23	23	23	22	22	22	21	21	21	20	20	19	19	19	18	18	18	17	17	17	16	16	15	15	15	14		587
May	14	13	13	13	12	12	12	11	11	10	10	10	9	9	9	9	8	8	8	7	7	7	7	6	6	6	5	5	5	5	5	272
Jun	4	4	4	4	4	3	3	3	3	3	2	2	2	2	2	2	2	2	1	1	1	1	1	1	1	1	1	1	1	1		63
Jul	1	1	1	1	1	1	1	1	0	0	0	0	0	0	0	0	0	0	0	0	0	0	0	0	0	0	0	0	0	0	0	8
Aug	0	0	0	0	0	0	0	0	0	0	0	0	0	0	0	1	1	1	1	1	1	1	1	1	1	1	1	1	1	2	2	18
Sep	2	2	2	2	2	3	3	3	3	3	4	4	4	4	4	5	5	5	6	6	6	7	7	7	8	8	9	9	10	10		151
Oct	10	11	11	12	12	13	13	13	14	14	15	15	15	16	16	16	17	17	17	18	18	18	18	19	19	19	20	20	20	20	20	496
Nov	21	21	21	21	21	22	22	22	22	23	23	23	24	24	24	24	25	25	25	26	26	27	27	27	28	28	29	29	29	30		739
Dec	30	31	31	32	32	32	33	33	33	34	34	34	35	35	35	36	36	36	37	37	37	37	38	38	38	38	39	39	39	39	39	1099

WIGWAM RESERVOIR, CT

Average Temperature in °F

	1	2	3	4	5	6	7	8	9	10	11	12	13	14	15	16	17	18	19	20	21	22	23	24	25	26	27	28	29	30	31	Month
Jan	25	25	24	24	24	24	24	24	24	24	23	23	23	23	23	23	23	23	23	23	23	23	23	23	23	23	23	23	23	23	23	23.4
Feb	23	23	23	23	23	23	24	24	24	24	24	24	25	25	25	25	25	26	26	26	27	27	27	28	28	28	28	29	29			25.3
Mar	29	30	30	31	31	31	32	32	33	33	33	34	34	34	35	35	35	36	36	36	37	37	37	38	38	38	39	39	39	40	40	34.9
Apr	40	41	41	41	41	42	42	42	43	43	43	44	44	45	45	45	46	46	46	47	47	47	48	48	49	49	50	50	50	51		45.2
May	51	52	52	52	53	53	54	54	54	55	55	56	56	56	57	57	57	58	58	58	59	59	59	59	60	60	60	61	61	61	61	56.7
Jun	62	62	62	62	63	63	63	64	64	64	64	65	65	65	65	65	66	66	66	66	67	67	67	67	68	68	68	68	68	69		65.3
Jul	69	69	69	70	70	70	70	70	70	70	70	71	71	71	71	71	71	71	71	71	71	71	71	71	71	71	71	71	71	71	71	70.5
Aug	71	71	70	70	70	70	70	70	70	69	69	69	69	69	69	69	68	68	68	68	68	67	67	67	68	68	66	66	66	66	65	68.4
Sep	65	65	65	65	64	64	64	63	63	63	62	62	62	61	61	61	60	60	60	59	59	59	58	58	57	57	57	56	56	55		60.7
Oct	55	54	54	54	53	53	52	52	52	51	51	50	50	50	49	49	49	48	48	47	47	47	46	46	46	46	45	45	45	44	44	49.1
Nov	44	44	43	43	43	42	42	42	41	41	41	41	40	40	40	39	39	38	38	38	37	37	37	36	36	36	35	35	34	34		39.2
Dec	34	33	33	33	32	32	31	31	31	30	30	30	30	29	29	29	28	28	28	28	27	27	27	27	26	26	26	26	25	25	25	28.9

Heating Degree Days in °F

	1	2	3	4	5	6	7	8	9	10	11	12	13	14	15	16	17	18	19	20	21	22	23	24	25	26	27	28	29	30	31	Month
Jan	40	40	41	41	41	41	41	41	41	42	42	42	42	42	42	42	42	42	42	42	42	42	42	42	42	42	42	42	42	42	42	1292
Feb	42	42	42	42	42	41	42	41	41	41	41	41	40	40	40	40	40	39	39	39	38	38	38	37	37	37	36	36				1113
Mar	36	35	35	34	34	34	33	33	33	32	32	32	31	31	30	30	30	29	29	29	28	28	28	27	27	27	26	26	26	26	25	936
Apr	25	25	24	24	24	23	23	23	22	22	22	21	21	21	20	20	19	19	19	18	18	18	17	17	16	16	16	15	15	14		596
May	14	13	13	13	12	12	11	11	11	10	10	10	9	9	9	8	8	8	7	7	7	6	6	6	6	5	5	5	5	5	4	265
Jun	4	4	4	3	3	3	3	3	3	3	2	2	2	2	2	2	2	2	1	1	1	1	1	0	0	1	1	1	1	1		62
Jul	1	1	1	1	1	1	0	1	0	0	0	0	0	0	0	0	0	0	0	0	1	0	0	0	0	0	0	0	0	0	0	8
Aug	0	0	0	0	0	0	0	0	0	0	0	0	0	0	0	0	0	1	0	1	0	0	1	0	0	1	1	1	1	0	2	15
Sep	2	2	2	2	2	2	3	3	3	3	3	4	4	4	4	4	5	5	6	6	6	7	7	7	8	8	9	9	9	10		150
Oct	10	11	11	11	12	12	13	13	14	14	14	15	15	15	16	16	16	17	17	18	18	18	19	19	19	19	20	20	20	21	21	494
Nov	21	21	22	22	22	23	23	23	24	24	24	25	25	25	25	26	26	26	27	27	28	28	28	29	29	29	30	30	31	31		774
Dec	31	32	32	32	33	33	34	34	34	35	35	35	36	36	36	36	37	37	37	37	38	38	38	38	39	39	39	40	40	40	40	1120

APPENDIX C
Daily/Monthly Station Normals 1971–2000
Cooling Degree Days/Total Precipitation*

FALLS VILLAGE, CT

Cooling Degree Days in °F

	1	2	3	4	5	6	7	8	9	10	11	12	13	14	15	16	17	18	19	20	21	22	23	24	25	26	27	28	29	30	31	Month
Jan	0	0	0	0	0	0	0	0	0	0	0	0	0	0	0	0	0	0	0	0	0	0	0	0	0	0	0	0	0	0	0	0
Feb	0	0	0	0	0	0	0	0	0	0	0	0	0	0	0	0	0	0	0	0	0	0	0	0	0	0	0	0				0
Mar	0	0	0	0	0	0	0	0	0	0	0	0	0	0	0	0	0	0	0	0	0	0	0	0	0	0	0	0	0	0	0	0
Apr	0	0	0	0	0	0	0	0	0	0	0	0	0	0	0	0	0	0	0	0	0	0	0	0	0	0	0	0	0	0		0
May	0	0	0	0	0	0	0	0	0	0	0	0	0	0	0	1	1	1	1	1	1	1	1	1	1	1	1	1	1	1	1	16
Jun	1	1	1	1	1	2	2	2	2	2	2	2	2	2	2	3	3	3	3	3	3	3	3	4	4	4	4	4	4	4		77
Jul	5	5	5	5	5	6	6	6	6	6	6	6	6	6	6	6	6	6	6	6	6	6	6	6	6	6	6	6	6	6	6	180
Aug	6	6	6	6	6	6	6	6	5	5	5	5	5	5	5	5	4	4	4	4	4	4	4	3	3	3	3	3	3	3	3	140
Sep	2	2	2	2	2	2	2	1	1	1	1	1	1	1	1	1	1	0	0	0	0	0	0	0	0	0	0	0	0	0		24
Oct	0	0	0	0	0	0	0	0	0	0	0	0	0	0	0	0	1	0	M	0	0	0	0	0	0	0	0	0	0	0	0	1
Nov	0	0	0	0	0	0	0	0	0	0	0	0	0	0	0	0	0	0	0	0	0	0	0	0	0	0	0	0	0	0		0
Dec	0	0	0	0	0	0	0	0	0	0	0	0	0	0	0	0	0	0	0	0	0	0	0	0	0	0	0	0	0	0	0	0

Total Precipitation (hundredths of an inch; months in inches)

	1	2	3	4	5	6	7	8	9	10	11	12	13	14	15	16	17	18	19	20	21	22	23	24	25	26	27	28	29	30	31	Month
Jan	11	11	12	12	12	12	12	12	12	12	12	12	12	12	12	12	12	12	11	11	11	11	11	11	11	11	11	11	10	10	10	3.54
Feb	10	10	10	10	10	10	10	9	9	9	9	9	9	9	9	9	9	9	9	9	9	10	10	10	10	10	10	10				2.66
Mar	10	11	11	11	11	11	11	11	11	12	12	12	12	12	12	12	12	12	12	12	12	12	12	12	12	12	12	12	12	13	13	3.62
Apr	12	12	12	12	12	12	13	13	12	12	12	12	12	13	13	13	13	13	13	13	13	13	13	13	13	13	13	13	13	13		3.77
May	13	13	13	13	13	13	13	13	13	14	14	14	14	13	13	13	13	13	13	13	13	13	13	13	13	14	14	14	14	14	14	4.26
Jun	14	14	14	14	14	14	14	14	14	14	14	14	14	14	14	14	14	14	14	14	14	14	14	15	15	14	14	14	14	14		4.17
Jul	14	14	14	14	14	14	14	14	14	14	14	14	14	14	14	14	14	14	14	14	14	15	15	15	15	14	14	14	14	14	14	4.41
Aug	15	15	15	14	14	14	14	14	14	14	14	14	14	14	14	14	14	14	14	14	14	14	14	15	14	14	14	14	14	14	14	4.37
Sep	14	14	14	14	14	14	14	13	13	13	13	13	13	13	13	13	13	13	13	13	13	13	13	13	13	13	13	13	13	13		3.98
Oct	13	13	13	13	13	12	13	12	13	13	13	13	13	13	13	13	12	12	12	12	12	12	12	12	12	12	12	12	13	13	13	3.81
Nov	12	12	12	12	12	12	12	13	13	13	13	13	13	13	13	13	13	12	12	12	12	11	11	11	12	12	12	12	12	12		3.74
Dec	12	12	12	12	12	12	11	11	11	11	11	11	11	11	12	11	11	12	11	11	11	11	11	11	11	12	12	12	11	12	12	3.49

*All information in Appendix C provided by the National Climatic Data Center-NOAA.

GROTON, CT

Cooling Degree Days in °F

	1	2	3	4	5	6	7	8	9	10	11	12	13	14	15	16	17	18	19	20	21	22	23	24	25	26	27	28	29	30	31	Month
Jan	0	0	0	0	0	0	0	0	0	0	0	0	0	0	0	0	0	0	0	0	0	0	0	0	0	0	0	0	0	0	0	0
Feb	0	0	0	0	0	0	0	0	0	0	0	0	0	0	0	0	0	0	0	0	0	0	0	0	0	0	0	0				0
Mar	0	0	0	0	0	0	0	0	0	0	0	0	0	0	0	0	0	0	0	0	0	0	0	0	0	0	0	0	0	0	0	0
Apr	0	0	0	0	0	0	0	0	0	0	0	0	0	0	0	0	0	0	0	0	0	0	0	0	0	0	0	0	0	0		0
May	0	0	0	0	0	0	0	0	0	0	0	0	0	0	0	0	0	0	0	0	0	0	0	0	0	1	1	1	1	1	1	6
Jun	1	1	1	1	1	1	1	1	1	1	1	1	2	2	2	2	2	2	2	3	3	3	3	3	3	4	4	4	4	4		64
Jul	5	5	5	5	6	6	6	6	6	6	7	7	7	7	7	7	7	7	7	7	7	8	8	8	8	8	8	8	8	8	8	213
Aug	8	8	7	7	7	7	7	7	7	7	7	7	7	6	6	6	6	6	6	6	6	5	5	5	5	5	4	4	4	4	4	186
Sep	3	3	3	3	3	3	2	2	2	2	2	2	1	1	1	1	1	1	1	1	1	1	0	0	0	0	0	0	0	0		40
Oct	M	M	0	0	0	0	0	0	0	0	0	0	0	0	0	0	0	0	0	0	0	0	0	0	0	0	0	0	0	0	0	0
Nov	0	0	0	0	0	0	0	0	0	0	0	0	0	0	0	0	0	0	0	0	0	0	0	0	0	0	0	0	0	0		0
Dec	0	0	0	0	0	0	0	0	0	0	0	0	0	0	0	0	0	0	0	0	0	0	0	0	0	0	0	0	0	0	0	0

Total Precipitation (hundredths of an inch; months in inches)

	1	2	3	4	5	6	7	8	9	10	11	12	13	14	15	16	17	18	19	20	21	22	23	24	25	26	27	28	29	30	31	Month
Jan	14	14	14	14	14	14	14	14	15	15	15	15	15	15	15	14	14	14	14	14	14	14	14	14	14	14	14	14	14	13	13	4.39
Feb	13	13	13	13	13	13	13	13	13	15	15	15	15	12	12	12	12	12	14	14	14	14	14	14	14	13	13	13				3.54
Mar	13	13	13	13	13	13	14	13	13	12	12	12	12	12	12	12	12	12	12	13	13	13	13	13	13	13	13	13	15	15	15	4.46
Apr	15	15	15	15	14	14	15	14	14	14	14	14	14	14	14	14	14	14	14	14	14	14	14	14	13	13	13	13	13	13		4.23
May	13	13	13	13	13	13	13	12	12	12	12	12	12	12	12	12	12	12	12	12	12	12	12	12	12	12	12	12	12	12	12	3.79
Jun	12	12	12	13	13	13	13	13	13	13	12	13	13	13	13	13	13	13	12	12	12	12	12	12	12	11	11	11	11	11		3.67
Jul	11	11	11	11	11	10	10	10	10	10	10	10	10	10	10	10	10	10	10	11	11	11	11	11	11	11	11	12	11	11	12	3.31
Aug	12	13	13	13	13	14	14	14	14	14	14	14	15	15	15	15	15	15	15	15	15	15	15	15	15	13	13	13	13	13	13	4.46
Sep	15	15	15	15	15	14	14	14	14	14	14	15	15	13	13	13	13	13	13	13	13	13	13	13	13	13	13	13	13	13		4.06
Oct	13	13	14	12	12	12	12	12	12	12	14	14	14	14	14	13	13	13	13	15	14	14	14	14	13	13	14	14	14	14	14	3.98
Nov	14	14	15	15	15	15	15	15	15	15	15	15	15	14	14	14	15	16	16	15	15	14	15	15	15	15	15	15	15	15		4.51
Dec	14	14	14	14	14	14	14	14	14	14	14	14	14	14	14	14	14	14	13	14	14	14	14	14	14	14	14	14	14	14	14	4.32

HARTFORD BRADLEY INTERNATIONAL AIRPORT, CT

Cooling Degree Days in °F

	1	2	3	4	5	6	7	8	9	10	11	12	13	14	15	16	17	18	19	20	21	22	23	24	25	26	27	28	29	30	31	Month
Jan	0	0	0	0	0	0	0	0	0	0	0	0	0	0	0	0	0	0	0	0	0	0	0	0	0	0	0	0	0	0	0	0
Feb	0	0	0	0	0	0	0	0	0	0	0	0	0	0	0	0	0	0	0	0	0	0	0	0	0	0	0	0	0			0
Mar	0	0	0	0	0	0	0	0	0	0	0	0	0	0	0	0	0	0	0	0	0	0	0	0	0	0	0	0	0	0	M	1
Apr	0	0	0	0	0	0	0	0	0	0	0	0	0	0	0	0	0	0	0	0	0	0	0	0	0	M	M	M	M	M		5
May	0	0	0	0	1	1	1	1	1	1	1	1	1	1	1	1	1	1	1	1	1	2	2	2	2	2	2	2	2	2	3	38
Jun	3	3	3	3	3	3	3	4	4	4	4	4	4	4	5	5	5	5	5	5	6	6	6	6	6	7	7	7	7	7		144
Jul	8	8	8	8	8	9	9	9	9	9	9	9	9	9	9	9	9	9	10	10	10	10	10	9	9	9	9	9	9	9	9	277
Aug	9	9	9	9	9	8	8	8	8	8	8	8	9	8	7	7	7	7	7	7	6	6	6	6	6	6	5	5	5	5	5	220
Sep	4	4	4	4	4	4	3	3	3	3	3	3	2	2	2	2	2	2	2	2	1	1	1	1	0	1	1	1	1	1		68
Oct	1	1	1	1	1	0	0	0	0	0	0	0	0	0	0	0	0	0	0	0	0	0	0	0	0	0	0	0	0	0	0	5
Nov	0	0	0	0	0	0	0	0	0	0	0	0	0	0	0	0	0	0	0	0	M	0	0	0	0	0	0	0	0	0		1
Dec	0	0	0	0	0	0	0	0	0	0	0	0	0	0	0	0	0	0	0	0	0	0	0	0	0	0	0	0	0	0	0	0

Total Precipitation (hundredths of an inch; months in inches)

	1	2	3	4	5	6	7	8	9	10	11	12	13	14	15	16	17	18	19	20	21	22	23	24	25	26	27	28	29	30	31	Month
Jan	12	12	12	12	12	12	13	13	13	13	13	13	13	13	13	13	13	13	13	13	12	12	12	12	12	12	12	12	12	11	11	3.84
Feb	11	11	11	11	11	11	11	11	10	10	10	10	10	10	10	10	10	10	10	10	11	11	11	11	11	11	11	11	12			2.96
Mar	11	11	11	11	11	11	12	11	10	10	10	10	10	10	10	10	10	10	10	10	13	13	13	13	13	13	13	13	13	13	13	3.88
Apr	13	13	13	13	13	13	13	13	13	13	13	13	13	13	13	13	13	13	13	13	13	13	13	13	13	13	13	13	13	13		3.86
May	14	14	14	14	14	14	14	14	14	14	14	14	14	14	15	15	15	15	15	14	14	14	14	14	14	14	14	14	14	14	14	4.39
Jun	14	14	14	14	14	13	13	13	13	13	13	13	13	13	13	13	13	13	13	13	12	12	12	12	12	12	12	12	12	12		3.85
Jul	12	12	12	12	12	12	12	12	12	12	12	12	11	11	11	11	11	12	12	12	12	12	12	12	12	12	12	12	12	12	12	3.67
Aug	12	12	12	12	12	12	12	12	12	13	13	13	13	13	13	13	13	13	13	14	13	13	13	13	13	13	13	13	14	14	14	3.98
Sep	14	14	14	14	14	14	14	14	14	14	14	14	14	14	14	14	14	14	14	14	14	14	14	14	13	13	13	13	14	14		4.13
Oct	13	13	13	13	13	13	13	13	13	13	13	13	12	12	12	12	12	12	12	13	13	13	13	13	13	13	13	13	13	13	13	3.94
Nov	13	13	13	13	14	14	14	14	14	14	14	14	14	14	14	14	14	14	14	14	13	13	13	13	13	13	13	13	13	13		4.06
Dec	13	12	12	12	12	12	12	12	12	12	12	11	11	11	12	12	11	11	11	11	11	11	11	11	12	12	12	12	12	12	12	3.60

HARTFORD BRAINARD FIELD, CT

Cooling Degree Days in °F

	1	2	3	4	5	6	7	8	9	10	11	12	13	14	15	16	17	18	19	20	21	22	23	24	25	26	27	28	29	30	31	Month
Jan	0	0	0	0	0	0	0	0	0	0	0	0	0	0	0	0	0	0	0	0	0	0	0	0	0	0	0	0	0	0	0	0
Feb	0	0	0	0	0	0	0	0	0	0	0	0	0	0	0	0	0	0	0	0	0	0	0	0	0	0	0	0	0			0
Mar	0	0	0	0	0	0	0	0	0	0	0	0	0	0	0	0	0	0	0	0	0	0	0	0	0	0	0	0	0	0	0	0
Apr	0	0	0	0	0	0	0	0	0	0	0	0	0	0	0	0	0	0	0	0	0	0	0	0	0	0	0	0	0	0		0
May	0	0	0	0	0	0	0	0	0	0	0	0	0	1	1	1	1	1	1	1	1	1	1	1	1	1	1	2	2	2	2	22
Jun	2	2	2	2	2	3	3	3	3	3	3	3	4	4	4	4	4	4	5	5	5	5	5	5	6	6	6	6	6	7		122
Jul	7	7	7	8	8	8	8	8	8	8	9	9	9	9	9	9	9	9	9	9	9	9	9	9	9	9	9	9	9	9	9	266
Aug	9	9	9	9	9	8	8	8	8	8	8	7	7	7	7	7	7	6	6	6	6	6	6	5	5	5	4	4	4	4	4	206
Sep	4	3	3	3	3	2	2	2	2	2	1	1	1	1	1	1	1	1	1	1	0	0	0	0	0	0	0	0	0	0		36
Oct	0	0	0	0	0	0	0	0	0	0	0	0	0	1	1	0	M	M	0	0	0	0	0	0	0	0	0	0	0	0	0	2
Nov	0	0	0	0	0	0	0	0	0	0	0	0	0	0	0	0	0	0	0	0	0	0	0	0	0	0	0	0	0	0		0
Dec	0	0	0	0	0	0	0	0	0	0	0	0	0	0	0	0	0	0	0	0	0	0	0	0	0	0	0	0	0	0	0	0

Total Precipitation (hundredths of an inch; months in inches)

	1	2	3	4	5	6	7	8	9	10	11	12	13	14	15	16	17	18	19	20	21	22	23	24	25	26	27	28	29	30	31	Month
Jan	12	12	12	12	12	12	12	12	12	12	12	12	12	12	12	12	12	12	12	12	12	12	12	12	12	11	11	11	11	11	11	3.66
Feb	10	10	10	10	10	10	10	10	10	10	9	9	9	9	9	9	9	9	9	9	9	9	9	9	9	10	10	10				2.65
Mar	10	10	10	10	10	10	11	11	11	11	11	11	12	12	12	12	12	12	12	12	12	12	12	12	13	13	13	13	13	13	13	3.61
Apr	12	12	12	12	12	12	12	12	13	13	13	13	13	13	13	13	13	13	13	13	13	13	13	13	13	13	13	13	13	13		3.82
May	13	13	13	13	13	13	13	13	13	13	13	13	13	13	13	13	13	13	13	13	13	13	13	13	13	13	13	12	12	12	12	3.99
Jun	13	13	13	13	13	13	13	13	13	13	13	13	13	13	13	13	13	13	13	13	13	13	13	12	12	12	12	12	12	12		3.83
Jul	13	13	13	13	13	13	13	13	13	13	13	13	13	13	13	13	13	13	13	13	13	12	12	12	12	12	12	12	12	12	12	3.93
Aug	13	13	13	13	13	13	13	13	13	13	13	12	12	12	12	12	12	12	12	12	12	12	12	12	12	12	12	12	12	12	12	3.83
Sep	12	13	12	12	12	12	12	13	13	13	13	13	13	13	13	13	13	13	13	13	13	13	13	13	13	13	13	13	13	13		3.83
Oct	13	13	13	13	13	13	13	13	13	13	13	13	12	12	12	13	13	13	13	13	13	13	13	13	13	13	12	12	12	13	13	3.91
Nov	13	13	13	13	13	13	13	13	11	13	13	13	13	13	13	13	13	13	13	12	12	12	12	12	12	12	12	12	11	11		3.79
Dec	12	12	11	11	11	11	11	11	11	11	11	11	11	11	11	11	11	11	11	11	11	11	11	11	11	11	11	11	11	11	12	3.44

MANSFIELD HOLLOW LAKE, CT

Cooling Degree Days in °F

	1	2	3	4	5	6	7	8	9	10	11	12	13	14	15	16	17	18	19	20	21	22	23	24	25	26	27	28	29	30	31	Month
Jan	0	0	0	0	0	0	0	0	0	0	0	0	0	0	0	0	0	0	0	0	0	0	0	0	0	0	0	0	0	0	0	0
Feb	0	0	0	0	0	0	0	0	0	0	0	0	0	0	0	0	0	0	0	0	0	0	0	0	0	0	0	0	0			0
Mar	0	0	0	0	0	0	0	0	0	0	0	0	0	0	0	0	0	0	0	0	0	0	0	0	0	0	0	0	0	0	0	0
Apr	0	0	0	0	0	0	0	0	0	0	0	0	0	0	0	0	0	0	0	0	0	0	0	0	0	0	0	0	0	0		0
May	0	0	0	0	0	0	0	0	0	0	0	0	0	0	0	0	0	0	0	0	0	0	0	0	1	1	1	1	1	1	1	7
Jun	1	1	1	1	1	1	1	1	1	2	2	2	2	2	2	2	2	2	2	3	3	3	3	3	3	3	3	4	4	4		65
Jul	4	4	4	5	5	5	5	5	5	5	5	5	5	5	5	6	6	6	6	6	6	6	6	6	6	6	6	6	6	5	5	164
Aug	5	5	5	5	5	5	5	5	5	5	5	5	5	5	4	4	4	4	4	4	4	3	3	3	3	3	3	3	2	2	2	124
Sep	2	2	2	2	1	1	1	1	1	1	1	1	0	0	0	0	0	0	0	0	0	0	0	0	0	0	0	0	0	0		16
Oct	0	0	0	0	0	0	0	0	0	0	0	0	0	0	0	0	0	0	0	0	0	0	0	0	0	0	0	0	0	0	0	0
Nov	0	0	0	0	0	0	0	0	0	0	0	0	0	0	0	0	0	0	0	0	0	0	0	0	0	0	0	0	0	0		0
Dec	0	0	0	0	0	0	0	0	0	0	0	0	0	0	0	0	0	0	0	0	0	0	0	0	0	0	0	0	0	0	0	0

Total Precipitation (hundredths of an inch; months in inches)

	1	2	3	4	5	6	7	8	9	10	11	12	13	14	15	16	17	18	19	20	21	22	23	24	25	26	27	28	29	30	31	Month
Jan	15	15	15	15	15	15	15	16	16	16	16	16	16	16	16	16	16	15	15	15	15	15	15	15	15	15	14	14	14	14	14	4.70
Feb	13	13	13	13	13	12	12	12	12	12	12	12	12	12	12	12	12	12	12	12	12	12	12	12	13	13	13	13				3.45
Mar	13	13	14	14	14	14	14	14	15	15	15	15	15	15	15	15	15	15	16	16	16	16	16	16	16	16	16	16	16	15	15	4.66
Apr	16	15	15	15	15	14	14	14	15	15	15	15	15	15	15	15	15	15	14	14	13	14	14	13	14	14	14	14	14	14		4.39
May	14	14	14	14	14	14	14	13	13	13	13	13	13	13	13	13	13	13	13	13	13	13	13	13	13	13	13	13	13	13	13	4.10
Jun	13	13	13	13	13	14	14	14	13	13	13	13	13	13	13	14	14	13	13	13	13	13	13	13	14	14	13	13	13	13		3.84
Jul	14	14	14	14	14	14	14	14	14	14	14	14	14	14	14	14	14	15	15	15	14	14	14	14	14	14	14	14	14	14	14	4.37
Aug	14	14	14	14	14	14	14	14	14	14	14	14	14	14	14	14	14	15	15	15	14	14	14	14	14	14	14	14	14	14	14	4.24
Sep	14	14	14	14	14	14	14	14	14	14	14	14	14	14	14	14	14	15	15	15	15	15	15	15	15	15	15	15	15	15		4.25
Oct	14	14	14	14	14	14	14	14	14	14	14	14	14	14	14	15	14	15	14	14	15	15	15	15	15	15	15	15	15	15	15	4.44
Nov	15	16	16	16	16	16	16	16	16	16	16	16	16	16	16	16	16	16	16	16	16	16	16	16	16	15	15	15	15	15		4.74
Dec	15	15	15	14	14	14	14	14	14	14	14	14	14	14	14	14	14	14	14	14	14	14	14	14	14	14	14	14	15	15	15	4.40

MIDDLETOWN 4 W (MERIDEN), CT
Cooling Degree Days in °F

	1	2	3	4	5	6	7	8	9	10	11	12	13	14	15	16	17	18	19	20	21	22	23	24	25	26	27	28	29	30	31	Month
Jan	0	0	0	0	0	0	0	0	0	0	0	0	0	0	0	0	0	0	0	0	0	0	0	0	0	0	0	0	0	0	0	0
Feb	0	0	0	0	0	0	0	0	0	0	0	0	0	0	0	0	0	0	0	0	0	0	0	0	0	0	0	0				0
Mar	0	0	0	0	0	0	0	0	0	0	0	0	0	0	0	0	0	0	0	0	0	0	0	0	0	0	0	0	0	0	0	0
Apr	0	0	0	0	0	0	0	0	0	0	0	0	0	0	0	0	0	0	0	0	0	0	0	0	0	0	0	0	0	0		0
May	0	0	0	0	0	0	0	0	0	0	0	1	1	1	1	1	1	1	1	1	1	1	1	1	1	2	2	2	2	2	2	26
Jun	2	2	2	3	3	3	3	3	3	3	4	4	4	4	4	4	5	5	5	5	5	5	6	6	6	6	6	6	7	7		121
Jul	7	7	7	8	8	8	8	8	8	8	8	8	8	9	9	9	9	9	9	9	9	9	9	9	9	9	9	9	8	8	8	262
Aug	8	8	8	8	8	8	8	8	7	7	7	8	8	9	9	9	9	9	9	9	9	9	9	9	9	9	9	9	7	8	4	197
Sep	4	3	3	3	3	3	3	8	7	7	7	7	7	7	7	7	6	6	6	6	6	6	5	5	5	5	5	4	4	0		50
Oct	M	M	M	3	3	3	3	2	2	2	2	2	2	2	2	1	1	1	1	1	1	1	1	1	1	0	1	0	0	0	0	3
Nov	0	0	0	0	0	0	0	0	0	0	0	0	0	0	0	0	0	0	0	0	0	0	0	0	0	0	0	0	0	0		0
Dec	0	0	0	0	0	0	0	0	0	0	0	0	0	0	0	0	0	0	0	0	0	0	0	0	0	0	0	0	0	0	0	0

Total Precipitation (hundredths of an inch; months in inches)

	1	2	3	4	5	6	7	8	9	10	11	12	13	14	15	16	17	18	19	20	21	22	23	24	25	26	27	28	29	30	31	Month
Jan	14	15	15	15	15	15	15	15	15	15	15	15	15	15	15	15	15	15	15	15	15	15	15	14	14	14	14	14	14	13	13	4.54
Feb	13	13	13	12	12	12	12	12	12	12	12	11	11	11	11	11	11	11	11	12	12	12	12	12	12	12	12	13	14	13		3.32
Mar	13	13	13	12	14	14	14	14	15	14	14	15	15	15	15	15	15	15	15	15	15	15	15	15	16	16	16	16	16	15	15	4.55
Apr	15	15	15	15	15	14	14	14	14	14	14	14	14	13	14	14	14	14	14	14	14	14	14	14	14	14	14	14	14	14		4.44
May	14	14	14	15	15	14	14	14	14	14	14	14	13	13	13	14	14	14	14	14	14	14	14	14	14	14	14	14	14	14	14	4.30
Jun	14	15	15	14	15	14	14	14	14	14	15	14	15	15	15	15	15	15	15	15	15	15	15	15	15	15	15	15	15	15		4.46
Jul	14	14	15	14	14	14	14	14	14	14	15	14	15	15	15	15	14	14	14	14	15	15	15	15	15	15	13	14	14	14	14	4.20
Aug	14	14	15	14	14	14	14	15	15	15	15	15	15	15	15	15	15	15	15	15	16	16	16	16	16	16	15	15	14	14	14	4.46
Sep	15	15	15	15	15	15	15	15	15	15	15	15	15	15	15	15	16	16	16	15	15	15	16	15	16	16	16	15	15	15		4.58
Oct	15	15	15	15	16	16	16	16	16	16	15	15	15	15	15	16	16	16	16	16	16	16	16	16	16	16	16	16	16	16	16	4.81
Nov	16	16	16	16	16	16	14	13	14	13	14	14	13	13	13	13	13	13	13	13	13	13	13	15	14	14	14	14	14	14		4.54
Dec	14	14	14	14	14	13	13	13	13	13	13	13	13	13	13	13	13	13	13	13	13	13	13	13	14	14	14	14	14	14	14	4.15

NORFOLK 2 SW, CT

Cooling Degree Days in °F

Month	1	2	3	4	5	6	7	8	9	10	11	12	13	14	15	16	17	18	19	20	21	22	23	24	25	26	27	28	29	30	31	Month
Jan	0	0	0	0	0	0	0	0	0	0	0	0	0	0	0	0	0	0	0	0	0	0	0	0	0	0	0	0	0	0	0	0
Feb	0	0	0	0	0	0	0	0	0	0	0	0	0	0	0	0	0	0	0	0	0	0	0	0	0	0	0	0				0
Mar	0	0	0	0	0	0	0	0	0	0	0	0	0	0	0	0	0	0	0	0	0	0	0	0	0	0	0	0	0	0	0	0
Apr	0	0	0	0	0	0	0	0	0	0	0	0	0	0	0	0	0	0	0	0	0	0	0	0	0	0	0	0	0	0		0
May	0	0	0	0	0	0	0	0	0	0	0	0	0	0	1	1	1	1	1	0	0	0	0	0	0	M	M	M	M	M	M	5
Jun	0	0	1	1	1	1	1	1	1	1	1	1	1	1	1	1	1	1	1	2	2	2	2	2	2	2	2	2	2	3		40
Jul	3	3	3	3	3	3	3	3	3	4	4	4	4	4	4	4	4	4	4	4	4	4	4	4	4	4	3	3	3	3	3	110
Aug	4	4	3	3	3	3	3	3	3	3	3	3	3	3	3	3	2	2	2	2	2	2	2	2	2	2	2	2	1	1	1	77
Sep	1	1	1	1	1	0	0	0	0	0	0	0	0	0	0	0	0	0	0	0	0	0	0	0	0	0	0	0	0	0		5
Oct	0	0	0	0	0	0	0	0	0	0	0	0	0	0	0	0	0	0	0	0	0	0	0	0	0	0	0	0	0	0	0	0
Nov	0	0	0	0	0	0	0	0	0	0	0	0	0	0	0	0	0	0	0	0	0	0	0	0	0	0	0	0	0	0		0
Dec	0	0	0	0	0	0	0	0	0	0	0	0	0	0	0	0	0	0	0	0	0	0	0	0	0	0	0	0	0	0	0	0

Total Precipitation (hundredths of an inch; months in inches)

Month	1	2	3	4	5	6	7	8	9	10	11	12	13	14	15	16	17	18	19	20	21	22	23	24	25	26	27	28	29	30	31	Month
Jan	14	14	14	14	15	15	15	15	15	15	15	15	15	15	15	15	15	15	15	14	14	14	14	14	14	14	14	14	14	13	13	4.47
Feb	13	13	13	13	13	13	13	13	13	13	12	12	12	12	12	12	12	12	12	12	13	13	13	13	13	13	13	13	14	13	13	3.58
Mar	14	14	14	14	14	14	14	14	14	14	14	14	15	14	15	14	15	15	15	15	15	15	15	15	15	15	14	15	15	15	15	4.57
Apr	15	15	15	15	15	15	15	15	15	15	15	15	15	15	15	15	15	15	15	15	15	15	15	15	15	15	16	15	16	16		4.53
May	15	15	15	15	15	15	16	16	16	16	16	16	16	16	16	16	16	16	16	16	16	16	15	15	15	15	15	15	15	15	15	4.81
Jun	15	15	15	15	15	15	16	16	16	16	16	16	16	16	16	16	16	16	16	16	16	16	15	15	15	16	15	16	15	15		4.49
Jul	15	15	15	15	15	15	16	16	16	16	16	16	16	16	16	16	16	16	16	16	16	16	16	15	16	16	15	16	16	16	16	4.90
Aug	16	16	16	16	16	16	16	16	16	16	16	16	16	16	16	16	16	16	16	16	16	16	16	15	16	15	15	15	15	15	15	4.74
Sep	15	15	15	15	15	15	15	15	15	15	15	15	15	15	15	15	15	15	15	14	14	14	14	14	15	15	15	15	14	14		4.47
Oct	14	14	14	14	14	15	14	14	14	14	14	14	14	14	14	14	14	14	14	14	14	15	14	15	14	15	15	15	15	15	15	4.40
Nov	15	15	15	15	15	15	16	16	16	16	16	16	16	16	16	16	16	16	16	16	16	15	15	15	15	15	15	15	15	15		4.65
Dec	15	14	14	14	14	14	14	14	14	14	14	14	14	14	14	14	13	13	13	13	14	14	14	14	14	14	14	14	14	14	14	4.31

NORWALK GAS PLANT, CT

Cooling Degree Days in °F

Day	1	2	3	4	5	6	7	8	9	10	11	12	13	14	15	16	17	18	19	20	21	22	23	24	25	26	27	28	29	30	31	Month
Jan	0	0	0	0	0	0	0	0	0	0	0	0	0	0	0	0	0	0	0	0	0	0	0	0	0	0	0	0	0	0	0	0
Feb	0	0	0	0	0	0	0	0	0	0	0	0	0	0	0	0	0	0	0	0	0	0	0	0	0	0	0	0				0
Mar	0	0	0	0	0	0	0	0	0	0	0	0	0	0	0	0	0	0	0	0	0	0	0	0	0	0	0	0	0	0	0	0
Apr	0	0	0	0	0	0	0	0	0	0	0	0	0	0	0	0	0	0	0	0	0	0	0	0	0	0	0	0	0	0		0
May	0	0	0	0	0	0	0	0	0	0	0	0	0	0	1	1	1	1	1	1	1	1	1	1	1	1	1	1	1	2	2	19
Jun	2	2	2	2	2	2	2	3	3	3	3	3	3	3	4	4	4	4	4	4	5	5	5	5	5	5	6	6	6	6		113
Jul	7	7	7	7	7	7	8	8	8	8	8	8	8	8	9	9	9	9	9	9	9	9	9	9	9	9	9	9	9	9	9	259
Aug	9	9	9	8	8	8	8	8	8	8	8	8	8	7	7	7	7	7	7	6	6	6	6	6	5	5	5	5	5	4	4	211
Sep	4	4	3	3	3	3	3	3	2	2	2	2	2	2	1	1	1	1	1	1	1	1	1	1	1	0	0	0	0	0		48
Oct	0	M	M	0	0	0	0	0	0	0	0	0	0	0	1	1	0	0	0	0	0	0	0	0	0	0	0	0	0	0	0	2
Nov	0	0	0	0	0	0	0	0	0	0	0	0	0	0	0	0	0	0	0	0	0	0	0	0	0	0	0	0	0	0		0
Dec	0	0	0	0	0	0	0	0	0	0	0	0	0	0	0	0	0	0	0	0	0	0	0	0	0	0	0	0	0	0	0	0

Total Precipitation (hundredths of an inch; months in inches)

Day	1	2	3	4	5	6	7	8	9	10	11	12	13	14	15	16	17	18	19	20	21	22	23	24	25	26	27	28	29	30	31	Month
Jan	13	14	14	14	14	14	14	14	14	14	14	14	14	14	14	14	14	14	14	14	14	13	13	13	13	13	13	13	12	12	12	4.20
Feb	13	12	12	11	11	11	11	11	11	10	10	10	10	10	10	10	10	10	10	11	11	11	11	11	11	11	12	12				3.03
Mar	12	12	12	12	13	13	13	14	14	14	14	14	15	15	15	14	14	14	14	15	15	14	14	15	15	14	15	14	15	15	15	4.33
Apr	15	15	15	14	15	15	15	14	14	14	14	14	15	15	14	14	14	14	14	14	14	14	14	14	14	14	14	14	14	14		4.37
May	15	15	14	14	14	14	14	14	14	15	14	14	13	13	14	14	14	14	13	13	13	14	13	13	13	13	14	14	14	14	14	4.36
Jun	14	14	14	14	14	13	13	13	13	13	13	13	13	13	13	13	13	13	13	12	12	12	12	12	12	12	13	13	13	13		3.94
Jul	13	13	13	13	13	13	13	13	13	13	13	13	12	12	12	12	12	12	12	12	12	12	12	12	12	12	12	12	12	12	12	3.83
Aug	12	12	12	12	12	12	12	12	12	12	12	12	13	13	13	14	14	14	14	13	13	14	14	14	14	14	14	14	14	14	14	3.89
Sep	14	15	14	15	15	15	15	15	15	15	15	16	16	16	16	16	16	16	15	15	15	15	15	15	15	15	14	14	14	14		4.54
Oct	14	14	14	13	13	13	13	13	13	13	13	14	14	14	14	14	14	14	14	13	13	14	14	14	13	13	13	13	13	13	13	3.89
Nov	13	13	13	13	13	13	13	13	13	13	13	13	13	14	14	14	14	14	14	13	13	13	13	13	13	13	13	13	13	13		4.04
Dec	13	13	13	13	13	13	13	13	13	13	13	13	12	12	12	12	13	13	13	13	13	13	13	13	13	13	13	13	13	13	13	3.96

NORWICH PUBLIC UTILITY PLANT, CT

Cooling Degree Days in °F

	1	2	3	4	5	6	7	8	9	10	11	12	13	14	15	16	17	18	19	20	21	22	23	24	25	26	27	28	29	30	31	Month
Jan	0	0	0	0	0	0	0	0	0	0	0	0	0	0	0	0	0	0	0	0	0	0	0	0	0	0	0	0	0	0	0	0
Feb	0	0	0	0	0	0	0	0	0	0	0	0	0	0	0	0	0	0	0	0	0	0	0	0	0	0	0	0				0
Mar	0	0	0	0	0	0	0	0	0	0	0	0	0	0	0	0	0	0	0	0	0	0	0	0	0	0	0	0	0	0	0	0
Apr	0	0	0	0	0	0	0	0	0	0	0	0	0	0	0	0	0	0	0	0	0	0	0	0	0	0	0	0	0	0		0
May	0	0	0	0	0	0	0	0	0	0	0	0	0	0	0	0	1	1	1	1	0	1	1	1	1	1	1	1	0	0	1	15
Jun	1	1	2	2	2	2	2	2	2	2	2	3	3	3	3	3	3	4	4	4	4	4	5	5	5	5	5	6	6	6		101
Jul	6	6	7	7	7	7	7	8	8	8	8	8	8	8	9	9	9	9	9	9	9	9	9	9	9	9	9	9	9	9	9	256
Aug	9	8	8	7	8	8	8	8	8	8	7	8	7	8	7	7	7	6	6	6	6	6	6	5	5	5	5	5	4	4	4	203
Sep	4	4	3	3	3	3	3	3	2	2	2	2	2	2	2	1	1	1	1	1	1	1	1	1	1	1	0	0	0	0		51
Oct	M	0	0	0	0	0	0	0	0	0	0	0	0	0	0	0	1	0	0	0	0	0	0	0	0	0	0	0	0	0	0	1
Nov	0	0	0	0	0	0	0	0	0	0	0	0	0	0	0	0	0	0	0	0	0	0	0	0	0	0	0	0	0	0		0
Dec	0	0	0	0	0	0	0	0	0	0	0	0	0	0	0	0	0	0	0	0	0	0	0	0	0	0	0	0	0	0	0	0

Total Precipitation (hundredths of an inch; months in inches)

	1	2	3	4	5	6	7	8	9	10	11	12	13	14	15	16	17	18	19	20	21	22	23	24	25	26	27	28	29	30	31	Month
Jan	15	15	15	15	16	16	16	16	16	16	16	16	16	16	16	16	15	15	15	15	15	15	15	15	15	15	15	15	14	14	14	4.74
Feb	14	14	14	14	14	14	14	14	13	13	13	13	13	13	13	13	13	13	14	14	14	14	14	14	14	14	14	14				3.82
Mar	15	15	15	15	15	15	16	16	16	16	16	16	16	16	16	16	16	16	16	16	16	16	17	17	17	16	16	16	16	16	16	4.93
Apr	16	16	16	16	16	16	16	16	16	16	16	16	16	16	15	16	15	16	15	15	15	16	15	15	15	15	14	14	14	14		4.58
May	14	14	14	14	14	14	14	14	14	14	13	13	13	13	13	13	13	13	13	13	13	13	13	13	13	13	13	13	13	13	13	4.13
Jun	13	13	13	13	13	13	13	13	13	13	13	13	12	13	12	13	12	12	12	12	12	12	12	12	12	12	12	12	11	11		3.68
Jul	11	11	11	11	11	11	11	11	11	11	13	11	11	11	11	12	12	12	12	12	12	12	12	13	13	13	12	13	13	14	14	3.67
Aug	14	14	14	15	15	15	15	15	16	16	16	16	16	16	16	16	16	16	16	16	16	16	16	16	16	16	16	16	16	16	16	4.85
Sep	15	15	15	15	15	15	15	15	15	16	16	16	14	16	16	15	14	14	14	15	14	15	15	16	16	16	14	14	14	14		4.29
Oct	14	14	14	14	14	14	14	14	14	14	14	14	14	14	14	15	15	15	15	15	14	15	15	15	16	15	16	15	16	16	16	4.53
Nov	16	16	16	16	16	16	16	16	16	16	16	16	17	17	17	17	17	16	16	16	16	16	16	16	16	16	16	16	16	16		4.86
Dec	16	16	16	16	16	15	15	15	15	15	15	15	15	15	16	15	15	15	15	15	15	15	15	15	15	15	15	15	15	15	15	4.70

Total Precipitation (hundredths of an inch; months in inches)

	1	2	3	4	5	6	7	8	9	10	11	12	13	14	15	16	17	18	19	20	21	22	23	24	25	26	27	28	29	30	31	Month
Jan	14	14	14	14	14	14	14	15	15	15	15	15	15	15	15	14	14	14	14	14	14	14	14	14	14	13	13	13	13	13	12	4.35
Feb	12	12	12	11	11	11	11	11	11	11	11	11	11	11	10	10	11	11	11	11	11	11	11	11	11	11	12	12				3.11
Mar	12	12	13	13	13	13	13	13	14	14	14	14	14	14	14	14	15	15	15	15	15	15	14	15	15	15	15	15	15	15	15	4.39
Apr	15	15	15	15	15	15	15	15	15	15	15	15	15	15	15	15	15	15	15	15	15	14	14	15	15	15	14	15	15	15		4.48
May	15	15	15	15	15	15	15	15	15	15	15	15	15	15	14	14	14	14	14	14	14	14	14	14	14	14	14	14	14	14	14	4.63
Jun	15	15	15	15	15	15	15	15	15	15	15	14	14	13	14	14	14	14	13	14	13	14	14	13	13	14	14	13	14	14		4.34
Jul	14	14	14	13	13	13	13	13	13	13	13	13	13	13	14	13	14	13	13	14	13	13	14	13	13	13	14	13	13	13	13	4.06
Aug	13	13	13	13	13	13	13	13	13	13	13	13	13	13	13	13	14	14	14	14	14	14	14	13	15	15	16	15	15	15	15	4.25
Sep	16	16	16	16	16	16	16	17	17	17	17	17	17	17	17	17	17	17	17	17	16	15	15	16	16	16	16	15	15	15		4.90
Oct	15	14	14	14	14	14	14	14	15	15	15	15	15	15	15	15	15	15	15	15	15	15	15	13	13	14	14	13	14	13	13	4.11
Nov	14	14	14	14	14	14	14	14	14	14	13	13	13	13	13	14	14	13	13	13	13	15	15	13	14	14	14	14	14	14	14	4.35
Dec	14	14	13	13	13	13	13	13	13	13	13	13	13	13	13	13	13	13	13	13	13	13	13	13	13	13	13	13	14	14	14	4.07

Total Precipitation (hundredths of an inch; months in inches)

	1	2	3	4	5	6	7	8	9	10	11	12	13	14	15	16	17	18	19	20	21	22	23	24	25	26	27	28	29	30	31	Month
Jan	12	12	12	12	12	12	12	12	12	12	12	12	12	12	12	12	12	12	12	12	12	12	12	12	12	12	12	11	11	11	11	3.68
Feb	11	11	11	10	10	10	10	10	10	10	10	10	10	10	10	10	10	10	10	10	10	10	10	10	11	11	11	11				2.87
Mar	11	11	12	12	12	12	12	12	12	12	12	13	13	13	13	13	13	13	14	13	13	13	13	13	13	13	13	13	13	13	13	3.90
Apr	13	13	13	14	13	13	13	13	13	13	13	13	13	13	14	13	14	14	14	14	14	14	14	14	14	14	14	13	13	13		4.04
May	14	14	14	14	14	14	14	14	14	14	14	14	15	15	14	15	15	15	15	15	15	15	15	14	14	14	14	14	14	14	14	4.47
Jun	14	14	14	14	14	14	14	14	14	14	14	14	14	14	13	14	13	14	13	13	13	13	13	14	14	14	14	14	14	14		4.11
Jul	14	14	14	14	14	14	14	14	14	14	14	14	14	14	14	14	14	14	14	14	15	15	15	15	15	14	15	14	15	15	15	4.45
Aug	15	15	15	15	15	15	15	15	15	15	15	15	15	15	15	15	15	16	16	16	16	16	16	16	16	16	15	15	15	15	15	4.73
Sep	15	15	15	15	15	15	15	15	15	14	13	13	14	14	14	15	15	15	13	15	13	15	15	15	14	14	14	14	14	14		4.44
Oct	14	14	14	14	14	14	14	14	14	14	14	14	14	14	14	14	14	14	14	14	14	14	14	14	13	13	13	13	13	13	14	4.21
Nov	14	14	14	14	14	14	14	14	14	14	12	12	12	12	11	11	11	11	11	11	11	11	11	11	11	11	13	12	13	13		4.14
Dec	13	13	13	12	12	12	12	12	12	12	12	12	12	12	12	12	11	11	11	11	11	11	11	11	11	11	12	12	12	12	12	3.62

ROUND POND, CT

Total Precipitation (hundredths of an inch; months in inches)

	1	2	3	4	5	6	7	8	9	10	11	12	13	14	15	16	17	18	19	20	21	22	23	24	25	26	27	28	29	30	31	Month
Jan	14	14	14	14	14	14	14	14	14	14	14	14	14	14	14	14	14	14	13	13	13	13	13	13	13	13	13	12	12	12	12	4.17
Feb	12	12	12	11	11	11	11	11	11	11	11	11	11	11	11	11	11	11	11	11	12	12	12	12	12	12	13	13				3.21
Mar	13	13	13	14	14	14	14	14	14	15	15	15	15	15	15	15	15	15	16	16	16	16	16	16	16	16	16	16	16	15	15	4.64
Apr	15	15	15	15	15	15	15	15	15	15	15	15	15	15	15	15	16	16	16	16	16	16	16	16	16	16	16	16	15	15		4.51
May	16	16	16	16	16	16	16	16	16	16	16	16	16	16	17	16	16	16	16	16	16	16	16	16	16	16	16	16	16	16	16	4.97
Jun	15	15	15	15	15	15	15	15	15	15	15	15	14	14	14	14	14	14	14	14	14	14	14	14	14	14	14	14	14	14		4.32
Jul	14	14	14	14	14	14	14	14	14	14	14	14	14	14	14	14	14	14	14	14	15	15	15	15	15	15	15	15	15	15	15	4.45
Aug	15	15	15	15	15	15	15	15	15	15	15	15	16	16	16	16	16	16	16	16	16	16	16	16	16	16	16	16	16	16	16	4.78
Sep	16	16	16	16	16	16	17	17	17	17	17	17	16	16	16	16	16	16	16	16	16	16	16	16	16	16	16	15	15	15		4.83
Oct	15	15	15	15	14	14	14	14	14	15	15	14	14	14	14	14	14	14	14	14	14	14	14	14	14	14	14	15	15	15	15	4.43
Nov	15	15	15	16	16	16	16	16	16	16	16	16	16	16	16	16	16	16	16	16	16	16	16	16	16	16	16	16	15	15		4.72
Dec	15	15	15	14	14	14	14	14	14	14	14	14	14	14	13	13	13	13	13	13	13	13	13	13	13	13	13	13	14	14	14	4.23

SAUGATUCK RESERVOIR, CT

Total Precipitation (hundredths of an inch; months in inches)

	1	2	3	4	5	6	7	8	9	10	11	12	13	14	15	16	17	18	19	20	21	22	23	24	25	26	27	28	29	30	31	Month
Jan	14	14	14	14	14	14	14	15	15	15	15	15	15	15	15	15	14	14	14	14	14	14	14	14	14	13	13	13	13	13	13	4.37
Feb	12	12	12	12	12	11	11	11	11	11	11	11	11	11	11	11	11	11	11	11	11	12	12	12	12	12	13	13				3.21
Mar	13	13	13	13	14	14	14	14	15	15	15	15	15	15	15	15	15	15	15	15	16	16	16	16	16	16	16	16	16	15	15	4.61
Apr	16	15	15	15	15	15	15	15	15	15	15	15	16	16	16	16	16	16	16	16	16	16	16	16	16	16	16	16	16	15		4.54
May	16	16	16	16	16	16	16	16	16	16	16	16	16	16	16	16	16	16	16	16	16	16	16	16	16	16	16	16	16	16	16	4.92
Jun	15	15	15	15	14	14	14	14	14	14	14	15	14	14	14	14	14	14	13	13	13	13	13	13	13	13	13	13	13	13		4.13
Jul	13	13	13	13	13	13	13	13	13	13	13	13	13	13	13	13	13	13	13	13	14	14	14	14	14	14	14	14	14	14	14	4.08
Aug	14	14	14	14	14	14	14	14	14	14	14	15	15	15	15	15	15	15	15	15	15	15	15	15	15	15	15	15	15	15	15	4.43
Sep	15	15	15	15	15	15	15	15	15	15	15	15	15	15	15	15	15	15	15	15	15	14	15	14	14	14	14	14	14	14		4.44
Oct	14	14	14	14	14	14	14	14	14	13	13	13	13	13	14	14	14	13	13	13	14	14	14	14	14	14	14	14	14	14	15	4.23
Nov	15	15	15	15	15	15	15	15	16	16	16	16	16	16	16	16	16	16	16	15	15	15	15	15	15	14	15	15	15	14		4.61
Dec	14	14	14	14	14	14	14	13	13	13	13	13	13	13	13	13	13	13	13	13	13	13	13	13	13	13	13	13	14	14	14	4.13

SHEPAUG DAM, CT
Cooling Degree Days in °F

	1	2	3	4	5	6	7	8	9	10	11	12	13	14	15	16	17	18	19	20	21	22	23	24	25	26	27	28	29	30	31	Month
Jan	0	0	0	0	0	0	0	0	0	0	0	0	0	0	0	0	0	0	0	0	0	0	0	0	0	0	0	0	0	0	0	0
Feb	0	0	0	0	0	0	0	0	0	0	0	0	0	0	0	0	0	0	0	0	0	0	0	0	0	0	0	0				0
Mar	0	0	0	0	0	0	0	0	0	0	0	0	0	0	0	0	0	0	0	0	0	0	0	0	0	0	0	0	0	0	0	0
Apr	0	0	0	0	0	0	0	0	0	0	0	0	0	0	0	0	0	0	0	0	0	0	0	0	0	0	0	0	0	0		0
May	0	0	0	0	0	0	0	0	0	0	0	0	0	0	0	0	0	0	0	0	0	0	0	0	0	0	M	M	M	M	M	5
Jun	0	0	1	1	1	1	1	1	1	1	1	1	1	1	1	1	1	2	2	2	2	2	2	2	2	2	3	3	3	3		45
Jul	3	3	3	4	4	4	4	4	4	4	4	4	4	4	4	5	5	5	5	5	5	5	5	5	5	5	5	5	5	4	4	135
Aug	4	4	4	4	4	4	4	4	4	4	4	4	4	3	3	3	3	3	3	3	3	3	2	2	2	2	2	2	2	2	2	97
Sep	1	1	1	1	1	1	1	0	0	0	0	0	0	0	0	0	0	0	0	0	0	0	0	0	0	0	0	0	0	0		0
Oct	0	0	0	0	0	0	0	0	0	0	0	0	0	0	0	0	0	0	0	0	0	0	0	0	0	0	0	0	0	0	0	0
Nov	0	0	0	0	0	0	0	0	0	0	0	0	0	0	0	0	0	0	0	0	0	0	0	0	0	0	0	0	0	0		0
Dec	0	0	0	0	0	0	0	0	0	0	0	0	0	0	0	0	0	0	0	0	0	0	0	0	0	0	0	0	0	0	0	0

Total Precipitation (hundredths of an inch; months in inches)

	1	2	3	4	5	6	7	8	9	10	11	12	13	14	15	16	17	18	19	20	21	22	23	24	25	26	27	28	29	30	31	Month
Jan	13	13	13	13	13	13	13	13	13	13	13	13	13	13	13	13	13	13	13	13	13	13	13	12	12	12	12	12	12	12	12	3.94
Feb	11	11	11	11	11	11	11	11	11	11	11	10	10	11	11	11	11	11	11	11	11	11	11	11	12	12	12	12				3.10
Mar	12	13	13	13	13	13	14	14	14	14	14	14	14	14	14	15	15	15	15	15	15	15	15	15	15	15	15	15	15	15	14	4.42
Apr	14	14	14	14	14	14	14	14	14	14	14	14	14	14	14	14	14	14	15	14	14	14	14	14	14	14	14	14	14	14		4.20
May	14	14	14	14	14	14	15	15	15	15	14	15	14	14	14	15	14	14	15	14	14	15	14	14	14	14	14	14	14	14	14	4.51
Jun	14	14	14	14	14	14	14	14	14	14	14	13	13	13	13	14	14	14	14	14	14	15	15	15	15	15	15	15	15	15		4.15
Jul	15	15	15	15	15	15	15	15	15	15	15	15	16	16	16	16	15	15	15	15	15	15	15	15	15	15	15	16	15	15	15	4.82
Aug	16	15	15	15	16	16	16	16	16	16	16	16	16	16	16	16	15	15	15	15	15	15	16	16	16	16	16	16	15	15	15	4.66
Sep	15	15	15	15	16	16	16	15	16	16	15	16	16	15	15	16	15	15	15	15	15	15	15	15	15	15	15	15	14	14		4.60
Oct	14	14	13	14	14	14	14	13	13	13	14	14	13	13	13	14	13	13	13	13	13	13	14	13	13	13	13	13	13	14	14	4.12
Nov	14	14	14	14	14	14	13	13	13	14	14	14	14	14	14	14	14	14	14	14	14	14	14	14	14	14	14	14	14	13		4.19
Dec	13	13	13	13	13	13	13	13	13	13	12	12	12	12	12	12	12	12	12	12	12	12	12	12	12	12	12	13	13	13	13	3.86

SHUTTLE MEADOW RESERVOIR, CT

Total Precipitation (hundredths of an inch; months in inches)

	1	2	3	4	5	6	7	8	9	10	11	12	13	14	15	16	17	18	19	20	21	22	23	24	25	26	27	28	29	30	31	Month
Jan	14	14	14	14	14	14	14	15	15	15	15	15	15	15	15	15	15	15	14	14	14	14	14	14	14	14	14	14	13	13	13	4.41
Feb	13	13	13	13	13	13	12	12	12	12	12	12	12	12	12	12	12	12	12	12	12	12	12	12	12	12	12	12				3.39
Mar	13	13	13	13	13	13	13	13	13	13	14	14	14	14	14	14	14	14	14	14	14	14	14	15	15	15	15	15	15	15	15	4.32
Apr	15	15	15	15	15	15	15	15	15	15	15	14	16	15	15	14	15	15	15	15	15	15	14	15	15	15	15	15	15	15		4.52
May	15	15	15	14	15	15	15	15	14	14	14	14	16	14	14	14	14	14	14	14	14	14	14	14	14	14	13	13	13	13	13	4.32
Jun	13	13	13	13	13	13	14	14	14	13	14	13	14	13	13	14	14	14	14	14	14	14	14	14	14	14	14	14	14	14		4.05
Jul	14	14	14	14	14	14	14	14	14	15	14	15	15	15	15	15	15	15	15	15	15	15	15	15	15	15	15	15	15	15	15	4.53
Aug	14	14	14	14	14	14	14	14	14	14	14	14	14	14	13	13	13	13	14	14	14	14	14	14	14	14	14	14	14	14	14	4.30
Sep	14	14	14	14	14	14	15	15	15	15	15	15	15	15	14	15	15	15	15	15	15	15	15	15	15	15	15	15	15	15		4.44
Oct	15	15	15	15	14	15	15	14	14	14	14	14	14	15	14	14	15	15	15	15	15	15	15	15	15	15	15	15	15	15	15	4.57
Nov	15	15	15	15	15	15	15	16	16	16	16	16	15	15	14	15	15	15	15	15	15	15	15	14	14	15	15	15	15	14		4.54
Dec	14	14	14	14	14	14	14	14	14	14	13	13	13	13	13	13	13	13	13	13	13	13	13	14	14	14	14	14	14	14	14	4.21

STAMFORD 5 N, CT

Cooling Degree Days in °F

	1	2	3	4	5	6	7	8	9	10	11	12	13	14	15	16	17	18	19	20	21	22	23	24	25	26	27	28	29	30	31	Month
Jan	0	0	0	0	0	0	0	0	0	0	0	0	0	0	0	0	0	0	0	0	0	0	0	0	0	0	0	0	0	0	0	0
Feb	0	0	0	0	0	0	0	0	0	0	0	0	0	0	0	0	0	0	0	0	0	0	0	0	0	0	0	0	0			0
Mar	0	0	0	0	0	0	0	0	0	0	0	0	0	0	0	0	0	0	0	0	0	0	0	0	0	0	0	0	0	0	0	0
Apr	0	0	0	0	0	0	0	0	0	0	0	0	0	0	0	0	0	0	0	0	0	0	0	0	0	0	0	0	0	0		0
May	0	0	0	0	0	0	0	0	0	0	0	0	0	1	1	1	1	1	1	1	1	1	1	1	1	2	2	2	2	2	2	24
Jun	2	2	2	3	3	3	3	3	3	3	3	4	4	4	4	4	4	5	5	5	5	5	5	6	6	6	6	6	7	7		128
Jul	7	7	7	8	8	8	8	8	8	8	8	9	9	9	9	9	9	9	9	9	9	9	9	9	9	9	9	9	9	9	9	265
Aug	9	9	9	9	9	8	8	8	8	8	8	8	8	8	7	7	7	7	7	7	6	6	6	6	6	6	5	5	5	5	4	218
Sep	4	4	4	3	3	3	3	3	3	2	2	2	2	2	2	1	1	1	1	1	1	1	1	1	0	1	0	0	0	0		53
Oct	M	M	M	M	0	0	0	0	0	0	0	0	0	0	0	0	0	0	0	0	0	0	0	0	0	0	0	0	0	0	0	4
Nov	0	0	0	0	0	0	0	0	0	0	0	0	0	0	0	0	0	0	0	0	0	0	0	0	0	0	0	0	0	0		0
Dec	0	0	0	0	0	0	0	0	0	0	0	0	0	0	0	0	0	0	0	0	0	0	0	0	0	0	0	0	0	0	0	0

Total Precipitation (hundredths of an inch; months in inches)

	1	2	3	4	5	6	7	8	9	10	11	12	13	14	15	16	17	18	19	20	21	22	23	24	25	26	27	28	29	30	31	Month
Jan	14	15	15	15	15	15	15	15	15	15	15	15	15	15	15	15	15	15	15	15	15	14	14	14	14	14	14	13	13	13	13	4.50
Feb	13	13	12	14	12	12	12	12	12	11	11	11	11	11	11	11	11	11	12	12	12	12	12	12	12	13	13	13	13	13	13	3.32
Mar	13	13	14	14	14	14	14	15	15	15	15	15	15	15	15	15	16	16	16	16	16	16	16	16	16	16	16	16	16	16	16	4.70
Apr	15	15	15	14	15	14	14	15	15	15	15	15	15	15	15	15	16	16	15	15	15	15	15	15	15	15	15	15	15	16		4.51
May	16	16	16	16	16	16	16	16	16	16	16	16	16	16	16	17	16	16	16	16	16	16	16	16	16	16	16	16	16	16	16	4.97
Jun	15	15	15	15	15	15	15	15	15	15	15	15	15	14	14	14	14	14	14	14	14	14	14	14	14	14	14	14	14	14		4.33
Jul	14	14	14	14	14	14	13	13	13	13	13	13	13	13	14	14	14	14	14	14	14	14	14	14	14	14	14	14	14	14	14	4.09
Aug	13	13	14	13	13	13	13	13	13	13	13	13	13	13	14	14	14	14	14	14	14	14	14	14	14	14	14	14	14	14	14	4.26
Sep	15	16	16	16	16	16	16	16	16	16	16	16	16	17	17	17	17	16	16	16	16	16	16	16	16	16	16	16	16	16		4.82
Oct	15	15	15	15	15	15	14	14	14	14	14	14	14	14	14	14	14	14	14	15	15	15	15	15	15	15	15	14	14	14	15	4.42
Nov	15	15	15	15	15	15	15	15	15	15	16	16	16	16	16	16	16	16	15	15	15	15	15	15	15	15	15	15	15	15		4.58
Dec	14	14	14	14	14	14	14	14	14	14	14	14	14	14	13	13	13	13	13	14	14	14	14	14	14	14	14	14	14	14	14	4.29

STEVENSON DAM, CT

Total Precipitation (hundredths of an inch; months in inches)

	1	2	3	4	5	6	7	8	9	10	11	12	13	14	15	16	17	18	19	20	21	22	23	24	25	26	27	28	29	30	31	Month
Jan	16	17	17	17	17	17	17	17	17	17	17	17	17	17	17	17	17	17	17	16	16	16	16	16	16	15	15	15	14	14	14	5.05
Feb	13	13	13	13	12	12	12	12	12	12	11	11	11	11	11	11	11	12	12	12	12	12	12	13	13	13	13	14				3.39
Mar	14	14	15	15	15	16	16	16	16	17	17	17	17	17	18	18	18	18	18	18	18	18	18	18	18	18	18	18	18	18	18	5.28
Apr	18	18	17	17	17	17	17	17	17	17	17	17	17	17	16	16	16	16	16	16	16	16	16	16	16	16	16	16	16	16		4.96
May	16	16	16	16	16	16	15	15	15	15	15	15	15	15	15	15	15	15	15	15	15	15	15	15	15	15	15	15	16	16	16	4.74
Jun	15	15	15	15	16	16	16	16	16	16	16	16	15	15	15	15	15	13	15	13	15	13	15	13	13	12	12	14	14	14		4.56
Jul	14	14	14	14	14	14	13	13	13	13	13	13	13	13	13	13	13	13	13	13	13	13	13	13	13	12	12	14	12	13	13	4.05
Aug	13	13	13	13	13	13	13	13	13	13	13	13	13	13	13	13	13	13	13	13	13	13	13	13	13	13	14	14	14	14	14	4.08
Sep	14	14	14	14	14	14	14	14	14	14	14	14	15	15	14	15	15	15	15	15	15	15	15	15	15	14	14	14	14	14		4.33
Oct	14	14	16	14	16	17	17	17	17	17	15	17	17	17	14	17	15	17	17	17	17	17	17	17	17	15	15	16	16	16	16	4.54
Nov	16	16	16	16	16	16	15	15	17	15	15	17	17	17	17	17	17	17	17	15	17	17	17	17	17	16	16	16	16	16		5.00
Dec	16	16	16	16	15	15	15	15	15	15	15	15	15	15	15	15	15	15	15	15	15	15	15	15	15	15	16	16	16	16	16	4.73

STORRS, CT

Cooling Degree Days in °F

	1	2	3	4	5	6	7	8	9	10	11	12	13	14	15	16	17	18	19	20	21	22	23	24	25	26	27	28	29	30	31	Month
Jan	0	0	0	0	0	0	0	0	0	0	0	0	0	0	0	0	0	0	0	0	0	0	0	0	0	0	0	0	0	0	0	0
Feb	0	0	0	0	0	0	0	0	0	0	0	0	0	0	0	0	0	0	0	0	0	0	0	0	0	0	0	0	0			0
Mar	0	0	0	0	0	0	0	0	0	0	0	0	0	0	0	0	0	0	0	0	0	0	0	0	0	0	0	0	0	0	0	0
Apr	0	0	0	0	0	0	0	0	0	0	0	0	0	0	0	0	0	0	0	0	0	0	0	0	0	0	0	0	0	0		0
May	0	0	0	0	0	0	0	0	0	0	0	0	0	0	0	0	0	0	0	0	0	0	0	0	1	1	1	1	1	1	1	7
Jun	1	1	1	1	1	1	1	1	1	2	2	2	2	2	2	2	2	2	2	3	3	3	3	3	3	3	4	4	4	4		66
Jul	4	4	5	5	5	5	5	5	5	5	5	5	5	5	6	6	6	6	6	6	6	6	6	6	6	6	6	6	6	6	5	167
Aug	6	5	5	5	5	5	5	5	5	5	5	5	5	4	4	4	4	4	4	4	4	4	3	3	3	3	3	3	3	2	2	127
Sep	2	2	2	2	2	2	1	1	1	1	1	1	1	1	1	1	0	0	0	0	0	0	0	0	0	0	0	0	0	0		22
Oct	0	0	0	0	0	0	0	0	0	0	0	0	0	0	0	1	M	0	0	0	0	0	0	0	0	0	0	0	0	0	0	1
Nov	0	0	0	0	0	0	0	0	0	0	0	0	0	0	0	0	0	0	0	0	0	0	0	0	0	0	0	0	0	0		0
Dec	0	0	0	0	0	0	0	0	0	0	0	0	0	0	0	0	0	0	0	0	0	0	0	0	0	0	0	0	0	0	0	0

Total Precipitation (hundredths of an inch; months in inches)

	1	2	3	4	5	6	7	8	9	10	11	12	13	14	15	16	17	18	19	20	21	22	23	24	25	26	27	28	29	30	31	Month
Jan	15	15	15	15	15	15	15	15	15	15	15	15	15	15	15	15	15	15	15	15	15	15	15	15	15	15	15	14	14	14	14	4.61
Feb	14	14	13	15	13	14	13	13	13	13	14	13	14	15	13	15	15	15	15	15	13	13	13	15	13	13	13	13	14	14	14	3.66
Mar	13	13	13	14	13	14	13	13	13	13	14	13	14	15	13	14	14	13	13	13	14	14	14	15	15	15	15	15	15	15	15	4.45
Apr	15	15	15	14	14	14	14	15	14	15	15	15	14	15	15	14	14	14	13	13	14	14	13	13	14	15	15	15	14	14		4.36
May	14	13	13	13	13	13	13	13	14	13	14	13	13	13	13	13	13	13	13	13	13	13	14	14	14	14	14	14	14	14	14	4.00
Jun	13	13	13	13	13	13	13	13	13	13	14	14	14	13	14	13	13	13	13	13	14	14	14	14	14	14	14	14	14	13		3.93
Jul	14	14	14	14	14	14	14	14	14	14	14	14	14	15	14	15	14	14	13	14	14	14	14	14	14	14	14	14	14	14	14	4.41
Aug	14	14	14	14	14	14	14	14	14	14	14	14	14	14	14	14	14	14	14	14	14	14	14	14	14	14	14	14	14	14	14	4.25
Sep	14	14	14	14	14	14	14	14	14	14	14	14	14	15	14	15	15	15	15	14	15	15	15	15	15	15	15	15	15	15		4.42
Oct	15	15	15	15	15	15	15	15	14	15	15	15	16	15	15	15	14	14	14	14	14	14	14	14	14	14	15	15	15	15	15	4.64
Nov	15	15	14	14	15	16	16	16	16	16	14	16	16	15	14	15	14	14	14	14	14	14	14	14	14	14	14	14	15	15	15	4.58
Dec	14	14	14	14	14	14	14	14	14	14	14	14	14	14	14	13	14	14	14	14	14	14	14	14	14	14	14	14	14	14	14	4.33

TORRINGTON, CT
Total Precipitation (hundredths of an inch; months in inches)

	1	2	3	4	5	6	7	8	9	10	11	12	13	14	15	16	17	18	19	20	21	22	23	24	25	26	27	28	29	30	31	Month
Jan	14	14	14	14	15	15	15	15	15	15	15	15	15	15	15	15	15	14	14	14	14	14	14	14	14	14	13	13	13	13	13	4.42
Feb	13	12	12	12	12	12	11	11	11	11	11	11	11	11	11	11	11	11	11	11	12	12	12	12	12	12	13	13				3.25
Mar	13	12	13	14	14	13	14	14	15	14	14	15	15	15	15	15	15	16	16	16	16	16	16	16	15	15	15	15	15	15	15	4.62
Apr	15	15	15	15	14	14	14	14	15	14	14	14	14	14	14	14	14	14	14	14	14	14	14	14	14	14	14	15	15	15		4.15
May	13	13	13	14	14	14	14	14	14	14	14	14	14	14	14	14	14	14	14	14	14	14	14	14	14	14	13	13	13	14	14	4.31
Jun	14	14	14	14	15	15	15	14	14	14	14	14	14	14	14	14	14	14	14	14	14	14	14	14	14	14	13	13	13	13		4.19
Jul	13	13	13	13	13	13	12	12	12	12	12	12	12	12	12	12	12	12	13	13	13	13	13	13	13	13	13	13	14	14	14	3.94
Aug	14	14	14	15	16	16	16	16	16	16	16	16	16	16	16	16	16	16	16	16	16	16	16	16	16	16	16	16	16	16	16	4.81
Sep	16	16	16	16	16	16	16	16	16	16	16	16	16	15	15	15	15	15	15	15	15	15	15	15	15	15	15	15	15	14		4.62
Oct	15	14	14	15	15	14	14	14	15	15	14	15	15	15	15	15	14	15	15	15	14	14	15	15	15	14	14	14	14	14	15	4.37
Nov	14	14	14	15	15	15	14	14	14	14	14	14	14	14	15	15	15	13	13	13	13	13	14	14	14	14	14	14	14	14		4.37
Dec	14	14	14	14	14	13	13	13	13	13	13	13	13	13	13	13	13	13	13	13	13	13	13	14	14	14	14	14	14	14	14	4.16

WEST HARTFORD, CT
Total Precipitation (hundredths of an inch; months in inches)

	1	2	3	4	5	6	7	8	9	10	11	12	13	14	15	16	17	18	19	20	21	22	23	24	25	26	27	28	29	30	31	Month
Jan	15	15	15	15	15	15	15	15	15	15	16	16	16	16	16	16	15	15	15	16	15	15	15	51	15	15	14	14	14	14	14	4.66
Feb	13	13	13	13	13	13	12	12	12	12	12	12	12	12	12	12	12	12	12	12	12	12	12	12	12	12	13	13				3.44
Mar	13	13	13	14	14	14	14	14	14	14	15	15	15	15	15	16	17	16	16	16	16	16	16	16	16	16	16	16	16	16	16	4.64
Apr	16	16	16	16	16	16	16	17	16	16	17	16	16	16	16	17	17	17	17	17	16	17	17	17	16	16	16	16	16	16		4.97
May	17	16	16	16	16	16	16	16	17	16	16	16	17	16	17	16	16	16	16	16	16	17	16	16	16	16	16	16	16	15	16	4.97
Jun	16	16	16	16	16	16	16	16	16	16	16	16	16	16	16	16	16	16	16	16	16	16	16	15	16	16	16	16	16	16		4.78
Jul	15	15	15	15	15	15	15	15	16	16	15	15	16	16	16	16	17	17	17	17	15	15	16	15	16	15	16	16	16	16	16	4.70
Aug	16	16	17	16	16	16	16	16	16	16	17	17	17	16	16	16	17	16	16	17	17	16	16	16	17	16	16	17	16	16	16	5.16
Sep	17	17	17	16	16	16	16	16	16	16	16	17	16	16	17	17	17	16	17	17	16	16	17	17	17	16	16	16	16	16		4.83
Oct	16	16	17	16	16	16	16	16	16	16	17	17	17	17	17	17	17	16	17	17	17	17	17	17	17	17	17	17	18	18	18	5.20
Nov	18	18	18	18	18	18	18	18	18	18	18	18	18	18	18	18	18	17	17	17	17	17	17	17	16	16	16	16	16	16		5.23
Dec	15	15	15	15	15	14	14	14	14	14	14	14	14	14	14	14	13	13	13	13	13	14	14	14	14	14	14	14	14	14	14	4.35

WEST THOMPSON LAKE, CT

Cooling Degree Days in °F

	1	2	3	4	5	6	7	8	9	10	11	12	13	14	15	16	17	18	19	20	21	22	23	24	25	26	27	28	29	30	31	Month
Jan	0	0	0	0	0	0	0	0	0	0	0	0	0	0	0	0	0	0	0	0	0	0	0	0	0	0	0	0	0	0	0	0
Feb	0	0	0	0	0	0	0	0	0	0	0	0	0	0	0	0	0	0	0	0	0	0	0	0	0	0	0	0				0
Mar	0	0	0	0	0	0	0	0	0	0	0	0	0	0	0	0	0	0	0	0	0	0	0	0	0	0	0	0	0	0	0	0
Apr	0	0	0	0	0	0	0	0	0	0	0	0	0	0	0	0	0	0	0	0	0	0	0	0	0	0	0	0	0	0		0
May	0	0	0	0	0	0	0	0	0	0	0	0	0	0	0	0	0	0	0	0	0	0	0	0	0	1	1	1	1	1	1	6
Jun	1	1	1	1	1	1	1	1	1	1	1	2	2	2	2	2	2	2	2	2	3	3	3	3	3	3	4	4	4	4		63
Jul	4	4	5	5	5	5	5	5	5	5	5	6	6	6	6	6	6	6	6	6	6	6	6	6	6	6	6	6	6	6	6	173
Aug	6	6	6	6	6	5	5	5	5	5	5	5	5	5	5	4	4	4	4	4	4	4	4	4	3	3	3	3	3	2	2	134
Sep	2	2	2	1	1	1	1	1	1	1	1	0	0	0	0	0	0	0	0	0	0	0	0	0	0	0	0	0	0	0		14
Oct	0	0	0	0	0	0	0	0	0	0	0	0	0	0	0	0	0	0	0	0	0	0	0	0	0	0	0	0	0	0	0	0
Nov	0	0	0	0	0	0	0	0	0	0	0	0	0	0	0	0	0	0	0	0	0	0	0	0	0	0	0	0	0	0		0
Dec	0	0	0	0	0	0	0	0	0	0	0	0	0	0	0	0	0	0	0	0	0	0	0	0	0	0	0	0	0	0	0	0

Total Precipitation (hundredths of an inch; months in inches)

	1	2	3	4	5	6	7	8	9	10	11	12	13	14	15	16	17	18	19	20	21	22	23	24	25	26	27	28	29	30	31	Month
Jan	15	15	15	15	15	15	15	16	16	16	16	16	16	16	16	16	16	15	15	15	15	15	15	15	15	14	14	14	14	14	13	4.68
Feb	13	13	13	13	12	12	12	12	12	12	12	12	11	11	11	11	11	11	11	11	12	12	12	12	12	12	12	12				3.32
Mar	13	13	13	13	13	13	14	14	14	14	14	14	14	14	14	15	15	15	15	15	15	14	15	14	15	15	12	12	15	14	15	4.44
Apr	15	15	15	15	15	15	15	15	15	15	14	14	14	14	14	15	15	15	15	15	14	14	14	14	14	14	14	14	14	13		4.40
May	14	13	13	13	13	13	13	13	13	13	13	13	13	13	13	13	13	12	12	12	12	12	12	12	12	13	12	12	13	13	13	3.94
Jun	13	13	13	13	13	13	13	13	13	13	13	13	13	13	13	13	13	13	13	13	14	14	14	14	14	14	14	14	14	14		4.00
Jul	14	14	14	14	14	14	14	14	14	14	14	15	15	15	15	15	15	15	15	15	14	15	14	14	14	14	14	15	14	15	14	4.55
Aug	15	15	15	15	15	15	15	15	15	15	15	15	15	15	14	14	14	14	14	14	14	15	14	14	14	13	15	15	14	15	15	4.47
Sep	14	14	14	14	14	14	14	14	14	14	14	14	14	14	14	14	14	14	14	14	14	13	13	13	13	13	13	13	14	14		4.00
Oct	13	13	14	14	14	14	14	14	14	14	14	14	14	14	14	14	14	14	14	14	15	15	15	15	15	15	15	15	15	15	15	4.43
Nov	15	15	16	16	16	16	16	16	16	16	16	16	16	16	16	16	16	16	16	16	16	16	15	14	14	14	15	15	15	15		4.70
Dec	15	14	14	14	14	14	14	14	14	14	14	14	14	14	13	13	13	14	14	14	14	14	14	14	14	14	14	14	14	14	15	4.32

WIGWAM RESERVOIR, CT
Cooling Degree Days in °F

	1	2	3	4	5	6	7	8	9	10	11	12	13	14	15	16	17	18	19	20	21	22	23	24	25	26	27	28	29	30	31	Month
Jan	0	0	0	0	0	0	0	0	0	0	0	0	0	0	0	0	0	0	0	0	0	0	0	0	0	0	0	0	0	0	0	0
Feb	0	0	0	0	0	0	0	0	0	0	0	0	0	0	0	0	0	0	0	0	0	0	0	0	0	0	0	0				0
Mar	0	0	0	0	0	0	0	0	0	0	0	0	0	0	0	0	0	0	0	0	0	0	0	0	0	0	0	0	0	0	0	0
Apr	0	0	0	0	0	0	0	0	0	0	0	0	0	0	0	0	0	0	0	0	0	0	0	0	0	0	0	0	0	0		0
May	0	0	0	0	0	0	0	0	0	0	0	0	0	0	0	0	0	0	0	0	0	0	0	1	1	1	1	1	1	1	1	8
Jun	1	1	1	1	1	1	1	1	2	2	2	2	2	2	2	2	2	2	3	3	3	3	3	3	3	4	4	4	4	4		69
Jul	4	5	5	5	5	5	5	5	6	6	6	6	6	6	6	6	6	6	6	6	6	6	6	6	6	6	6	6	6	6	6	177
Aug	6	5	5	5	5	5	5	5	5	5	5	4	4	4	4	4	4	4	4	3	3	3	3	3	3	3	3	2	2	2	2	120
Sep	2	2	2	2	1	1	1	1	1	1	1	1	1	1	1	1	0	0	0	0	0	0	0	0	0	0	0	0	0	0		20
Oct	0	0	0	0	0	0	0	0	0	0	0	0	0	0	M	1	0	0	0	0	0	0	0	0	0	0	0	0	0	0	0	1
Nov	0	0	0	0	0	0	0	0	0	0	0	0	0	0	0	0	0	0	0	0	0	0	0	0	0	0	0	0	0	0		0
Dec	0	0	0	0	0	0	0	0	0	0	0	0	0	0	0	0	0	0	0	0	0	0	0	0	0	0	0	0	0	0	0	0

Total Precipitation (hundredths of an inch; months in inches)

	1	2	3	4	5	6	7	8	9	10	11	12	13	14	15	16	17	18	19	20	21	22	23	24	25	26	27	28	29	30	31	Month
Jan	13	13	13	14	14	14	14	14	14	13	13	13	15	15	13	15	15	13	13	13	13	13	13	13	13	12	12	12	12	12	12	4.03
Feb	12	11	11	11	11	11	11	11	11	13	13	13	11	11	11	11	11	11	13	13	13	12	12	12	12	12	13	13				3.17
Mar	13	13	13	13	14	14	14	14	11	15	11	15	15	15	15	15	15	15	14	14	15	16	16	16	15	15	15	15	15	15	15	4.57
Apr	15	15	15	14	14	14	14	14	15	15	14	15	14	15	14	14	14	14	15	14	15	16	14	16	14	14	14	14	14	14		4.29
May	14	14	14	14	14	14	14	15	14	14	14	14	15	15	14	14	14	14	15	14	15	15	14	14	15	14	14	14	14	14	14	4.50
Jun	14	14	14	14	14	14	14	14	14	14	15	14	13	15	14	13	14	13	15	14	14	15	14	14	14	14	14	14	14	14		4.20
Jul	14	14	14	14	14	14	14	14	13	13	13	14	14	14	14	14	13	13	14	14	14	15	14	14	14	14	14	14	14	14	14	4.20
Aug	14	14	14	14	14	14	14	13	14	14	14	14	14	14	14	14	14	14	14	14	14	15	14	14	15	15	15	15	15	15	15	4.44
Sep	15	15	15	15	15	15	15	16	16	16	16	16	16	16	16	16	16	16	16	16	15	15	15	15	15	15	15	15	15	15		4.63
Oct	15	15	15	15	15	15	15	16	15	16	16	14	14	14	15	14	14	14	15	14	14	14	15	14	14	14	14	14	14	14	15	4.44
Nov	14	14	14	15	14	14	14	15	15	14	14	15	14	15	15	15	14	15	15	15	15	15	14	14	14	14	14	14	14	14		4.39
Dec	14	14	14	14	14	14	14	14	14	14	14	14	14	13	13	13	13	13	13	13	13	13	13	13	13	13	13	14	13	13	14	4.17

Daily Climate Extremes

BAKERSVILLE, CT   Maximum Temperature Records (1990–2008)

Day	Jan °F	Year	Feb °F	Year	Mar °F	Year	Apr °F	Year	May °F	Year	Jun °F	Year	Jul °F	Year	Aug °F	Year	Sep °F	Year	Oct °F	Year	Nov °F	Year	Dec °F	Year
1	48	2005	46	2001	57	2004	72	2006	89	2001	90	1999	88	2002	92	1999	86	1995	75	2002	74	2003	65	2001
2	53	2000	47	2006	60	2004	65	2000	92	2001	89	2000	93	2002	94	2006	87	1999	81	2002	70	2001	64	2006
3	61	2000	56	2006	61	1991	73	2002	93	2001	87	2007	93	2002	95	2006	91	1999	80	2007	75	2003	60	1998
4	58	2000	58	1991	61	1991	63	2000	91	2001	86	2005	93	2002	94	2006	89	1993	76	2001	69	2005	68	1998
5	58	2007	60	1991	51	1992	68	1991	84	2000	87	2005	94	2003	91	1995	83	1999	81	2007	75	1994	65	2001
6	66	2007	64	1991	63	1992	72	1991	88	2000	85	2005	95	2003	87	2001	87	1998	80	2007	75	1994	70	2001
7	47	2007	53	1991	64	2000	79	1991	92	2000	97	1999	91	2003	87	2001	86	2001	82	2007	62	1994	70	2004
8	51	2008	50	2005	62	2000	87	1991	93	2000	95	1999	93	1993	88	2001	88	2007	82	1990	65	2004	72	1998
9	53	2008	47	2005	72	2000	87	1991	93	2000	89	2005	90	1993	90	2001	90	2007	80	1990	65	1996	49	2006
10	58	2008	50	2001	67	2006	83	1991	88	2007	90	2004	90	2007	95	2001	85	2002	73	2003	70	1999	53	2004
11	49	2000	51	1999	55	2006	73	2006	87	2001	89	2000	91	2007	90	2002	85	2002	76	1990	65	2002	57	1991
12	47	2007	52	1999	54	2007	69	2006	90	1993	90	2002	87	1993	90	2002	87	2005	73	2001	65	2002	51	2006
13	55	2005	51	1998	61	2007	75	2006	84	1993	88	2005	85	1997	91	2005	86	2005	76	1995	60	2005	51	2003
14	57	2005	45	2000	70	2007	77	2002	86	1991	87	2001	90	1994	92	2002	85	2005	81	1995	60	2005	49	1991
15	58	1992	53	2006	65	2000	83	2003	87	1998	88	2001	94	1995	90	2002	83	1998	75	2000	68	1993	58	1990
16	60	1995	57	2006	66	2000	90	2002	86	1998	88	1991	96	1995	90	2002	85	1993	72	1990	73	1993	55	1991
17	57	1995	51	2006	68	2003	94	2002	87	1991	88	2000	94	1999	90	2002	86	1991	73	1996	66	2006	50	2006
18	55	2006	53	2008	66	1999	91	2002	84	1991	89	1994	95	1999	93	2002	86	1991	74	1998	65	2006	61	2000
19	52	1999	55	2008	57	1996	88	2004	83	1998	94	1994	92	2006	89	2002	81	1992	73	2007	60	2003	55	2006
20	55	1996	57	1994	56	2001	81	2006	88	1996	90	1995	95	1991	83	2003	82	1998	70	2007	70	1991	51	1996
21	58	2006	59	2002	67	2003	86	2005	95	1996	91	1995	95	1991	86	2005	83	1998	73	2000	70	1991	48	2002
22	42	2002	56	1997	63	2003	86	2001	90	1996	90	1997	93	1991	89	1995	81	2007	70	2007	61	1991	54	2002
23	49	2002	68	1997	69	2000	80	2007	91	1992	89	2002	91	2002	85	1996	79	2002	75	2007	67	1999	57	1990
24	55	1999	63	2000	70	2000	88	2007	91	1992	90	1999	92	2001	89	1996	75	2007	76	2001	66	1992	59	1990
25	51	1999	53	2002	67	2000	80	1994	87	2007	92	2003	94	2001	89	1998	80	2007	75	2001	59	2004	61	1990
26	47	2002	62	2002	71	2004	74	1993	91	2007	91	2005	90	2005	89	2007	85	2007	72	2000	60	2004	55	1996
27	56	2002	53	1997	81	1998	76	1991	82	2007	95	2003	92	2005	90	1993	88	2007	68	1991	60	2007	51	1994
28	57	2002	65	1997	84	1998	89	1994	86	1998	95	1999	88	2006	92	1993	80	2007	71	1991	62	2003	46	1994
29	63	2002	51	1996	79	1998	78	2004	86	1998	92	1999	92	1999	92	1993	75	1990	68	1999	60	2005	46	1994
30	50	2002	—		84	1998	80	1998	89	1999	90	1999	92	1999	86	2007	76	1990	64	1999	62	2001	53	2003
31	47	2001	—		90	1998	—		89	1999	—		91	1999	88	1991	—		73	1999	—		55	2003

	Jan		Feb		Mar		Apr		May		Jun		Jul		Aug		Sep		Oct		Nov		Dec	
Monthly High	66	6th	68	23rd	90	31st	94	17th	95	21st	97	7th	96	16th	95	10th	91	3rd	82	8th	75	6th	72	7th

BAKERSVILLE, CT   Minimum Temperature Records (1990–2008)

Day	Jan °F	Year	Feb °F	Year	Mar °F	Year	Apr °F	Year	May °F	Year	Jun °F	Year	Jul °F	Year	Aug °F	Year	Sep °F	Year	Oct °F	Year	Nov °F	Year	Dec °F	Year
1	0	1997	-2	1996	-1	2008	21	1991	29	1992	34	2001	47	1991	48	1998	43	1995	28	1992	26	2002	12	1995
2	-1	1999	-9	1994	2	1994	21	1995	29	2005	38	1998	46	2007	49	1992	38	1991	29	1993	23	1992	16	2007
3	-1	2008	-9	1994	-1	2003	17	1995	29	1994	39	1994	42	2001	49	1992	39	1992	30	2003	25	2002	8	2002
4	-4	2008	-3	1994	-6	2003	17	1995	29	1994	37	1998	47	1992	52	1999	43	1995	28	1996	22	1998	8	2000
5	-5	1996	-9	1996	4	2005	14	1995	27	2005	38	1993	52	1995	53	2007	41	2000	27	1996	22	2006	12	2005
6	-8	1996	-7	1996	0	2007	14	1995	28	1992	40	1993	47	2000	44	1992	39	2000	27	1996	19	1991	12	1991
7	-7	1996	-15	1995	-10	2003	17	2002	26	2001	37	2007	47	2001	45	1994	39	2000	28	1992	19	1991	3	2002
8	0	1999	-14	1995	2	2007	22	2007	28	1995	41	2000	46	2000	44	1995	45	2000	27	1999	17	1993	10	2002
9	-1	2004	-6	1995	2	2007	22	1995	31	1997	43	1994	50	2000	46	1995	36	1990	26	2001	14	1992	4	2002
10	-5	2004	-4	1994	-4	1996	21	1997	37	2003	44	1994	46	1991	48	1999	37	1990	30	2001	14	1992	6	1992
11	-8	2004	-1	1994	-3	2003	20	2007	33	1994	44	2004	45	2002	44	2007	34	1995	22	1993	18	2004	4	1995
12	-4	2004	-1	2001	4	1996	25	1997	34	2005	40	2004	45	2002	45	2006	34	1995	24	1993	20	1999	7	1995
13	6	2001	-9	2003	7	1998	24	1992	27	2005	47	1991	46	2001	45	2006	37	1992	26	1994	18	1996	1	2005
14	-7	2004	-13	2003	12	1993	26	2003	27	1996	46	1991	48	2001	47	2006	37	1992	21	1993	18	2001	-7	2005
15	-7	2004	-7	1994	2	1993	23	1992	29	1996	41	1997	51	1999	49	2007	37	2001	22	1993	14	1996	-6	2005
16	-13	1994	-4	1994	4	1993	22	1992	31	2000	41	1992	51	1991	47	1994	36	2001	28	2006	11	1996	10	2004
17	-10	2004	-2	2004	7	1992	23	1992	36	1999	41	1997	53	2002	47	1994	35	2007	29	1994	14	1996	5	1991
18	-6	2000	5	1994	5	1993	26	1995	30	2003	46	1997	53	1993	45	2000	31	1990	26	1992	19	1997	5	1991
19	-10	1994	-3	1996	-7	1993	25	1991	32	2002	49	1999	53	2000	44	2007	31	1990	26	1999	14	1997	4	1991
20	-10	1994	-5	1993	-2	1993	25	2001	28	2002	45	2004	46	1997	41	1995	30	1993	27	2003	15	1997	2	2004
21	-18	1994	-3	1993	10	1992	26	1994	31	2002	42	2004	47	1997	42	1995	30	1993	25	1991	15	1992	-1	2004
22	-17	1994	0	1993	9	1992	24	1994	31	2002	47	1992	52	2007	43	1993	32	1991	25	2002	22	2006	-1	2004
23	-9	1991	5	1999	8	2004	25	1994	35	2002	43	2005	49	2000	43	1993	32	1991	26	1992	17	2000	9	1997
24	-5	1991	6	2008	8	1992	25	1994	39	2006	41	2007	51	1992	43	1994	33	1998	24	2002	12	2000	8	2000
25	-2	2004	3	1993	9	1992	27	1999	37	1996	45	1993	48	1992	48	1995	32	1992	23	2003	11	2000	6	2000
26	-6	1991	-7	1993	13	1992	28	2001	32	1992	45	1992	49	2002	43	1995	32	1992	24	2003	10	2005	6	2000
27	-20	1994	-2	2003	15	2001	25	2002	34	1992	43	2004	44	2001	45	1995	34	2000	24	2006	13	1994	-1	1993
28	-20	1994	3	1994	17	1996	27	1993	31	1994	40	1995	45	2001	48	1995	30	1991	26	2005	8	2002	-1	1993
29	-5	2005	-1	2008	21	2001	28	2001	34	1994	44	1995	49	1992	45	1995	28	2000	23	2002	13	1996	-4	1993
30	3	2000	—		23	1996	29	2006	34	2004	46	2007	46	1997	47	1999	29	1991	25	2001	11	1995	-4	1993
31	2	1999	—		20	1991	—		37	1993	—		47	2001	43	1995	—		21	2001	—		2	1993
Monthly Low	-20	28th	-15	7th	-10	7th	14	6th	26	7th	34	1st	42	3rd	41	20th	28	29th	21	31st	8	28th	-7	14th

BARKHAMSTED, CT   Maximum Temperature Records (2000–2008)

Day	Jan °F	Year	Feb °F	Year	Mar °F	Year	Apr °F	Year	May °F	Year	Jun °F	Year	Jul °F	Year	Aug °F	Year	Sep °F	Year	Oct °F	Year	Nov °F	Year	Dec °F	Year
1	48	2005	46	2001	50	2004	73	2006	82	2004	85	2007	93	2001	90	2002	86	2000	78	2006	70	2006	64	2006
2	49	2005	46	2001	58	2004	74	2006	87	2001	89	2006	92	2002	96	2006	84	2000	80	2002	75	2003	67	2001
3	51	2000	47	2006	60	2004	64	2000	93	2001	90	2000	95	2002	96	2006	84	2005	86	2002	71	2001	50	2001
4	53	2005	56	2006	58	2002	64	2002	92	2001	77	2005	95	2002	96	2006	84	2007	80	2001	76	2003	52	2001
5	51	2007	48	2006	50	2004	64	2000	90	2001	84	2005	96	2002	93	2005	83	2000	80	2007	68	2000	60	2001
6	59	2007	54	2005	53	2004	60	2005	76	2006	88	2005	91	2003	94	2005	77	2005	86	2007	73	2005	66	2001
7	68	2007	49	2005	56	2004	70	2005	80	2002	84	2005	88	2003	91	2001	80	2007	87	2007	59	2005	69	2001
8	55	2008	51	2005	63	2000	74	2005	92	2000	87	2005	88	2003	95	2001	90	2007	75	2007	65	2004	60	2001
9	60	2008	53	2005	64	2000	72	2000	93	2000	92	2005	90	2007	95	2001	91	2007	80	2007	59	2005	54	2004
10	60	2008	49	2001	74	2000	76	2002	94	2000	93	2004	93	2002	99	2001	93	2002	78	2006	66	2006	51	2006
11	48	2002	50	2002	68	2006	71	2005	88	2004	90	2000	94	2007	92	2002	90	2002	74	2006	67	2002	50	2006
12	50	2000	44	2000	55	2006	69	2006	86	2001	92	2000	90	2005	92	2002	81	2006	76	2001	66	2002	48	2006
13	51	2006	38	2002	55	2007	68	2006	89	2004	81	2007	84	2005	93	2002	88	2005	77	2001	59	2006	42	2007
14	57	2005	42	2001	60	2007	74	2006	80	2004	91	2005	86	2002	96	2002	90	2005	76	2001	61	2005	51	2001
15	53	2006	53	2006	71	2007	73	2002	77	2004	89	2005	90	2006	97	2002	89	2005	80	2000	61	2005	56	2006
16	43	2007	54	2006	64	2000	83	2003	88	2004	89	2004	89	2002	92	2002	84	2005	76	2000	64	2001	50	2006
17	42	2001	58	2006	70	2000	87	2002	86	2007	87	2004	93	2006	92	2002	79	2006	66	2001	69	2001	56	2000
18	52	2006	54	2008	70	2003	83	2002	78	2004	87	2004	95	2006	90	2002	80	2005	70	2007	64	2006	60	2000
19	56	2006	55	2008	63	2003	88	2002	76	2004	94	2006	96	2006	95	2002	80	2006	75	2007	62	2004	50	2006
20	48	2005	51	2002	46	2001	87	2004	79	2003	90	2006	91	2005	90	2002	81	2005	70	2007	61	2003	47	2002
21	55	2006	52	2002	54	2001	86	2005	83	2003	92	2001	86	2005	88	2004	90	2005	70	2007	56	2005	56	2002
22	58	2006	60	2002	65	2003	77	2004	80	2004	86	2002	89	2006	90	2005	82	2007	74	2001	62	2001	49	2006
23	40	2002	48	2000	65	2007	86	2001	72	2007	90	2002	92	2005	90	2003	83	2005	80	2007	61	2007	48	2003
24	50	2002	50	2000	53	2007	85	2007	85	2004	89	2006	94	2002	81	2006	80	2005	75	2007	53	2003	57	2004
25	45	2002	66	2000	67	2000	87	2001	87	2007	91	2003	95	2001	84	2007	81	2007	78	2001	61	2004	54	2003
26	40	2002	53	2002	68	2000	72	2004	91	2007	94	2005	96	2001	90	2007	86	2007	78	2001	62	2004	44	2006
27	50	2002	60	2002	70	2004	70	2006	84	2007	95	2005	94	2005	83	2005	90	2007	76	2000	59	2007	45	2006
28	56	2002	52	2000	64	2007	80	2004	81	2006	95	2007	95	2005	86	2003	86	2007	67	2007	58	2006	46	2003
29	62	2006	48	2004	63	2003	80	2003	83	2007	90	2007	94	2005	90	2004	74	2007	63	2006	62	2003	51	2003
30	62	2002	—		68	2003	79	2003	88	2006	87	2002	91	2002	88	2007	73	2007	57	2004	61	2005	55	2003
31	48	2002	—		66	2006	—		87	2006	—		89	2002	87	2007	—		62	2005	—		49	2003
Monthly High	Jan 68	7th	Feb 66	25th	Mar 74	10th	Apr 88	19th	May 94	10th	Jun 95	28th	Jul 96	26th	Aug 99	10th	Sep 93	10th	Oct 87	7th	Nov 76	4th	Dec 69	7th

181

BARKHAMSTED, CT   Minimum Temperature Records (2000–2008)

Day	Jan °F	Year	Feb °F	Year	Mar °F	Year	Apr °F	Year	May °F	Year	Jun °F	Year	Jul °F	Year	Aug °F	Year	Sep °F	Year	Oct °F	Year	Nov °F	Year	Dec °F	Year
1	10	2002	2	2005	1	2008	24	2003	30	2002	37	2001	52	2007	50	2001	50	2003	39	2005	24	2001	23	2007
2	10	2002	2	2005	12	2006	24	2003	30	2002	38	2001	48	2007	58	2001	48	2007	38	2003	24	2002	15	2007
3	0	2008	6	2005	4	2003	23	2008	34	2007	40	2003	46	2001	60	2001	45	2007	33	2003	27	2002	9	2002
4	-2	2008	6	2001	-5	2003	23	2008	33	2005	42	2002	47	2001	61	2000	49	2001	33	2003	27	2006	8	2002
5	3	2008	6	2001	-4	2003	23	2004	29	2005	42	2002	55	2005	56	2000	44	2003	36	2003	26	2006	12	2002
6	12	2001	1	2007	-2	2007	22	2007	34	2005	46	2007	55	2001	52	2000	44	2000	31	2003	25	2006	12	2007
7	9	2004	0	2007	-8	2003	19	2002	28	2001	40	2007	50	2001	49	2004	44	2000	31	2003	29	2006	5	2002
8	7	2004	0	2007	0	2003	22	2007	28	2001	40	2007	50	2001	49	2004	44	2000	30	2000	24	2002	6	2002
9	0	2004	4	2003	0	2007	24	2003	30	2001	46	2000	56	2005	51	2002	52	2002	28	2001	21	2003	6	2002
10	-10	2004	11	2007	-1	2005	26	2007	40	2001	48	2001	52	2004	54	2002	44	2003	28	2000	18	2004	4	2002
11	-10	2004	5	2008	0	2003	24	2007	43	2003	48	2006	48	2002	48	2007	45	2005	30	2001	20	2004	8	2000
12	4	2004	-2	2001	0	2003	25	2007	42	2002	44	2004	48	2002	50	2006	39	2006	36	2006	22	2007	15	2005
13	8	2001	-6	2003	20	2001	30	2007	31	2005	50	2004	48	2002	48	2006	42	2006	32	2006	21	2001	6	2005
14	-10	2004	-10	2003	2	2003	26	2000	34	2007	47	2000	49	2001	49	2006	47	2007	30	2006	28	2003	0	2005
15	-8	2004	-10	2003	12	2003	27	2003	38	2002	48	2000	52	2001	50	2006	40	2001	27	2002	25	2003	-1	2005
16	-12	2004	0	2003	20	2005	28	2005	35	2002	48	2002	56	2001	56	2007	40	2001	28	2002	24	2003	0	2005
17	-8	2004	0	2004	19	2007	29	2004	35	2002	48	2002	56	2002	56	2004	39	2007	31	2006	26	2003	12	2004
18	-6	2000	2	2004	10	2000	28	2003	32	2003	50	2002	56	2002	48	2000	40	2007	35	2003	26	2001	10	2004
19	-7	2003	0	2007	16	2000	28	2001	32	2002	50	2002	57	2003	48	2007	42	2007	31	2001	26	2000	12	2004
20	-3	2005	0	2007	14	2004	26	2001	29	2002	49	2004	38	2000	52	2007	40	2004	30	2003	21	2000	2	2004
21	-5	2005	12	2008	15	2007	26	2001	33	2002	52	2000	54	2001	54	2007	46	2006	30	2003	20	2000	-4	2004
22	-11	2005	5	2001	11	2002	34	2005	35	2002	53	2007	54	2007	50	2004	42	2006	28	2002	23	2006	0	2005
23	-2	2000	6	2001	11	2004	33	2005	37	2002	48	2007	49	2000	50	2000	42	2006	27	2002	20	2000	7	2000
24	-4	2005	8	2008	15	2004	30	2002	42	2006	46	2007	55	2005	50	2003	45	2005	26	2002	12	2000	6	2000
25	-4	2005	10	2007	20	2008	28	2002	41	2006	48	2007	52	2002	50	2003	41	2006	26	2003	12	2000	8	2000
26	-4	2007	0	2003	18	2001	30	2006	40	2006	53	2000	51	2002	52	2005	42	2003	26	2003	14	2005	4	2000
27	-4	2007	-2	2003	16	2006	27	2002	46	2006	48	2004	47	2001	55	2002	36	2000	27	2006	14	2000	8	2000
28	-7	2005	-2	2003	16	2001	30	2001	49	2005	58	2004	48	2001	56	2003	40	2001	27	2006	2	2002	4	2004
29	-7	2005	0	2008	21	2001	30	2001	48	2004	60	2003	52	2001	50	2003	30	2000	26	2002	10	2002	8	2004
30	4	2004	—		20	2008	30	2006	39	2004	50	2007	52	2001	52	2003	29	2000	26	2002	21	2002	7	2000
31	4	2004	—		25	2008	—		40	2001	—		49	2001	48	2003	—		24	2001	—		14	2001
Monthly Low	-12	16th	-10	15th	-8	7th	19	7th	28	8th	37	1st	38	20th	48	31st	29	30th	24	31st	2	28th	-4	21st

BURLINGTON, CT Maximum Temperature Records (1961–2008)

Day	Jan °F Year	Feb °F Year	Mar °F Year	Apr °F Year	May °F Year	Jun °F Year	Jul °F Year	Aug °F Year	Sep °F Year	Oct °F Year	Nov °F Year	Dec °F Year
1	64 1966	59 1988	61 1976	85 1998	83 1985	91 1987	94 1964	95 1999	92 1973	86 1986	73 1999	65 2006
2	58 1966	59 1989	64 1972	74 2006	88 2001	89 2006	94 1968	95 2006	92 1961	85 2002	78 1974	68 2006
3	55 2000	54 1988	63 2004	75 1963	92 2001	90 1989	95 2002	98 1975	94 1980	86 2002	80 1982	63 1982
4	64 2000	60 1991	59 1991	74 2002	92 2001	86 1967	97 1966	95 2007	90 1999	82 1967	79 2003	62 1998
5	58 2000	64 1991	66 1974	75 1974	91 2001	87 1966	96 2002	92 2002	93 1973	82 2007	77 1994	70 1998
6	62 2007	66 1991	62 1992	73 1985	82 2000	89 1966	96 1999	92 2007	90 1983	88 2007	78 1994	68 1982
7	72 2007	55 1991	58 2004	73 1991	88 2000	91 1968	96 1999	91 1989	92 1983	89 2007	73 1978	68 1998
8	54 1998	52 2005	66 1974	87 1991	93 2000	95 1999	98 1993	93 2007	89 2007	88 1963	72 1975	68 1998
9	63 2008	55 1990	66 1987	80 1991	92 2000	94 1984	96 1988	92 1983	93 2007	84 2007	72 1975	75 1998
10	62 2008	59 1990	72 2000	75 2005	94 2000	93 1984	94 1981	95 2001	90 2002	80 2006	69 1986	60 1980
11	57 1983	53 2002	70 1977	72 2005	91 1979	94 1974	97 1988	92 1973	90 1989	81 1997	73 1999	64 1966
12	58 1980	58 1981	70 1977	75 1987	90 1985	93 1984	94 1988	93 1988	95 1983	75 1995	67 2002	61 1966
13	52 2006	55 1999	66 1973	85 1977	90 2004	91 1973	95 1966	92 2002	91 1961	83 1962	63 1982	61 1979
14	60 2005	55 1974	77 1990	85 1977	86 1991	92 1984	95 1966	96 1988	90 2005	80 1995	72 1993	66 1979
15	62 1995	53 1990	69 2007	76 2002	78 1985	92 1988	95 1965	96 2002	89 2005	82 2000	70 1989	63 1984
16	60 1995	57 1967	79 1990	84 2003	89 2004	94 1988	92 1997	95 2002	85 1993	81 1975	75 1993	57 2006
17	59 1995	60 2006	80 1990	89 2002	88 1965	94 1967	96 1980	95 2002	90 1991	80 1964	72 1990	59 1975
18	58 2006	62 1981	71 2003	94 2002	91 1974	90 1994	95 1999	96 2002	88 1991	81 1968	67 2006	60 2000
19	62 1990	67 1981	67 1989	91 2002	92 1962	94 1994	96 1991	94 2002	84 1972	79 1968	70 1963	61 2000
20	58 1986	64 1981	66 1976	93 1976	95 1962	94 1994	99 1991	92 1966	90 1983	79 1963	67 1991	55 1996
21	56 2006	58 1994	73 1976	86 2005	95 1996	91 1964	100 1991	91 1983	92 1983	78 1969	72 1991	52 1998
22	60 2006	62 2002	62 2003	80 1985	92 1996	92 1997	100 1991	89 1976	88 1980	79 1979	72 1991	57 2002
23	53 1986	69 1997	70 1979	86 2001	92 1992	92 1997	92 1994	91 1976	92 1970	85 1979	64 2007	56 1994
24	60 1967	65 1990	70 1979	87 2007	93 1964	91 1975	94 1991	89 1996	90 1970	79 1978	69 1992	58 1998
25	61 1967	70 1985	72 1988	85 2001	91 1975	92 2003	94 1999	91 1998	84 1964	75 1963	68 1979	62 1990
26	58 1978	67 1976	74 1963	80 1982	91 2007	94 1999	94 2001	92 2007	88 2007	81 1963	70 1979	57 1996
27	57 1978	63 1976	71 2004	80 1991	90 1965	95 2003	94 1963	90 1993	91 2007	82 1963	64 1979	61 1964
28	63 1974	66 1997	81 1998	91 1962	89 1991	97 1966	93 2005	93 1993	86 1998	82 1963	64 2001	60 1982
29	54 2006	63 1976	83 1998	90 1990	87 1991	94 1963	93 1970	95 1993	79 1987	77 1989	70 1990	54 1988
30	65 2002	—	78 1986	87 1974	92 1987	93 1991	93 1999	91 1977	81 1987	73 1971	65 1968	63 1984
31	54 1974	—	82 1998	—	90 1987	—	95 1999	93 1973	—	74 1989	—	56 1990
Monthly High	Jan 72 7th	Feb 70 25th	Mar 83 29th	Apr 94 18th	May 95 21st	Jun 97 28th	Jul 100 22nd	Aug 98 3rd	Sep 95 12th	Oct 89 7th	Nov 80 3rd	Dec 75 8th

183

BURLINGTON, CT   Minimum Temperature Records (1961–2008)

Day	Jan °F	Year	Feb °F	Year	Mar °F	Year	Apr °F	Year	May °F	Year	Jun °F	Year	Jul °F	Year	Aug °F	Year	Sep °F	Year	Oct °F	Year	Nov °F	Year	Dec °F	Year
1	-9	1963	-13	1971	0	1980	13	1969	30	1978	35	2001	41	1989	48	1964	40	1965	30	1992	22	1988	8	1976
2	-10	1968	-12	1971	0	1967	19	1964	30	1964	39	1993	48	1978	43	1992	40	1991	30	1992	24	1965	4	1989
3	-8	1968	-9	1971	4	1962	20	1962	27	1966	37	1964	40	1995	50	1976	42	2001	32	2003	19	1984	0	1976
4	-6	1981	-10	1965	3	1982	19	1962	30	1966	39	1965	40	1995	46	1966	43	1987	32	2003	23	1998	2	1976
5	-6	1981	-12	1965	4	2003	16	1995	29	1966	40	1993	45	1986	45	1972	40	1989	29	1996	24	1989	6	1989
6	-3	1976	-7	1988	2	2007	16	1995	28	1992	39	1964	45	1961	44	1972	38	1988	26	1984	20	1991	8	1966
7	-3	1976	-10	1995	-3	2003	14	1982	29	2001	39	1964	46	1965	46	1964	39	1984	27	1984	18	1962	8	2002
8	0	1981	-10	1963	3	1986	14	1982	29	2001	41	1987	50	1979	49	1994	41	1988	29	1999	20	1993	3	1964
9	-12	1968	-10	1963	3	2007	17	1989	29	1974	41	2002	42	1963	45	1989	40	1990	28	1988	16	1992	3	1989
10	-8	1968	-5	1975	-1	1984	22	1985	30	1985	37	1980	47	1963	42	1964	38	1975	25	1989	18	2004	1	1968
11	-13	1988	-12	1962	0	1984	24	2007	26	1966	27	1972	48	1983	46	1964	40	1975	25	1993	20	1961	2	1968
12	-13	1988	-8	1979	0	1984	20	1976	30	1969	37	1980	48	1978	47	1968	39	1985	21	1964	19	1976	-3	1988
13	-10	1981	-11	1967	5	1984	21	1967	32	1969	42	1990	44	1989	47	1972	40	1985	20	1976	20	1996	-3	1988
14	-8	1988	-10	1979	12	1993	20	1991	29	1996	43	1970	43	1989	44	1964	34	1963	25	1993	11	1986	-1	1976
15	-14	1988	-6	1979	4	1993	23	1997	34	1996	38	1978	51	2001	46	1964	35	1963	26	1993	10	1986	1	1976
16	-13	1994	-10	1987	7	1992	25	1992	35	2000	43	1985	50	1966	46	1994	35	1964	27	1978	16	1996	4	1961
17	-14	1971	-4	2003	11	1967	22	1988	34	1983	41	1964	50	1966	46	1979	37	1984	29	1978	18	1967	2	1988
18	-12	1982	-7	1979	2	1967	25	1962	33	1983	46	1986	53	1989	46	1979	34	1990	25	1978	22	1980	-3	1980
19	-12	1982	-11	1979	-6	1967	27	1990	33	1985	42	1986	51	1971	45	1973	35	1990	23	1976	19	1997	1	1989
20	-10	1976	-6	1966	6	1993	28	2001	38	2002	46	1986	47	1965	40	1988	32	1979	23	1974	10	1986	-1	1989
21	-8	1971	-2	1993	8	1986	28	1981	36	1964	43	1968	47	1966	45	1992	31	1991	21	1972	10	1986	-3	1962
22	-18	1984	-2	1968	11	1988	26	1994	38	1994	44	1990	49	1965	40	1992	24	1991	20	1988	1	1987	-2	1962
23	-9	1976	-3	1972	11	2004	25	1989	38	1990	42	1992	52	1977	41	1988	36	1997	25	1997	11	1989	-1	1989
24	-9	1976	-3	1972	14	1992	26	1989	35	1963	40	1972	49	1985	44	1987	27	1989	20	1969	7	1989	-7	1989
25	-5	1963	3	1993	16	1974	26	1965	35	1967	42	1972	51	1992	41	1987	32	1974	20	1969	10	1989	-8	1989
26	-4	1963	-5	1990	16	1974	27	1989	34	1972	42	1979	49	1976	46	1989	34	1966	26	2003	10	1993	-13	1980
27	-6	1994	-4	1990	14	1975	30	1987	34	1968	46	1965	49	2001	47	1964	30	1989	25	1987	12	1993	-10	1980
28	-16	1994	-3	1964	11	1982	23	1989	39	1983	42	1995	48	2001	47	1964	29	1965	20	1976	13	2002	0	1993
29	-6	1971	0	1964	12	1974	29	1996	33	1994	46	1995	47	1968	39	1986	30	2000	21	1976	16	1996	0	1993
30	-4	1977	—		11	1970	28	1989	30	1992	40	1988	49	1968	35	1965	32	1991	25	1988	12	1976	-2	1987
31	-10	1965	—		17	1970	—		36	1965	—		49	1964	36	1965	—		19	1988	—		-12	1962
Monthly Low	-18	22nd	-13	1st	-6	19th	13	1st	26	11th	27	11th	40	4th	35	30th	24	22nd	19	31st	1	22nd	-13	26th

DANBURY, CT   Maximum Temperature Records (1937–2008)

Day	Jan °F	Year	Feb °F	Year	Mar °F	Year	Apr °F	Year	May °F	Year	Jun °F	Year	Jul °F	Year	Aug °F	Year	Sep °F	Year	Oct °F	Year	Nov °F	Year	Dec °F	Year
1	48	2005	46	2001	57	2004	72	2006	89	2001	90	1999	88	2002	92	1999	86	1995	75	2002	74	2003	65	2001
2	53	2000	47	2006	60	2004	65	2000	92	2001	89	2000	93	2002	94	2006	87	1999	81	2002	70	2001	64	2006
3	61	2000	56	2006	61	1991	73	2002	93	2001	87	2007	93	2002	95	2006	91	1999	80	2002	75	2003	60	1998
4	58	2000	58	1991	61	1991	63	2000	91	2001	86	2005	93	2002	94	2006	89	1993	76	2001	69	2005	68	1998
5	58	2007	60	1991	51	1992	68	1991	84	2000	87	2005	94	2003	91	1995	83	1999	81	2007	75	1994	65	2001
6	66	2007	64	1991	63	1992	72	1991	88	2000	85	2005	95	2003	87	2001	87	1998	80	2007	75	1994	70	2001
7	47	2007	53	1991	64	2000	79	1991	92	2000	97	1999	91	2003	87	2001	86	2001	82	2007	62	1994	72	1998
8	51	2008	50	2005	62	2000	87	1991	93	2000	95	1999	93	1993	88	2001	88	2007	82	2007	65	2004	49	2006
9	53	2008	47	2005	72	2000	87	1991	93	2000	89	2005	90	1993	90	2001	90	2007	82	1990	65	1996	53	2004
10	58	2008	50	2001	67	2006	83	1991	88	2007	90	2004	90	2007	95	2001	90	2007	80	1990	65	1996	57	1991
11	49	2000	51	1999	55	2006	73	2006	87	2001	89	2000	91	2007	90	2002	85	2002	73	2003	70	1999	51	2006
12	47	2007	52	1999	54	2007	69	2006	90	1993	90	2002	87	1993	90	2002	85	2002	76	1990	65	2002	51	2003
13	55	2005	51	1998	61	2007	75	2006	84	1993	88	2005	85	1997	91	2005	87	2005	73	2001	65	2005	49	1991
14	57	2005	45	2000	70	2007	77	2002	86	1991	87	2001	90	1994	92	2002	86	2005	76	1995	60	2005	58	1990
15	58	1992	53	2006	65	2000	83	2003	87	1998	88	2001	94	1995	92	2002	85	2005	81	1995	60	2005	55	1991
16	60	1995	57	2006	66	2000	90	2002	86	1998	88	1991	96	1995	90	2002	83	1998	75	2000	68	1993	50	2006
17	57	1995	51	2006	68	2003	94	2002	87	1991	88	2000	94	1999	90	2002	85	1993	72	1990	73	1993	61	2000
18	55	2006	53	2008	66	1999	91	2002	84	1991	89	1994	95	1999	93	2002	86	1991	73	1996	66	2006	55	2006
19	52	1999	55	2008	57	1996	88	2004	83	1998	94	1994	92	2006	89	2002	86	1991	74	1998	65	2006	51	1996
20	55	1996	57	1994	56	2001	81	2006	88	1996	90	1995	95	1991	83	2003	81	1992	73	2007	60	2003	48	2002
21	58	2006	59	2002	67	2003	86	2005	95	1996	91	1995	95	1991	86	2005	82	1998	73	2000	70	1991	54	2002
22	42	2002	56	1997	63	2003	86	2001	90	1996	90	1997	93	1991	89	1995	83	1998	70	2007	61	1991	57	1990
23	49	2002	68	1997	69	2000	80	2007	91	1992	89	2002	91	2002	85	1996	81	2007	75	2007	67	1999	59	1990
24	55	1999	63	2000	70	2000	88	2007	91	1992	90	1999	92	2001	89	1996	79	2002	76	2001	66	1992	61	1990
25	51	1999	53	2002	67	2000	80	1994	87	2007	92	2003	94	2001	89	1998	75	2007	75	2001	59	2004	55	1996
26	47	2002	62	2002	71	2004	74	1993	91	2007	91	2005	90	2005	89	2007	85	2007	72	2000	60	2004	51	1994
27	56	2002	53	1997	81	1998	76	1991	82	2007	95	2003	92	2005	90	1993	88	2007	68	1991	60	2007	46	1994
28	57	2002	65	1997	84	1998	89	1994	86	1998	95	1999	88	2006	92	1993	80	2007	71	1991	62	2003	46	1994
29	63	2002	51	1996	79	1998	78	2004	86	1998	92	1999	92	1999	92	1993	75	1990	68	1999	60	2005	53	2003
30	50	2002	—		84	1998	80	1998	89	1999	90	1999	92	1999	86	2007	76	1990	64	1999	62	2001	55	2003
31	47	2001	—		90	1998			89	1999	—		91	1999	88	1991	—		73	1999	—		55	1990
Monthly Low	66	6th	68	23rd	90	31st	94	17th	95	21st	97	7th	96	16th	95	10th	91	3rd	82	8th	75	6th	72	7th

DANBURY, CT   Minimum Temperature Records (1937–2008)

Day	Jan °F	Year	Feb °F	Year	Mar °F	Year	Apr °F	Year	May °F	Year	Jun °F	Year	Jul °F	Year	Aug °F	Year	Sep °F	Year	Oct °F	Year	Nov °F	Year	Dec °F	Year
1	2	1997	-12	1948	3	1980	15	1970	28	1943	35	1938	38	1943	47	1964	42	1942	31	1947	22	1937	8	1976
2	-5	1968	-7	1961	0	1967	17	1964	32	1978	41	1993	40	1943	44	1947	40	1949	27	1997	23	1976	8	1967
3	-1	1981	-7	1961	4	1950	16	1944	29	1966	36	1964	40	1978	44	1959	36	1941	27	1942	20	1980	-4	1938
4	-12	1981	-8	1985	-3	1950	15	1954	29	1985	38	1944	45	1944	45	1966	40	1946	25	1945	18	1939	5	1976
5	-6	1981	-7	1996	2	1948	17	1995	28	1974	39	1939	45	1979	47	1972	40	1997	24	1943	16	1942	9	1976
6	-7	1996	-3	1996	-4	1948	17	1982	33	1996	35	1939	44	1979	44	1951	35	1938	24	1984	21	1991	10	1976
7	2	1942	-8	1948	-2	2003	14	1982	27	1996	36	1944	46	1979	46	1964	35	1984	24	1984	20	1962	3	1964
8	-16	1942	-6	1963	6	1986	18	1982	30	1974	40	1949	40	1942	45	1950	37	1984	25	1954	17	1993	5	1964
9	-14	1942	-10	1948	-1	1943	20	1996	28	1956	38	1980	43	1948	49	1995	34	1938	27	1953	15	1992	7	1960
10	-6	1968	-10	1979	-3	1996	20	1985	25	1947	36	1957	47	1983	41	1964	34	1938	16	1943	20	2004	2	1949
11	-14	1942	-9	1979	5	1996	20	1938	28	1947	36	1980	47	1954	40	1941	34	1943	23	1993	14	1956	-1	1958
12	-13	1981	-10	1979	4	1984	16	1943	31	1938	37	1980	46	1978	47	1968	28	1943	24	1996	18	1937	4	1962
13	-7	1981	-10	1967	3	1948	22	1967	30	1967	40	1979	48	1973	41	1941	27	1943	26	1981	19	1996	1	1943
14	-7	1954	-6	1979	4	1948	20	1942	26	1996	42	1978	52	2000	37	1941	35	1963	23	1993	16	1939	1	2005
15	-9	1957	-12	1943	5	1993	22	1944	30	1984	38	1978	48	1950	44	1964	33	1975	24	1937	14	1996	-2	1943
16	-8	1994	-16	1943	14	1980	18	1943	29	1939	41	1961	46	1942	45	1972	33	1964	25	1939	10	1996	0	1943
17	-8	1971	-7	1943	10	1967	25	1962	33	1956	41	1965	44	1946	43	1979	32	1948	18	1937	15	1967	-11	1942
18	-13	1982	-8	1943	-1	1967	24	1948	30	1944	38	1958	49	1956	37	1941	32	1943	22	1978	16	1959	-1	1942
19	-16	1938	0	1996	-9	1967	25	1944	34	2002	41	1956	40	1939	40	1943	34	1959	19	1948	17	1997	-10	1944
20	-8	1994	-2	1978	1	1949	27	1974	31	2002	43	1959	49	1997	41	1949	29	1941	24	1972	16	1992	-11	1942
21	-16	1994	-6	1950	10	1986	25	1956	31	2002	42	1968	45	1944	40	1941	30	1956	20	1972	16	1984	-10	1944
22	-17	1984	-2	1946	12	1986	26	1994	33	2002	45	1963	43	1939	39	1982	31	1948	23	1983	16	1969	-11	1942
23	-8	1970	-5	1972	13	1940	25	1982	32	1976	45	2007	49	1977	45	1957	32	1947	19	1997	12	1942	-3	1945
24	-7	1948	-1	1948	10	1940	29	2002	32	1963	44	1944	46	1985	42	1957	28	1963	20	1969	13	2000	1	1975
25	-4	1961	4	1964	12	1956	28	1956	30	1956	40	1942	50	1953	42	1971	29	1950	21	1939	10	1938	-10	1980
26	-8	1994	0	1950	10	1960	28	1963	32	1938	40	1979	47	1976	42	1995	32	1947	23	1952	0	1938	-11	1980
27	-18	1994	-1	1950	15	2001	29	2002	34	1968	46	1965	47	1977	44	1943	27	1947	25	1976	12	1949	-8	1948
28	-6	1939	2	1950	13	1966	28	1972	32	1994	43	1995	46	1977	38	1941	25	1947	20	1976	11	1996	-6	1950
29	-4	1963	6	1980	15	1974	27	1947	35	1957	46	1995	50	1968	37	1941	26	1942	24	1942	12	1996	-2	1944
30	-5	1948			14	1970	28	1944	33	1938	40	1938	47	1968	38	1965	23	1941	23	1948	12	1976	0	1962
31	-10	1965			18	1964			32	1941			46	1956	38	1976			21	1966			-7	1963
Monthly Low	Jan -18	27th	Feb -16	16th	Mar -9	19th	Apr 14	7th	May 25	10th	Jun 35	6th	Jul 38	1st	Aug 37	29th	Sep 23	30th	Oct 16	10th	Nov 0	26th	Dec -11	26th

FALLS VILLAGE, CT   Maximum Temperature Records (1916–2008)

Day	Jan °F	Jan Year	Feb °F	Feb Year	Mar °F	Mar Year	Apr °F	Apr Year	May °F	May Year	Jun °F	Jun Year	Jul °F	Jul Year	Aug °F	Aug Year	Sep °F	Sep Year	Oct °F	Oct Year	Nov °F	Nov Year	Dec °F	Dec Year
1	59	1966	63	1989	65	1972	84	1998	87	2001	93	1937	95	1968	100	1917	95	1953	86	1927	80	1950	66	2001
2	58	1979	54	1981	68	1991	72	1967	90	2001	91	1919	96	1934	96	1917	101	1953	90	1927	81	1982	62	2006
3	57	2000	59	1991	68	1991	77	1981	91	2001	100	1919	98	1966	99	1930	99	1953	85	1922	76	2003	61	1998
4	63	1950	61	1991	65	1974	79	1950	90	2001	97	1919	101	1919	97	1926	96	1929	83	1931	77	1994	69	1998
5	62	1950	64	1991	68	1976	84	1928	90	1949	94	1930	98	1919	100	1955	90	1983	88	1941	75	1994	65	2001
6	67	2007	57	1991	67	1976	80	1928	89	1930	94	1925	97	1999	95	1931	93	1983	88	1941	74	1948	70	2001
7	57	1930	54	2005	67	1974	87	1991	91	2000	97	1925	97	1988	101	1918	91	1943	85	1963	73	1975	72	1998
8	58	1930	62	1933	66	2000	87	1991	90	2000	94	1984	98	1988	94	2001	89	2007	83	1990	72	1975	61	1951
9	59	2008	60	1925	73	2000	83	1991	94	2000	100	1933	100	1936	99	2001	92	1936	82	1949	73	1975	63	1966
10	54	1937	55	1955	71	1977	83	1922	92	2000	93	2004	100	1926	98	1949	94	1931	86	1949	73	1931	65	1946
11	59	1924	61	1960	72	1977	81	1922	90	1979	93	1984	97	1936	98	1966	94	1983	85	1949	69	2002	63	1966
12	58	1980	58	1981	65	1977	89	1945	90	2004	91	1973	96	1922	98	1944	91	1961	86	1928	66	1964	64	1979
13	65	1932	57	1951	75	1990	88	1945	87	1991	92	1984	96	1966	96	2002	91	1947	84	1954	70	1964	61	1984
14	65	1932	60	1946	75	1990	83	1945	88	1991	94	1956	96	1995	98	2002	91	1948	82	1954	70	1989	60	1920
15	64	1937	61	1954	78	1990	84	1941	90	2004	95	1945	99	1995	94	2002	89	1939	82	1956	73	1993	58	1975
16	62	1932	72	1954	81	1990	88	2002	92	1932	94	1981	96	1995	95	2002	92	1939	82	1947	70	1928	58	1982
17	59	1990	60	1981	79	1945	92	2002	88	1977	93	1957	97	2006	96	1935	89	1939	85	1947	70	1928	64	2000
18	63	1990	65	1981	72	1927	90	1976	92	1962	96	1957	97	1953	95	2002	88	1948	82	1928	72	1928	58	1928
19	60	1949	64	1981	65	1927	90	1976	93	1962	94	1923	99	1991	93	2002	90	1983	82	1963	71	1941	51	1957
20	58	1951	65	1930	77	1945	90	1941	92	1996	96	1931	100	1991	95	1937	92	1983	78	1965	73	1985	60	1957
21	56	2006	65	1953	79	1921	87	1923	91	1996	98	1921	99	1930	93	1955	87	1980	79	1979	72	1931	61	1957
22	60	1959	70	1997	79	1938	86	1973	90	1992	98	1921	102	1926	95	1916	90	1931	84	1979	68	1931	60	1990
23	60	1957	66	1985	80	1938	84	2001	94	1930	92	1965	99	1933	95	1916	89	1970	85	1947	73	1931	65	1990
24	59	1999	70	1985	72	1988	85	2001	93	1930	95	1919	95	2001	93	1947	88	1959	78	2001	69	1931	61	1990
25	58	1938	66	1976	72	1987	84	1942	92	1932	94	1949	95	2001	96	1947	88	1970	78	1963	66	1979	62	1964
26	69	1950	63	2002	76	2004	81	1925	95	1932	98	1952	93	1963	100	1948	88	1930	79	1963	66	1979	60	1964
27	63	1974	65	1997	79	1998	90	1962	88	1991	98	1941	95	1955	99	1948	87	1933	81	1963	65	1979	59	1964
28	58	2002	65	1997	83	1998	89	1990	89	1972	94	1941	96	1929	96	1948	82	1959	76	1971	70	1990	61	1949
29	60	2002	61	1976	83	1945	93	1990	95	1931	103	1933	96	1964	96	1945	87	1921	78	1918	68	1990	71	1984
30	55	2006	—		85	1998	85	1974	95	1921	96	1964	96	1917	97	1953	87	1986	78	1946	65	1933	67	1984
31	61	1947	—		88	1998	—		91	1999	—		97	1933	95	1953	—		77	1946	—		61	1932
Monthly High	69	26th	72	16th	88	31st	93	29th	95	30th	103	29th	102	22nd	101	7th	101	2nd	90	2nd	81	2nd	72	7th

187

FALLS VILLAGE, CT   Minimum Temperature Records (1916–2008)

Day	Jan °F	Year	Feb °F	Year	Mar °F	Year	Apr °F	Year	May °F	Year	Jun °F	Year	Jul °F	Year	Aug °F	Year	Sep °F	Year	Oct °F	Year	Nov °F	Year	Dec °F	Year
1	-17	1918	-23	1948	-10	1934	8	1923	22	1931	30	1924	39	1936	42	1964	38	1946	25	1947	12	1925	0	1936
2	-23	1918	-26	1918	-5	1920	10	1923	21	1943	31	1933	38	1978	39	1947	38	1994	27	1997	15	1923	-6	1945
3	-9	1918	-18	1971	-4	1950	9	1924	21	1946	32	1964	37	1929	40	1956	33	1941	25	1994	12	1923	-7	1976
4	-14	1981	-18	1965	-11	1950	6	1954	25	1986	32	2002	39	1929	41	1966	31	1946	22	1945	16	1939	-5	1976
5	-14	1996	-15	1965	-4	1969	10	1995	22	1920	32	1944	39	1927	42	1972	36	1994	23	1935	15	1952	-1	1971
6	-16	1996	-16	1935	-18	1948	12	1944	25	1954	33	1964	40	1979	40	1934	36	2000	22	1984	14	1954	0	1976
7	-14	1996	-21	1995	-10	2003	16	2002	20	1970	34	1958	37	1979	40	1964	33	1962	21	1992	14	1916	1	1964
8	-18	1942	-16	1967	-15	1920	11	1982	25	1968	30	1944	41	1979	38	1929	35	1978	18	1964	12	1960	-1	1964
9	-20	1968	-26	1934	-6	1943	12	1982	23	1956	32	1980	41	1969	43	1923	32	1938	22	2001	12	1992	-5	1949
10	-20	1968	-24	1948	-5	1984	17	1982	20	1947	35	1957	41	1954	37	1964	32	1978	18	1929	13	1954	-10	1949
11	-22	1968	-19	1936	-2	1939	17	1938	24	1966	34	1972	43	1954	37	1941	28	1995	16	1929	10	1954	-6	1958
12	-25	1981	-21	1979	-4	1916	13	1967	26	1941	33	1972	39	1945	40	1930	29	1933	18	1964	12	1926	-9	1962
13	-24	1981	-14	1967	-6	1948	17	1967	26	1938	37	1980	41	1973	39	1930	25	1933	21	1917	11	1920	-7	1962
14	-18	1957	-15	1944	-3	1948	14	1940	24	1928	35	1979	45	1940	33	1941	27	1946	18	1953	12	1971	-9	2005
15	-18	1957	-21	1916	4	1993	13	1940	25	1947	33	1978	42	1929	38	1964	30	1975	20	1937	10	1942	-7	2005
16	-17	1994	-7	1916	4	1993	14	1943	27	1947	35	1921	36	1946	40	1968	28	1964	17	1939	5	1933	-7	1943
17	-22	1971	-15	1930	-5	1916	19	1995	27	1939	33	1926	40	1954	37	1979	29	1950	16	1937	9	1924	-10	1951
18	-24	1957	-19	1979	-8	1956	18	1962	27	1983	34	1958	40	1946	35	1941	30	1950	18	1978	11	1924	-12	1919
19	-23	1971	-6	1948	-9	1967	19	1926	26	1944	37	1956	42	1944	39	1962	29	1929	13	1921	1	1924	-15	1919
20	-19	1994	-20	1936	-7	1949	20	1961	26	2002	35	1926	38	1929	38	1995	27	1993	16	1972	7	1986	-15	1942
21	-26	1994	-14	1936	0	1956	18	1925	27	2002	35	1940	42	1965	39	1953	27	1962	14	1972	11	1987	-15	1942
22	-30	1961	-13	1916	2	1965	19	1947	28	2002	33	1940	39	1944	34	1982	29	1962	14	1948	9	1916	-14	1944
23	-22	1961	-13	1963	5	1934	20	1994	29	1932	36	1940	43	1977	39	1923	27	1947	15	1930	6	1972	-10	1960
24	-20	1961	-9	1948	6	1992	20	1930	27	1963	36	1932	42	1947	37	1971	24	1963	19	1980	5	1989	-15	1989
25	-16	1935	-18	1934	7	1940	19	1936	25	1956	34	1979	42	1953	31	1940	24	1950	17	1939	5	1936	-14	1980
26	-17	1948	-10	1950	3	1960	19	1947	30	1956	32	1979	41	1976	37	1942	18	1947	17	1952	-8	1938	-16	1980
27	-27	1994	-15	1963	9	2001	23	1969	30	1969	41	1979	43	1977	39	1969	18	1947	17	1976	7	1932	-12	1948
28	-26	1935	-18	1934	8	1982	19	1933	26	1994	36	1995	43	1946	35	1941	17	1947	11	1936	1	1938	-20	1933
29	-17	1925	0	1980	2	1923	19	1934	30	1949	40	1995	43	1968	34	1941	24	1947	15	1941	2	1932	-17	1933
30	-16	1965	—		6	1970	24	1976	30	1949	39	1988	41	1968	34	1965	21	1941	16	1941	4	1947	-20	1917
31	-19	1948	—		12	1947	—		28	1947	—		42	2001	32	1976	—		16	1925	—		-17	1917
Monthly Low	-30	22nd	-26	9th	-18	6th	6	4th	20	10th	30	8th	36	16th	31	25th	17	28th	11	28th	-8	26th	-20	30th

GROTON, CT   Maximum Temperature Records (1957–2008)

Day	Jan °F	Year	Feb °F	Year	Mar °F	Year	Apr °F	Year	May °F	Year	Jun °F	Year	Jul °F	Year	Aug °F	Year	Sep °F	Year	Oct °F	Year	Nov °F	Year	Dec °F	Year
1	62	1966	55	1982	59	2004	66	1975	80	1957	88	1987	95	1964	94	2006	92	2005	80	1986	75	1982	69	2001
2	56	2005	55	1973	62	1985	71	1986	86	2001	84	1961	91	2002	99	1975	90	1966	82	2002	71	1982	62	1968
3	60	2000	57	1991	62	1991	77	1967	82	2001	81	1985	97	1966	94	2006	90	1973	78	2000	74	2003	60	1998
4	62	1998	59	1991	60	1974	63	2001	87	2001	84	1971	96	2002	90	1995	91	1973	81	1967	74	1975	69	1998
5	58	1993	63	1991	63	1985	66	2005	79	2000	84	2005	98	1999	91	1979	88	1983	82	2002	70	1975	65	2001
6	64	2007	55	2008	58	1984	72	1991	76	1993	88	1968	94	1999	91	1977	89	1985	83	1959	68	1959	66	2001
7	57	2007	52	2005	63	1987	79	1991	83	2004	88	1999	91	1981	90	2001	91	1983	84	2005	67	1975	69	1998
8	58	2007	52	1965	69	1987	77	1991	85	2000	96	2005	92	1981	92	2001	91	1985	82	2007	65	1996	61	1966
9	60	2008	53	1990	61	2002	72	1970	82	2000	92	1984	94	1993	94	2001	89	1959	78	2003	72	1975	67	1991
10	65	2006	54	2001	59	1977	67	2002	91	1979	94	2005	94	1993	90	1973	88	1961	78	1997	70	1985	59	1987
11	60	1980	56	1981	63	1986	66	1987	84	2001	92	1984	91	1981	90	1977	93	1983	75	1960	66	1984	67	1971
12	56	1975	55	1984	61	2001	84	1977	86	1991	92	1973	90	1966	89	1988	90	1961	80	1969	66	1982	60	1979
13	59	1972	53	2008	77	1990	76	1977	77	2004	90	1983	96	1979	90	2005	93	2005	77	1995	66	1964	61	1983
14	61	1995	55	1992	64	2002	71	2002	79	1985	89	2005	91	1995	89	2003	87	1981	79	1990	67	1993	58	2001
15	59	1995	58	1967	67	1990	78	1960	82	1976	91	1988	95	1995	92	1985	87	2005	78	1975	73	1993	60	2001
16	59	1995	57	2006	65	2000	84	2003	80	1991	94	1957	93	1983	91	1970	87	1991	78	1963	67	2006	62	1971
17	57	1995	63	1976	65	2001	88	2002	87	1974	91	1957	93	2006	95	2005	89	1991	78	1963	66	2006	56	1984
18	58	1990	65	1981	67	1999	82	2002	87	1977	85	1995	95	1991	92	1987	81	1965	74	2006	66	1987	61	1984
19	55	1996	61	1997	59	2001	78	1976	82	1998	92	1994	95	1977	90	2002	87	2005	76	1963	65	1991	56	1990
20	53	1986	61	1997	67	2001	80	1976	89	1996	92	1995	97	1991	94	1983	88	1983	77	1984	68	1991	58	2002
21	57	2006	60	1981	62	1979	75	2007	86	1996	91	1964	101	1991	90	1976	83	1980	78	1963	67	1991	60	1973
22	55	1973	61	1991	68	1979	79	1960	87	1992	87	1965	95	1957	93	2005	87	1980	74	2007	62	2007	55	1998
23	58	1974	57	1992	65	1994	81	1973	87	1964	89	1983	94	1991	88	1976	89	1970	74	1978	65	1982	58	2004
24	65	1967	60	1985	65	1987	85	2001	85	1981	91	1983	87	1984	87	1974	83	1959	75	1973	68	1979	56	2003
25	53	1990	67	1976	62	1987	79	1960	89	1991	90	2003	93	2001	90	1969	80	2007	73	2001	65	1979	58	1994
26	55	1978	57	1976	63	2000	80	1985	87	1965	89	2003	95	1979	87	1993	85	1958	74	1971	65	2001	63	1982
27	62	1974	66	1976	76	1998	82	1990	82	1977	94	1980	93	1963	89	1980	84	2005	75	1964	62	1966	60	1973
28	57	2002	61	1976	75	1991	80	1990	88	1991	88	2001	94	1963	90	1959	82	2005	74	1989	66	1990	57	1982
29	63	2002	58	1972	78	1998	79	1974	87	1969	95	1991	91	2002	88	1973	79	1959	77	1971	64	1963	65	1984
30	53	1974	—		75	1977	77	1985	91	1987	95	1964	92	2002	91	1973	80	1986	70	1989	62	2001	54	2003
31	58	1974	—		73	1986	—		87	1987	—		90	2002	90	1973	—		73	2005	—		60	1965
Monthly High	65	24th	67	25th	78	29th	88	17th	91	30th	96	8th	101	21st	99	2nd	93	13th	84	7th	75	1st	69	7th

189

GROTON, CT   Minimum Temperature Records (1957–2008)

Day	Jan °F	Year	Feb °F	Year	Mar °F	Year	Apr °F	Year	May °F	Year	Jun °F	Year	Jul °F	Year	Aug °F	Year	Sep °F	Year	Oct °F	Year	Nov °F	Year	Dec °F	Year
1	4	1997	-2	1961	5	1980	16	1964	33	1967	38	1967	47	1988	51	1964	45	1975	32	1992	26	1968	8	1989
2	-1	1968	-8	1961	8	1962	20	1964	33	1964	42	1971	50	1978	54	1961	45	1991	32	1992	25	1976	11	1989
3	4	1962	-9	1961	7	1962	23	1965	30	1966	40	1986	49	1957	50	1959	42	1967	33	1975	24	1965	5	1976
4	-1	1981	-12	1965	7	2003	24	1962	30	1966	42	1984	48	1986	50	1964	48	1975	33	1974	27	1998	6	1989
5	-3	1981	-10	1978	11	1978	20	1995	33	1961	42	1964	49	1979	47	1972	46	1989	30	1974	27	1998	9	1976
6	-1	1996	0	1978	6	2007	19	1982	33	1992	42	1964	49	1979	50	1972	45	1976	26	1965	26	1967	12	1957
7	7	1996	-2	1993	7	2003	14	1982	31	1967	43	1958	49	1960	51	1957	40	1962	31	1984	21	1962	12	2002
8	-5	1968	-1	1963	7	1986	17	1982	32	1974	45	2000	49	1960	50	1957	43	1962	33	1999	19	1960	9	1964
9	-8	1968	-1	1978	9	2007	22	1977	33	1977	43	1997	52	2000	51	1964	43	1990	30	1988	21	1971	6	1968
10	0	2004	-2	1979	7	1984	25	1997	34	1977	42	1957	52	1963	44	1964	40	1975	31	1980	23	1995	4	1968
11	-10	1982	-5	1979	9	1960	24	2007	31	1966	40	1980	52	1957	50	1974	41	1995	28	1993	17	1973	1	1958
12	-11	1981	-10	1979	10	1984	21	1976	34	1972	39	1972	50	1978	49	1968	40	1958	26	1964	19	1957	5	1958
13	1	1981	-9	1967	15	1998	23	1990	34	1963	44	1979	49	1973	44	1957	43	1985	31	1981	22	1986	4	1976
14	-2	1981	-11	1979	16	1993	26	1973	34	1996	46	1980	53	1999	45	1964	40	1975	29	1958	18	1986	2	1976
15	-5	1988	0	1987	11	1993	24	1992	38	1986	39	1978	55	1999	45	1964	37	1975	29	1979	20	1967	6	1960
16	-4	1994	3	1991	16	1979	28	1981	39	1959	43	1961	53	1960	48	1972	37	1964	29	1978	18	1996	7	1989
17	-6	1965	-2	1979	12	1967	29	1971	35	1967	45	1965	53	1962	49	1981	38	1960	26	1978	16	1967	3	1963
18	-13	1982	-5	1979	6	1967	25	1962	36	1983	39	1958	52	1958	49	1979	36	1959	24	1978	20	1959	6	1980
19	-7	1965	5	1996	0	1967	30	1990	37	2003	47	1986	54	1957	49	1963	37	1959	25	1974	21	1986	7	1989
20	-1	1971	1	1958	12	1967	28	1961	38	2002	46	1959	52	1965	49	1958	34	1979	26	1972	17	1986	4	1980
21	-7	1961	3	1978	13	1986	26	1979	38	1994	46	1970	50	1966	47	1977	33	1962	23	1972	8	1989	2	1962
22	-14	1961	5	1968	15	1988	31	1984	37	1990	46	1963	53	1958	48	1969	33	1962	25	1974	14	1987	-7	1989
23	-6	1991	1	1972	16	2004	27	1982	39	1976	48	1992	50	1977	46	1957	38	1963	26	1997	13	1972	0	1989
24	-4	1961	10	2006	20	1960	30	1978	37	1963	47	1958	54	1992	45	1957	32	1963	24	1969	10	1989	0	1989
25	0	1963	9	1967	16	1960	31	1971	38	1967	49	1985	52	1957	45	1971	34	1963	26	1962	17	2000	-6	1980
26	0	1991	3	1990	11	1960	30	1967	36	1972	47	1986	52	1976	46	1981	37	1966	29	1969	11	2000	-10	1980
27	-5	1994	7	1990	15	1975	30	1972	36	1972	49	1965	51	1977	49	1989	30	1957	28	1976	13	1978	4	1993
28	-13	1961	9	1964	16	1966	28	1972	39	1997	48	1995	51	1977	47	1986	29	1957	24	1976	18	1996	3	1960
29	-2	1961	5	1992	16	1974	31	1992	38	1962	49	1995	54	1977	44	1982	31	1957	25	1959	20	1989	5	1993
30	1	1965	—		13	1970	30	1967	38	1970	49	1988	51	1968	42	1965	32	2000	25	1983	12	1989	-5	1962
31	-1	1965	—		19	1964	—		33	1961	—		52	1964	41	1965	—		22	1966	—		-10	1962
Monthly Low	-14	22nd	-12	4th	0	19th	14	7th	30	4th	38	1st	47	1st	41	31st	29	28th	22	31st	8	21st	-10	31st

HARTFORD BRADLEY INTERNATIONAL AIRPORT, CT

Maximum Temperature Records (1949–2008)

Day	Jan °F	Year	Feb °F	Year	Mar °F	Year	Apr °F	Year	May °F	Year	Jun °F	Year	Jul °F	Year	Aug °F	Year	Sep °F	Year	Oct °F	Year	Nov °F	Year	Dec °F	Year
1	61	1966	67	1989	60	1991	78	1967	88	2001	91	2007	101	1964	98	1955	96	1961	87	1950	81	1974	70	2001
2	57	1979	54	1981	64	2004	77	1967	93	2001	91	1961	99	1966	101	1975	101	1953	87	2002	83	1950	64	1970
3	62	2000	61	1991	63	1991	77	1981	93	2001	91	1970	102	1966	97	2006	101	1953	85	1950	78	1990	61	1998
4	62	1950	64	1991	67	1974	77	1974	91	2001	92	1966	101	1949	95	1995	96	1973	86	2007	78	1987	71	1998
5	63	1993	67	1991	63	1974	75	1985	94	1949	93	1966	99	1999	101	1955	93	1983	87	2007	76	1994	68	2001
6	72	2007	57	1991	60	1974	80	1991	87	2000	95	1968	99	1999	95	2001	96	1983	89	2007	72	1959	74	2001
7	52	2008	52	1951	69	1974	90	1991	93	2000	98	1999	99	1993	98	2001	93	2007	91	1963	74	1975	76	1998
8	62	2008	54	1990	69	1987	89	1991	92	2000	96	1984	97	1993	98	2001	95	2007	85	1990	77	1975	63	1966
9	63	2008	58	1990	72	2000	85	1991	97	1979	96	1984	96	1981	102	2001	91	2002	83	1949	76	1975	61	1991
10	52	1972	53	1990	70	2006	78	1955	96	1979	97	1974	99	1988	100	1949	94	1983	88	1949	74	1999	63	1966
11	60	1983	61	1981	75	1977	79	1955	92	1993	98	1973	95	1988	96	1949	99	1983	86	1949	69	1977	64	1966
12	55	1980	54	1999	69	1977	88	1977	90	2004	97	1973	97	1966	95	1988	92	1961	88	1954	65	1982	66	1979
13	57	1972	55	1976	79	1990	86	1977	86	1991	96	1984	99	1966	98	2002	91	2005	85	1995	73	1964	60	1984
14	60	2005	53	1990	69	1990	81	1968	85	1961	97	1956	100	1965	99	2002	89	2005	81	2000	74	1973	58	2006
15	63	1995	66	1954	73	1990	82	1994	89	2004	97	1988	100	1995	97	1996	88	1993	85	1975	78	1993	63	1975
16	62	1995	68	1954	79	1990	90	2002	91	1965	96	1967	96	1983	97	2002	92	1991	84	1956	72	1990	60	1971
17	60	1973	64	1981	70	1990	95	2002	93	1977	95	1957	97	1999	95	1987	90	1991	83	1968	67	2006	63	2000
18	63	1990	68	1981	70	1999	95	1976	87	1989	95	1994	99	1982	96	2002	88	1972	80	1968	73	1963	57	1984
19	58	1951	67	1981	64	1976	96	1976	94	1962	95	1995	100	1991	95	1966	93	1983	82	1963	67	1985	52	1967
20	58	2006	61	1994	76	1976	89	1976	99	1996	96	1995	100	1991	95	1983	95	1983	81	1969	73	1991	61	1957
21	61	2006	62	2002	67	2003	86	1957	93	1996	99	1953	101	1991	93	1995	91	1965	78	1963	64	1956	60	1957
22	57	1959	69	1997	72	1979	90	1977	95	1992	94	1997	97	1955	93	1976	94	1970	85	1979	65	2007	59	1990
23	60	1967	68	1990	72	1979	88	2007	96	1964	97	1965	99	1978	90	1996	92	1970	78	2007	72	1992	61	1990
24	65	1967	73	1985	74	1988	88	2001	95	1964	94	1975	96	1987	94	1969	89	1959	80	1972	68	1999	59	1996
25	53	1972	70	1976	76	1964	83	1982	93	2007	95	1949	98	2001	95	1968	90	2007	80	1963	71	1979	64	1964
26	66	1950	65	1976	72	1986	81	1970	94	1965	101	1952	95	1989	94	1993	93	2007	81	1963	65	1979	61	1982
27	64	1974	65	1997	82	1998	94	1962	94	1965	98	1966	96	1964	97	1949	88	1998	83	1963	64	1976	60	1949
28	58	2002	66	1976	84	1998	94	1990	93	1977	97	1969	96	1970	99	1993	83	1959	79	1971	71	1990	59	1982
29	66	2002	64	1976	80	1981	91	1974	93	1987	95	1959	96	1949	96	1953	84	1959	76	1971	63	2005	74	1984
30	56	1974	—		87	1977	85	1985	93	1987	100	1964	98	1988	98	1973	91	1986	76	1989	64	2006	59	1984
31	57	1974	—		89	1998	—		95	1987	—		95	1975	97	1973	—		74	1999	—		65	1965
Monthly	Jan		Feb		Mar		Apr		May		Jun		Jul		Aug		Sep		Oct		Nov		Dec	

HARTFORD BRADLEY INTERNATIONAL AIRPORT, CT
Minimum Temperature Records (1949–2008)

Day	Jan °F	Year	Feb °F	Year	Mar °F	Year	Apr °F	Year	May °F	Year	Jun °F	Year	Jul °F	Year	Aug °F	Year	Sep °F	Year	Oct °F	Year	Nov °F	Year	Dec °F	Year
1	-4	1964	-8	1971	3	1980	9	1970	30	1961	38	2001	46	1988	51	1987	44	1975	30	1992	24	1988	9	1976
2	-6	1968	-21	1961	4	1962	20	1964	32	1978	42	1998	44	1962	51	1987	43	1967	32	1960	23	1978	7	1989
3	-3	2008	-9	1961	-2	1950	17	1954	30	1964	37	1986	45	2001	46	1956	40	1967	32	1975	20	1980	6	1976
4	-7	1981	-8	1965	-8	1950	15	1954	28	1985	42	1957	49	1986	49	1964	44	1987	30	1996	22	1951	5	1976
5	-10	1981	-13	1996	10	1950	19	1995	30	2005	42	1964	46	1979	47	1972	44	1989	29	1996	20	1952	3	1976
6	-6	1976	-5	1988	3	2007	17	1982	32	1992	37	1964	48	1962	45	1951	40	1984	24	1984	21	1991	8	1976
7	2	1996	-9	1995	-6	2003	14	1982	28	2001	38	1958	46	1979	48	1957	37	1984	26	1984	19	1962	-1	1964
8	-7	1968	-13	1967	4	1986	20	1982	31	1968	42	2002	46	1969	46	1950	39	1984	27	1954	15	1960	-3	1964
9	-9	1968	-2	1959	4	2007	23	1977	28	1956	41	1949	46	1963	48	1989	38	1986	28	2001	18	1952	4	1968
10	-7	1958	-7	1979	1	1984	21	1985	33	1986	38	1957	49	1963	45	1964	37	1978	29	1989	18	2004	-3	1949
11	-14	1988	-9	1979	3	1996	25	2007	32	1966	40	1980	51	2002	49	2007	39	1995	25	1993	12	1956	-6	1958
12	-14	1981	-13	1979	6	1984	22	1976	32	1983	40	1980	48	2002	47	2006	36	1958	24	1964	20	1976	-3	1988
13	-9	1981	-7	1967	11	1998	24	1990	32	2005	43	1980	51	1973	45	1957	40	1985	28	1981	18	2001	-1	1962
14	-12	1957	-9	1979	14	1993	24	1959	32	1987	45	1979	54	1999	47	1964	37	1963	25	1993	15	1986	-2	2005
15	-15	1957	-4	1987	6	1993	24	1957	34	1996	44	1985	49	1950	46	1964	35	1975	26	1978	19	1996	-4	1960
16	-8	1994	0	1987	9	1992	25	1957	36	2000	39	1961	51	1987	47	1972	33	1964	23	1978	16	1996	1	1951
17	-9	1971	-5	1979	11	1961	28	1995	33	1956	45	1961	50	1954	45	1979	34	1984	25	1978	16	1967	-6	1951
18	-17	1957	-9	1979	1	1956	24	1962	31	1984	40	1958	50	1956	46	1979	36	1986	17	1978	18	1959	-3	1980
19	-12	1971	1	1996	-6	1967	29	1991	35	2002	44	1950	51	1956	46	1977	33	1956	18	1974	14	1986	1	1960
20	-13	1971	-5	1950	4	1949	27	1960	30	2002	47	1959	51	2001	42	1949	30	1979	23	1972	9	1986	-4	1980
21	-13	1961	-5	1950	10	1986	27	1961	34	2002	47	1970	50	1974	45	2000	31	1962	19	1972	13	1987	-4	1955
22	-26	1961	3	1963	13	1956	28	1984	35	2002	46	1986	52	1974	41	1982	32	1962	24	1983	14	1969	-1	1958
23	-19	1961	-2	1972	15	2004	26	1989	37	1976	46	1992	49	1977	42	1988	34	1974	24	1982	12	1972	-5	1989
24	-19	1961	9	1967	16	1956	29	1971	35	1963	46	1988	49	1985	43	1971	30	1974	21	1969	1	1989	-9	1989
25	-3	1961	-1	1959	9	1956	26	1956	33	1956	50	1986	51	1992	44	1971	30	1963	24	2003	12	2000	-13	1980
26	0	1994	-4	1990	6	1960	30	1989	36	1992	47	1986	50	1984	46	1989	33	1978	23	1952	12	1993	-14	1980
27	-10	1994	-2	1990	15	1951	30	2002	37	1969	47	1979	49	2001	45	1954	30	1978	22	1950	12	1949	-1	1962
28	-12	1961	-3	1950	17	1956	29	1972	38	1997	44	1995	48	2001	43	1957	31	1965	23	1974	10	1951	-6	1950
29	-10	1963	8	2008	10	1959	27	1949	37	1962	47	1970	51	1977	39	1982	30	2000	24	2001	13	1996	1	1963
30	-7	1952			15	1970	31	1978	33	1949	44	1988	48	1968	39	1965	27	1951	26	1962	12	1995	-9	1962
31	-8	1965			17	1970			33	1961			50	1956	36	1965			21	1988			-8	1963
Monthly	Jan		Feb		Mar		Apr		May		Jun		Jul		Aug		Sep		Oct		Nov		Dec	

HARTFORD BRAINARD FIELD, CT   Maximum Temperature Records (1904–1999)

Day	Jan °F	Jan Year	Feb °F	Feb Year	Mar °F	Mar Year	Apr °F	Apr Year	May °F	May Year	Jun °F	Jun Year	Jul °F	Jul Year	Aug °F	Aug Year	Sep °F	Sep Year	Oct °F	Oct Year	Nov °F	Nov Year	Dec °F	Dec Year
1	61	1966	56	1988	64	1976	85	1998	84	1985	95	1937	98	1968	100	1917	98	1973	89	1927	77	1950	65	1908
2	58	1979	65	1989	60	1991	76	1934	88	1913	90	1919	95	1966	96	1975	101	1953	87	1954	83	1950	62	1970
3	60	1913	56	1983	65	1973	72	1967	90	1919	97	1919	100	1911	102	1975	96	1953	85	1919	79	1982	65	1998
4	60	1950	60	1991	62	1965	74	1950	85	1944	98	1919	99	1919	99	1975	95	1929	86	1959	77	1990	64	1998
5	59	1998	65	1991	63	1974	82	1921	93	1949	96	1925	98	1919	101	1955	95	1973	88	1941	78	1987	71	1982
6	62	1993	67	1991	64	1935	81	1921	89	1930	96	1925	98	1911	95	1931	90	1959	89	1959	73	1994	67	1912
7	62	1907	56	1991	68	1974	90	1929	93	1930	96	1925	97	1934	100	1918	92	1945	88	1963	72	1938	65	1998
8	59	1930	63	1933	64	1987	88	1991	90	1936	98	1999	97	1994	94	1916	95	1983	83	1916	72	1975	75	1998
9	64	1937	54	1990	68	1987	86	1991	91	1936	96	1984	98	1912	97	1949	92	1959	83	1949	72	1945	62	1980
10	60	1978	57	1990	69	1955	84	1922	92	1965	96	1984	100	1936	100	1949	95	1931	89	1949	76	1975	67	1946
11	59	1983	58	1966	68	1977	78	1955	93	1979	96	1984	100	1993	98	1949	94	1983	86	1955	71	1985	64	1971
12	62	1975	61	1981	75	1977	79	1945	91	1993	96	1984	97	1988	98	1944	93	1983	88	1954	74	1909	64	1931
13	59	1932	59	1937	72	1946	86	1977	87	1956	94	1973	95	1966	96	1944	91	1957	87	1954	74	1964	64	1979
14	70	1932	55	1949	78	1946	86	1977	88	1907	98	1956	97	1954	97	1988	92	1931	82	1954	71	1959	62	1984
15	63	1995	69	1954	68	1945	88	1941	88	1951	96	1956	94	1984	95	1947	90	1915	83	1960	72	1973	59	1918
16	64	1995	72	1954	74	1990	79	1994	90	1951	98	1988	95	1968	96	1988	92	1941	84	1947	77	1993	60	1971
17	62	1995	56	1992	76	1990	79	1976	87	1991	95	1957	98	1980	96	1913	91	1991	90	1908	72	1928	59	1982
18	64	1990	63	1981	68	1927	91	1976	90	1977	94	1957	98	1968	97	1987	92	1991	80	1908	74	1963	61	1984
19	64	1973	68	1981	72	1999	93	1976	93	1962	93	1994	100	1991	95	1966	92	1906	81	1945	71	1941	57	1984
20	62	1996	69	1930	81	1945	92	1976	92	1959	96	1953	100	1991	96	1937	95	1983	80	1947	72	1942	60	1957
21	59	1906	63	1930	82	1921	87	1976	99	1996	96	1953	101	1991	97	1955	91	1914	82	1920	71	1985	61	1957
22	58	1906	61	1925	75	1948	83	1985	94	1996	95	1921	101	1991	93	1916	92	1970	77	1920	72	1931	60	1973
23	60	1906	65	1997	73	1938	89	1977	94	1992	94	1997	97	1955	92	1976	93	1970	85	1979	75	1931	59	1990
24	65	1967	66	1990	70	1979	83	1973	93	1992	92	1963	98	1991	93	1947	89	1959	79	1978	71	1992	60	1990
25	58	1999	74	1985	78	1915	87	1915	92	1975	95	1943	97	1987	95	1948	87	1926	79	1963	69	1979	64	1964
26	65	1950	64	1976	74	1922	83	1908	92	1965	100	1952	96	1963	99	1948	90	1958	80	1963	74	1979	60	1982
27	67	1916	61	1951	76	1945	90	1915	94	1914	95	1966	95	1964	98	1948	86	1998	80	1963	67	1979	62	1982
28	65	1974	67	1997	83	1945	91	1990	90	1939	95	1983	96	1949	98	1993	86	1998	81	1919	62	1984	60	1949
29	54	1994	67	1976	86	1945	93	1990	92	1969	98	1934	96	1933	98	1953	86	1945	77	1918	69	1990	60	1982
30	60	1947	—		79	1998	86	1974	92	1987	97	1964	97	1949	97	1953	85	1922	83	1946	69	1933	63	1984
31	59	1947	—		82	1977	—		93	1987	—		97	1988	98	1953	—		82	1946	—		66	1965
Monthly High	Jan 70	14th	Feb 74	25th	Mar 86	29th	Apr 93	29th	May 99	21st	Jun 100	26th	Jul 101	22nd	Aug 102	3rd	Sep 101	2nd	Oct 90	17th	Nov 83	2nd	Dec 75	8th

193

HARTFORD BRAINARD FIELD, CT   Minimum Temperature Records (1904-1999)

Day	Jan °F	Year	Feb °F	Year	Mar °F	Year	Apr °F	Year	May °F	Year	Jun °F	Year	Jul °F	Year	Aug °F	Year	Sep °F	Year	Oct °F	Year	Nov °F	Year	Dec °F	Year
1	-8	1918	-8	1948	2	1980	11	1923	31	1999	39	1967	48	1912	50	1964	44	1996	26	1996	17	1996	8	1996
2	-8	1918	-10	1961	2	1980	18	1919	26	1999	43	1946	45	1962	50	1947	41	1963	33	1972	22	1996	10	1989
3	0	1918	-4	1955	4	1962	17	1954	30	1966	40	1964	46	1957	48	1959	42	1967	33	1945	15	1980	5	1940
4	-2	1918	-8	1985	2	1950	14	1954	30	1978	41	1984	46	1962	47	1964	45	1946	20	1996	17	1996	2	1906
5	-6	1910	-11	1918	4	1948	20	1982	32	1966	42	1910	48	1979	52	1972	42	1963	26	1996	20	1996	3	1976
6	-3	1996	-5	1910	-4	1948	20	1943	32	1961	40	1964	47	1963	47	1957	43	1962	21	1996	22	1998	10	1989
7	1	1912	-6	1910	8	1920	13	1982	25	1984	42	1980	45	1960	47	1957	34	1984	20	1996	19	1962	3	1964
8	-6	1942	-11	1934	7	1999	15	1982	31	1968	43	1932	50	1959	47	1957	39	1962	27	1984	20	1960	0	1906
9	-9	1968	-15	1934	1	1997	22	1982	31	1956	42	1957	45	1963	51	1955	41	1956	30	1953	19	1952	5	1968
10	-8	1958	-7	1948	3	1997	23	1982	28	1947	42	1957	48	1963	43	1964	35	1956	26	1980	19	1980	2	1949
11	-10	1942	-9	1948	7	1984	23	1909	32	1966	40	1980	47	1984	46	1963	36	1917	21	1996	16	1996	-2	1958
12	-10	1981	-10	1979	4	1984	21	1976	32	1907	39	1980	48	1945	49	1968	38	1958	21	1996	17	1996	2	1988
13	-7	1981	-7	1979	5	1984	24	1976	27	1984	42	1980	52	1980	46	1957	40	1943	24	1996	14	1996	2	1988
14	-12	1912	-5	1979	7	1948	24	1963	33	1958	45	1980	52	1962	46	1983	35	1963	24	1996	15	1996	2	1958
15	-7	1988	-18	1943	10	1993	24	1957	32	1996	41	1953	52	1950	46	1964	37	1975	20	1996	10	1996	0	1904
16	-7	1988	-24	1943	4	1997	21	1943	35	1947	42	1984	50	1946	47	1968	34	1984	25	1996	10	1996	-4	1917
17	-6	1971	-6	1922	6	1916	25	1908	30	1984	42	1926	49	1954	46	1979	33	1984	24	1996	5	1996	-6	1942
18	-11	1954	-5	1979	4	1967	23	1962	31	1984	40	1958	51	1956	45	1941	37	1959	22	1996	13	1996	-6	1919
19	-16	1948	-2	1979	-4	1967	29	1979	35	1944	43	1956	52	1956	44	1963	32	1959	21	1974	12	1924	-3	1942
20	-8	1997	-3	1936	2	1949	26	1961	38	1945	45	1959	49	1965	46	1949	34	1979	20	1974	13	1986	-10	1942
21	-15	1984	-2	1950	12	1997	28	1962	36	1964	44	1918	46	1966	43	1984	30	1956	19	1972	15	1996	-6	1942
22	-17	1961	-2	1916	12	1934	22	1999	26	1999	41	1940	52	1944	43	1982	31	1962	22	1940	14	1987	-5	1942
23	-8	1961	-3	1907	9	1934	28	1982	36	1999	45	1940	49	1977	43	1957	33	1973	25	1996	10	1972	-5	1945
24	-9	1907	-4	1907	7	1906	27	1930	35	1963	47	1958	51	1923	45	1952	29	1963	21	1969	12	1989	-4	1989
25	-5	1976	-2	1914	7	1997	27	1919	31	1956	49	1979	50	1912	38	1940	33	1963	24	1996	12	1938	-10	1980
26	-8	1948	3	1990	10	1960	26	1919	35	1972	46	1979	49	1984	42	1963	34	1925	23	1952	7	1938	-8	1980
27	-6	1994	2	1950	18	1975	29	1963	36	1969	49	1940	49	1977	46	1963	29	1957	23	1950	6	1996	-8	1914
28	-10	1961	0	1907	8	1923	30	1940	40	1994	42	1980	49	1977	45	1905	29	1957	18	1940	12	1996	-5	1963
29	-6	1963	0	1992	4	1923	30	1949	36	1956	45	1980	52	1984	38	1982	29	1957	20	1940	13	1940	-11	1933
30	-4	1961	—		16	1915	32	1960	37	1949	48	1988	50	1968	39	1982	31	1951	23	1962	6	1996	-18	1917
31	-12	1948	—		13	1923	—		34	1961	—		49	1956	38	1965	—		22	1996	—		-15	1917
Monthly Low	-17	22nd	-24	16th	-4	19th	11	1st	25	7th	39	12th	45	9th	38	31st	29	29th	18	28th	5	17th	-18	30th

MANSFIELD HOLLOW LAKE, CT   Maximum Temperature Records (1952–2007)

Day	Jan °F	Year	Feb °F	Year	Mar °F	Year	Apr °F	Year	May °F	Year	Jun °F	Year	Jul °F	Year	Aug °F	Year	Sep °F	Year	Oct °F	Year	Nov °F	Year	Dec °F	Year
1	66	1966	57	2001	63	1976	84	1998	83	1985	91	1987	97	1964	94	1955	93	1953	85	1986	71	2004	63	2006
2	59	1979	65	1989	65	1972	74	1967	88	2001	88	2006	98	1964	95	2006	100	1953	85	1954	77	1982	70	2001
3	57	1979	57	1983	62	2004	74	1967	91	2001	87	1989	96	1963	100	1975	100	1953	84	1968	80	1982	64	1998
4	59	1998	59	1991	68	1991	73	1967	91	2001	89	1952	97	1966	95	2006	91	1953	81	1954	78	2003	62	1998
5	60	1998	65	1991	69	1974	70	1974	89	2001	88	1953	97	1955	97	1955	90	1973	84	1959	76	1990	69	1998
6	61	1993	65	1991	65	1979	76	1985	81	1953	91	1953	98	1999	95	1955	81	1983	82	1967	73	2005	67	2001
7	54	1998	55	1991	58	1974	74	1954	82	1986	92	1968	94	1999	92	2001	93	1983	87	1959	72	1959	71	2001
8	69	2007	53	2005	65	1974	75	1997	84	2004	92	1984	95	1993	97	2001	93	1983	88	1963	75	1975	75	1998
9	59	1998	54	1990	69	1987	85	1991	87	1957	94	1984	94	1988	96	2001	89	1985	82	1990	70	1975	65	1966
10	58	1965	57	1990	66	2002	82	1991	91	1979	93	1984	94	1981	100	2001	89	2002	79	2006	75	1975	61	1991
11	59	1983	57	1960	69	1977	79	1955	91	1979	93	1967	99	1988	94	2005	92	1983	81	1997	70	1985	62	1966
12	60	1975	61	1981	74	1977	75	1955	88	1993	94	1967	96	1988	92	2005	98	1983	87	1954	64	1995	65	1971
13	54	1975	56	1999	67	1977	83	1977	89	1959	92	1973	93	1966	93	2002	91	2005	87	1954	67	1964	65	1979
14	60	2005	55	1984	76	1990	84	1977	83	1970	94	1956	94	1979	97	2005	90	2005	82	1995	69	1964	64	1983
15	64	1995	67	1954	67	2007	76	1968	85	1961	94	1957	95	1995	95	2002	90	2005	86	1956	71	1993	56	2006
16	63	1995	72	1954	81	1990	79	1960	86	2004	95	1988	97	1997	93	1988	85	1957	84	1956	75	1993	59	1975
17	61	1995	60	2006	76	1990	88	2002	86	1965	95	1957	96	1983	94	1970	88	1991	81	1956	71	2001	59	1982
18	58	1973	62	1981	66	1990	93	2002	89	1974	95	1957	97	1968	94	1987	87	1991	81	1968	72	1953	62	2000
19	63	1973	67	1981	70	1989	91	1976	88	1986	92	1957	97	1999	93	2002	85	1955	78	1961	72	1963	57	1996
20	58	1996	62	1997	65	1954	91	1976	95	1962	95	1953	97	1991	92	2002	92	1983	83	1963	72	1953	60	1957
21	55	2006	61	1994	72	1976	86	1976	92	1996	98	1953	100	1991	93	1983	93	1983	79	1984	70	1985	60	1957
22	60	1959	61	2002	64	1979	80	1985	91	1996	93	1988	100	1991	90	1995	88	1980	79	1963	64	1953	59	1973
23	56	1973	63	1997	71	1979	85	2001	92	1992	93	1988	98	1955	93	1976	90	1980	86	1979	64	1963	61	1994
24	61	1967	62	1990	70	1979	84	2007	92	1964	93	1965	95	1991	88	1976	89	1970	79	1978	71	1992	62	1990
25	62	1967	69	1985	68	1994	83	2001	92	1975	91	2003	94	1987	90	1969	88	1959	78	2001	70	1979	59	1996
26	60	1978	69	1976	74	1963	78	1982	88	1981	98	1952	94	2001	92	1968	85	1968	81	1963	72	1979	64	1964
27	57	1978	60	2002	71	1963	81	1957	91	1965	96	1952	94	1989	93	1993	88	1958	82	1963	66	1979	61	1982
28	64	1974	63	1997	76	1998	89	1990	87	1982	94	1983	94	1970	93	1983	84	1998	83	1963	63	1984	59	1973
29	57	2002	64	1976	79	1998	91	1990	90	1959	95	1963	94	1970	95	1953	85	1952	79	1989	68	1990	61	1984
30	66	2002	—		79	1998	86	1974	90	1987	94	1959	94	1970	96	1953	83	1959	78	1989	64	1963	71	1984
31	55	1959	—		82	1977	—		92	1987	—		95	1988	95	1953	—		75	1989	—		57	1990
Monthly High	69	8th	72	16th	82	31st	93	18th	95	20th	98	26th	100	22nd	100	10th	100	3rd	88	8th	80	3rd	75	8th

MANSFIELD HOLLOW LAKE, CT   Minimum Temperature Records (1952–2007)

Day	Jan °F Year	Feb °F Year	Mar °F Year	Apr °F Year	May °F Year	Jun °F Year	Jul °F Year	Aug °F Year	Sep °F Year	Oct °F Year	Nov °F Year	Dec °F Year
1	-13 1964	-11 1971	2 1980	9 1970	27 1961	32 1967	40 1988	41 1964	39 1975	25 1992	18 1964	6 1976
2	-14 1968	-20 1961	1 1978	12 1964	26 1964	36 1993	40 1962	47 1987	38 1963	25 1992	19 1976	4 1989
3	-11 1968	-16 1961	4 1994	18 1995	24 1961	32 1953	37 1957	40 1959	36 1967	27 1957	18 1980	5 1976
4	-4 1981	-21 1965	4 1982	6 1954	26 1964	36 1957	41 1962	41 1964	33 1987	27 1957	21 1998	3 1976
5	-8 1996	-19 1996	6 1954	14 1954	25 1974	36 1964	43 1953	42 1972	35 1989	24 1963	13 1952	4 1976
6	-11 1996	-19 1996	2 2007	12 1995	26 1969	31 1964	42 1979	45 1957	38 1989	22 1984	17 1967	4 1976
7	-10 1996	-11 1966	1 1990	15 1982	26 2001	30 1958	41 1965	41 1957	31 1962	24 1984	16 1962	0 1964
8	-7 1970	-16 1967	4 2007	16 1982	26 1968	35 1958	45 1959	42 1957	35 1962	20 1954	12 1993	-3 1964
9	-11 1968	-15 1967	3 2007	17 1955	22 1956	36 1957	43 1969	44 1989	35 1990	22 1953	12 1952	2 1989
10	-12 1958	-10 1975	-6 1996	20 1977	28 1962	30 1957	42 1953	37 1964	32 1956	25 2001	14 2004	-7 1958
11	-22 1988	-14 1962	4 1996	21 1960	25 1966	37 1980	43 1957	42 1974	35 1956	21 1956	8 1956	-9 1958
12	-20 1981	-18 1979	-1 1960	21 1976	31 1972	34 1972	43 1978	42 1968	33 1967	19 1964	13 1957	-2 1988
13	-18 1981	-19 1967	8 1984	21 1956	27 1963	37 1979	46 1973	39 1957	35 1958	22 1957	16 1976	0 1988
14	-21 1954	-13 1987	14 1998	20 1959	27 1996	39 1979	47 1962	38 1961	33 1963	18 1953	11 1986	-5 1958
15	-17 1988	-8 1979	7 1993	17 1957	30 1996	33 1953	50 2001	31 1975	31 1975	21 1993	15 1996	-8 1960
16	-14 1988	-6 1969	6 1993	19 1957	26 2002	33 1961	42 1954	41 1964	28 1964	23 1961	10 1996	-5 2005
17	-20 1971	-4 1979	6 1993	25 1995	28 1952	37 1961	37 1954	42 1957	30 1960	25 1978	11 1996	-3 1970
18	-26 1957	-12 1979	-8 1967	18 1962	29 1983	31 1958	45 1958	41 1957	31 1959	20 1978	18 1959	-7 1980
19	-20 1957	-3 1979	-16 1967	25 1962	30 2002	35 1956	45 1956	38 1953	27 1959	17 1974	15 1997	-8 1989
20	-15 1982	-6 1978	-2 1967	21 1961	28 2002	38 1956	45 1965	41 1953	30 2004	18 1974	7 1986	-8 1980
21	-15 1994	-1 1978	3 1956	23 1962	28 2002	41 1970	43 1966	40 1981	26 1962	16 1972	11 1986	-7 1980
22	-27 1961	-3 1977	7 1956	24 1975	31 2002	40 1963	46 1958	37 1982	25 1962	19 1974	9 1969	-8 1958
23	-22 1961	-10 1972	10 2004	22 1982	34 1990	39 1958	45 1977	39 1988	29 1953	19 1997	7 1964	-13 1955
24	-17 1961	-3 1972	13 1992	24 1971	28 1963	39 1958	46 1985	36 1957	24 1963	15 1969	1 1989	-15 1989
25	-17 1961	-5 1959	6 1956	21 1956	26 1956	43 1985	43 1953	38 1987	25 1963	17 1969	2 1989	-13 1989
26	-8 1987	-5 1959	3 1960	23 1963	30 1956	40 1979	44 1976	38 1963	30 1966	15 1952	11 1978	-18 1980
27	-15 1994	-3 1990	15 1975	25 2002	30 1969	42 1979	45 2001	40 1963	23 1957	16 1976	11 1957	-15 1980
28	-23 1961	-3 1964	11 1956	22 1972	32 1994	41 1995	43 1962	39 1957	20 1957	18 1976	12 1996	-4 1960
29	-21 1961	1 1956	7 1959	25 1963	27 1956	41 1970	45 1968	37 1986	22 1957	18 1976	13 1952	-3 1993
30	-16 1965		11 1970	27 1992	33 1970	43 1956	43 1968	33 1965	30 2000	20 1969	11 1976	-10 1963
31	-18 1965		15 1957		28 1961		43 1956	32 1965		16 1966		-18 1963
Monthly Low	-27 22nd	-21 4th	-16 19th	6 4th	22 9th	30 10th	37 17th	32 31st	20 28th	15 26th	1 24th	-18 31st

NORFOLK, CT   Maximum Temperature Records (1884–2008)

Day	Jan °F	Year	Feb °F	Year	Mar °F	Year	Apr °F	Year	May °F	Year	Jun °F	Year	Jul °F	Year	Aug °F	Year	Sep °F	Year	Oct °F	Year	Nov °F	Year	Dec °F	Year
1	56	1966	55	2002	55	1976	85	1998	78	2004	86	1999	89	1964	89	1954	89	1953	81	1986	68	2006	61	2006
2	53	1985	57	1989	62	1972	71	1986	83	2001	84	2006	90	1964	92	2006	87	1953	77	1953	73	1950	63	2006
3	52	2000	50	1981	61	1991	66	1967	87	2001	87	1943	90	2002	92	2006	93	1953	78	2002	75	1982	60	2001
4	54	2000	52	2006	66	1991	78	2002	87	2001	88	1943	91	1966	89	2006	90	1953	76	1967	70	2003	58	2001
5	58	1950	54	1991	59	1974	72	1950	88	1944	82	1967	92	1949	98	2001	87	1953	77	2007	72	1994	63	1973
6	60	2007	58	1991	65	1976	75	1985	85	1949	84	1966	90	1999	93	1955	89	1953	80	2007	70	1994	61	1982
7	62	2007	49	1991	53	2004	74	1991	82	1980	85	1968	91	1999	88	1955	87	1943	80	2007	67	1978	64	2001
8	52	2008	53	2005	60	1974	81	1991	87	2000	88	1999	91	1993	89	2001	86	2007	78	1990	69	1975	67	1998
9	57	2008	52	1886	64	2002	82	1991	86	2000	90	1984	92	1988	87	1983	90	1943	78	1990	66	1975	55	1980
10	54	2008	52	1990	70	2000	77	1991	88	2000	87	1984	88	2007	93	2001	89	2002	75	1949	68	1975	63	1966
11	52	1983	50	2002	64	1977	78	1945	85	1979	89	1984	91	1988	93	1949	86	2002	79	1949	66	1999	58	1966
12	54	1975	54	1981	66	1977	76	1945	84	1993	88	1973	88	1988	92	1944	89	1983	79	1949	65	2002	57	1946
13	45	2006	49	1999	63	1946	82	1945	85	1959	87	1973	88	1987	93	1944	85	1961	79	1954	66	1964	59	1979
14	56	2005	55	1951	70	1990	81	1977	81	1985	88	1988	89	1966	91	1944	83	2005	77	1995	64	1964	56	1984
15	56	1995	49	1886	69	2007	75	1960	83	1961	91	1945	89	1966	88	2005	83	1942	75	1954	65	1989	53	1991
16	58	1995	56	1954	79	1990	81	2003	83	2004	91	1988	89	1995	89	1944	83	1942	77	1947	67	1993	54	1975
17	54	1995	66	1954	79	1990	85	1994	82	1998	88	1988	87	1999	89	1944	84	1942	76	1964	64	2006	54	1975
18	54	1990	53	2008	65	1990	89	2002	83	1977	87	1994	89	2006	89	1987	82	1946	74	1980	62	2001	55	1982
19	55	2006	57	1981	63	1989	87	1976	86	1962	91	1957	91	1953	86	1956	83	1948	74	1945	63	1963	59	2000
20	54	1949	60	1981	73	1945	88	1976	87	1962	86	1995	92	1991	84	1987	83	1983	73	1963	65	1991	49	1954
21	54	1951	56	1994	67	1946	81	2002	88	1996	87	1995	91	1991	85	1983	87	1983	74	1965	67	1985	52	1957
22	55	1959	58	1953	68	1946	80	1957	84	1996	88	1943	91	1957	88	1955	83	1998	73	1979	61	1953	56	1957
23	54	1957	63	1997	59	1979	84	1973	84	1959	89	1943	90	1957	85	1976	84	1970	77	1979	61	1953	58	1990
24	55	1999	58	1990	65	1979	82	2007	86	1964	87	1999	90	2002	85	1947	82	1970	70	2007	62	1992	60	1990
25	53	1999	63	1985	65	1988	83	2001	86	1975	89	1943	90	2001	87	1947	80	1961	73	2001	63	1979	56	1990
26	51	1990	59	1976	68	1945	77	1962	85	2007	91	1943	90	2001	90	2007	83	1970	72	2001	69	2001	55	1982
27	62	1950	61	1976	71	1949	81	1990	85	1965	91	1952	90	2001	92	1948	85	2007	72	2001	69	2001	57	1964
28	54	1974	60	1997	80	1945	86	1962	85	1965	89	2007	89	1955	89	1949	82	1998	72	2001	57	1988	50	1973
29	53	2002	56	1976	81	1945	88	1990	83	1959	89	1944	90	1949	90	1993	78	1943	71	1964	65	1990	58	1982
30	55	1947	—		73	1986	82	1974	83	1998	89	1948	89	1949	89	1953	78	1948	73	1946	57	2005	64	1984
31	51	2002	—		79	1998	—		84	2006	—		90	1949	90	1953	—		71	1946	—		54	1884
	Jan		Feb		Mar		Apr		May		Jun		Jul		Aug		Sep		Oct		Nov		Dec	
Monthly High	62	27th	66	17th	81	29th	89	18th	88	21st	91	27th	92	20th	98	5th	93	3rd	81	1st	75	3rd	67	8th

197

NORFOLK, CT   Minimum Temperature Records (1884–2008)

Day	Jan °F	Year	Feb °F	Year	Mar °F	Year	Apr °F	Year	May °F	Year	Jun °F	Year	Jul °F	Year	Aug °F	Year	Sep °F	Year	Oct °F	Year	Nov °F	Year	Dec °F	Year
1	-12	1963	-16	1971	-8	1886	7	1969	26	1978	33	1945	41	1943	44	1964	41	1975	27	1992	14	1885	4	1976
2	-10	1968	-15	1961	-6	1980	13	1956	26	1974	37	1998	41	1885	44	1947	38	1886	28	1997	20	1965	1	1989
3	-10	1968	-14	1955	-11	1950	17	1978	26	1966	32	1986	43	2001	44	1976	35	1885	29	1997	19	1980	-4	1976
4	-11	1981	-13	1955	-9	1950	6	1954	24	1885	36	1965	43	1962	43	1964	38	1946	25	1945	14	1951	-5	1976
5	-13	1981	-17	1886	-5	1948	12	1995	25	1974	32	1964	43	1961	44	1972	40	1974	26	1965	17	1951	0	1989
6	-10	1996	-12	1886	-7	1948	10	1943	28	1954	35	1964	42	1962	42	1951	35	1885	21	1965	13	1951	3	1989
7	-9	1996	-15	1885	-8	2003	7	1982	26	1970	36	1958	44	1979	43	1885	35	1984	24	1984	16	1951	5	1949
8	-9	1887	-16	1963	-5	1990	7	1982	26	1956	37	1957	46	2000	44	1950	37	1978	25	1964	15	1960	3	1964
9	-20	1968	-17	1963	-9	1943	15	1977	25	1956	36	1980	42	1963	45	1989	39	1990	28	2000	14	1992	0	1976
10	-19	1968	-14	1948	-4	1984	17	1997	25	1966	34	1957	44	1953	41	1964	34	1956	26	1989	15	2004	-3	1968
11	-13	2004	-15	1979	-1	1984	19	1985	27	1966	33	1980	46	1983	44	1974	33	1885	21	1943	13	1956	-5	1958
12	-16	1886	-17	1979	-2	2003	14	1976	27	1885	35	1972	43	1886	45	1968	35	1967	24	1964	16	1956	-8	1977
13	-15	1981	-16	1979	-6	1885	17	1976	27	1967	38	1979	47	1886	40	1957	34	1943	26	1964	17	1983	-6	1988
14	-13	1988	-15	1979	0	1948	22	1973	27	1996	40	1970	51	2001	42	1961	34	1963	23	1993	10	1986	-5	2005
15	-21	1957	-22	1943	1	1993	16	1943	29	1971	36	1978	44	1950	42	1964	33	1975	26	1993	11	1986	-3	2005
16	-22	1957	-25	1943	2	1993	15	1943	32	2002	37	1961	44	1946	41	1885	31	1964	27	1978	11	1967	-2	1943
17	-15	1994	-25	1943	-2	1885	22	1946	29	1952	39	1965	43	1954	42	1979	31	1959	18	1886	11	1967	-8	1942
18	-17	1982	-16	1979	-10	1885	21	1962	27	1983	35	1958	45	1956	44	1981	32	1990	22	1978	10	1967	-8	1942
19	-15	1971	-15	1979	-8	1993	25	1990	29	1944	37	1950	47	1956	42	1977	31	1959	18	1974	12	1959	-16	1884
20	-16	1971	-10	1966	-7	1949	23	1974	29	2002	41	1959	45	1965	42	1964	29	1979	17	1974	8	1986	-23	1884
21	-13	1994	-12	1950	-3	1885	22	1981	31	2002	43	1970	43	1966	40	1984	28	1956	20	1974	10	1987	-15	1942
22	-16	1984	-11	1950	-2	1885	19	1947	33	1950	41	1950	46	1944	37	1982	30	1962	22	1974	4	1987	-11	1962
23	-16	1976	-10	1972	6	1885	25	1989	35	1971	42	1958	45	1977	42	1988	29	1947	21	1969	9	1972	-7	1989
24	-15	1976	-10	1972	1	1885	26	1965	29	1956	42	2000	45	1886	41	1971	26	1963	18	1969	8	1989	-11	1989
25	-15	1945	-2	1964	5	1956	24	1949	29	1956	43	1979	41	1953	40	1971	28	1963	21	1969	8	1989	-19	1980
26	-14	1945	-8	1970	-7	1960	25	1972	31	1956	38	1979	45	1976	41	1885	30	1947	21	1952	11	2005	-20	1980
27	-21	1994	-9	1963	0	1960	26	2002	30	1968	46	1979	45	2001	41	1989	26	1947	20	1976	6	1949	-11	1968
28	-19	1994	-7	1963	9	1975	22	1947	32	1994	42	1995	45	1977	36	1885	27	1965	19	1976	5	1951	-6	1989
29	-14	1885	-2	1980	7	1959	24	1949	34	1956	41	1970	48	1989	37	1982	29	2000	20	1976	6	1951	-5	1993
30	-13	1948	—		2	1885	28	1975	31	1949	41	1988	43	1956	38	1986	29	2000	22	1983	6	1976	-6	1987
31	-14	1948	—		8	1970	—		30	1961	—		44	1964	35	1965	—		18	1966	—		-14	1962
Monthly Low	Jan -22	16th	Feb -25	17th	Mar -11	3rd	Apr 6	4th	May 24	4th	Jun 32	5th	Jul 41	25th	Aug 35	31st	Sep 26	27th	Oct 17	20th	Nov 4	22nd	Dec -23	20th

NORWICH, CT   Maximum Temperature Records (1956–2008)

Day	Jan °F	Year	Feb °F	Year	Mar °F	Year	Apr °F	Year	May °F	Year	Jun °F	Year	Jul °F	Year	Aug °F	Year	Sep °F	Year	Oct °F	Year	Nov °F	Year	Dec °F	Year
1	63	1973	62	1989	63	1972	72	1967	82	1985	91	1987	97	1964	96	1999	88	2000	81	1986	79	1982	64	2001
2	58	1979	57	1973	63	1972	76	1967	92	2001	93	1960	97	1963	96	2006	93	1980	82	1995	76	1982	68	2001
3	58	1998	62	1991	67	1991	77	1967	93	2001	94	1960	100	1966	100	2006	93	1980	84	2002	79	1990	66	1998
4	61	2000	66	1991	65	1974	65	1968	93	2001	88	1985	98	2002	99	1995	89	1980	82	1967	78	2003	71	1998
5	60	2000	68	1991	62	1979	72	1985	93	2001	89	1966	101	1999	94	2002	91	1983	86	1967	73	1994	62	2001
6	59	2007	57	1991	58	2008	77	1991	87	1993	92	2005	100	1999	96	2005	95	1983	87	1997	73	2005	68	2001
7	63	2007	51	2005	68	1987	84	1991	83	2000	96	1999	95	1986	91	2001	92	1959	84	2007	72	1959	77	1998
8	60	1998	57	1965	72	1987	87	1991	92	2000	94	1999	95	1993	96	2001	88	1985	83	1963	68	1996	66	1966
9	61	2008	58	1990	61	2002	82	1991	93	2000	93	2005	96	1981	97	2001	90	1971	84	2007	68	1983	67	1966
10	61	2008	55	1990	69	2000	78	2001	95	1979	94	2004	98	1993	102	2001	94	1971	85	1997	71	2006	59	1966
11	60	1975	58	1960	69	1990	73	2005	91	1993	96	1959	96	1988	94	2001	97	1983	81	1961	72	1999	63	1971
12	58	2008	58	1999	62	1985	73	1987	88	2001	94	1973	92	1966	93	2005	91	1961	82	1969	66	2002	60	1979
13	60	1995	56	1971	80	1990	82	1968	90	2004	95	1988	96	1966	94	2002	93	1961	82	1995	70	1964	65	1983
14	65	1995	57	1990	64	1983	78	1968	83	2004	95	1961	96	1995	97	2005	91	2005	81	1990	72	1993	59	1991
15	64	1995	60	1967	77	1990	77	2002	87	1998	98	1988	101	1995	96	2002	86	1982	88	1963	77	1993	57	2001
16	63	1995	57	1992	72	1990	82	1960	89	1998	91	1957	96	1999	92	1995	90	1991	88	1956	72	1990	63	1971
17	58	1995	68	1981	67	2000	86	2002	87	1974	96	1957	99	1999	93	1995	88	1991	82	1963	72	1975	68	1984
18	65	1990	72	1981	72	2003	94	2002	87	1989	91	1994	98	1999	94	2002	85	1972	79	1963	75	1975	66	1984
19	58	2006	64	1981	65	2003	90	2002	89	1986	94	1994	98	1977	95	2002	89	1983	84	1963	75	1975	57	1990
20	54	1991	62	1994	60	1985	78	2002	98	1996	95	1995	100	1991	95	2002	90	1983	83	1963	70	1991	60	1957
21	55	2006	59	1989	72	1959	85	2005	94	1996	93	1988	101	1991	93	1995	87	1965	77	1971	72	1985	60	1957
22	59	1959	64	1991	73	1979	87	1957	95	1992	91	1997	96	1957	92	1959	90	1980	85	1979	64	1983	62	1957
23	59	1967	60	1985	70	1994	82	2001	94	1964	91	2002	100	1957	90	2003	87	1959	77	2007	69	1992	61	1990
24	67	1967	60	1985	70	1994	79	2007	91	1964	92	1966	92	2002	90	1972	91	1959	77	1985	73	1979	60	1990
25	67	1967	64	2000	73	1987	80	2001	91	1991	92	1980	94	1999	92	1993	88	1959	80	1963	78	1979	63	1964
26	58	1978	59	1957	74	1963	82	1962	94	2007	95	2003	96	2001	95	1993	84	2007	79	1963	64	1988	62	1982
27	62	1974	64	1957	80	1998	89	1990	89	1981	94	2003	96	2005	95	1993	87	2007	79	1963	66	1999	62	1973
28	58	2002	58	1997	78	1991	91	1990	90	1991	98	1963	95	1963	95	1959	81	2003	82	1963	69	1990	59	1982
29	56	2006	58	1972	81	1998	82	1974	92	1959	96	1991	94	1999	90	1991	81	1959	78	1989	64	1990	73	1984
30	68	2002	—		81	1977	83	2003	94	1987	98	1964	96	1988	92	1991	84	1986	76	1989	65	1960	58	1984
31	58	1988	—		85	1998	—		92	1987	—		94	2002	91	1966	—		75	1982	—		64	1965
Monthly High	68	30th	72	18th	85	31st	94	18th	98	20th	98	30th	101	21st	102	10th	97	11th	88	16th	79	3rd	77	7th

199

NORWICH, CT   Minimum Temperature Records (1956–2008)

Day	Jan °F	Year	Feb °F	Year	Mar °F	Year	Apr °F	Year	May °F	Year	Jun °F	Year	Jul °F	Year	Aug °F	Year	Sep °F	Year	Oct °F	Year	Nov °F	Year	Dec °F	Year
1	-2	1963	-4	1977	4	1980	17	1964	31	1978	37	1967	43	1988	48	1964	43	1975	33	1993	24	1990	11	1989
2	0	1968	-7	1961	7	1962	20	1964	31	1986	41	1963	47	1978	52	1990	40	1991	34	1972	23	1976	7	1989
3	4	1977	-7	1961	-1	1962	19	1964	31	1966	39	1986	45	1957	48	1959	42	1968	34	2003	21	1980	1	1976
4	0	1981	-5	1985	5	2003	24	1962	31	1986	40	1976	47	1986	48	1964	44	1989	32	1996	24	1998	5	1989
5	-3	1981	-17	1996	6	2003	17	1995	32	1976	40	1997	48	1979	46	1972	42	1989	30	1996	23	1998	8	1989
6	-3	1959	0	1996	8	2007	17	1982	33	1961	38	1964	45	1979	50	1981	41	1989	27	1968	20	1991	8	1976
7	-2	1959	-5	1995	3	2003	17	1982	29	1996	40	1958	49	1979	49	1994	39	1962	30	1958	23	1991	7	2002
8	-5	1968	-4	1995	4	2003	21	1982	31	2001	41	1977	50	1979	48	1957	41	1962	30	1991	19	1960	6	1964
9	-10	1968	-2	1963	8	2007	20	1990	27	1985	40	1980	52	1989	48	1989	37	1990	27	1978	20	2003	6	1976
10	-4	1968	-2	1979	6	1984	23	1997	33	1983	33	1983	46	1991	48	1964	39	1978	28	1989	20	2004	1	1968
11	-10	1988	-5	1979	9	1960	26	2007	35	1983	39	1980	50	1983	47	1972	38	1995	26	1993	14	1956	1	1958
12	-10	1981	-9	1979	2	1960	23	1976	34	1983	36	1980	46	1978	45	1974	40	2006	25	1994	19	1957	0	1988
13	0	1981	-9	1967	8	1984	24	1967	32	1963	42	1980	51	1973	47	1957	39	1991	28	1981	20	2001	4	1982
14	-8	1957	-6	1979	15	1968	27	1990	30	1996	43	1979	47	1980	45	1964	39	1963	25	1993	17	1986	-1	1982
15	-11	1957	-2	2003	13	1968	22	1957	32	1980	40	1978	44	1971	45	1964	35	1975	28	1987	15	1996	3	1960
16	-10	1957	2	1962	14	1979	26	1957	26	1964	41	1961	51	1966	45	1972	35	1964	28	1978	12	1996	4	2005
17	-6	1982	-2	1979	10	1967	28	1971	34	1984	44	1961	51	1987	43	1979	36	1960	29	1994	19	1996	5	1958
18	-13	1957	-5	1979	8	1967	25	1985	31	1983	41	1958	50	1958	47	1979	35	1990	23	1972	17	1959	6	1980
19	-12	1982	4	1958	4	1967	25	1979	34	2003	44	1986	52	1976	46	1963	34	1956	22	1974	17	1997	-1	1989
20	-4	1994	2	1966	3	1967	26	1979	33	2002	45	1959	52	1997	48	1998	30	1979	23	1970	15	1986	7	1989
21	-5	1985	-1	1972	10	1986	17	1981	31	1964	48	1986	47	1966	47	2000	33	1993	21	1972	17	1987	2	1962
22	-13	1984	4	1959	15	1988	26	1976	36	1990	45	1986	52	1958	43	1982	33	1991	24	1974	15	1987	-1	1958
23	-7	1991	-15	1972	16	2004	27	1989	34	1963	46	1958	51	1977	43	1988	34	1976	23	1997	12	1989	0	1989
24	-6	1961	5	1963	18	2004	26	1971	37	1963	46	1988	51	1985	40	1957	30	1963	24	1973	6	1989	-6	1989
25	0	1961	3	1967	17	1971	20	1967	36	1972	47	1986	51	2002	41	1977	32	1963	26	2003	14	2000	-7	1980
26	-9	1982	-1	1990	14	1974	28	1989	33	1968	45	1979	49	1976	43	1963	36	1987	26	1972	11	1970	-13	1980
27	-2	1994	1	1990	16	1975	30	2002	38	1997	45	1979	50	2001	45	1989	31	1957	25	1976	17	2005	-1	1993
28	-11	1961	-4	1973	16	1966	28	1975	37	1962	50	1974	49	1977	45	1986	31	1957	20	1970	14	2002	1	1993
29	-9	1961	8	1980	14	1972	32	2001	38	1957	47	1995	50	2001	40	1986	29	1957	26	1970	14	2002	6	2004
30	-3	1977	—		23	2008	29	1987	38	1957	48	1988	50	1968	40	1986	30	1991	18	1980	11	1958	2	1987
31	-7	1965	—		21	1964	—		34	1961	—		51	1964	45	1986	—		21	1988	—		-5	1963
Monthly Low	Jan		Feb		Mar		Apr		May		Jun		Jul		Aug		Sep		Oct		Nov		Dec	
	-13 22nd		-17 5th		-1 3rd		17 21st		26 16th		33 10th		43 1st		40 30th		29 29th		18 30th		6 24th		-13 26tt	

STORRS, CT   Maximum Temperature Records (1888–2008)

Day	Jan °F	Year	Feb °F	Year	Mar °F	Year	Apr °F	Year	May °F	Year	Jun °F	Year	Jul °F	Year	Aug °F	Year	Sep °F	Year	Oct °F	Year	Nov °F	Year	Dec °F	Year
1	59	1966	58	1988	61	1976	71	1967	84	1899	91	1937	93	1964	96	1917	92	1973	85	1927	73	1950	66	2001
2	61	1890	63	1989	60	1991	73	1918	85	1930	91	1895	95	1901	92	1999	97	1953	87	1927	82	1950	68	2001
3	57	1913	55	1988	61	1991	75	1892	83	1942	95	1919	99	1911	96	1975	92	1929	81	1891	78	1982	62	1998
4	58	1998	57	1991	65	1991	74	1928	85	1944	95	1919	98	1911	92	2006	91	1929	84	1891	75	2003	62	1998
5	59	1950	64	1890	68	1974	77	1928	89	1949	91	1925	95	1911	95	1955	90	1973	85	1941	75	1987	67	1998
6	59	1890	63	1991	64	1979	77	1910	87	1931	92	1925	101	1919	93	1918	92	1900	83	1959	72	1994	66	2001
7	67	2007	52	1991	64	1946	84	1929	88	1930	92	1925	92	1999	94	1918	92	1983	83	2007	72	1938	69	2001
8	58	1930	60	1933	64	1974	84	1991	89	1930	92	1999	93	1937	93	2001	92	1983	80	1916	70	2005	73	1998
9	62	2008	52	1990	66	1987	84	1991	87	1936	91	1933	96	1937	92	2001	87	1915	80	1990	70	2005	62	1966
10	58	2008	56	1990	73	2000	81	1922	90	1896	89	2004	98	1911	97	1949	90	1931	85	1939	74	1931	66	1946
11	58	1983	57	2002	67	1977	77	1922	89	1979	95	1984	95	1911	95	1944	90	1931	83	1949	69	1999	61	1911
12	59	1975	60	1981	71	1977	78	1945	86	1993	95	1984	92	1908	96	1944	95	1983	85	1938	72	1909	63	1911
13	58	1932	58	1951	68	1946	84	1945	86	2004	91	1892	94	1894	94	1944	90	1931	81	1930	67	1964	65	1979
14	65	1932	54	1946	74	1990	83	1977	88	1900	92	1956	90	1979	93	2005	88	1915	80	1995	67	1902	63	1901
15	65	1932	66	1954	66	2007	86	1941	90	1900	92	1945	88	1909	92	2002	87	1915	83	1956	69	1993	61	1918
16	59	1932	69	1954	81	1990	85	1896	85	1932	92	1957	93	1900	92	1944	89	1915	86	1897	74	1993	60	1975
17	53	1913	58	2006	75	1990	87	2002	83	1991	91	1957	93	1968	94	1944	86	1991	82	1938	70	1928	72	1912
18	58	1973	60	1981	67	2003	91	2002	87	1974	88	1929	96	1953	91	1987	87	1906	89	1908	71	1963	61	2000
19	63	1973	64	1981	69	1989	89	1976	92	1962	89	1994	92	2006	90	2002	87	1906	82	1963	73	1941	59	1899
20	59	1951	65	1930	78	1945	90	1976	89	1903	93	1953	93	1916	94	1937	90	1983	77	1965	70	1953	58	1957
21	68	1906	60	1930	74	1918	84	1923	92	1996	93	1953	98	1916	94	1937	92	1983	79	1947	70	1931	60	2002
22	61	1906	62	1925	75	1938	82	1902	92	1911	91	1943	97	1918	89	1924	92	1914	75	1979	69	1931	58	1973
23	60	1967	63	1997	77	1938	84	2001	90	1992	94	1888	96	1918	90	1976	93	1914	84	1979	72	1931	59	1994
24	60	1967	61	1990	69	1979	81	2007	89	1964	90	1919	97	1916	88	1919	88	1970	77	1978	68	1992	60	1990
25	57	1967	69	1985	76	1910	86	1915	89	1975	93	1943	92	1892	91	1948	85	1926	78	1963	69	1979	63	1889
26	65	1950	66	1976	75	1910	80	1915	89	1914	95	1952	91	2001	96	1948	85	1930	79	1963	70	1979	64	1964
27	65	1916	60	2002	78	1945	87	1915	91	1914	92	1941	98	1964	92	1949	85	2007	81	1963	64	2001	62	1964
28	62	1974	64	1976	81	1945	87	1990	88	1939	92	1963	95	1894	93	1948	82	1998	83	1919	63	1984	57	1973
29	57	2002	62	1976	83	1945	90	1990	90	1919	93	1934	94	1894	93	1953	83	1945	86	1919	67	1990	59	1982
30	64	2002	—		76	1910	84	1974	89	1931	92	1964	94	1933	93	1953	81	1922	79	1946	70	1933	69	1984
31	57	1947	—		80	1977	—		91	1944	—		94	1988	93	1953	—		77	1946	—		64	1965
Monthly High	68	21st	69	25th	83	29th	91	18th	92	22nd	95	26th	101	6th	97	10th	97	2nd	89	18th	82	2nd	73	8th

STORRS, CT   Minimum Temperature Records (1888–2008)

Day	Jan °F	Year	Feb °F	Year	Mar °F	Year	Apr °F	Year	May °F	Year	Jun °F	Year	Jul °F	Year	Aug °F	Year	Sep °F	Year	Oct °F	Year	Nov °F	Year	Dec °F	Year
1	-12	1918	-14	1920	1	1938	13	1923	30	1978	35	1907	45	1988	46	1891	42	1975	28	1888	20	1923	5	1936
2	-11	1899	-12	1961	0	1891	14	1919	28	1931	39	1933	32	1909	39	1927	40	1906	25	1899	22	1976	5	1938
3	-7	1904	-7	1931	0	1950	15	1894	28	1903	37	1986	43	1929	48	1940	40	1938	27	1899	19	1891	3	1938
4	-10	1904	-5	1905	-3	1950	10	1954	30	1917	41	1976	45	1986	40	1976	43	1909	25	1945	18	1891	-4	1940
5	-10	1910	-9	1918	-1	1948	16	1995	29	1951	38	1947	46	1927	47	1972	39	1906	29	1965	21	1951	4	1906
6	-13	1896	-12	1996	-6	1948	17	1938	28	1891	39	1891	43	1962	45	1934	34	1902	26	1984	20	1951	2	1926
7	-10	1896	-14	1910	-1	1890	14	1982	30	1970	41	1987	48	1906	46	1951	34	1984	29	1984	19	1927	7	1902
8	-10	1942	-8	1963	-1	1923	17	1982	30	1956	38	1951	48	1906	43	1903	41	1978	26	1954	19	1931	-3	1906
9	-13	1968	-20	1934	2	2007	20	1977	28	1985	39	1980	46	1918	45	1899	38	1990	28	1937	13	1931	4	1934
10	-9	1958	-10	1899	3	1984	20	1900	25	1947	39	1928	47	1890	46	1964	36	1938	26	1980	18	1976	-9	1902
11	-9	1942	-10	1962	-1	1939	18	1909	25	1900	36	1980	45	1898	46	1894	38	1981	24	1943	18	2004	-4	1929
12	-9	1981	-12	1914	4	1984	17	1926	27	1907	37	1980	47	1913	46	1889	34	1917	28	1964	12	1956	-2	1929
13	-13	1912	-9	1967	5	1984	21	1926	32	1941	39	1907	45	1933	44	1941	38	1985	24	1925	17	1894	-4	1898
14	-12	1912	-17	1914	5	1948	20	1940	29	1939	40	1912	49	1933	45	1964	35	1911	25	1993	17	1894	-4	1898
15	-14	1957	-19	1943	9	1932	19	1940	30	1947	40	1912	46	1950	46	1964	34	1975	28	1937	10	1905	-1	1904
16	-10	2004	-17	1943	6	1893	20	1926	31	1947	35	1926	48	1946	46	1964	35	1899	21	1939	12	1905	-6	1917
17	-8	1994	-13	1896	6	1916	21	1908	30	1895	43	1954	44	1946	43	1905	33	1948	20	1937	8	1924	-7	1942
18	-10	1982	-7	1979	-1	1967	21	1948	35	1984	41	1954	48	1946	43	1923	35	1922	20	1939	10	1933	-10	1919
19	-19	1948	-3	1936	-3	1967	20	1926	29	1944	37	1939	42	1890	46	1918	33	1956	23	1974	10	1924	-6	1919
20	-8	1901	-9	1936	-5	1949	19	1897	34	1976	40	1926	47	1914	41	1976	31	1979	24	1972	9	1894	-13	1942
21	-4	1994	-8	1950	5	1906	21	1897	33	1936	38	1918	46	1890	43	1977	31	1956	22	1972	11	1888	-17	1942
22	-10	1984	-6	1916	6	1916	25	1947	31	1907	40	1940	45	1937	42	1940	29	1904	19	1940	11	1987	-7	1944
23	-8	1976	-8	1907	2	1906	20	1933	35	1950	41	1940	45	1923	40	1923	30	1904	22	1925	9	1888	-6	1902
24	-13	1907	-9	1894	9	1960	23	1927	31	1907	41	1932	47	1950	42	1927	32	1963	22	1969	5	1897	-5	1943
25	-13	1935	-12	1894	9	1960	22	1936	34	1956	45	1985	49	1953	37	1940	28	1925	25	1969	8	1936	-11	1980
26	-8	1927	-2	1990	3	1960	24	1919	35	1972	43	1979	45	1936	40	1981	32	1950	20	1933	1	1938	-11	1980
27	-15	1925	-7	1900	13	1975	29	1933	33	1949	39	1902	44	1940	41	1940	30	1940	21	1950	5	1932	-4	1968
28	-15	1935	-9	1934	2	1923	24	1933	27	1902	42	1902	45	1903	42	1944	29	1947	18	1936	7	1936	-10	1933
29	-4	1928	5	1980	4	1923	24	1934	33	1902	45	1902	47	1925	40	1982	29	1914	20	1891	6	1930	-14	1933
30	-7	1898			10	1974	28	1922	35	1915	42	1988	47	1928	39	1986	26	1941	20	1928	5	1891	-17	1917
31	-7	1908			8	1923			32	1961			45	1895	38	1976			16	1925			-13	1917
Monthly Low	-19	19th	-20	9th	-6	6th	10	4th	25	11th	35	16th	32	2nd	37	25th	26	30th	16	31st	1	26th	-17	30th

NEW HAVEN - TWEED AIRPORT, CT   Maximum Temperature Records (1948-1999)

Day	Jan °F	Year	Feb °F	Year	Mar °F	Year	Apr °F	Year	May °F	Year	Jun °F	Year	Jul °F	Year	Aug °F	Year	Sep °F	Year	Oct °F	Year	Nov °F	Year	Dec °F	Year
1	60	1966	52	2008	56	1976	69	1955	81	1957	82	1951	95	1963	90	1975	89	1961	84	1950	69	2003	64	2006
2	48	2007	48	1970	58	2004	71	1955	80	1951	85	2007	95	1966	95	1975	91	1966	82	1954	75	1968	56	1962
3	53	1960	53	2006	58	1967	75	1967	78	1969	80	1959	97	1966	95	1975	90	1977	78	1968	71	2003	58	1972
4	52	1951	51	2006	55	1974	65	1960	85	1965	84	1971	93	2002	89	2002	87	1959	79	2007	76	1975	60	1973
5	55	1950	52	2005	62	1974	66	1955	81	1955	85	1966	90	1949	94	2005	89	1961	83	1967	72	1975	62	2001
6	66	2007	51	2008	57	1949	64	1948	78	1949	88	1968	88	2003	93	1977	86	1977	82	1959	69	1959	64	2001
7	55	2007	51	1951	60	1974	68	1954	82	2004	85	1968	89	1971	91	1977	83	1969	79	2007	68	1975	60	2001
8	59	1949	51	1965	57	2008	76	1959	78	1964	86	1976	91	1971	92	2007	83	2007	84	2007	71	1975	62	1951
9	62	2008	57	1949	62	2002	73	1968	78	1964	86	1976	91	1974	91	1977	90	1959	80	1961	73	1975	60	1966
10	49	2002	51	2002	66	2006	78	1955	82	1970	93	1974	90	1974	92	1949	85	2002	81	1949	67	1948	58	1966
11	56	1975	53	1960	64	1977	75	1955	81	1953	86	1967	91	2005	93	1949	86	1961	81	1949	65	1966	60	1966
12	50	2008	53	1966	63	1973	87	1977	82	1959	86	1973	89	1966	88	2002	88	1952	79	1969	64	1955	56	1959
13	54	2005	55	1951	60	1977	78	1977	86	1956	92	1956	92	1952	91	2005	89	1952	77	1954	67	1964	56	1956
14	60	1950	52	1949	63	1957	75	1949	73	1975	89	2005	91	1952	90	2002	85	1961	75	1970	69	1959	57	1973
15	52	1962	58	1954	59	1977	76	2006	80	1976	88	1956	90	1974	89	1970	80	1969	78	1956	66	1973	60	1975
16	53	1953	59	1954	61	1977	84	2003	80	1951	91	1957	92	1953	91	1970	83	1971	76	1956	69	2001	55	1975
17	55	1949	65	1976	62	2003	85	2002	80	1974	96	1957	94	1953	89	2002	80	2005	79	1963	67	1953	53	2006
18	57	2006	54	2008	61	2003	86	2002	82	1977	85	2006	95	1977	91	2002	83	1965	74	1968	67	1975	54	2006
19	54	1951	59	1976	57	1974	82	1976	83	1962	87	1957	97	1977	89	1956	83	1977	77	1963	64	1957	56	1967
20	57	1951	55	1949	67	1948	81	1952	85	1975	86	1969	92	1952	93	1955	81	1955	73	1953	67	1948	57	2002
21	56	2006	58	2002	60	1959	83	1957	84	1962	93	1953	96	1977	91	1955	82	1965	79	1963	63	2003	60	1973
22	53	1973	59	1954	74	1948	80	1960	80	1974	88	1949	100	1957	89	1975	88	1970	78	1975	63	1953	55	1949
23	54	1974	50	1954	62	1953	78	1952	80	1977	87	1965	92	1955	87	1976	89	1970	75	2007	62	1953	57	2006
24	65	1967	57	1961	65	1948	77	1957	85	1975	92	1966	90	1976	89	1969	84	1961	74	1970	62	2006	54	2003
25	50	1967	62	1976	62	1964	82	1960	84	2007	93	1952	87	1965	90	1959	83	1970	74	2001	61	2004	61	1964
26	56	1950	57	1954	67	1954	76	1969	83	2007	92	1949	92	2005	97	1948	82	1958	70	1963	63	2001	55	1964
27	63	1974	66	1976	73	2007	74	1949	83	2006	90	1949	89	2005	100	1948	81	1970	74	1963	60	1966	65	1973
28	54	2006	67	1976	68	1960	73	1962	83	1959	91	1963	90	1970	90	1948	82	1948	73	1977	65	2001	55	1949
29	66	2002	55	1976	64	1977	78	1974	92	1969	91	1965	92	2002	97	1953	82	1959	70	1966	63	1957	52	2007
30	56	2002	—		73	1977	76	2007	85	1969	93	1964	92	2002	90	1977	80	1959	75	1961	62	2001	54	1948
31	54	1974	—		65	1962	—		82	1969	—		91	1954	89	1953	—		73	1950	—		57	1965
Monthly High	Jan 66	29th	Feb 67	28th	Mar 74	22nd	Apr 87	12th	May 92	29th	Jun 96	17th	Jul 100	22nd	Aug 100	27th	Sep 91	2nd	Oct 84	8th	Nov 76	4th	Dec 65	27th

NEW HAVEN - TWEED AIRPORT, CT   Minimum Temperature Records (1948–1999)

Day	Jan °F	Year	Feb °F	Year	Mar °F	Year	Apr °F	Year	May °F	Year	Jun °F	Year	Jul °F	Year	Aug °F	Year	Sep °F	Year	Oct °F	Year	Nov °F	Year	Dec °F	Year
1	7	1963	0	1961	14	1963	17	1969	34	2002	40	1967	52	1952	55	1953	49	1975	41	1974	27	2002	15	1967
2	2	1968	-5	1961	9	1962	21	1964	34	1964	47	1971	52	2007	55	1953	46	1949	39	1956	29	1965	16	1967
3	7	2008	0	1955	8	1962	17	1954	33	1966	42	1964	52	2007	53	1959	45	1967	38	1966	25	2002	11	1976
4	7	2008	4	1963	5	1950	17	1954	34	2005	44	1957	54	1954	52	1966	51	1960	37	1974	24	1951	13	1966
5	5	1977	3	1965	7	1948	25	1964	35	2003	45	1958	51	1954	54	1951	50	1963	33	1965	25	1951	15	1966
6	10	1976	11	1961	1	1948	24	1970	35	1969	44	1964	52	1962	35	2004	48	1962	21	2005	26	1967	13	2002
7	7	1968	-2	1948	4	2003	24	2007	32	1967	44	1958	53	1967	31	2004	46	1962	34	1954	24	2002	14	1970
8	-1	1968	-4	1963	14	2007	28	2004	33	1974	46	2002	53	1948	49	1948	44	1962	32	1954	20	1960	13	1970
9	-5	1968	3	1948	9	2007	27	1977	32	1956	44	1957	52	1963	54	1964	47	1956	32	1953	22	2003	8	1968
10	0	2004	0	1948	16	2003	26	1977	34	1966	42	1957	54	1953	48	1964	42	1975	36	1976	20	2003	5	1968
11	1	1968	-1	1962	12	1960	26	1948	35	1966	49	1960	50	2002	53	2007	45	1969	32	1964	16	1956	4	1958
12	2	1968	6	1967	14	1948	28	1976	39	1969	47	2004	53	2002	52	1968	42	1958	27	1964	22	1952	8	1960
13	5	1958	-3	1967	13	1948	26	1967	34	2005	46	1974	55	1973	50	1957	43	1955	33	1963	19	2001	6	1960
14	-1	1954	6	2003	15	1948	27	1950	37	2007	46	1974	59	1962	53	1964	42	1963	32	1958	24	1950	7	1958
15	-6	1957	8	1958	21	1968	29	1957	39	1966	45	1953	56	1950	52	1964	42	1964	32	2006	19	1967	7	1960
16	-3	2004	6	2003	18	1956	26	1957	38	1966	47	1961	55	1960	50	1968	42	1964	34	2006	21	1967	10	1962
17	1	1971	4	1958	12	1967	30	2005	37	1956	47	1961	53	1954	52	1957	39	1950	38	1976	20	1976	7	1951
18	-3	1957	1	1958	10	1967	27	1962	36	2003	41	1958	55	1976	53	1961	38	1959	32	2001	21	1959	12	2007
19	-8	1948	7	2003	5	1967	31	1962	38	2003	45	1956	59	2003	50	1953	41	1959	26	1976	21	2005	11	1960
20	4	1971	3	1950	8	1949	31	1962	35	2002	47	1959	55	1965	51	1958	42	2004	31	2003	23	1951	3	1955
21	-2	1961	1	1950	17	1965	30	1961	38	1950	48	2004	52	1951	48	1949	35	1956	31	1960	21	1951	1	1955
22	-7	1961	6	1968	19	2002	26	1975	36	2002	51	1950	55	1958	51	1969	37	1948	30	1974	20	1969	7	1958
23	0	1976	9	1963	15	2004	30	1975	40	2002	51	2005	55	1977	52	1957	38	1953	30	1955	18	1964	6	1955
24	0	1961	10	1948	21	1956	29	2002	38	1963	50	2007	53	1971	46	1952	37	1974	28	2002	19	1956	8	1975
25	2	2004	13	2005	16	1956	32	2003	37	1967	51	1961	53	1953	48	1956	34	1963	27	2003	20	1956	3	1948
26	2	1948	6	1970	12	1960	31	1963	38	1956	53	1965	53	1953	51	2004	40	1967	25	1952	20	2005	2	1968
27	4	2003	5	1950	20	1951	28	2002	37	1961	48	2004	52	1977	52	1969	36	1957	27	2006	17	1949	-3	1948
28	-3	1961	11	2006	19	1966	34	1948	37	1961	52	2004	54	1977	49	1968	34	1957	29	2001	14	1951	0	1950
29	-2	2005	11	2008	20	1974	32	1948	42	1970	53	1970	53	1968	50	1965	36	1957	27	1959	19	1955	15	1976
30	2	1948			19	1970	34	1977	40	2004	53	1956	52	1968	47	1965	36	1951	27	1966	.15	1976	-2	1962
31	-1	1948			22	1964			36	1961			53	1956	43	1976			24	1966			-2	1962
Monthly Low	-8	19th	-5	2nd	1	6th	17	4th	32	9th	40	1st	50	11th	31	7th	34	28th	21	6th	14	28th	-3	27th

APPENDIX E
Snow Totals and Freeze Date Probabilities, 1971–2000

Month	Snow fall mean	Snow fall median	Snow depth mean	Snow depth median	Highest daily snow fall	Year	Day	Highest monthly snow fall	Year	Highest daily snow depth	Year
Jan	8.5	6.1	2	1	15.7	1978	20	28.1	1978	20+	1996
Feb	7.2	5.8	1	1	12.6	1994	11	27.9	1994	20	1994
Mar	4.3	3.1	#	1	10.6	1993	13	13.7	1993	9+	1993
Apr	.9	.0	#	0	6.0	1982	6	11.8	1996	6+	1982
May	#	#	#	0	#	1977	9	#	1977	0	N/A
Jun	.0	.0	0	0	.0	N/A	N/A	.0	N/A	0	N/A
Jul	.0	.0	0	0	.0	N/A	N/A	.0	N/A	0	N/A
Aug	.0	.0	#	0	.0	N/A	N/A	.0	N/A	#	1990
Sep	.0	.0	0	0	.0	N/A	N/A	.0	N/A	0	N/A
Oct	.0	.0	0	0	.5	1987	4	.5	1987	0	1987
Nov	.7	.0	#	0	6.2	1989	23	6.6	1989	#+	1989
Dec	3.2	2.4	#	0	7.1	1990	28	13.8	1995 Jan	10	1995
Ann	24.8	17.4	N/A^c	N/A^c	15.7	1978	20	28.1	1978 Jan	20+	1996

+ Also occurred on an earlier date(s)

#Denotes trace amounts

@ Denotes mean number of days greater than 0 but less than .05

[a] Derived from Snow Climatology and 1971–2000 daily data

[b] Derived from 1971–2000 daily data

[c] Annual statistics for Mean/Median snow depths are not appropriate

205

BRIDGEPORT SIKORSKY AIRPORT, CT

Spring Freeze Dates (Month/Day)
Probability of later date in spring (thru Jul 31) than indicated[a]

Temp (F)	.10	.20	.30	.40	.50	.60	.70	.80	.90
36	5/01	4/27	4/25	4/23	4/20	4/18	4/16	4/14	4/10
32	4/22	4/18	4/15	4/13	4/11	4/08	4/06	4/03	3/30
28	4/07	4/03	4/01	3/29	3/27	3/25	3/22	3/20	3/16
24	4/02	3/28	3/25	3/23	3/20	3/18	3/15	3/12	3/08
20	3/24	3/19	3/15	3/11	3/08	3/05	3/02	2/26	2/20
16	3/17	3/11	3/07	3/03	2/28	2/24	2/20	2/16	2/10

Fall Freeze Dates (Month/Day)
Probability of earlier date in fall (beginning Aug 1) than indicated[a]

Temp (F)	.10	.20	.30	.40	.50	.60	.70	.80	.90
36	10/03	10/08	10/12	10/15	10/18	10/21	10/24	10/27	11/01
32	10/20	10/25	10/29	11/01	11/04	11/07	11/10	11/14	11/19
28	11/04	11/09	11/13	11/16	11/19	11/22	11/26	11/29	12/05
24	11/14	11/20	11/23	11/27	11/30	12/02	12/06	12/09	12/15
20	11/22	11/29	12/03	12/07	12/11	12/15	12/18	12/23	12/29
16	12/06	12/11	12/15	12/18	12/21	12/25	12/28	1/01	1/06

[a] Probability of observing a temperature as cold, or colder, later in the spring or earlier in the fall than the indicated date.

BURLINGTON, CT

Snow (inches)

| | Snow totals Means/Medians[a] | | | | Extremes[b] | | | | | | |
| | Snow fall mean | Snow fall median | Snow depth mean | Snow depth median | Highest daily snow fall | Year | Day | Highest monthly snow fall | Year | Highest daily snow depth | Year |
Month											
Jan	9.8	9.6	1	0	15.0	1983	16	25.0	1978	13	1994
Feb	8.5	5.1	2	0	20.0	1983	12	29.5	1983	18	1972
Mar	4.4	1.0	1	0	7.0	1984	29	23.5	1984	18	1994
Apr	.6	.0	0	0	8.0	1971	7	8.0	1971	0	N/A
May	.0	.0	0	0	.5	1977	9	.5	1977	0	N/A
Jun	.0	.0	0	0	.0	N/A	N/A	.0	N/A	0	N/A
Jul	.0	.0	0	0	.0	N/A	N/A	.0	N/A	0	N/A
Aug	.0	.0	0	0	.0	N/A	N/A	.0	N/A	0	N/A
Sep	.0	.0	0	0	.0	N/A	N/A	.0	N/A	0	N/A
Oct	.2	.0	0	0	3.5	1979	11	3.5	1979	0	N/A
Nov	1.0	.0	#	0	6.5	1980	18	7.0	1987	15	1971
Dec	3.3	4.0	1	0	7.0	1975	21	7.0	1974	14	1992
Ann	27.8	19.7	N/A[c]	N/A[c]	20.0	Feb 1983	12	29.5	Feb 1983	18+	Mar 1994

+ Also occurred on an earlier date(s)
[#]Denotes trace amounts
@ Denotes mean number of days greater than 0 but less than .05
-9.9 represents missing values
[a] Derived from Snow Climatology and 1971–2000 daily data
[b] Derived from 1971–2000 daily data
[c] Annual statistics for Mean/Median snow depths are not appropriate

BURLINGTON, CT

Spring Freeze Dates (Month/Day)

Probability of later date in spring (thru Jul 31) than indicated[a]

Temp (F)	.10	.20	.30	.40	.50	.60	.70	.80	.90
36	5/26	5/21	5/17	5/14	5/11	5/09	5/06	5/02	4/27
32	5/18	5/12	5/07	5/04	4/30	4/27	4/23	4/19	4/13
28	5/04	4/29	4/25	4/21	4/18	4/15	4/11	4/07	4/02
24	4/17	4/12	4/09	4/06	4/04	4/01	3/30	3/26	3/22
20	4/08	4/03	3/31	3/28	3/26	3/23	3/21	3/18	3/13
16	4/01	3/27	3/23	3/20	3/17	3/15	3/11	3/08	3/03

Fall Freeze Dates (Month/Day)

Probability of earlier date in fall (beginning Aug 1) than indicated[a]

Temp (F)	.10	.20	.30	.40	.50	.60	.70	.80	.90
36	9/19	9/22	9/25	9/27	9/28	9/30	10/02	10/05	10/08
32	9/26	9/30	10/04	10/07	10/10	10/12	10/15	10/19	10/24
28	10/03	10/09	10/13	10/17	10/20	10/23	10/27	10/31	11/06
24	10/19	10/26	10/30	11/03	11/07	11/10	11/14	11/19	11/25
20	10/31	11/06	11/11	11/15	11/19	11/23	11/27	12/01	12/08
16	11/17	11/22	11/26	11/30	12/03	12/06	12/10	12/14	12/19

[a] Probability of observing a temperature as cold, or colder, later in the spring or earlier in the fall than the indicated date.

DANBURY, CT

Snow (inches)

Month	Snow totals Means/Medians[a]				Extremes[b]						
	Snow fall mean	Snow fall median	Snow depth mean	Snow depth median	Highest daily snow fall	Year	Day	Highest monthly snow fall	Year	Highest daily snow depth	Year
Jan	11.9	10.0	3	2	14.5	1996	8	38.3	1996	36	1996
Feb	11.0	9.2	3	3	24.0	1983	12	30.0	1983	28	1983
Mar	6.7	5.8	1	#	17.0	1993	14	28.7	1993	19	1993
Apr	1.8	.1	#	#	10.0	1982	6	10.2	1982	10	1982
May	.0	.0	#	0	1.0	1977	9	1.0	1977	#	1998
Jun	.0	.0	0	0	.0	N/A	N/A	.0	N/A	0	N/A
Jul	.0	.0	#	0	.0	N/A	N/A	.0	N/A	#	1996
Aug	.0	.0	0	0	.0	N/A	N/A	.0	N/A	0	N/A
Sep	.0	.0	0	0	.0	N/A	N/A	.0	N/A	0	N/A
Oct	.2	.0	0	0	3.0	1979	10	3.0	1979	3	1979
Nov	1.1	.1	#	#	5.5	1971	25	5.5	1971	5	1971
Dec	6.1	5.0	1	#	13.4	2000	30	17.6	2000	18	1995
Ann	38.8	30.2	N/A[c]	N/A[c]	24.0	Feb 1983	12	38.3	Jan 1996	36	Jan 1996

+ Also occurred on an earlier date(s)
# Denotes trace amounts
@ Denotes mean number of days greater than 0 but less than .05
[a] Derived from Snow Climatology and 1971–2000 daily data
[b] Derived from 1971–2000 daily data
[c] Annual statistics for Mean/Median snow depths are not appropriate

DANBURY, CT

Spring Freeze Dates (Month/Day)
Probability of later date in spring (thru Jul 31) than indicated[a]

Temp (F)	.10	.20	.30	.40	.50	.60	.70	.80	.90
36	5/26	5/22	5/18	5/15	5/13	5/10	5/07	5/04	4/29
32	5/15	5/10	5/07	5/04	5/01	4/28	4/25	4/21	4/16
28	4/29	4/24	4/21	4/18	4/15	4/13	4/10	4/07	4/02
24	4/14	4/10	4/07	4/04	4/02	3/31	3/28	3/25	3/21
20	4/08	4/03	3/31	3/28	3/25	3/23	3/20	3/16	3/12
16	3/29	3/23	3/19	3/16	3/12	3/09	3/06	3/02	2/24

Fall Freeze Dates (Month/Day)
Probability of earlier date in fall (beginning Aug 1) than indicated[a]

Temp (F)	.10	.20	.30	.40	.50	.60	.70	.80	.90
36	9/15	9/19	9/22	9/24	9/26	9/28	9/30	10/03	10/07
32	9/26	10/01	10/04	10/06	10/09	10/11	10/14	10/17	10/22
28	10/05	10/11	10/15	10/18	10/22	10/25	10/29	11/02	11/08
24	10/16	10/23	10/27	10/31	11/04	11/08	11/12	11/16	11/23
20	10/30	11/06	11/11	11/15	11/19	11/23	11/27	12/02	12/09
16	11/19	11/24	11/28	12/01	12/04	12/07	12/10	12/14	12/20

[a] Probability of observing a temperature as cold, or colder, later in the spring or earlier in the fall than the indicated date.

FALLS VILLAGE, CT

Snow (inches)

Month	Snow totals Means/Medians[a]				Extremes[b]						
	Snow fall mean	Snow fall median	Snow depth mean	Snow depth median	Highest daily snow fall	Year	Day	Highest monthly snow fall	Year	Highest daily snow depth	Year
Jan	12.6	12.0	5	2	10.0	1996	9	22.3	1984	34	1971
Feb	9.0	7.8	4	2	17.0	1983	12	22.5	1972	26	1971
Mar	4.3	4.5	1	#	18.0	1993	14	18.0	1993	22	1993
Apr	2.4	.0	#	0	15.0	1971	7	17.7	1971	18	1982
May	.0	.0	0	0	.0	N/A	N/A	.0	N/A	0	N/A
Jun	.0	.0	0	0	.0	N/A	N/A	.0	N/A	0	N/A
Jul	.0	.0	0	0	.0	N/A	N/A	.0	N/A	0	N/A
Aug	.0	.0	0	0	.0	N/A	N/A	.0	N/A	0	N/A
Sep	.0	.0	0	0	.0	N/A	N/A	.0	N/A	0	N/A
Oct	.1	.0	0	0	3.0	1979	10	3.0	1979	0	N/A
Nov	1.3	.0	#	0	10.0	1971	25	16.0	1971	14	1971
Dec	8.5	7.9	1	#	10.0	1981	16	20.2	1981	30	1971
							Mar		Feb		Jan
Ann	38.2	32.2	N/A[c]	N/A[c]	18.0	1993	14	22.5	1972	34	1971

+ Also occurred on an earlier date(s)
# Denotes trace amounts
@ Denotes mean number of days greater than 0 but less than .05
-9.9 represents missing values
[a] Derived from Snow Climatology and 1971–2000 daily data
[b] Derived from 1971–2000 daily data
[c] Annual statistics for Mean/Median snow depths are not appropriate

FALLS VILLAGE, CT

Spring Freeze Dates (Month/Day)

Probability of later date in spring (thru Jul 31) than indicated[a]

Temp (F)	.10	.20	.30	.40	.50	.60	.70	.80	.90
36	6/17	6/11	6/06	6/03	5/30	5/27	5/23	5/18	5/12
32	6/01	5/27	5/23	5/19	5/16	5/13	5/10	5/06	5/01
28	5/14	5/10	5/07	5/05	5/02	4/30	4/27	4/24	4/20
24	4/29	4/25	4/22	4/19	4/16	4/14	4/11	4/08	4/03
20	4/17	4/13	4/09	4/07	4/04	4/02	3/30	3/27	3/23
16	4/03	3/30	3/27	3/24	3/22	3/20	3/17	3/15	3/11

Fall Freeze Dates (Month/Day)

Probability of earlier date in fall (beginning Aug 1) than indicated[a]

Temp (F)	.10	.20	.30	.40	.50	.60	.70	.80	.90
36	9/03	9/08	9/11	9/14	9/16	9/19	9/21	9/24	9/29
32	9/13	9/18	9/22	9/24	9/27	9/30	10/03	10/06	10/11
28	9/22	9/28	10/01	10/05	10/08	10/11	10/14	10/18	10/23
24	10/07	10/12	10/16	10/18	10/21	10/24	10/27	10/30	11/04
20	10/19	10/24	10/29	11/01	11/05	11/08	11/12	11/16	11/22
16	11/01	11/08	11/13	11/17	11/21	11/24	11/29	12/03	12/10

[a] Probability of observing a temperature as cold, or colder, later in the spring or earlier in the fall than the indicated date.

Snow (inches)

	Snow totals Means/Medians[a]				Extremes[b]						
	Snow fall	Snow fall	Snow depth	Snow depth	Highest daily snow fall			Highest monthly snow fall		Highest daily snow depth	
Month	mean	median	mean	median		Year	Day		Year		Year
Jan	6.7	4.5	1	#	9.5	1978	20	19.5	1996	14	1996
Feb	6.8	4.5	1	#	11.2	1978	6	26.5	1994	15	1978
Mar	2.7	1.5	#	#	7.0	1999	15	11.3	1978	9	1978
Apr	.6	.0	#	0	6.0	1982	6	9.5	1996	6	1982
May	#	.0	0	0	#	1977	9	#	1977	0	N/A
Jun	.0	.0	0	0	.0	N/A	N/A	.0	N/A	0	N/A
Jul	.0	.0	0	0	.0	N/A	N/A	.0	N/A	0	N/A
Aug	.0	.0	0	0	.0	N/A	N/A	.0	N/A	0	N/A
Sep	.0	.0	0	0	.0	N/A	N/A	.0	N/A	0	N/A
Oct	#	.0	#	0	#	2000	29	#+	2000	#+	2000
Nov	.7	.0	#	0	6.4	1989	23	6.4	1989	6	1989
Dec	2.9	2.1	#	#	6.0	1976	29	13.9	Feb 1995	8	Feb 1995
Ann	20.4	12.6	N/A[c]	N/A[c]	11.2	1978	6	26.5	1994	15	1978

+ Also occurred on an earlier date(s)
# Denotes trace amounts
@ Denotes mean number of days greater than 0 but less than .05
[a] Derived from Snow Climatology and 1971–2000 daily data
[b] Derived from 1971–2000 daily data
[c] Annual statistics for Mean/Median snow depths are not appropriate

Spring Freeze Dates (Month/Day)

Probability of later date in spring (thru Jul 31) than indicated[a]

Temp (F)	.10	.20	.30	.40	.50	.60	.70	.80	.90
36	5/18	5/13	5/10	5/07	5/04	5/01	4/28	4/25	4/20
32	4/28	4/25	4/22	4/20	4/18	4/16	4/14	4/11	4/08
28	4/20	4/15	4/12	4/09	4/07	4/04	4/01	3/29	3/25
24	4/08	4/04	3/31	3/29	3/26	3/24	3/21	3/18	3/13
20	4/02	3/28	3/25	3/22	3/19	3/16	3/14	3/10	3/05
16	3/27	3/21	3/17	3/13	3/10	3/07	3/03	2/27	2/21

Fall Freeze Dates (Month/Day)

Probability of earlier date in fall (beginning Aug 1) than indicated[a]

Temp (F)	.10	.20	.30	.40	.50	.60	.70	.80	.90
36	9/24	9/29	10/03	10/05	10/08	10/11	10/14	10/17	10/22
32	10/04	10/09	10/13	10/16	10/19	10/22	10/25	10/29	11/03
28	10/19	10/25	10/28	11/01	11/04	11/07	11/10	11/14	11/20
24	11/01	11/07	11/12	11/15	11/19	11/22	11/26	11/30	12/06
20	11/17	11/22	11/26	11/29	12/02	12/05	12/08	12/11	12/16
16	11/26	12/02	12/06	12/10	12/13	12/16	12/20	12/24	12/30

[a] Probability of observing a temperature as cold, or colder, later in the spring or earlier in the fall than the indicated date.

HARTFORD BRADLEY INTERNATIONAL AIRPORT, CT

Snow (inches)

Month	Means/Medians[a]				Extremes[b]						
	Snow fall mean	Snow fall median	Snow depth mean	Snow depth median	Highest daily snow fall	Year	Day	Highest monthly snow fall	Year	Highest daily snow depth	Year
Jan	14.3	10.5	3	1	14.1	1978	20	42.8	1996	38	1996
Feb	10.7	9.0	3	2	12.8	1978	6	29.4+	1994	26	1983
Mar	7.7	5.3	1	1	12.3	1993	13	31.1	1993	16	1993
Apr	1.5	.3	#	0	14.1	1982	6	14.3	1982	14	1982
May	.1	.0	#	0	1.3	1977	9	1.3	1977	#	1977
Jun	.0	.0	0	0	.0	N/A	N/A	.0	N/A	0	N/A
Jul	.0	.0	0	0	.0	N/A	N/A	.0	N/A	0	N/A
Aug	.0	.0	0	0	.0	N/A	N/A	.0	N/A	0	N/A
Sep	.0	.0	0	0	.0	N/A	N/A	.0	N/A	0	N/A
Oct	.1	.0	#	0	1.7	1979	10	1.7	1979	1	1979
Nov	2.5	.7	#	0	7.6	1971	25	8.7	1986	8+	1971
Dec	8.4	6.7	1	0	10.8	1977	14	23.4	1977	13+	1995
Ann	45.3	32.5	N/A	N/A	14.1+	1982	6 Apr	42.8	1996 Jan	38	1996

+ Also occurred on an earlier date(s)
# Denotes trace amounts
@ Denotes mean number of days greater than 0 but less than .05
[a] Derived from Snow Climatology and 1971–2000 daily data
[b] Derived from 1971–2000 daily data
[c] Annual statistics for Mean/Median snow depths are not apppropriate

HARTFORD BRADLEY INTERNATIONAL AIRPORT, CT

Spring Freeze Dates (Month/Day)

Probability of later date in spring (thru Jul 31) than indicated[a]

Temp (F)	.10	.20	.30	.40	.50	.60	.70	.80	.90
36	5/22	5/17	5/14	5/11	5/08	5/05	5/02	4/29	4/24
32	5/10	5/05	5/02	4/29	4/26	4/23	4/20	4/16	4/11
28	4/22	4/18	4/15	4/12	4/10	4/08	4/05	4/02	3/29
24	4/10	4/05	4/02	3/30	3/28	3/26	3/23	3/20	3/15
20	3/31	3/27	3/24	3/22	3/20	3/18	3/15	3/13	3/09
16	3/27	3/23	3/19	3/16	3/14	3/11	3/08	3/05	2/28

Fall Freeze Dates (Month/Day)

Probability of earlier date in fall (beginning Aug 1) than indicated[a]

Temp (F)	.10	.20	.30	.40	.50	.60	.70	.80	.90
36	9/19	9/23	9/26	9/28	9/30	10/03	10/05	10/08	10/12
32	9/26	10/01	10/04	10/07	10/09	10/12	10/14	10/17	10/22
28	10/08	10/13	10/17	10/20	10/23	10/26	10/29	11/02	11/07
24	10/20	10/26	10/31	11/04	11/08	11/12	11/16	11/21	11/27
20	11/02	11/09	11/14	11/18	11/22	11/26	12/01	12/06	12/13
16	11/20	11/25	11/28	12/01	12/04	12/07	12/10	12/13	12/18

[a] Probability of observing a temperature as cold, or colder, later in the spring or earlier in the fall than the indicated date.

MANSFIELD HOLLOW LAKE, CT

Snow (inches)

	Means/Medians[a]				Extremes[b]						
	Snow fall	Snow fall	Snow depth	Snow depth	Highest daily snow fall			Highest monthly snow fall		Highest daily snow depth	
Month	mean	median	mean	median		Year	Day		Year		Year
Jan	10.7	9.0	3	2	10.0	1978	21	27.0	1978	24	1996
Feb	7.4	6.0	3	2	23.0	1978	7	24.0	1978	28	1978
Mar	4.7	4.0	1	#	8.0	1978	17	13.0	1996	18	1978
Apr	1.7	.0	#	0	14.0	1982	7	15.0	1982	14	1982
May	.0	.0	#	0	.0	1977	10	.0	1977	#	1977
Jun	.0	.0	0	0	.0	N/A	N/A	.0	N/A	0	N/A
Jul	.0	.0	0	0	.0	N/A	N/A	.0	N/A	0	N/A
Aug	.0	.0	0	0	.0	N/A	N/A	.0	N/A	0	N/A
Sep	.0	.0	0	0	.0	N/A	N/A	.0	N/A	0	N/A
Oct	.1	.0	#	0	2.0	1979	11	2.0	1979	1	1979
Nov	1.4	.0	#	0	6.0	1986	19	7.0	1986	6	1986
Dec	5.3	4.0	1	#	6.0	1989	16	18.0	1995	12	1995
Ann	31.3	23.0	N/A	N/A	23.0	1978 Feb	7	27.0	1978 Jan	28	1978 Feb

+ Also occurred on an earlier date(s)
#Denotes trace amounts
@ Denotes mean number of days greater than 0 but less than .05
[a] Derived from Snow Climatology and 1971–2000 daily data
[b] Derived from 1971–2000 daily data
[c] Annual statistics for Mean/Median snow depths are not appropriate

MANSFIELD HOLLOW LAKE, CT

Spring Freeze Dates (Month/Day)

Probability of later date in spring (thru Jul 31) than indicated[a]

Temp (F)	.10	.20	.30	.40	.50	.60	.70	.80	.90
36	6/07	6/02	5/28	5/25	5/22	5/18	5/15	5/11	5/05
32	5/22	5/18	5/14	5/11	5/09	5/06	5/03	4/30	4/26
28	5/06	5/02	4/29	4/27	4/25	4/23	4/20	4/17	4/13
24	4/22	4/17	4/13	4/10	4/07	4/04	4/01	3/28	3/23
20	4/03	3/31	3/28	3/26	3/24	3/23	3/21	3/18	3/15
16	4/02	3/28	3/24	3/20	3/17	3/14	3/11	3/07	3/01

Fall Freeze Dates (Month/Day)

Probability of earlier date in fall (beginning Aug 1) than indicated[a]

Temp (F)	.10	.20	.30	.40	.50	.60	.70	.80	.90
36	9/08	9/12	9/15	9/18	9/20	9/22	9/25	9/28	10/02
32	9/20	9/24	9/27	9/29	10/01	10/03	10/06	10/08	10/12
28	10/03	10/07	10/10	10/12	10/14	10/17	10/19	10/22	10/26
24	10/14	10/19	10/22	10/25	10/28	10/31	11/03	11/06	11/11
20	10/23	10/29	11/03	11/07	11/11	11/15	11/19	11/24	12/01
16	11/06	11/13	11/17	11/21	11/25	11/28	12/02	12/07	12/13

[a] Probability of observing a temperature as cold, or colder, later in the spring or earlier in the fall than the indicated date.

NORFOLK 2 SW, CT

Snow (inches)

Month	Snow totals / Means/Medians[a]				Extremes[b]						
	Snow fall mean	Snow fall median	Snow depth mean	Snow depth median	Highest daily snow fall	Year	Day	Highest monthly snow fall	Year	Highest daily snow depth	Year
Jan	21.0	20.5	8	6	14.0	1987	23	50.5	1987	39	1996
Feb	17.8	16.5	12	10	17.6	1983	12	39.9	1972	34	1978
Mar	15.9	12.7	8	6	25.0	1977	23	42.6	1993	37	1993
Apr	7.7	4.6	2	#	21.0	1997	1	31.1	1997	26	1971
May	.7	.0	#	0	10.5	1977	10	20.0	1977	13	1977
Jun	.0	.0	0	0	.0	N/A	N/A	.0	N/A	0	N/A
Jul	.0	.0	0	0	.0	N/A	N/A	.0	N/A	0	N/A
Aug	.0	.0	0	0	.0	N/A	N/A	.0	N/A	0	N/A
Sep	.0	.0	0	0	.0	N/A	N/A	.0	N/A	0	N/A
Oct	.8	.0	#	0	6.5	1979	11	9.5	1987	10	1987
Nov	5.8	4.3	1	#	10.5	1971	25	24.1	1971	15	1971
Dec	17.2	16.9	4	3	16.5	1996	7	33.8	1996	29	1996
Ann	86.9	75.5	N/A[c]	N/A[c]	25.0	1977 Mar	23	50.5	1987 Jan	39	1996 Jan

+ Also occurred on an earlier date(s)

#Denotes trace amounts

@ Denotes mean number of days greater than 0 but less than .05

[a] Derived from Snow Climatology and 1971-2000 daily data

[b] Derived from 1971-2000 daily data

[c] Annual statistics for Mean/Median snow depths are not appropriate

NORFOLK 2 SW, CT

Spring Freeze Dates (Month/Day)

Probability of later date in spring (thru Jul 31) than indicated[a]

Temp (F)	.10	.20	.30	.40	.50	.60	.70	.80	.90
36	6/07	6/02	5/29	5/26	5/22	5/19	5/16	5/12	5/07
32	5/23	5/19	5/15	5/12	5/10	5/07	5/04	5/01	4/26
28	5/08	5/04	5/01	4/28	4/26	4/23	4/20	4/17	4/13
24	4/23	4/19	4/16	4/14	4/12	4/10	4/08	4/05	4/01
20	4/12	4/08	4/05	4/03	4/01	3/29	3/27	3/24	3/20
16	4/06	4/02	3/30	3/27	3/25	3/23	3/20	3/17	3/13

Fall Freeze Dates (Month/Day)

Probability of earlier date in fall (beginning Aug 1) than indicated[a]

Temp (F)	.10	.20	.30	.40	.50	.60	.70	.80	.90
36	9/11	9/15	9/18	9/20	9/22	9/25	9/27	9/30	10/03
32	9/20	9/25	9/29	10/02	10/05	10/07	10/10	10/14	10/19
28	10/03	10/08	10/11	10/14	10/17	10/19	10/22	10/26	10/30
24	10/18	10/23	10/27	10/30	11/02	11/05	11/08	11/12	11/17
20	10/29	11/04	11/07	11/11	11/14	11/17	11/20	11/24	11/29
16	11/14	11/18	11/21	11/24	11/26	11/28	12/01	12/04	12/08

[a] Probability of observing a temperature as cold, or colder, later in the spring or earlier in the fall than the indicated date.

NORWICH PUBLIC UTILITY PLANT, CT

Snow (inches)

Month	Snow fall mean	Snow fall median	Snow depth mean	Snow depth median	Highest daily snow fall	Year	Day	Highest monthly snow fall	Year	Highest daily snow depth	Year
Jan	3.3	2.5	2	#	8.0	1974	9	8.0	1974	25	1996
Feb	7.2	3.6	2	1	10.0	1994	11	21.3	1994	16	1978
Mar	3.2	.1	#	0	7.7	1978	16	12.7	1978	9	1978
Apr	1.0	.0	#	0	9.0	1996	10	14.0	1996	3	1996
May	#	.0	0	0	#	1977	9	#	1977	0	N/A
Jun	.0	.0	0	0	.0	N/A	N/A	.0	N/A	0	N/A
Jul	.0	.0	0	0	.0	N/A	N/A	.0	N/A	0	N/A
Aug	.0	.0	0	0	.0	N/A	N/A	.0	N/A	0	N/A
Sep	.0	.0	0	0	.0	N/A	N/A	.0	N/A	0	N/A
Oct	.0	.0	0	0	.0	N/A	N/A	.0	N/A	0	N/A
Nov	.3	.0	#	0	4.0	1980	17	4.0	1980	5	1986
Dec	3.7	2.3	#	#	5.5	1995	14	16.3	1995	10	1995
Ann	18.7	8.5	N/A[c]	N/A[c]	10.0	1994	11	21.3 Feb	1994	25 Jan	1996

+ Also occurred on an earlier date(s)
#Denotes trace amounts
@ Denotes mean number of days greater than 0 but less than .05
-9.9 represents missing values
[a] Derived from Snow Climatology and 1971–2000 daily data
[b] Derived from 1971–2000 daily data
[c] Annual statistics for Mean/Median snow depths are not appropriate

---

NORWICH PUBLIC UTILITY PLANT, CT

Spring Freeze Dates (Month/Day)
Probability of later date in spring (thru Jul 31) than indicated[a]

Temp (F)	.10	.20	.30	.40	.50	.60	.70	.80	.90
36	5/27	5/22	5/18	5/15	5/12	5/09	5/05	5/01	4/26
32	5/10	5/06	5/02	4/29	4/27	4/24	4/21	4/18	4/13
28	4/26	4/22	4/18	4/15	4/12	4/10	4/07	4/03	3/29
24	4/11	4/06	4/03	3/31	3/29	3/26	3/23	3/20	3/15
20	4/05	3/31	3/27	3/24	3/21	3/18	3/15	3/12	3/07
16	3/26	3/21	3/16	3/13	3/09	3/06	3/02	2/26	2/20

Fall Freeze Dates (Month/Day)
Probability of earlier date in fall (beginning Aug 1) than indicated[a]

Temp (F)	.10	.20	.30	.40	.50	.60	.70	.80	.90
36	9/18	9/22	9/25	9/27	9/29	10/01	10/04	10/06	10/10
32	9/30	10/04	10/07	10/09	10/11	10/13	10/16	10/19	10/22
28	10/08	10/13	10/17	10/20	10/23	10/26	10/29	11/02	11/07
24	10/24	10/30	11/03	11/07	11/10	11/13	11/17	11/21	11/27
20	11/08	11/14	11/18	11/21	11/25	11/28	12/01	12/05	12/11
16	11/23	11/28	12/02	12/05	12/08	12/12	12/15	12/19	12/24

[a] Probability of observing a temperature as cold, or colder, later in the spring or earlier in the fall than the indicated date.

Index

flooding (*continued*)
103–4; of 1982, 104–5; of 1984, 105–6; of 1992, 106–7; in nineteenth century, 94–96; sources of, 93–94, 108; during Tropical Storm Floyd, 83; of 2005, 107; of 2006, 107–8

Floyd, Tropical Storm, 82–83

forecast equations, 124

Fort William (New London Harbor), 67

Franklin, Benjamin, 66, 111

Franklin's Hurricane, 66

freeze dates: Bridgeport Sikorsky Airport station, 1971–2000, 205; Burlington station, 1971–2000, 206; Danbury station, 1971–2000, 207; Falls Village station, 1971–2000, 208; Groton station, 1971–2000, 209; Hartford Bradley International Airport station, 1971–2000, 210; Mansfield Hollow Lake station, 1971–2000, 211; Norfolk 2 SW station, 1971–2000, 212; Norwich Public Utility Plant station, 1971–2000, 213

French Storm (1778), 67

Fujita scale, 85

geologic time scale, 116, 117

Georgetown, 104

Gilbert, Raleigh, 17, 18

glaciers, 117–20, 127

Glastonbury, 68

Gloria, Hurricane, 46, 47, 81–82

Grasso, Ella, 49, 88

Great Colonial Hurricane (1635), 64–65

Great World War I Cold Wave, 36–37

greenhouse gases, 4, 121, 124, 125

Greenwich: blizzard of January 2005 in, 61; Presidents' Day storm of 2003 in, 59

Groton: annual snowfall and total precipitation, 10; blizzard of April 1982 in, 53; cooling degree days, 1971–2000, 161; daily average temperature, 1971–2000, 147; daily minimum/maximum

temperatures, 1971–2000, 133; daily total precipitation, 1971–2000, 161; heating degree days, 1971–2000, 147; Hurricane Bob in, 82; maximum temperature records, 1957–2008, 189; minimum temperature records, 1957–2008, 190; snow totals and freeze date probabilities, 1971–2000, 209; storm of April 2006 in, 108; twentieth-century winters in, 42, 53, 54; twenty-first-century winters in, 60, 61

Guilford: hurricane of 1938 in, 72; snow of winter of 1740–41 in, 21

Gulf Stream, 8, 15, 94

Haddam, 44

Hague, Patrick, 56–57

Hamden: late eighteenth-century winters in, 23; nineteenth-century winters in, 25; tornado of 1989 in, 11, 85, 91, 91, 92, 92

Hartford: Blizzard of February 1978 in, 49, 50–52; blizzard of April 1982 in, 53; Blizzard of 1996 in, 58; Charter Oak Hurricane of 1856 in, 70; Civic Center roof collapses, 48–49; colonial winters in, 22; flood of 1770 in, 94; flood of 1936 in, 97, 97, 98, 98; flood of August 1955 in, 102; flood of 1984 in, 106; Great World War I Cold Wave in, 36, 37; Hurricane Diane in, 79; hurricane of 1938 in, 75, 75; hurricane of 1944 in, 76; Hurricane Wilma in, 107; ice storm of 1973 in, 47; late eighteenth-century winters in, 22–23, 24; nineteenth-century winters in, 26; 90-degree days in, 109, 110–11; Presidents' Day storm of 2003 in, 59; record high snow accumulation in, 57; summer temperatures during twentieth century, 122; twentieth-century winters in, 38, 39, 40, 42, 43,

Kent, Don, 71
Killingly, 86

Lamed, Otis, 95
Late Season Hurricane of 1770, 66–67
Lewis, Francis, 21
Lindsay Storm, 43
Litchfield: snowstorm of December 1992
    in, 56; tornado of 1989 in, 91
Little Ice Age, 17, 19, 23, 35, 68, 112,
    119–20
Long Island Sound: cooling effect of,
    109; eighteenth-century winters on,
    20, 21, 23; freezes in 1970s, 48; glacier
    in formation of, 117–19; hurricanes
    on, 66, 67, 69, 70, 72; nineteenth-
    century winters on, 26; snowfall
    affected by, 8–9
Long Meadow Pond Dam, 108
Long Storm (November 1798), 24
Lyman, John, 37

mail delivery, 42
Manchester: snowstorm of January 2004
    in, 60; snowstorm of March 2007 in,
    62
Mansfield, 56
Mansfield Hollow Lake: annual snowfall
    and total precipitation, 10; cooling
    degree days, 1971–2000, 164; daily
    average temperature, 1971–2000, 150;
    daily minimum/maximum tempera-
    tures, 1971–2000, 136; daily total pre-
    cipitation, 1971–2000, 164; heating
    degree days, 1971–2000, 150; maxi-
    mum temperature records, 1952–2007,
    195; minimum temperature records,
    1952–2007, 196; snow totals and
    freeze date probabilities, 1971–2000,
    211
Mather, Cotton, 19, 20
methane, 4, 121, 123, 125
Middlebury, 88
Middletown: Blizzard of 1888 in, 29;

cooling degree days, 1971–2000, 165;
    daily average temperature, 1971–2000,
    151; daily minimum/maximum tem-
    peratures, 1971–2000, 137; daily total
    precipitation, 1971–2000, 165; flood
    of 1984 in, 106; flood of 2006 in, 107;
    heating degree days, 1971–2000,
    151; ice storm of 1973 in, 48; late
    eighteenth-century winters in, 23;
    nor'easter of December 2005 in, 61;
    snowstorm of March 2007 in, 62
Milford: flood of 1982 in, 105; Hurricane
    Gloria in, 82; hurricane of 1938 in, 72;
    twentieth-century winters in, 56
Mill River, 108
Misquamicut, 72
Montville, 61
Mood Indigo (Allen), 38
Moore, Dudley, 11
Mount Hope River, 95

Naugatuck: flood of 1982 in, 105; flood
    of October 2005 in, 107
Naugatuck River: flooding during Hurri-
    cane Diane, 79; flood of 1853, 96;
    flood of 1955, 99; flood of August
    1955, 99, 101; flood of 1982, 104; flood
    of 2006, 108
New Britain: during flood of 1936, 97;
    twentieth-century winters in, 42
New Hartford, 97–98
New Haven: Blizzard of 1888 in, 29,
    30–34; blizzard of April 1982 in, 53;
    colonial winters in, 21; elevation
    and weather variation in, 9; flood of
    1982 in, 105; flood of October 2005
    in, 107; freezing of harbor in 1970s,
    48; Great World War I Cold Wave
    in, 36, 37; Ephraim Howe's voyage,
    65; hurricanes in, 67, 68, 71; late
    eighteenth-century winters in, 22,
    23, 24; nineteenth-century winters in,
    25, 26, 27, 28; Presidents' Day storm
    of 2003 in, 59; snowstorm of October

Norwich (*continued*)
1956–2008, 200; twentieth-century winters in, 56; twenty-first-century winters, 62. *See also* Norwich Public Utility Plant

Norwich Public Utility Plant: cooling degree days, 1971–2000, 168; daily average temperature, 1971–2000, 154; daily minimum/maximum temperatures, 1971–2000, 140; daily total precipitation, 1971–2000, 168; heating degree days, 1971–2000, 154; snow totals and freeze date probabilities, 1971–2000, 213

October Hurricane of 1749, 66

Old Lyme, 26

Old Saybrook: Hurricane Carol in, 77; hurricane of 1938 in, 72; twentieth-century winters in, 56; twenty-first-century winters in, 60

100-hour storm (1969), 43

O'Neill, William A., 53, 82

Oxford: drought in year without a summer (1816), 27; flood of October 2005 in, 107

Park River: flooding during Hurricane Diane, 79; flood of 1936, 97, 98; flood of 1982, 104

peaches, 37

Perfect Storm of 1991, 63

Pierce, Charlie, 71

Pilgrims, 18–19, 63

Plainfield, 68

plowing roads, 13

Plymouth, 28

Plymouth colony (Massachusetts), 17–18, 64

polar easterlies, 5

polar high, 5

Pomfret, 86

Popham, George, 17, 18

Poquonock, 89

power outages: in flood of 1936, 97; in flood of 1982, 105; in flood of 1992, 106; in Hurricane Gloria, 82; in ice storm of 1973, 46, 47–48; in snowstorm of October 1987, 55; in snowstorm of December 1992, 56; in snowstorm of April 1997, 59; in storm of April 2006, 108

precipitation: annual total at Connecticut stations, 10; Connecticut's annual total, 9–10; daily total, 1971–2000, 160–78; likelihood of trends in, 128; uniformity across state over the year, 10. *See also* rain; snow

Presidents' Day Blizzard (1979), 52

Presidents' Day storm (2003), 59–60

pressure, barometric. *See* barometric pressure

prevailing westerlies, 5, 10

Project Stormfury, 80–81

Providence, 77

Putnam: flooding during hurricane of 1938, 75; flood of August 1955 in, 100, 101; Hurricane Diane in, 79; twentieth-century winters in, 42, 43, 56, 59; twenty-first-century winters in, 60

Putnam Lake, daily total precipitation at, 1971–2000, 169

"quiet corner," 42

Quinebaug River: flooding during Hurricane Diane, 79; flooding during hurricane of 1938, 75; flood of 1801, 95

Quinnipiac River, 83, 108

radiation balance, 4, 4–5

radiative forcing, 123, 125

radioactive dating, 115

rain: in drought of 1965 and 1966, 10; formation of, 5–6; records of October 2005, 107. *See also* flooding; thunderstorms

Redfield, William, 69

Rell, Jodi, 108

twentieth century, 122; year without a (1816), 9, 12, 25, 27–28, 120
sunlight, amount that reaches Earth, 3–4

Tambora, Mount, 27
Tammy, Tropical Storm, 107
temperature: average daily, 1971–2000, 146–59; daily minimum/maximum normal, 1971–2000, 132–45; daily minimum/maximum records, 179–204; estimated changes in, 126, 127; fluctuation during last three thousand years, 119, 119; fluctuation through twentieth century, 120, 120; general trend in, 121; global and continental change, 1900–2000, 124; Great World War I Cold Wave, 36–37; likelihood of trends in, 128; long-term global, 5; multi-model averages and assessed ranges for surface warming, 126; over past two million years, 116, 118; sea breezes keep down, 8; summer in selected Connecticut cities during twentieth century, 122; thermometers come into use, 22; variation of sea-surface, 116, 118; winter in selected Connecticut cities during twentieth century, 122. See also cold; heat
Terryville, 56
Thames River, 21, 96
thermometers, 22, 111
thunderstorms: average number per year, 85; flooding caused by, 94; in flood of 1982, 104; July as biggest month for, 11, 110; local precipitation variation caused by, 10; in snowstorms, 41, 51; with tornadoes, 86, 91
tornadoes, 84–92; average number per year, 85; in colonial period, 84; density increases damage from, 11; in eighteenth century, 86–87; FE scale for, 85–86; Fujita scale for, 85; in

Hamden in 1989, 11, 85, 91, 91, 92, 92; in nineteenth century, 87; threat rating of Connecticut, 84; in twentieth century, 87–92; in Windsor Locks in 1979, 11, 84, 85, 85, 88–91; in Worcester in 1953, 85, 87–88
Torrington: daily total precipitation, 1971–2000, 176; flood of August 1955 in, 99; hurricanes in, 78, 79; ice storm of 1973 in, 47; tornadoes in, 92; twentieth-century winters in, 44, 59
Trade Wind Belt, 63
training, 94
tree rings, 115
Twain, Mark, 11
Tweed Airport. See New Haven Tweed Airport

Union: Presidents' Day storm of 2003 in, 59; snow melt after blizzard of 1978 in, 9; snowstorm of December 1992 in, 56
Unionville, 101
Upson, Helen, 34
Utley, Vine, 26

Vernon, 9
Vikings, 17, 18, 119

Wallingford: Blizzard of 1888 in, 29; tornado of 1878 in, 87; twentieth-century winters in, 38
Warren, Harry, 38
Washington, George, 22, 111, 114–15
water: balancing water budget, 6; vapor, 4, 121, 125. See also droughts; flooding; ice; precipitation; rain
Waterbury: Blizzard of 1888 in, 29; blizzard of April 1982 in, 53; flood of August 1955 in, 99, 103; Hurricane Diane in, 79; Hurricane Gloria in, 82; snowstorm of January 2004 in, 60; tornadoes in, 86, 88

About the Author

From the time he was a young boy, Dr. Mel Goldstein has been fascinated by the weather. So fascinated, he started a meteorology club when he was in the eighth grade, and decades later, the club is still in existence. Dr. Mel earned a Ph.D. in Meteorology from New York University and holds honorary doctorates from Albertus Magnus College and Mitchell College.

Now Dr. Mel is interpreting the weather for Connecticut viewers on News Channel 8 throughout the day and evening.

A popular meteorologist, Dr. Mel wears many hats. Since 1970, Mel has taught at Western Connecticut State University, where he developed the first and only Bachelor's degree program in meteorology in Connecticut. He also developed a severe-storm prediction index used by numerous electric utilities across the country.

He has been a consultant to firms such as IBM, Union Carbide, General Electric, Detroit Edison, Philadelphia Electric, Northeast Utilities, and United Illuminating.

Mel's media career began with a single radio station, and by 1976 his broadcasts were on dozens of radio stations nationwide. He then began doing television. In the 1980s his forecasts were seen across the country on the Satellite News Channel, an all-news cable effort of ABC and Westinghouse. He became the Chief Meteorologist at Connecticut's WTNH-TV in 1986.

In addition, Dr. Mel has made the transition to author by writing *The Complete Idiot's Guide to Weather*. It's a quick and easy guide that can answer any question about weather. The profits from this book are donated to cancer research. Dr. Mel also wrote a weekly column for the *Hartford Courant* in *Northeast Magazine* for twenty years.

All of Mel's hard work has not gone unnoticed. He has received the President's Award from Western Connecticut State University for his teaching and community service, the Connecticut Bloomer Award for contributions to the state of Connecticut, and a nomination for an Emmy award for a series of educational vignettes about the weather.

He recently won the prestigious Silver Circle Award from the National Academy of Television Arts and Sciences for twenty-five years of on-air performance and public service.

Dr. Mel also won the Best of Connecticut poll for an on-air meteorologist in each of the past nine years. This readers' poll is conducted by *Connecticut*

Dr. Mel at Western Connecticut State University, 1983.

Governor Grasso meets Dr. Mel Goldstein, head of the West Connecticut Environmental Center, 1979.

*Dr. Mel Goldstein,
News Channel 8.*

Magazine. He was also inducted into the magazine's Hall of Fame, and he has also won several polls for best TV personality from the New Haven Advocate.

He has served as director on several boards, including the Connecticut Academy for Education, the Long Island Sound Foundation, and the Ronald McDonald House. He also has an endowed research foundation in his name at Yale University. The research is for multiple myeloma.

A scholarship fund has been created in his honor for meteorology students at Western Connecticut State University.

When he is not in front of the camera, Dr. Mel can be found playing jazz piano at his home overlooking Long Island Sound, or digging for crabs with his grandson Eric, daughter Laura, and wife, Arlene.